Valentyna Romanova, Andreas Umland (eds.)

UKRAINE'S DECENTRALIZATION

Challenges and Implications of the
Local Governance Reform after the Euromaidan Revolution

Bibliografische Information der Deutschen Nationalbibliothek
Die Deutsche Nationalbibliothek verzeichnet diese Publikation in der Deutschen Nationalbibliografie; detaillierte bibliografische Daten sind im Internet über http://dnb.d-nb.de abrufbar.

Bibliographic information published by the Deutsche Nationalbibliothek
Die Deutsche Nationalbibliothek lists this publication in the Deutsche Nationalbibliografie; detailed bibliographic data are available in the Internet at http://dnb.d-nb.de.

ISBN-13: 978-3-8382-1162-6
© *ibidem*-Verlag, Hannover • Stuttgart 2024
Alle Rechte vorbehalten

Das Werk einschließlich aller seiner Teile ist urheberrechtlich geschützt. Jede Verwertung außerhalb der engen Grenzen des Urheberrechtsgesetzes ist ohne Zustimmung des Verlages unzulässig und strafbar. Dies gilt insbesondere für Vervielfältigungen, Übersetzungen, Mikroverfilmungen und elektronische Speicherformen sowie die Einspeicherung und Verarbeitung in elektronischen Systemen.

All rights reserved. No part of this publication may be reproduced, stored in or introduced into a retrieval system, or transmitted, in any form, or by any means (electronic, mechanical, photocopying, recording or otherwise) without the prior written permission of the publisher. Any person who does any unauthorized act in relation to this publication may be liable to criminal prosecution and civil claims for damages.

Printed in the EU

Soviet and Post-Soviet Politics and Society (SPPS) Vol. 183
ISSN 1614-3515

General Editor: Andreas Umland,
Stockholm Centre for Eastern European Studies, andreas.umland@ui.se

Commissioning Editor: Max Jakob Horstmann,
London, mjh@ibidem.eu

EDITORIAL COMMITTEE*

DOMESTIC & COMPARATIVE POLITICS
Prof. **Ellen Bos**, *Andrássy University of Budapest*
Dr. **Gergana Dimova**, *Florida State University*
Prof. **Heiko Pleines**, *University of Bremen*
Dr. **Sarah Whitmore**, *Oxford Brookes University*
Dr. **Harald Wydra**, *University of Cambridge*

SOCIETY, CLASS & ETHNICITY
Col. **David Glantz**, *"Journal of Slavic Military Studies"*
Dr. **Marlène Laruelle**, *George Washington University*
Dr. **Stephen Shulman**, *Southern Illinois University*
Prof. **Stefan Troebst**, *University of Leipzig*

POLITICAL ECONOMY & PUBLIC POLICY
Prof. **Andreas Goldthau**, *University of Erfurt*
Dr. **Robert Kravchuk**, *University of North Carolina*
Dr. **David Lane**, *University of Cambridge*
Dr. **Carol Leonard**, *University of Oxford*
Dr. **Maria Popova**, *McGill University, Montreal*

FOREIGN POLICY & INTERNATIONAL AFFAIRS
Dr. **Peter Duncan**, *University College London*
Prof. **Andreas Heinemann-Grüder**, *University of Bonn*
Prof. **Gerhard Mangott**, *University of Innsbruck*
Dr. **Diana Schmidt-Pfister**, *University of Konstanz*
Dr. **Lisbeth Tarlow**, *Harvard University, Cambridge*
Dr. **Christian Wipperfürth**, *N-Ost Network, Berlin*
Dr. **William Zimmerman**, *University of Michigan*

HISTORY, CULTURE & THOUGHT
Dr. **Catherine Andreyev**, *University of Oxford*
Prof. **Mark Bassin**, *Södertörn University*
Prof. **Karsten Brüggemann**, *Tallinn University*
Prof. **Alexander Etkind**, *Central European University*
Prof. **Gasan Gusejnov**, *Free University of Berlin*
Prof. **Leonid Luks**, *Catholic University of Eichstaett*
Dr. **Olga Malinova**, *Russian Academy of Sciences*
Dr. **Richard Mole**, *University College London*
Prof. **Andrei Rogatchevski**, *University of Tromsø*
Dr. **Mark Tauger**, *West Virginia University*

ADVISORY BOARD*

Prof. **Dominique Arel**, *University of Ottawa*
Prof. **Jörg Baberowski**, *Humboldt University of Berlin*
Prof. **Margarita Balmaceda**, *Seton Hall University*
Dr. **John Barber**, *University of Cambridge*
Prof. **Timm Beichelt**, *European University Viadrina*
Dr. **Katrin Boeckh**, *University of Munich*
Prof. em. **Archie Brown**, *University of Oxford*
Dr. **Vyacheslav Bryukhovetsky**, *Kyiv-Mohyla Academy*
Prof. **Timothy Colton**, *Harvard University, Cambridge*
Prof. **Paul D'Anieri**, *University of California*
Dr. **Heike Dörrenbächer**, *Friedrich Naumann Foundation*
Dr. **John Dunlop**, *Hoover Institution, Stanford, California*
Dr. **Sabine Fischer**, *SWP, Berlin*
Dr. **Geir Flikke**, *NUPI, Oslo*
Prof. **David Galbreath**, *University of Aberdeen*
Prof. **Frank Golczewski**, *University of Hamburg*
Dr. **Nikolas Gvosdev**, *Naval War College, Newport, RI*
Prof. **Mark von Hagen**, *Arizona State University*
Prof. **Guido Hausmann**, *University of Regensburg*
Prof. **Dale Herspring**, *Kansas State University*
Dr. **Stefani Hoffman**, *Hebrew University of Jerusalem*
Prof. em. **Andrzej Korbonski**, *University of California*
Dr. **Iris Kempe**, *"Caucasus Analytical Digest"*
Prof. **Herbert Küpper**, *Institut für Ostrecht Regensburg*
Prof. **Rainer Lindner**, *University of Konstanz*

Dr. **Luke March**, *University of Edinburgh*
Prof. **Michael McFaul**, *Stanford University, Palo Alto*
Prof. **Birgit Menzel**, *University of Mainz-Germersheim*
Dr. **Alex Pravda**, *University of Oxford*
Dr. **Erik van Ree**, *University of Amsterdam*
Dr. **Joachim Rogall**, *Robert Bosch Foundation Stuttgart*
Prof. **Peter Rutland**, *Wesleyan University, Middletown*
Prof. **Gwendolyn Sasse**, *University of Oxford*
Prof. **Jutta Scherrer**, *EHESS, Paris*
Prof. **Robert Service**, *University of Oxford*
Mr. **James Sherr**, *RIIA Chatham House London*
Dr. **Oxana Shevel**, *Tufts University, Medford*
Prof. **Eberhard Schneider**, *University of Siegen*
Prof. **Olexander Shnyrkov**, *Shevchenko University, Kyiv*
Prof. **Hans-Henning Schröder**, *SWP, Berlin*
Prof. **Yuri Shapoval**, *Ukrainian Academy of Sciences*
Dr. **Lisa Sundstrom**, *University of British Columbia*
Prof. **Philip Walters**, *"Religion, State and Society"*, *Oxford*
Prof. **Zenon Wasyliw**, *Ithaca College, New York State*
Dr. **Lucan Way**, *University of Toronto*
Dr. **Markus Wehner**, *"Frankfurter Allgemeine Zeitung"*
Dr. **Andrew Wilson**, *University College London*
Prof. **Jan Zielonka**, *University of Oxford*
Prof. **Andrei Zorin**, *University of Oxford*

---

* While the Editorial Committee and Advisory Board support the General Editor in the choice and improvement of manuscripts for publication, responsibility for remaining errors and misinterpretations in the series' volumes lies with the books' authors.

Soviet and Post-Soviet Politics and Society (SPPS)
ISSN 1614-3515

Founded in 2004 and refereed since 2007, SPPS makes available affordable English-, German-, and Russian-language studies on the history of the countries of the former Soviet bloc from the late Tsarist period to today. It publishes between 5 and 20 volumes per year and focuses on issues in transitions to and from democracy such as economic crisis, identity formation, civil society development, and constitutional reform in CEE and the NIS. SPPS also aims to highlight so far understudied themes in East European studies such as right-wing radicalism, religious life, higher education, or human rights protection. The authors and titles of all previously published volumes are listed at the end of this book. For a full description of the series and reviews of its books, see www.ibidem-verlag.de/red/spps.

Editorial correspondence & manuscripts should be sent to: Dr. Andreas Umland, Department of Political Science, Kyiv-Mohyla Academy, vul. Voloska 8/5, UA-04070 Kyiv, UKRAINE; andreas.umland@cantab.net

Business correspondence & review copy requests should be sent to: *ibidem* Press, Leuschnerstr. 40, 30457 Hannover, Germany; tel.: +49 511 2622200; fax: +49 511 2622201; spps@ibidem.eu.

Authors, reviewers, referees, and editors for (as well as all other persons sympathetic to) SPPS are invited to join its networks at www.facebook.com/group.php?gid=52638198614
www.linkedin.com/groups?about=&gid=103012
www.xing.com/net/spps-ibidem-verlag/

Recent Volumes

175 *Eduard Klein*
Bildungskorruption in Russland und der Ukraine
Eine komparative Analyse der Performanz staatlicher Antikorruptionsmaßnahmen im Hochschulsektor am Beispiel universitärer Aufnahmeprüfungen
Mit einem Vorwort von Heiko Pleines
ISBN 978-3-8382-0995-1

176 *Markus Soldner*
Politischer Kapitalismus im postsowjetischen Russland
Die politische, wirtschaftliche und mediale Transformation in den 1990er Jahren
Mit einem Vorwort von Wolfgang Ismayr
ISBN 978-3-8382-1222-7

177 *Anton Oleinik*
Building Ukraine from Within
A Sociological, Institutional, and Economic Analysis of a Nation-State in the Making
ISBN 978-3-8382-1150-3

178 *Peter Rollberg, Marlene Laruelle (Eds.)*
Mass Media in the Post-Soviet World
Market Forces, State Actors, and Political Manipulation in the Informational Environment after Communism
ISBN 978-3-8382-1116-9

179 *Mikhail Minakov*
Development and Dystopia
Studies in Post-Soviet Ukraine and Eastern Europe
With a foreword by Alexander Etkind
ISBN 978-3-8382-1112-1

180 *Aijan Sharshenova*
The European Union's Democracy Promotion in Central Asia
A Study of Political Interests, Influence, and Development in Kazakhstan and Kyrgyzstan in 2007–2013
With a foreword by Gordon Crawford
ISBN 978-3-8382-1151-0

181 *Andrey Makarychev, Alexandra Yatsyk (Eds.)*
Boris Nemtsov and Russian Politics
Power and Resistance
With a foreword by Zhanna Nemtsova
ISBN 978-3-8382-1122-0

182 *Sophie Falsini*
The Euromaidan's Effect on Civil Society
Why and How Ukrainian Social Capital Increased after the Revolution of Dignity
With a foreword by Susann Worschech
ISBN 978-3-8382-1131-2

Contents

Acknowledgements and Caveats 7

Tables, Figures, and Maps 9

Introduction: Taking Stock of Ukraine's Decentralization
Andreas Umland and Valentyna Romanova 13

1. Ukraine's Early Decentralization Attempts
   Valentyna Romanova and Andreas Umland 23

2. Ukraine's Local Governance Reform and Territorial Consolidation in 2014-20
   Valentyna Romanova and Andreas Umland 35

3. Fiscal Decentralization in Ukraine, 2014-17: Prospects and Challenges for Amalgamated Territorial Communities
   Maryna Rabinovych 59

4. Decentralization Reform in Ukraine: Political Context, Key Results, Public Attitudes
   Oleksii Sydorchuk 91

5. State Fragility and the Risks of Decentralization in Ukraine
   Max Bader 121

6. The Effects of Decentralization on Party Politics in Ukraine
   Melanie Mierzejewski-Voznyak 149

7. Trends in Ukrainian Regions in 2015-17: Toward a Decentralized Model of Regional Development
   Igor Dunayev 183

8. Spatial Planning in Ukraine's Sustainable Development and European Integration: The National, Regional, and Local Levels
   Yuriy Palekha 205

9. From Decentralization to Wartime Resistance: Building a Cohesive Ukraine
   Oleksandra Deineko and Aadne Aasland 227

10. Ukraine's Social Inclusion Policies Toward Internally Displaced Persons: Has Local Amalgamation Made a Difference?
    Valentyna Romanova 257

11. Four Geopolitical Dimensions of Ukraine's Decentralization
    Andreas Umland and Valentyna Romanova 277

The Contributors 297

Acknowledgements and Caveats

The production of this volume has taken an unusually long time. Its planning started in 2017 and publication was originally planned for the year 2020. Yet, the completion and editing of the collection was completed only in late 2023, for a number of reasons. Disruptions in the professional and private biographies of the editors who switched their places and countries of work during this period, as well as in the initially assumed project funding led to an initial delay. In early 2022, the Russia's large-scale invasion again interrupted our work, but also gave us a chance to include some more recent chapters in the volume.

Some of the contributions to this volume and author affiliations are thus dated by the publication year 2024. We apologize for this circumstance to our contributors, reviewers, and readers, as well as warn readers that the authors of these older texts should not be held responsible for possible non-consideration of relevant recent new primary or secondary sources not yet considered in these papers. In a way, the contributions to the volume document not only the course of Ukraine's decentralization, but also the evolution, over time, of its perception by the experts assembled here.

The volume has benefitted from largely indirect support by a whole number of institutions who funded the editors' work during the time of its collection. They include, in Valentyna Romanova's case, the Institute of Developing Economies—Japan External Trade Organization (IDE-JETRO) as well as European Cooperation in Science and Technology (COST), and, in Andreas Umland's case, the Kyiv-Mohyla Academy (NaUKMA), German Corporation for International Cooperation (GIZ), Czech Institute of International Relations (UMV), Ukrainian Institute for the Future (UIM), Research Council of Norway (NFR), as well as the foreign ministries of Germany (AA) and Sweden (UD). We are also grateful to the various institutions which have supported the volume's authors.

Special thanks from Andreas Umland go to Andreas von Schumann, head of the former GIZ Bureau for Political Communication at Kyiv, Babara-Maria Monheim, director of the former

Democracy Study Centre at the German-Polish-Ukrainian Society in Kyiv, and Dr. Martin Kragh, deputy director for research at the Stockholm Centre for Eastern European Studies.

Andreas Umland and Valentyna Romanova
Kyiv and Tokyo, March 2024

Tables, Figures, and Maps

Figure 2.1. Inter-municipal cooperation in 2021 39

Figure 2.2. Local revenues share in Ukraine's overall GDP 43

Figure 2.3. Local budgets share in Ukraine's overall budget 43

Table 3.1. The Conditions of Successful Fiscal Decentralization. 66

Table 3.2. Subnational budgets' tax revenue before and after fiscal decentralization. 79

Table 4.1. How would you evaluate solving the following issues in your city (town)?(%, November 2014) 93

Table 4.2. Are you satisfied with activities of the following government bodies?(%, November 2014) 94

Table 4.3. Territorial regime of Ukraine should be ... (%, April 2014) 99

Figure 4.1. Total amounts of local budgets in 2014–2016 (excluding non-controlled territories in Crimea and Donbas, UAH bn) 102

Figure 4.2. Revenues and expenses of local budgets in 2014–2016 (excluding non-controlled territories in Crimea and Donbas, UAH bn) 104

Figure 4.3. Do you support the measures that the government implements in the framework of decentralization of power? (%) 114

Figure 4.4. During 2015–2016, revenues of local budgets has significantly increased. Have you seen any results of use of these funds? (%) 117

Figure 4.5. Has the process of amalgamation of communities changed conditions of life in your community? (among those who already live in ATCs, %) 118

Figure 6.1. "Have you heard anything about the work of any party's local offices in your region?" (in percentages) 165

Figure 7.1. Total number of projects of international technical assistance to Ukraine for years, pcs. (as of April 2017). 187

Figure 7.2. Experts' responses to the survey question: "What issues have the most negative impact on regional bodies' adaptation to their enhanced role and responsibilities in the course of decentralization?", in % 188

Figure 7.3. Experts' responses to the survey question: "What prevents a region from benefiting from intraregional and interregional cooperation/integration?", in % 189

Figure 7.4. Experts' responses to the survey question: "What do regional authorities mostly incline to?", in %. 190

Figure 7.5. Experts' responses to the survey questions: 191

A) Do you think that the decisions of regional authorities are made on time or delayed, in %.? 191

B) Do you think that the decisions of regional authorities are more focused on mitigation rather than preventing negative phenomena? 191

Figure 7.6. Aggregated results of experts' assessment of economic and political impact factors that can help overcoming inertia in decision making at the regional level, in % 192

Figure 7.7. Aggregated results of experts' assessment of social and communicational impact factors that can help overcoming inertia in decision making at the regional level, in % 193

Figure 7.8. Respondents' answers to the survey question: "What contradictions and conflicts are most evident at the regional level during the implementation of decentralization reforms?", in % 194

Figure 7.9. Experts' responses to the survey question: "In the next 3-5 years, can Ukrainian regions change their economic agenda so that they could realize their own potential to the full and become self-sufficient?", in % 195

Figure 8.1. The hierarchical levels of spatial planning documentation in Ukraine.. 208

Figure 9.1. Perceived effects of the decentralization reform on the work of local government, in % (N=2,103) a nationwide sample. 239

Table 9.3. Types of volunteering during the war (in %)............. 248

Table 9.4 Satisfaction with activities of mayors/hromada heads, and heads of regional military-civilian administrations (in %, July 2022, N=1507) 250

Introduction
Taking Stock of Ukraine's Decentralization

Andreas Umland and Valentyna Romanova

This volume seeks to contribute to the emerging body of English-language analytical literature on Ukraine's decentralization. It explains why the reform started, how it proceeded in 2014-2020, and how its first deliverables have affected state capacity, party politics, and territorial cohesion. Over the last years, at first, domestic experts have, in Ukrainian language, examined Ukraine's local governance structure and decentralization reform, discussing its successes and failures.[1] These studies were then supplemented with Ukrainian studies in Western languages as well as with more and more studies by foreign scholars.[2] This volume complements this

---

1   Among early seminal Ukrainian-language general surveys are: Anatolii Tkachuk, *Mistseve samovryaduvannya ta detsentralizatsiya: Praktychnyy posibnyk* (Kyiv: Sofiia, 2012); Yuriy Hanushchak, *Reforma terytorial'noi orhanizatsii vlady* (Kyiv: DESPRO, 2012; 3rd edn, 2015); Anatolii Tkachuk, *Derzhavna rehionalna polityka: Vid asymetrii do solidarnosti (robochyi zoshyt)* (Kyiv: Lehalnyi status, 2013); Anatoliy Tkachuk, *Pro detsentralizatsiiu, federalizatsiiu, separatystiv ta ul'tymatumy: zapytannia ta vidpovidi* (Kyiv: Lehalnyi status, 2014). Some of the most recent relevant think-tank papers, coauthored by Valentyna Romanova, include Ya. A. Zhalilo et al., *Detsentralizatsiya vlady: Yak zberehty uspishnist' v umovakh novykh vyklykiv?* (Kyiv: NISD, 2018); Ya. A. Zhalilo et al., *Detsentralizatsiya vlady: Poriadok dennyy na sredn'ostrokovu perspektyvu* (Kyiv: NISD, 2019). An early relevant English-language study by Ukrainian experts was: Viktor Chumak and Ihor Shevliakov, *Local Government Functioning and Reform in Ukraine: An Overview of Analytical Studies of Local Government System and Local Services Provision in Ukraine* (Oslo: Norwegian Institute for Urban and Regional Research, 2009).
2   See, among the relevant English-language publications, in chronological order: *Local Governance and Decentralization Assessment: Implications of Proposed Reforms in Ukraine* (Washington, DC: USAID, 2014); Yuliya Bila, "Decentralize or Perish", *Foreign Policy*, 14 April 2015. http://foreignpolicy.com/2015/04/14/dece ntralize-or-perish-ukraine-kiev-russia/; Galyna Kalachova, "Budget Decentralization: Life or Death for Ukrainian Cities and Towns", *Vox Ukraine*, 21 November 2016 https://voxukraine.org/2016/11/21/budget-decentralization-en/; Kirill Mikhailov, "Ukraine's Decentralization and Donbas 'Special Status:' What You Need to Know", *Euromaidan Press*, 1 September 2015 http://euromaidanpress.com/2015/09/01/ukraines-decentralization-and-donbas-special -status-what-you-need-to-know/#arvlbdata; William Partlett, "Agendas of

Constitutional Decentralization in Ukraine", *ConstitutionNet*, 23 July 2015. http://www.constitutionnet.org/news/agendas-constitutional-decentralization-ukraine; Oleksii Sydorchuk, *Decentralization: Results, Challenges and Prospects* (Kyiv: Ilko Kucheriv Democratic Initiatives Foundation, 2016); Ivan Lukerya, Olena Halushka, "10 ways decentralization is changing Ukraine", *Kyiv Post*, 7 December 2016, https://www.kyivpost.com/article/opinion/op-ed/ivan-lukerya-olena-halushka-10-ways-decentralization-changing-ukraine.html; Balázs Jarábik, Yulia Yesmukhanova, "Ukraine's Slow Struggle for Decentralization", *Carnegie Europe*, 8 March 2017 http://carnegieendowment.org/2017/03/08/ukraine-s-slow-struggle-for-decentralization-pub-68219; Tony Levitas and Jasmina Djikic, *Caught Mid-Stream: "Decentralization", Local Government Finance Reform, and the Restructuring of Ukraine's Public Sector 2014 to 2016* (Kyiv: SIDA-SKL, 2017), http://sklinternational.org.ua/wp-content/uploads/2017/10/UkraineCaughtMidStream-ENG-FINAL-06.10.2017.pdf; *Report on Municipal Amalgamation and Possible Impact on Territorial Reform of Upper Tiers of Government* (Strasbourg: Centre of Expertise for Local Government Reform of the Council of Europe, 2017). http://www.slg-coe.org.ua/wp-content/uploads/2017/12/CoE_Report_Municipal_amalgamation_CELGR_2017_4_.pdf; *Decentralization in Ukraine: Achievements, Expectations and Concerns* (Kyiv: International Alert & Ukrainian Center for Independent Political Research 2017). https://www.international-alert.org/sites/default/files/Ukraine_Decentralization_EN_2017.pdf; Maryna Rabinovych, Anthony Levitas, Andreas Umland, "Revisiting Decentralization After Maidan: Achievements and Challenges of Ukraine's Local Governance Reform", *Kennan Cable*, no. 34, 2018, www.wilsoncenter.org/publication/kennan-cable-no-34-revisiting-decentralization-after-maidan-achievements-and-challenges; Angela Boci, "Latent Capacity of the Budgets of Amalgamated Territorial Communities: How Can It be Unleashed?" *Vox Ukraine*, 30 August 2018, voxukraine.org/en/latent-capacity-of-the-budgets-of-amalgamated-territorial-communities-how-can-it-be-unleashed/; *Maintaining the Momentum of Decentralization in Ukraine* (Kyiv: OECD, 2018). www.oecd.org/countries/ukraine/maintaining-the-momentum-of-decentralization-in-ukraine-9789264301436-en.htm; Andreas Umland, "International Implications of Ukraine's Decentralization", *Vox Ukraine*, 30 January 2019, voxukraine.org/en/international-implications-of-ukraine-s-decentralization/. Among the first German-language studies were: Ruben Werchan, "Dezentralisierung: Der Weg zu einer effizienteren Regierung, Wirtschaftswachstum und dem Erhalt der territorialen Integrität?", in Evgeniya Bakalova et al., eds., *Ukraine – Krisen – Perspektiven: Interdisziplinäre Betrachtungen eines Landes im Umbruch* (Berlin: WVB, 2015), 187-212; Natalia Shapovalova, "Mühen der Ebenen: Dezentralisierung in der Ukraine", *Osteuropa* 65, no. 4 (2015): 143-152; Robert Sperfeld, "Dezentralisierung in der Ukraine: Kein wirksames Mittel zur Befriedung", *Heinrich-Böll-Stiftung*, 20 July 2015 https://www.boell.de/de/2015/07/20/vom-kopf-auf-die-fuesse-gestellt; Oesten Baller, "Korruptionsbekämpfung und Dezentralisierung auf dem Prüfstand des Reformbedarfs in der Ukraine", *Jahrbuch für Ostrecht*, no. 2 (2017): 235-268; Anatolij Tkatschuk, "Zur Dezentralisierung: Erfolge, Risiken und die Rolle des Parlamentes", *Ukraine-Nachrichten*, 26 January 2017, https://ukraine-nachrichten.de/dezentralisierung-erfolge-risiken-rolle-parlamentes_4568; Jurij Hanuschtschak, Oleksij Sydortschuk, Andreas Umland, "Die ukrainische Dezentralisierungsreform nach der Euromajdan-

emerging body of literature, engages critically with previously published investigations of the post-Euromaidan decentralization reform, and shares new research results.

We start here with the pre-history of the recent reforms. Consideration of research findings regarding Ukraine's earlier decentralization attempts advances understanding of both, the post-2014 changes and post-Euromaidan continuities in center-periphery relations and territorial politics. Our perspective, for instance, helps explaining why the constitutionally enshrined status of regional (*oblast*) and upper subregional (*rayon*) authorities appeared difficult to challenge during the implementation of the post-Euromaidan decentralization reform. In a way, the cover of this book is thus actually misleading in that it shows the banners of Ukraine's regions which were not the primary locus of the reform processes that are analyzed here and that have been mainly happening at lower levels.

One critical issue of the post-1991 decentralization reforms in Ukraine was the balance of responsibilities between central state authorities, on the one hand, and self-governing bodies, on the other, at the level of regions (*oblasts*) and upper subregional districts (*rayons*).[3] Prior to 2014, "a specific feature of the local reforms in Ukraine [was] the status of regional and district authorities, which have been repeatedly municipalized in times of decentralization and stratified in times of centralization".[4] In 2014-2015 and 2019-2020, domestic reformers attempted to implement, but ended up postponing, a constitutional reform aimed at granting regional and upper subregional councils the right to establish their executive committees. Thus, the constitutional status of regional and district authorities was not changed.

Revolution 2014–2017: Vorgeschichte, Erfolge, Hindernisse", *Ukraine-Analysen*, no. 183 (2017): 2-11, http://www.laender-analysen.de/ukraine/pdf/Ukraine Analysen183.pdf; Marian Madela, *Der Reformprozess in der Ukraine 2014-2017: Eine Fallstudie zur Reform der öffentlichen Verwaltung* (Stuttgart: ibidem-Verlag, 2018).

3   Kimitaka Matsuzato, "Local Reforms in Ukraine 1990-1998: Elite and Institutions", in Osamu Ieda, ed., *The Emerging Local Governments in Eastern Europe and Russia: Historical and Post-Communist Development* (Hiroshima: Keisuisha, 2000), 25-54.

4   Ibid., 45.

A key difference between the early attempts to implement territorial reforms and the post-2014 decentralization policy was Kyiv's new attention to the municipal level. A community amalgamation reform and redivision of responsibilities between substate authorities to the benefit of local authorities as well as the introduction of direct inter-budgetary relations between the central budget and local budgets. A nuanced analysis of the post-2014 fiscal decentralization in Ukraine revealed a shift in

> "the center [of] gravity of Ukraine's subnational order from 2nd (rayon) and 3rd (oblast) tier local governments towards cities and amalgamated gromada[s] [i.e. territorial communities or municipalities]. Or put more prosaically, the last few years have seen the significant municipalization of oblast power and the beginnings of what might best be called the 'gromadization' of rayon power".[5]

Despite some tensions and inconsistencies, this shift contributed to territorial consolidation at the local level. Moreover, it reshaped Ukraine's center-periphery relations from the bottom up.

Paradoxically, at their time, Kyiv's centralization policies of the mid-1990s reflected Ukraine's ambition to "return to Europe". In that period, domestic policymakers understood democratic state-building in a way that conformed to patterns of early post-World War II Europe rather than to later European Union (EU) prerogatives established by the 1992 Maastricht Treaty.[6] Over time, domestic reformers' understanding of EU policies changed. Their cooperation with Western counterparts at various international organizations (e.g., the Council of Europe) as well as the sharing of foreign expertise in various international technical assistance programs and projects enabled this shift. The post-2014 decen-

---

5   Tony Levitas and Jasmina Djikic, Caught Mid-Stream: "Decentralization", Local Government Finance Reform, and the Restructuring of Ukraine's Public Sector 2014 to 2016 (Kyiv: SIDA-SKL, 2017), http://sklinternational.org.ua/wp-content/uploads/2017/10/UkraineCaughtMidStream-ENG-FINAL-06.10.2017.pdf
6   Kataryna Wolczuk, "Catching up with 'Europe'? Constitutional Debates on the Territorial-Administrative Model in Independent Ukraine", *Regional and Federal Studies* 12, no. 2 (2002): 65-88.

tralization reform contributed to Ukraine's Europeanization.[7] The major component of that reform, namely the local amalgamation policy, reflected the reformers' commitment to introducing the principle of subsidiarity found in the EU. Simultaneously, the reform's deliverables demonstrated that domestic policymakers failed to strengthen Ukraine's regional authority, despite of the fact that this goal also corresponds to EU notions of good governance and democratic accountability.

Research results on Ukraine's regional policy and fiscal decentralization in the 2000s warn that domestic policy initiatives can generate ambiguous outcomes even when they benefit from international donor support and foreign expertise.[8] Thus, acknowledgement of potential limitations to the intended eventual impact of external financial injections driving this or that reform agenda forward seems apt.[9] In any way, soon after the post-Euromaidan decentralization reform was launched, the reformers' efforts were greatly enhanced by an unprecedented degree of international technical and financial assistance.[10] A key role has been played by the multi-donor "U-LEAD [Ukraine—Local Empowerment, Accountability and Development] with Europe" initiative, with its House of Decentralization in Kyiv; by substantial, mainly EU-provided funds; and by regional bureaus and partner offices in Ukraine's 24

---

7 Andreas Umland, "Chotyry heopolitychni vymiry detsentralizatsii Ukrainy", *Dzerkalo tyzhnya*, no. 1 (2019) https://dt.ua/internal/chotiri-geopolitichni-vimiri-decentralizaciyi-ukrayini-299352_.html.
8 Duncan Leitch, *Assisting Reform in Post-Communist Ukraine, 2000–2012: The Illusions of Donors and the Disillusion of Beneficiaries* (Stuttgart: ibidem-Verlag, 2016).
9 See also, in German: Stefanie Bailer, "Förderung von Zivilgesellschaft und Drittem Sektor? Eine Untersuchung der Demokratieförderung der Europäischen Union in der Ukraine und ihrer gesellschaftlichen Wirkung", in: Markus Kaiser, ed., *WeltWissen: Entwicklungszusammenarbeit in der Weltgesellschaft* (Bielefeld: transcript-Verlag, 2003), 107-132; Andreas Umland, "Westliche Förderprogramme in der Ukraine: Einblicke in die europäisch-nordamerikanische Unterstützung ukrainischer Reformbestrebungen seit 1991", *Arbeitspapiere und Materialien der Forschungsstelle Osteuropa Bremen*, no. 63 (December 2004). http://www.forschungsstelle-osteuropa.de/con/images/stories/pdf/ap/fsoAP63.pdf.
10 "EU supports Decentralization and Regional Policy reforms in Ukraine with €55 millions", *European Commission*, 27 November 2014. http://europa.eu/rapid/press-release_IP-14-2221_en.htm.

oblasts. U-LEAD's extent across the whole country was one of its core assets: it helped collect data at the local scale and then produce data-driven policy analysis for the benefit of Ukraine's policymakers. Among the particularly supportive countries—including Germany (BMZ/GIZ), Sweden (SIDA), Switzerland (SDC/DESPRO)[11] and Poland (Polish Aid)—the United States launched two large multimillion-dollar programs in support of the reform: PULSE (Policy for Ukraine Local Self-Governance) and DOBRE (Decentralization Offering Better Results and Efficiency).[12]

The UNDP's Recovery and Peacebuilding Program in Ukraine too had a special focus on decentralization.[13] Moreover, since 2017, Ukraine has received additional specialized advice on decentralization from Germany via Georg Milbradt, its Special G7 Envoy for the Ukrainian Reform Agenda and the former Prime Minister of the East German Free State of Saxony.[14] Finally, Ukraine benefited from legal expertise on a number of draft laws provided within several Council of Europe programs, including the "Decentralization and Local Government Reform in Ukraine" project.

In a departure from previous practice, international donors established an institution, the Council of Donors, aimed at coordinating their efforts and sharing information about project results. Notably, the Council of Donors was chaired by both a representative of the international donors (on a rotating basis) and the head of the Ukrainian ministry responsible for implementing the reform (*Minregion*). Thus, in the case of the post-2014 decentralization reform, generous Western developmental support and data-driven policy advice proved to be highly beneficial. International donors made efforts to coordinate their input and opted for long-term

---

11 Oksana Myshlovska, "Democratizing Ukraine by Promoting Decentralization? A Study of Swiss-Ukraine Cooperation", *International Development Policy Working Papers*, 4 May 2015. http://journals.openedition.org/poldev/2010.
12 Rabinovych, Levitas and Umland, "Revisiting Decentralization After Maidan".
13 "Our Focus: Recovery and Peacebuilding", *UNDP in Ukraine*. http://www.ua.undp.org/content/ukraine/en/home/recovery-and-peacebuilding.html.
14 Christian F. Trippe, "Special Envoy Georg Milbradt: Ukraine Has Achieved Major Success", *Deutsche Welle*, 19 August 2017. www.dw.com/en/special-envoy-georg-milbradt-ukraine-has-achieved-major-success/a-40154634.

cooperation with the Ukrainian authorities responsible for the reform implementation.

This volume surveys the decentralization reform's prehistory before 2014; the post-Euromaidan administrative, fiscal, and political decentralization policy provisions; public attitudes toward decentralization; party politics; regional and spatial development; territorial cohesion; the risks raised by the reform; its impact on the social inclusion of internally displaced persons (IDPs); and the reform's international dimensions.

Chapter 1 by Romanova and Umland outlines the domestic origins of the post-Euromaidan decentralization reform. It presents the results of a retrospective analysis, from the eve of Ukraine's independence, and highlights the legacy of local governance reforms. The chapter explains how the experience of twenty years of attempts to balance center-periphery relations paved the way for more successful and domestically driven decentralization reforms launched in 2014.

Chapter 2 by Romanova and Umland examines the first phases of the local governance reform and its major deliverable: territorial consolidation on the municipal level. From 2014-2020, the reform faced two principal challenges. First, it was difficult to start implementing the reform in Spring-Summer 2014 before that year's October re-election of parliament and its forthcoming support for the government's new policy proposals. Second, getting the second phase of the reform on track was complicated by three rounds of nationwide voting in the course of Ukraine's 2019 presidential and parliamentary elections. President Poroshenko, who was strongly associated with the decentralization reform, lost the 2019 general elections.

Many domestic decentralization experts associated the reform with Poroshenko's policy agenda and were initially afraid that President Zelenskyy would abandon the undertaking. However, the newly elected president opted to also promote decentralization, in line with the previously drafted policy agenda. As a result of a local amalgamation, the authority of subnational executive organs over local self-governmental authorities declined, while the interconnectedness between central and municipal authorities increased.

Chapter 3 by **Rabinovych** investigates fiscal decentralization in Ukraine in 2014-2017 and presents research results in the light of theoretical and comparative lessons drawn from the literature on the interplay between fiscal decentralization and political and economic transition. Rabinovych argues that fiscal decentralization contributes to democratization by improving the fiscal capacities of substate authorities responsible for introducing principles of good governance in multilevel polities. However, fiscal decentralization does not automatically boost economic growth and needs to be accompanied by a strengthening not only of local but also of regional authorities.

Chapter 4 by **Sydorchuk** explains the dynamics of public attitudes toward decentralization in post-Euromaidan Ukraine. Based on analysis of data from public opinion polls, Sydorchuk argues that the majority of Ukrainians are in favor of decentralization, but not of federalization. Additionally, the chapter investigates the matter of the failed constitutional changes concerning decentralization in 2015 and argues that their failure was determined by their direct link to the highly controversial Minsk Agreements and fulfilment of conditions for a putative conflict resolution in Donbas. Although, as the chapter highlights, people were mostly in favor of post-Euromaidan decentralization, they were also concerned about "the threat of excessive concentration of powers and resources in the hands of elected mayors and heads of communities ... especially after the central government lost its right to monitor the legality of the acts of local elected authorities". Reformers should take note of this concern in designing the postwar phase of decentralization.

Chapter 5 by **Bader** investigates interconnections between state fragility and decentralization in post-Euromaidan Ukraine. Bader presents a comprehensive and nuanced review of comparative research results on the implications of decentralization reforms on state capacity, economic growth, and democratic accountability. According to Bader's assessment, Ukraine was a weak state in 2014, and this affected the reform's outcomes and deliverables. His findings are based on his extensive fieldwork in Odesa Oblast, revealing citizens' engagement in decision-making at the grassroots level during local amalgamation. He identifies potential risks in the diffusion of corrupt practices and reduction of state capacity at the local level.

Chapter 6 by Mierzejewski-Voznyak explores the effects of decentralization on party politics in post-Euromaidan Ukraine, particularly the territorial dimension of party competition and party organization. Although Ukraine's party system has been heavily regionalized for a long time, according to her findings, "[t]he development of local party branches with independent manifestos and campaign strategies is a relatively new issue for Ukrainian political parties".[15] The first phase of the decentralization reform motivated political parties to intensify their competition at local scales because there was now more at stake in local self-government. Under these circumstances, most parliamentary parties failed, however, to address the need for applying a locally tailored approach to campaigns in local elections, while local party projects failed to invest time and effort into fostering a state-wide network of local party organizations.

Chapter 7 by Dunayev investigates the relationship between decentralization and regional policy in Ukraine in 2014-2017. Based on results of an expert survey of the drafting and implementation of strategies for regional and local development in Ukraine, Dunayev describes the input of empowered local authorities into promoting local development. The chapter finds that the institutional capacity of regional authorities to foster economic growth remained limited at the first stage of the post-Euromaidan decentralization reform.

Chapter 8 by Palekha investigates the interplay between decentralization and spatial planning in Ukraine. It highlights those institutional changes that can help Ukraine meet the EU's requirements and standards of spatial planning and contribute to the sustainable development of territorial communities.

---

15 Sarah Birch, "Interpreting the Regional Effect in Ukrainian Politics", *Europe-Asia Studies* 52, no. 6 (2000): 1017-1041.

Chapter 9 by Deineiko and Aasland examines the impact of the decentralization reform on social cohesion since the Russian military invasion. The authors apply both qualitative and quantitative methods to establish that social capital generated at the local level was augmented during the war. "Greater trust in heads of ATCs [amalgamated territorial committees] and city mayors has fostered greater responsibility and local attachment to local leaders, who have proved their leadership by personally supporting and participating in military and civil resistance in all parts of Ukraine".

Chapter 10 by Romanova studies the input of local amalgamation reform into Ukraine's social inclusion policies related to IDPs. It compares social policy provisions and their deliverables since Russia annexed Ukraine's Autonomous Republic of Crimea and fueled armed conflict in Donbas, as well as since its large-scale invasion of Ukraine in 2022. The chapter finds that Ukraine's local amalgamation reform moderately contributed to ensuring stability of IDPs' regular income, but that its input into providing IDPs with communal housing was crucial.

The final chapter by Umland and Romanova presents four international dimensions of the post-2014 local governance reform in Ukraine. The chapter claims that the reform increases resilience, improves cohesion, contributes to Ukraine's Europeanization, and has the potential to inspire local governance reforms in other decentralizing unitary states around the globe.

1. Ukraine's Early Decentralization Attempts*

Valentyna Romanova and Andreas Umland

The local governance reform in Ukraine that started after the Revolution of Dignity has gained increasing international attention. However, the origins and determinants of the reform often remain unclear or, worse, misunderstood. The transformation of Ukrainian center-periphery relations is sometimes seen as driven by foreign factors, such as Kyiv's Association Agreement with the EU or the Minsk Agreements with Russia. This chapter aims to remedy this gap and to explain the prehistory of the post-Euromaidan decentralization reform. To better understand the historic roots of Ukraine's recent decentralization, we briefly consider the legacy of previous reform efforts aimed at both improving multilevel governance and introducing more meaningful self-government.[1] To be sure, these earlier attempts, as reported below, were for the most part abortive. However, these efforts are still important to understand not only the background and sources of the present transitions, but also their nature and prospects within the context of Ukraine's post-Soviet political life and public administration.

By the start of decentralization in spring 2014, Ukraine was—despite some regions' and cities' de facto and, in the case of Crimea, de jure autonomy—still a formally centralized state with administrative and territorial structures largely inherited from the USSR.[2] Crimea and Sevastopol were illegally annexed by Russia in March

---

* This chapter is based on our older *Kennan Cable*, no. 44, 2019.
1 Among early seminal Ukrainian-language surveys were: Anatolii Tkachuk, *Mistseve samovryaduvannya ta detsentralizatsiya: Praktychnyy posibnyk* (Kyiv: Sofiia, 2012); Yuriy Hanushchak, *Reforma terytorial'noi orhanizatsii vlady* (Kyiv: DESPRO, 2012, 3rd edn 2015); Anatolii Tkachuk, *Derzhavna rehionalna polityka: Vid asymetriï do solidarnosti (robochyi zoshyt)* (Kyiv: Lehalnyi status, 2013); Anatoliy Tkachuk, *Pro detsentralizatsiiu, federalizatsiiu, separatystiv ta ul'tymatumy: zapytannia ta vidpovidi* (Kyiv: Lehalnyi status, 2014).
2 Kyiv and Sevastopol are two Ukrainian cities with a special status acknowledged in the Constitution and regulated by separate laws.

2014, and the Moscow-fueled conflict in Donbas started shortly after. These events, though instigated from outside, illustrated the vulnerability of the Ukrainian state's regional and local structures. The country suffered from a lack of territorial cohesion, large intranational disparities, and limited intercommunal cooperation. These conditions were not sufficient to generate an armed uprising on their own but certainly facilitated Russian intrusion into Ukraine.[3]

Before 2014, subnational self-governance remained weak and allowed little room for local development. In the 24 regions (*oblasts*) and 490 districts (*rayons*) of unified Ukraine, only directly elected councils in villages, towns and cities had the constitutional right to establish "executive organs" (*vykonavchi orhany*). The smaller towns

---

3   Some early contributions to the ongoing heated debate about the weight of domestic versus foreign factors in the outbreak of the Donbas war—a discussion that is also of interest to some issues touched upon here—include, in chronological order: Nikolai Mitrokhin, "Infiltration, Instruktion, Invasion: Russlands Krieg in der Ukraine", *Osteuropa* 64, no. 8, 2014, 3-16; Sergiy Kudelia, "Domestic Sources of the Donbas Insurgency", *PONARS Eurasia Policy Memos*, no. 351, 2014, www.ponarseurasia.org/memo/domestic-sources-donbas-insurgency; Andreas Umland, "In Defense of Conspirology: A Rejoinder to Serhiy Kudelia's Anti-Political Analysis of the Hybrid War in Eastern Ukraine", *PONARS Eurasia*, 30 September 2014, www.ponarseurasia.org/article/defense-conspirology-rejoinder-serhiy-kudelias-anti-political-analysis-hybrid-war-eastern;   Sergiy Kudelia, "Reply to Andreas Umland: The Donbas Insurgency Began At Home", *PONARS Eurasia*, 8 October 2014, www.ponarseurasia.org/article/reply-andreas-umland-donbas-insurgency-began-home; Lawrence Freedman, "Ukraine and the Art of Limited War", *Survival* 56, no. 6, 2014-2015, 7-38; Nikolai Mitrokhin, "Infiltration, Instruction, Invasion: Russia's War in the Donbass", *Journal of Soviet and Post-Soviet Politics and Society* 1, no. 1, 2015, 219-250; Oleksandr Zadorozhnii, "Hybrid War or Civil War? The Interplay of Some Methods of Russian Foreign Policy Propaganda with International Law", *Kyiv-Mohyla Law and Politics Journal*, no. 2, 2016, 117-128; Andrew Wilson, "The Donbas in 2014: Explaining Civil Conflict Perhaps, but not Civil War", *Europe-Asia Studies* 68, no. 4, 2016, 631-652; Ivan Katchanovski, "The Separatist War in Donbas: A Violent Break-up of Ukraine?" *European Politics and Society* 17, no. 4, 2016, 473-489; Serhiy Kudelia, "The Donbas Rift", *Russian Politics and Law* 54, no. 1, 2016, 5-27; Gwendolyn Sasse and Alice Lackner, "War and Identity: The Case of the Donbas in Ukraine", *Post-Soviet Affairs* 34, nos. 2-3, 2018, 139-157; Elise Giuliano, "Who Supported Separatism in Donbas? Ethnicity and Popular Opinion at the Start of the Ukraine Crisis", *Post-Soviet Affairs* 34, nos. 2-3, 2018, 158-178; Andreas Umland, "The Glazyev Tapes, Origins of the Donbas Conflict, and Minsk Agreements", *Foreign Policy Association*, 13 September 2018, foreignpolicyblogs.com/2018/09/13/the-glazyev-tapes-origins-of-the-donbas-conflict-and-minsk-agreements/.

and villages that elected their mayors and councils and established executive committees, however, had too little institutional and financial capacity to properly provide basic services. They were thus dependent on subregional, regional, and central authorities.

Directly elected councils in regions and districts still have no constitutional right to establish executive committees on their own. Thus, they delegate implementation of their decisions to substate executives appointed directly by the center. Weak self-government in regions and districts, combined with a centrally imposed executive vertical, were designed as a means to implement Kyiv's decisions all over Ukraine. In practice, the prerogatives of the *oblast* and *rayon* councils, on the one hand, and the central executive vertical, on the other, partly duplicate each other.[4] This peculiar constitutional arrangement was the result of a compromise between the president and parliament in 1996 and reflected the central government's effort to secure loyalty of regional elites.[5]

At the local level, only certain so-called "cities of *oblast* significance" had enough power and resources to enjoy some kind of genuine local self-government. Their residents elected mayors as well as city councils that established executive committees and received a generous share of the Personal Income Tax for their local budgets. Although smaller towns and villages also elected mayors and councils, and the latter established executive committees, they

---

4   The most prominent partial exception, in formal terms, was the Autonomous Republic of Crimea (ARC), where the directly elected regional parliament appointed the head of the regional government, i.e., the Prime-Minister of the ARC, who was then approved by the President of Ukraine, and appointed the ministers of the regional government, on suggestion of the Prime-Minister of the ARC. In practical terms, by February 2014, the top personnel of the regional government in ARC was largely represented by the so-called *makedontsy*. These were ministers lobbied, first, by the former Prime-Minister of the ARC Vasyl Dzharty from the Party of Regions and, later, by his successor Anatolyi Mohyliov from the same party, and jokingly referred to as "Macedonians", after Yanukovych's Donbas home town Makiivka. More on this: Andrew Wilson, "The Crimean Tatar Question: A Prism for Changing and Rival Versions of Eurasianism", *Journal of Soviet and Post-Soviet Politics and Society* 3, no. 2, 2017, 1-46.
5   Kimitaka Matsuzato, "Local Reforms in Ukraine 1990-1998: Elite and Institutions", in: Osamu Ieda, ed., *The Emerging Local Governments in Eastern Europe and Russia: Historical and Post-Communist Development* (Hiroshima: Keisuisha, 2000), 25-54.

were assigned very modest shares of the taxes and thus lacked the financial capacity to provide public services at local scales. Instead, regional and subregional executives assumed key duties related to public service provision.

Nevertheless, prior to 2014, there had already been some first efforts at decentralization. The majority of these reflected power struggles either between president and parliament (in 1991-1996),[6] or between the president and the prime minister (in 2005-2013).[7] Already on the eve of independence, the Ukrainian Soviet Republic's newly elected national parliament introduced a legislative framework for local self-governance. On 7 December 1990, it approved the Law "On Local Councils and Local & Regional Self-Governance", which allowed all directly elected councils to exert more authority over their jurisdictions. It also made these councils responsible for fulfilling the functions of regional or local self-government as well as of central state power. This proved to be so attractive that even very small villages sought to establish their own legislative and executive bodies.

Thus, soon after Ukraine gained independence in 1991, the number of local self-governing units increased dramatically. In the early 1990s, approximately 10,000 self-administering local communities appeared. However, with an average population of approximately 1,500 inhabitants, they were very often far too small to provide, unaided, even basic public services, to say nothing of their ability to effectively promote local development. In newly independent Ukraine, policymakers thus tended to prioritize the regional and upper subregional (district or county) levels of governance while often ignoring the municipal level. Local matters of public service delivery were—with the notable exception of some dynamic cities—largely overlooked.

---

6   Kimitaka Matsuzato, "All Kuchma's Men: The Reshuffling of Ukrainian Governors and the Presidential Election of 1999", *Post-Soviet Geography and Economics* 42, no. 6, 2001, 416-439.

7   Valentyna Romanova, "The Role of Centre-Periphery Relations in the 2004 Constitutional Reform in Ukraine", *Regional & Federal Studies* 21, no. 3, 2011, 321-339.

There was a baffling back-and-forth with prerogatives provided to regional and local self-governmental bodies and then again canceled, during the first years of independence.[8] In 1992, the Law "On the Presidential Representative" and the new edition of the Law "On Local Councils and Local & Regional Self-Governance" were passed. They abolished the recently created executive bodies, appointed by directly elected regional and subregional councils, and introduced presidential representatives as *oblast* and *rayon* executives. These centrally appointed governors and county managers were tasked with implementing Kyiv's decisions on the subnational levels and of ensuring the center's oversight of decision-making within directly elected regional and subregional councils.

Only two years later, in 1994, however, the national parliament approved the Law "On the Establishment of Local Power Institutions and Self-Government". This law abolished the regional executives and transferred their responsibilities back to executive committees appointed by elected regional and subregional councils.[9] This provoked a chaotic form of regionalization and eventually failed to strengthen self-governing bodies' capacity to properly deliver public services.

In general, there were severe challenges to basic state building after the collapse of the USSR. One outcome of this was that, in 1995, the newly elected President Leonid Kuchma and national parliament signed a peculiar constitutional agreement. Among other provisions, this treaty converted the directly elected regional and subregional councils' executive committees into state administrations headed by officials appointed by the president. This mixed or hybrid model finally became entrenched in Ukraine's new 1996 Constitution.[10] Directly elected *oblast* and *rayon* councils served as (sub)regional self-government bodies, but centrally appointed

---

8   Andrew Wilson, "Ukraine", in: Robert Elgie (ed.), *Semi-Presidentialism in Europe* (Oxford: Oxford University Press, 1999), 260–280.
9   Matsuzato, "Local Reforms in Ukraine 1990-1998: Elite and Institutions".
10 Wolczuk, "Catching up with 'Europe'? Constitutional Debates on the Territorial-Administrative Model in Independent Ukraine".

regional and upper subregional state administrations had executive power.

As part of its accession to the Council of Europe, Ukraine signed the European Charter on Local Self-Government in 1996 and ratified it in 1997. As a consequence, it had once more to pass new domestic legislation that, again, redefined the prerogatives of municipalities and specified anew the responsibilities of subnational executives. Ukraine thus adopted the Law "On Local Self-Government in Ukraine" in 1997 and the Law "On Regional State Administrations" in 1999, thereby strengthening once again regionally and locally elected bodies.

These changes, however, proved to be insufficient to establish a sustainable model of multilevel governance, one that would secure enough leeway for genuine self-government. In practice, the regional executives reporting to the president continued to concentrate most power in their hands.[11] Many local self-governmental bodies, with the partial exception of those in certain large cities, continued to heavily depend on transfers and subsidies from Kyiv, allocated in an often-nontransparent manner. Bargaining continued to flourish. Interregional disparities did not decline; in some cases, they even worsened.

There were also noteworthy attempts to reform Ukraine's territorial division and subnational budgets. For instance, the 1998 so-called "Concept of Administrative Reform in Ukraine", approved by Presidential Decree No. 810, included an ambitious plan to introduce new forms of governance and territorial divisions.[12] For a variety of reasons, however, this "Concept" ultimately failed to impact real policymaking. Its vague formulations left the tasks and expected results of the suggested changes unclear.

An early attempt to reform the Budget Code of Ukraine was more successful. In 2001, Ukraine introduced a formula-method into certain parts of the central budget allocations to regions,

---

11 Matsuzato, "All Kuchma's Men: The Reshuffling of Ukrainian Governors and the Presidential Election of 1999".
12 Valentyna Romanova, *Decentralization and Multilevel Elections in Ukraine: Reform Dynamics and Party Politics in 2010–2021* (Stuttgart: ibidem-Verlag, 2022), 39.

districts, and localities.[13] Thanks to this change, the system of intergovernmental transfers was improved. It enhanced overall state capacity and transparency of public finances.[14] However, a more coherent system of multilevel governance, as well as an appropriate territorial structure, were still lacking.

A new fundamental reform attempt was contained in the project for a constitutional amendment, Draft Law 3207-1 submitted to parliament in 2003. It proposed a redefinition of the administrative-territorial structure of Ukraine via, among others, an

a) introduction of the concept of *hromady* (or *gromadas*, i.e. communities) instead of cities, towns, and villages,
b) subordination of regional executives to the Council of Ministers (thereby excluding the President from this part of intragovernmental relations), and
c) establishment of "executive organs" (*vykonavchi orhany*) appointed by elected regional and subregional councils.

However, the severe tension between the then outgoing President Leonid Kuchma and the opposition in 2003-2004 — a confrontation that eventually culminated in the Orange Revolution — ensured that the amendment failed to gain support.

During the 2004 electoral uprising, a constitutional reform, known in Ukraine as *politreforma*, was negotiated between the governing coalition and opposition forces. This far-reaching rearrangement of institutional power weakened the Office of the President and introduced the present parliamentary-presidential republic in which the prime minister formally holds about as much power as the president — and, in some ways, more. However, this transition did not tackle the issue of decentralization. The reform merely resubordinated regional executives to both the president and the prime minister, thereby creating an additional source of confusion.

---

13 Leitch, Assisting Reform in PostCommunist Ukraine, 2000–2012.
14 Jorge Martinez-Vazquez and Signe Zeikate, "Ukraine: Assessment of the Implementation of the New Formula Based Inter-Governmental Transfer System", *Andrew Young School of Policy Studies Working Papers*, no. 8, 2004. https://www.academia.edu/19727028/Ukraine_Assessment_of_the_Implementation_of_th e_New_Formula_Based_Inter-Governmental_Transfer_System.

The president and prime minister's newly shared responsibility for (sub)regional state administrations was expected to provide an institutional stimulus to compromise and cooperation.[15] In reality, however, it became yet another object of competition between them.[16]

Things were on the path towards change, however. After the triumph of the Orange Revolution in late December 2004, the new postrevolutionary government made decentralization and the territorial restructuring of Ukraine a priority. In 2005, a team led by the new First Deputy Prime Minister Roman Bezsmertnyi designed and promoted a so-called "Concept of Administrative-Territorial Reform" that aimed to improve self-governmental capacity to provide services to citizens and to boost regional development. The draft "Concept" suggested introducing a three-level administrative-territorial system that would consist of

- territorial local communities (*hromady, gromadas*) with no fewer than 5,000 residents;
- subregional districts (*rayony*) with no fewer than 70,000 residents, but also including so-called "*rayon*-cities" or towns with more than 70,000 residents;
- regions, including all *oblasts*, Crimea as well as Sevastopol, and so-called "region-cities", i.e., metropolises with no fewer than 750,000 residents.

According to this scheme—forecasting changes that started to become a reality in 2015—the then existing smaller local communities would have to merge to improve their capacity to provide basic services to local residents. Bezsmertnyi's "Concept" thus already explicitly linked the issue of a new administrative-territorial division to the ability to deliver public services—an idea that has

---

15 Robert K. Christensen, Edward R. Rakhimkulov and Charles R. Wise, "The Ukrainian Orange Revolution Brought More than a New President: What Kind of Democracy Will the Institutional Changes Bring?" *Communist and Post-Communist Studies* 38, no. 2, 2005, 207-230; Oleksyi Protsyk, "Troubled Semi-Presidentialism: Stability of the Constitutional System and Cabinet in Ukraine", *Europe-Asia Studies* 55, no. 7, 2003, 1077-1095.

16 Romanova, "The Role of Centre-Periphery Relations in the 2004 Constitutional Reform in Ukraine".

prominently informed the decentralization ongoing since 2014. The number of *rayons* would significantly shrink, but their size would grow. Moreover, *rayons* would lose a significant share of their responsibilities due to the empowerment of new territorial communities emerging out of amalgamation.

The 2005 draft Concept highlighted the special role of cities, as they would be given enlarged budgets and more responsibilities regarding service provision and local development. Moreover, the draft Concept suggested strengthening regional and subregional council executive committees and drawing a clear dividing line between their competencies and those of the centrally appointed regional executives. After the 2004 *politreforma*, however, such radical changes required once more amending the Constitution and adopting up to 300 new laws—or so Bezsmertnyi then claimed.[17] Due to a lack of political will on the part of central and regional stakeholders and the absence of any relevant draft laws, Bezsmertnyi's ambitious plan fell into oblivion after a personnel rotation within the government in the fall of 2005.

In 2005, the State Law on the Stimulation of Regional Development and, a year later, the State Strategy on the Stimulation of Regional Development were passed by parliament. They provided institutional frameworks for identifying priorities in regional development and for allocating money for certain tasks. One instrument that they recommended was the use of agreements between regions and the center, signed by regional councils and the central government. In practice, however, such regional agreements did not serve the purpose of improving economic development. They quickly became targets of lobbyism by oligarchs who promoted their own enterprises rather than the national interest in different regions.

The governments that followed blocked rather than promoted changes to the division of power between the center, the regions and the municipalities. They stalled reform of Ukraine's dated

---

17 Roman Bezsmertnyi, "Derzhava, yak i budyvlya, pochynaet'sya z fundamentu", *Uryadovyi kur'er*, 22 April 2005. http://crimea-portal.gov.ua/kmu/co ntrol/uk/publish/printable_article?art_id=15884111.

administrative and territorial architecture. Most telling was the sad fate of the originally promising "Concept of Reforming Local Self-Government", which had been designed in the newly established Ministry of Regional Development and was approved by the Cabinet of Ministers on 29 July 2009. In contrast to previous cases, the relevant Working Group immediately supported the Concept with a package of urgent draft laws. This package included amendments to the 1997 Law "On Local Self-Government in Ukraine" and to the 1999 Law "On Regional State Administrations", as well as new draft laws on the amalgamation of communities (*hromady*) and on changes to the administrative-territorial division of Ukraine, to improve public service provision.[18] Despite the emergence of such a comprehensive and concrete reform agenda, the Cabinet of Ministers did not hasten its implementation. This turned out to be a fateful lapse.

A very different political period, the presidency of Viktor Yanukovych which succeeded in 2010-2014, witnessed a new concentration of power in Kyiv. The deeply presidential and centralizing 1996 Constitution came into force again in 2010. A rare concession that indicated, at least, some policy-making commitment to regional interests was the 2010 establishment of the Council of Regions. However, this Council only acted as a consultative institutional platform for central political actors, regional executives, and heads of regional councils. Its main function was to serve as a complementary organ for implementing the central government's regional policies. The creation of the Council of Regions — while itself perhaps a good idea — was not designed to promote genuine devolution of power.

Ukrainian policymakers' first efforts at promoting decentralization were not particularly fruitful. Yet, the various failures and abortive moves were not entirely meaningless. These and similar experiences eventually paved the way for a more successful and domestically driven decentralization reform that started in 2014.

In the early 1990s, elite struggles were evident at a state-wide level: the president and parliament competed for power in Kyiv;

---

18 N. Aleksandrova and I. Koliushko, eds., *Rozvytok publichnoho prava v Ukraini (dopovid za 2009-2010)* (Kyiv: Centre for Political and Legal Reforms, 2011).

regional elites attempted to capture resources and to strengthen their positions at substate scales. Since the mid-1990s, Kyiv gradually succeeded in imposing a centralized vertical of power. However, it failed to improve the state's capacity to deliver public services of a reasonable quality. The quality of services has become the major issue that the recent decentralization reform prioritized. Despite being informed by certain foreign examples, especially by a similar reform in Poland in the 1990s, the Ukrainian decentralization's priorities neither came out of the blue nor were they imported from outside, as is sometimes assumed even by otherwise well-informed Western observers.

After the victory of the Euromaidan revolution in spring 2014, a complex of external pressures and new domestic challenges rapidly increased the impetus for territorial and administrative reform of Ukraine. Some Ukrainian think-tank experts and policymakers quickly converted previously proposed documents, both published and unpublished, into drafts for a comprehensive decentralization agenda. This did not mean, of course, that policy implementation always went smoothly. However, the historic learnings from the above-sketched attempts, along with some Ukrainian experts' increasing familiarity with foreign—above all Polish—decentralization schemes finally bore some real fruit.[19]

---

19 E.g.: Poland: *Decentralization and Reform of the State* (Washington, DC: World Bank, 1992); Anthony Levitas and Jan Herczyński, "Decentralization, Local Governments and Education Reform and Finance in Poland: 1990–1999", in: Kenneth Davey, ed., *Balancing National and Local Responsibilities: Education Management and Finance in Four Central European Countries* (Budapest: CEU Press, 2003), 113-191; Paweł Swianiewicz, "Poland and Ukraine: Contrasting Paths of Decentralization and Territorial Reform", *Local Government Studies* 32, no. 5 (2006), 599-622; Anthony Levitas, "Local Government Reform as State Building: What the Polish Case tells us about 'Decentralization'", *Studies in the International Development* 52 (2017), 23-44.

2. Ukraine's Local Governance Reform and Territorial Consolidation in 2014-20*

Valentyna Romanova and Andreas Umland

Introduction

This chapter examines the core aspects of the post-2014 decentralization reform: local amalgamation and fiscal decentralization. Taken together, these two policies radically changed the division of responsibilities and finances at substate scales and aided Ukraine's territorial consolidation. The 2019 shift of the balance of power in Kyiv did not alter the reform's trajectory. Indeed, the newly elected President Zelenskyy fostered, as we show, implementation of the reform by approving the previously drafted laws on decentralization whose progress had stalled prior to 2019-2020. Evidence of this commitment was the policy of merging *rayons* (upper subregional units) that was quickly implemented once nationwide local amalgamation was completed.

The Political Context

Democratization often leads to decentralization in so far as more political pluralism generates societal demands for redivision of power between central and subnational levels of government.[1] However, until the 2013-2014 Euromaidan (literally: European Square) uprising or Revolution of Dignity, the EU and OECD's occasional reports regularly concluded that state power in Ukraine

---

* The chapter's first sections are partly based on an older Chatham House report from 2019.
1 We use "decentralization" here as a lose summary term for various interrelated processes, and as an antonym of centralization. "Decentralization" can—depending on the concrete context—mean devolution, deconcentration or downward delegation of this or that set of prerogatives, competencies, and responsibilities.

was highly concentrated.² The Ukrainian state's centralization did not lead to the center's greater administrative capacity or an improved ability to deliver public services. On the contrary, formal centralism and weak local self-government generated extreme territorial fragmentation, large interregional disparities in economic development, and poor public administration.

A series of events—the victory of the Euromaidan uprising in February 2014, the beginning of Russia's intervention in Ukraine shortly thereafter, and two subsequent rounds of presidential and parliamentary national elections in 2014—changed the composition of Ukraine's ruling elites. The great and unexpected threat to Ukraine's territorial integrity demonstrated the weakness of its centralized yet regionally diverse state. Moreover, post-Euromaidan civil society pressured policymakers to an enact substantial rather than cosmetic reforms.³

In 2014-2015, the post-Euromaidan reformers launched a whole battery of simultaneous and radical changes aimed at improving multilevel governance and promoting local democracy.⁴ The reform's ambitious decentralization plan included empowering communities' self-government and realigning the country's administrative-territorial organization to improve the state's capacity to deliver public services. According to the "Concept of Reforming Local Self-Government and the Territorial Division of Power", approved on 1 April 2014, 10,961 local communities were expected to

---

2   For example: *OECD Territorial Reviews: Ukraine 2013* (Paris: OECD Publishing, 2014). https://doi.org/10.1787/9789264204836-en.
3   Anatolij Tkatschuk, "Zur Dezentralisierung: Erfolge, Risiken und die Rolle des Parlaments", *Ukraine-Nachrichten*, 26 January 2017. https://ukraine-nachrichte n.de/dezentralisierung-erfolge-risiken-rolle-parlamentes_4568; Natalia Shapovalova and Olga Burlyuk, eds., *Civil Society in Post-Euromaidan Ukraine: From Revolution to Consolidation* (Stuttgart: *ibidem*-Verlag, 2018).
4   Some of the first English-language surveys included Roger Myerson and Tymofiy Mylovanov, "Fixing Ukraine's Fundamental Flaw", *Kyiv Post*, 7 March 2014. https://www.kyivpost.com/article/opinion/op-ed/fixing-ukraines-fun damental-flaw-338690.html; Editorial Board, "Decentralization: Second Try", *Vox Ukraine*, 16 July 2015. https://voxukraine.org/2015/07/16/decentralizatio n-second-try/; Ivan Lukerya and Olena Halushka, "Decentralization as a Remedy for Bad Governance in Ukraine", *Euromaidan Press*, 5 December 2016. http:/ /euromaidanpress.com/2016/12/05/decentralization-governance-ukraine-re form/.

voluntarily merge into approximately 1,500 so-called amalgamated territorial communities (ATCs). Initially, the 2014 Concept envisioned changing the institutional structure of *rayons* and *oblasts* to introduce executive committees so as to transform them into properly self-governing bodies, and to enshrine this change in the Constitution. However, this task was not completed. The reform's most notable changes, instead, affected the local level and thus contributed to a remake of Ukraine's center-periphery relations from the bottom up.

In late 2014, Ukraine introduced fiscal decentralization, and in early 2015, the voluntary amalgamation of small territorial communities into larger and more sustainable ones began. Local ATC budgets were given a higher share of taxes (most importantly, 60% of the Personal Income Tax) and obtained new direct transfers from the central state budget (i.e., blocks of grants for covering the costs for primary and secondary education). The purpose was to make ATCs capable of delivering basic public services at local scales.[5]

Thanks to the voluntary aspect of local amalgamation, since 2015 many Ukrainians have gained valuable experience in organizing collective undertakings and resources while engaging in debates—often rather heated—on municipal issues and taking responsibility for joint decision-making. Once the new ATCs were established, voters were asked to elect more powerful local self-governmental bodies responsible for distributing public funds and administering the regulative functions that had previously been the province of regional and subregional state bodies.

Territorial fragmentation at the local level was reduced. Notably, both rural and urban municipalities, including many so-called "cities of *oblast* significance", joined the voluntary amalgamation process. The inclusion of these cities explains why the populations of ATCs differ enormously, ranging from a mere 1,002 to as many as 373,164 inhabitants, with an average of 10,563 people per ATC.[6]

---

5   Levitas and Djikic, "Caught Mid-Stream".
6   Valentyna Romanova and Andreas Umland, "Ukraine's Decentralization Reforms Since 2014: Initial Achievements and Future Challenges", *Chatham House*, September 2019. https://www.chathamhouse.org/sites/default/files/2019-09-24-UkraineDecentralization.pdf.

Certain new ATCs extend over such large territories that they replicate the boundaries of Ukrainian upper subregional administrative units, the so-called *rayons*.

Due to their increased local budgets and direct relations with the state budget, ATCs grew strong enough to take responsibility for public services that the centrally directed *rayons* used to take care of. Subsequently, in the last stage of local amalgamation, a radical decrease in the number of *rayons* was achieved either through their amalgamation or the establishment of brand-new subregional units. In mid-2020, 490 old *rayons* were merged into 136 new *rayons*. The local amalgamation reform thus significantly changed Ukrainian state's structure and functioning.

Ambitious Plans vs. Modest Progress in 2014

On 1 April 2014, the early postrevolutionary government adopted the mentioned new Concept which outlined how Kyiv intended to empower local self-governments, improve state capacity to deliver public services, and fundamentally redesign Ukraine's administration. The reform's proclaimed objectives were ambitious. They included significant empowerment of self-government at the local level and a thoroughgoing readjustment of Ukraine's territorial division. Additionally, the Concept proposed introducing executive committees to regional and subregional assemblies and redesigning Ukraine's administrative-territorial divisions at the subregional level. In practice, however, local amalgamation became the reformers' major priority.

Although post-Euromaidan policymakers demonstrated enough political will to announce the start of the reform in Spring 2014, political fragmentation in the national parliament, the *Verkhovna Rada* (Supreme Council), prior to the October 2014 parliamentary snap elections prevented progress in implementation. At that stage, the reformers only managed to carry through some substantial changes in intermunicipal cooperation and regional development.

First, on 17 June 2014, the law on intermunicipal cooperation was approved. It provided a legal framework that allowed territorial communities to join forces to better tackle common challenges.

The 2014 law did not foresee financial benefits accompanying the new institutional framework; it simply eliminated some legal obstacles that had previously prevented municipalities' effective cooperation. Although the 2014 law benefited local communities and their authorities, the latter did initially not make much use of it, as is evident from the low degree of intermunicipal cooperation. While, in 2014-2017, 535 territorial communities completed 118 intermunicipal cooperation projects, in 2021 alone, 153 intermunicipal cooperation projects were implemented by 296 ATCs.

A brief data analysis of the latter reveals that 50 out of these 153 projects (see Figure 2.1 for their geographical location) concerned public service provision in the areas of education, healthcare, and social policy. The largest number of ATCs engaged in intermunicipal cooperation were in the Rivne, Lviv, and Ivano-Frankivsk *oblasts* in Western Ukraine. The largest number of intermunicipal cooperation projects, however, were implemented in the Dnipropetrovsk, Kharkiv, and Zaporizhzhya *oblasts* in Eastern Ukraine. Such cooperations required treaties to be signed by local governments and their collaboration to cope with various matters related to healthcare, education, energy efficiency, administrative services, etc.

Figure 2.1. Intermunicipal cooperation in 2021

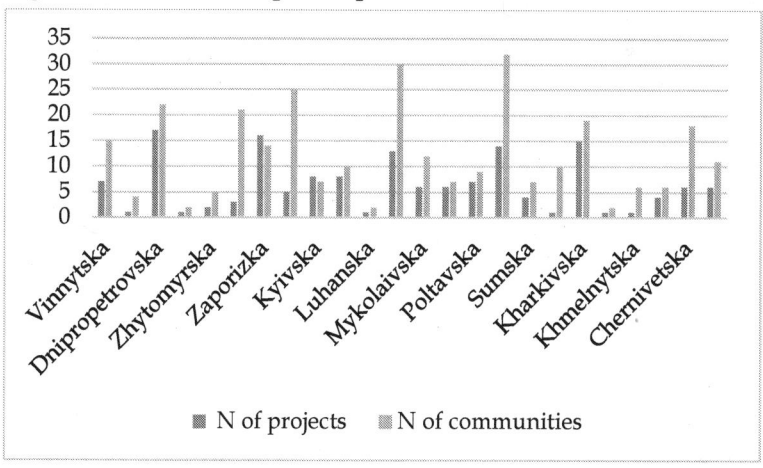

Source: Our own compilation based on: "Monitoring of power decentralization and local self-government reform in Ukraine", *Detsentralizatsiya*, 10 January 2022. https://decentralization.gov.ua/uploads/library/file/800/10.01.2022.pdf

Second, in order to minimize interregional disparities, Kyiv also amended the institutional and financial framework to foster local development via central subsidies. On 6 August 2014, the national parliament approved the State Strategy for Regional Development until 2020 (SSRD-2020). The SSRD-2020 aimed to ensure the territorial integrity of the state, promoting sustainable economic development, fostering the regions' competitiveness, and stimulating interregional cooperation. It applied planning and budgeting standards and methods that were also used in the EU. This was meant to improve multilevel institutional coordination in the area of regional development.

The SSRD imposed horizontal coordination mechanisms for the state bodies that influenced regional development, as well as vertical coordination between central and regional institutions that developed and supported regional development projects. Horizontal coordination was guided by *Minregion*, which was charged with engaging other executive bodies in the reform. Vertical coordination was meant to ensure that every regional development strategy was formulated according to the SSRD priorities and that every local development plan was harmonized with the relevant regional development strategy.[7] These mechanisms were meant to help implementing coherent and coordinated plans for regional and local development within a new institutional setting.

These two policy changes, i.e. intermunicipal cooperation and regional development, were modest when compared to the ambitious reform agenda adopted on 1 April 2014. They nevertheless impressed representatives of the Council of Europe who likened their progress to Kyiv's previous decentralization attempts of 2010-2013.[8] Most importantly, the newly introduced changes inspired

---

7   Maintaining *the Momentum of Decentralization in Ukraine* (Kyiv: OECD, 2018). www.oecd.org/countries/ukraine/maintaining-the-momentum-of-decentralization-in-ukraine-9789264301436-en.htm.
8   "U 2014 rotsi dlya detsentralizatsii zrobleno bilshe, nizh za dekilka porerednikh rokiv, - predstavnyky Kongresu mistsevykh i regionalnykh vlad Rady Yevropy", *Detsentralizatsiya*, 9 December 2014. https://decentralization.gov.ua/news/133.

the domestic reformers to move forward with implementing their plans soon after the 2014 early parliamentary elections.

Fiscal Decentralization and Voluntary Amalgamation in 2015-19

In late 2014 and early 2015, the core policy initiatives to foster Ukraine's territorial consolidation were launched. First, fiscal decentralization was introduced. In December 2014, the *Verkhovna Rada* amended the Budget and Tax Codes of Ukraine and introduced fiscal decentralization. These changes were intended to provide the new ATCs with financial prerogatives similar to those enjoyed by the so-called "cities of *oblast* significance", which, until 2014, were the only municipalities with meaningful local self-government.[9] The *Verkhovna Rada* grated to the ATCs direct inter-budgetary relations with the central government and allowed them an impressive share of the tax revenue, including, as already stated, 60% of the Personal Income Tax (PIT).

In addition, ATC budgets received a set of subsidies from the center, including, until 2020, for constructing the institutional and social infrastructure of the reformed self-government bodies. Special equalization grants were introduced to mitigate disparities between territorial communities' local development. Separate block grants in the areas of healthcare (until July 2018), education, and administrative services further improved the financial capacities of ATCs, allowing them to take on more responsibility for delivering public services. ATCs became, for instance, responsible for managing primary and secondary education in their territories—in contrast to non-amalgamated communities whose self-governance was weak and dependent on the guidance of centrally appointed upper subregional executives.

Fiscal decentralization advanced quickly. In December 2018, the National Institute for Strategic Studies, Kyiv's main governmental think-tank, proudly reported:

---

9   *Maintaining the Momentum of Decentralization in Ukraine.*

"Nearly 15% of Ukraine's GDP is distributed through local budgets. In 2018, local budgets' share of properly owned incomes accounted (in total) for 7.1% of GDP (in 2014, it was 5.1%), and local budgets' properly owned incomes rose from UAH68.6 billion in 2015 to UAH189.4 billion [in 2018]. Local budgets' share (including transfers [from the center]) in Ukraine's overall budget rose from 45.6% in 2015 to 51.5% in 2018. [...] In comparison to 2014, [central] state support for the development of territorial communities and the improvement of their infrastructure was 39 times greater. [Central] subsidies for the formation of [administrative] structures of the ATCs was, in 2018, UAH1.9 billion, [and], for 2019, [these] subsidies are forecast [to reach] UAH2.1 billion".[10]

Additionally, the central government increased its financial support for regional and local development. According to *Minregion*'s official records, in 2013, Ukraine spent UAH0.5 billion for this purpose. By contrast, in 2018, it invested approximately UAH19.37 billion in regional and local development.[11]

Some shortcomings regarding local fiscal autonomy remained.[12] Still, in 2015-21, the capacity of local communities to generate their own income grew steadily (Figure 2.2), and the share of local budget revenues in the consolidated budget of Ukraine increased (Figure 2.3).

---

10 Zhalilo et al., Detsentralizatsiya vlady (2018), 12-13.
11 "Finansovi rezul'taty mistsevykh byudzhetiv za 5 misyatsiv 2018 roku [Local Budgets' Financial Results During the First Five Months of 2018]", *Detsentralizatsiya*, 19 June 2018. https://decentralization.gov.ua/news/9047.
12 Manuela Söller-Winkler, "Financial autonomy: At the heart of local government!" *Detsentralizatsiya*, 3 June 2021. https://decentralization.gov.ua/en/news/13610?page=3.

Figure 2.2. Local revenue share of Ukraine's overall GDP

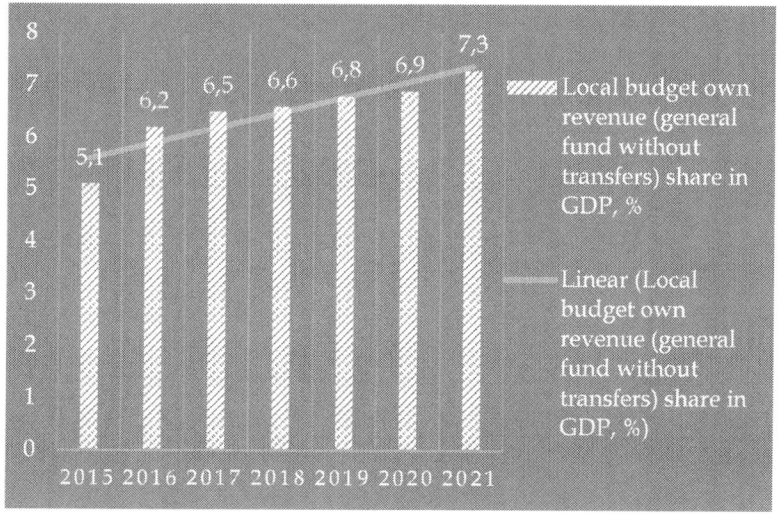

Source: Our compilation based on "Monitoring of power decentralization and local self-government reform in Ukraine", *Decentralization*, 10 January 2022. https://decentralization.gov. ua/uploads/library/file/800/10.01.2022.pdf

Figure 2.3. Local budgets' share of Ukraine's overall budget

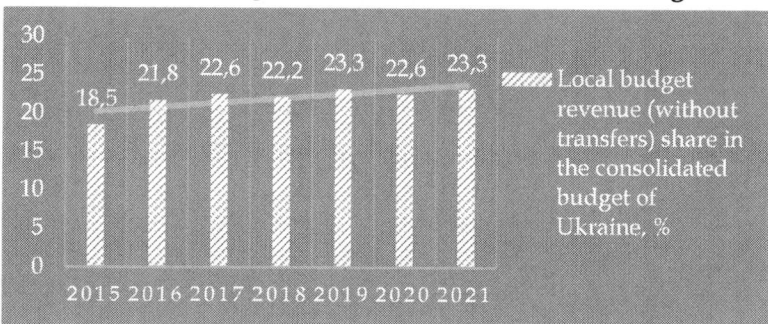

Source: Our compilation based on: "Monitoring of power decentralization and local self-government reform in Ukraine", *Detsentralizatsiya*, 10 January 2022. https://decentralization.gov. ua/uploads/library/file/800/10.01.2022.pdf

The central government often touted advances in fiscal decentralization as a major achievement. However, international experts warned that it was risky for the government to assume that the prospect of financial benefit would act as a reliable incentive for local communities to voluntarily merge.[13] The central government continued to highlight the promise of financial gains to ATCs nonetheless.

The government introduced the legal framework for voluntary local amalgamation in February 2015. In line with the 2015 law on voluntary local amalgamation, rural and urban municipalities could merge into ATCs which assume full responsibility for local development and the provision of basic public services. To do so, they had to follow a detailed procedure set out in the official "Methodology for Establishing Sustainable Territorial Communities" approved by the Cabinet of Ministers on 8 April 2015.[14]

The new ATCs needed to meet certain criteria for the government to accept them as self-sustaining. For example, it was possible for local self-governing units to amalgamate contiguous territories in the same region that had historical, natural, ethnic, cultural, or other unifying characteristics. The distance of potential amalgamation partners should be no more than 25–30 km from the ATC center, while the ATC center itself should be a relatively large local governmental unit with its own administrative and social infrastructure.

The government's policy implied that ATC centers were expected to become major drivers and beneficiaries of local amalgamation. Core providers of public services for the residents of a newly established ATC were expected to be located in the ATC center; this concerns above all schools, hospitals, centers for administrative service provision, etc. The local council of a newly established ATC elected by voters in different localities belonging to the ATC was expected to carry out its functions in the ATC center. By contrast, local communities (villages, settlements) which were part of an ATC would, once local amalgamation was complete, no longer elect their local councils.

The ATCs' institutional design was meant to ensure representation for residents from all of their localities, but there was a telling

---

13 Levitas and Djikic, "Caught Mid-Stream".
14 "Postanova vid 8 kvitnya 2015 r. No. 214, Kyiv, 'Pro zatverdzhennya Metodyky formuvannya spromozhnykh terytorial'nykh hromad'", *Kabinet ministriv Ukrainy*, 8 April 2015. https://zakon.rada.gov.ua/laws/show/214-2015-%D0%BF#n10.

nuance. The new entities' self-government bodies consisted of a directly elected ATC *holova* (head); a directly elected territorial council, with its own executive committee; and *starosty* (literally, elders). However, a *starosta*—a representative from the villages and towns outside the administrative center of the ATC—was so far directly elected only once as there were no direct elections of *starosty* during the 2020 local elections.[15]

In 2015, the government simultaneously introduced two distinct voluntary local amalgamation procedures. On the one hand, local initiative played a key role: local authorities or residents invited potential local partners to join a discussion about amalgamating into one ATC, following the government's methodology on choosing the ATC center, developing the prospective ATC's infrastructure, etc. If a positive outcome had been reached, they drew up the local councils' draft decision and passed it on to the respective regional state administration (regional executive) to double check that it complied with the Constitution and domestic laws. If it passed, the local councils took the final decision to establish the ATC. Then they communicated with the regional state administration again. This time, the latter was entitled to officially communicate with the Central Electoral Commission and request that it announces the first election of the newly established ATC's local authorities.

On the other hand, the central government requested all regional state administrations to draft (and every regional assembly to approve) a so-called "prospect plan" of ATCs in their respective regions. In doingthis, the regional authorities were expected to follow the above-mentioned so-called Methodology's guidelines on how to choose the ATC center, how to develop the infrastructure of the prospective ATC, etc. The completed "prospect plans" were approved by the central government, which is supposed to ensure that potential ATCs has enough resources to assume responsibility for public service delivery at alocal level. Finally, after completion of local amalgamation, the residents of the newly established ATC

---

15 Valentyna Romanova, *Decentralization and Multilevel Elections in Ukraine: Reform Dynamics and Party Politics in 2010–2021* (Stuttgart: ibidem-Verlag, 2022), 39.

elected their self-governing bodies, which then obtained additional budgetary funds as well as new administrative prerogatives.

Voluntary amalgamation in Ukraine was surprisingly quick. In 2015, the first year of the process, 159 ATCs were created in Ukraine.[16] These united 795 old communities. In 2016, 944 territorial communities amalgamated into 207 ATCs. Thus, by the end of 2016, 366 ATCs were made from 1,739 localities. In 2017, 1,525 old territorial communities merged into 333 ATCs, raising the total, by the end of that year, to 699 ATCs composed of 3,264 rural and urban municipalities. In 2018, the number increased to 874 ATCs. Finally, 899 ATCs were established by May 2019, when Petro Poroshenko lost the presidential election and Volodymyr Zelenskyy became head of state.

It was clear that voluntary amalgamation was still far from being completed. Only 4,187 or 38.2% of the old small local communities had united by May 2019, representing 38.9% of Ukraine's overall territory.[17] A little more than a quarter of the population of Ukraine (27.2%) lived in ATCs, where local self-governance was strengthened, while another 42.85% lived in "cities of *oblast* significance" that already enjoyed strong and sustainable local self-government even without participating in the process of amalgamation. Together, these two groups comprised 66.1% of the population of Ukraine.

Yet, almost one-third of the population of Ukraine (30.13%) still lived in communities with weak local self-government.[18] Several factors prevented voluntary local amalgamation proceeding

---

16 Most of the statistics used to illustrate the progress of Ukraine's decentralization reform typically exclude the Autonomous Republic of Crimea and the city of Sevastopol, illegally annexed by Russia, the temporarily occupied territories of the Donetsk and Luhansk *oblasts*, and the city of Kyiv, which enjoys a special status within Ukraine's territorial-administrative structure.
17 Zhalilo et al., *Detsentralizatsiya vlady* (2018), 5.
18 *Monitorynh protsesu detsentralizatsii vlady ta reformuvannya mistsevoho samovryaduvannya stanom na 12 bereznya 2019* (Kyiv: MinRegion, 2019), https://storage.decentralization.gov.ua/uploads/library/file/389/10.03.2019.pdf.

more quickly.[19] Below, we highlight two factors that cast light on the agency of local and regional authorities.

First, the unamalgamated communities in over half of Ukraine's territory were hesitant to merge because they did not trust the government's promise that fiscal decentralization would greatly benefit them. Their skepticism closely accorded with the warnings of international experts already mentioned.[20] These skeptical unamalgamated communities did not want to take on additional responsibilities for managing social infrastructure, in line with so-called "sectoral decentralization", in such fields as school education, delivery of administrative services, etc. For example, ATCs were tasked with establishing so-called educational districts including foundational or hub schools (*oporni shkoly*) with the best available teaching and learning practices as well as these hub schools' local branches or divisions (*filii*), or administrative centers for public service provision and their subdivisions in remote territories.[21] However, this sometimes required more funds than the ATC budgets gained.

Moreover, some of the reforms could have contradictory aims or their logic could unexpectedly change. Perhaps, most prominently, the parallel ongoing post-Euromaidan health care reform foresaw a certain (re)centralization of transfers to local medical service providers. By May 2019, there was still a lack of clarity about the final arrangement of the newly emerging hospital districts across the country.[22]

---

19 The older local communities that were lucky to have profitable businesses on their territory, and collected taxes from them, were, out of self-interest, less keen to amalgamate with poorer communities, whose and social and other expenses they would have to cover. Sometimes, small local communities were reluctant to amalgamate with larger neighbors for fear that their interests would be insufficiently represented in the new ATC.
20 Levitas and Djikic, "Caught Mid-Stream".
21 "Innovations in decentralization: The very first Ukraine Mobile Administrative Service Centre began operating in Slavuta community with support of U-LEAD with Europe Programme", *Detsentralizatsiya*, 1 December 2017. https://decentralization.gov.ua/en/news/7724.
22 Olesya Shutkevych, "Detsentralizatsiya + medreforma: Na rasshyrennom pravitel'stvennom soveshchanii v Vinnitse rukovoditeli gromad rasskazali, kak delayut uslugi vracha dostupnymi dlia vsekh [Decentralization + Health Care

By 2019, ATCs had assumed responsibility for 335 of the 785 foundational or hub schools then established in Ukraine. ATCs and "cities of *oblast* significance" had taken over the responsibility for approximately 44.4% of Ukrainian schools. Upper subregional executives remained in charge of the remaining 55.6% of the schools in unamalgamated communities. As of this writing in 2021, ATCs were responsible for 540 of the existing 1,272 divisions (or branches) of the foundational or hub schools in Ukraine.

Second, some regional (*oblast*) and upper subregional (*rayon*) councils and their state administrations could be unwilling to give transfer their resources and functions to ATCs. One telling case was the regional executive of the Transcarpathian (*Zakarpatska*) *oblast*, which only allowed ATCs to voluntarily emerge on its territory in early 2019. Somewhat understandably, some administrations and councils were not supportive of the reform, not wanting to lose their jobs as a result of municipal amalgamation and the accompanying transfer of their funds and functions to the new ATCs.[23] On the other hand, some of the members of the gradually dissolving old state bodies ran for local office in the newly established ATCs.[24]

Even if local amalgamation was voluntary in 2015-19, regional authorities could have a considerable impact on its speed as well as on the composition of ATCs. Regional executives contributed to

---

Reform: At an Extended Governmental Meeting, Heads of Communities Explained How They Make Healthcare Services Accessible to Everyone]", *Den'*, 10 April 2018. https://day.kyiv.ua/ru/article/ekonomika/decentralizaciya-m edreforma.

23 Yuriy Hanushchak "Nynishni rayony potribni lishe chynovnykam, a lyudiam potribni yakisni posluhy [Only public servants need the rayons that exist in Ukraine currently: Ordinary people need public services of a good quality]", *Detsentralizatsiya*, 21 February 2019. https://decentralization.gov.ua/news/col umns/10655.

24 "Ostatochnii zvit za rezultatamy sposterezhennya OPORY na pershyh mistsevykh vyborakh u OTH 29 zhovtnya ta 24 hrudnya 2017 roku", *OPORA*, 15 March 2018. https://www.oporaua.org/report/vybory/pershi-vybory-v-o biednanikh-gromadakh/45292-ostatochnyi-zvit-za-rezultatamy-sposterezhen-nia-opory-na-pershykh-mistsevykh-vyborakh-u-obiednanykh-terytorialnykh-hromadakh-29-zhovtnia-ta-24-hrudnia-2017-roku; "Detsentralizovani krainy mayut menshe koruptsii na mistsiakh—spetsposlannyk Nimechchyny z pytan reform v Ukraini [There is less corruption in decentralized states—Special Envoy of Germany for the Ukrainian Reform Agenda]", *Detsentralizatsiya*, 19 March 2019. https://decentralization.gov.ua/news/10765.

organizing voluntary local amalgamation according to the government's guidelines. Regional councils could block local amalgamation if they believed it did not sufficiently reflect regional interests (as represented in regional councils). When the local amalgamation reform was implemented, their power over local authorities increased rather than declined. Regional authorities could either promote public discussion among potential local partners or discourage local residents and local authorities from pursuing local amalgamation.

An important distinction existed between regional executives and regional councils in terms of accountability. While regional executives were subordinate to the central government and, thus, obliged to report on the progress of voluntary local amalgamation and their own input into it, the directly elected regional councils remained relatively autonomous from the executive branch and were not obliged to approve their regions' ATC "prospect plan" if they did not accord with their interests. Last, but not least, regional authorities expected that local amalgamation—once implemented—would limit their prerogatives. This prompted many of them to drag out the process of approving ATC "prospect plans" and to discourage their local counterparts from pursuing local amalgamation.

Still, the agency of local authorities and the local public gradually increased during voluntary local amalgamation as, at least officially, initiation and discussion of the communities' unification was to arise from below. It rapidly increased once the process was completed as local authorities obtained a number of important prerogatives, and local budgets benefited from direct relations to the central budget. During voluntary amalgamation, local publics, to this or that degree, took an active part in discussions regarding the geographical and administrative structures of the prospective ATCs. To be sure, this did not necessarily mean that people supported each and every change triggered by the decentralization reform. As various reform steps were introduced and implemented, sometimes vicious confrontations between various stakeholders and the public took place. However, these political conflicts allowed people to gain valuable experience in articulating their interests and making use of their representation in the new local self-governmental bodies.

The voluntary amalgamation of territorial communities, together with fiscal stimuli, helped consolidate Ukraine from the bottom up. These changes remained incomplete, however. Moreover, their finalization had a certain urgency, as the amalgamation of territorial communities was meant to be completed before Ukrainian local elections regularly scheduled for October 2020.

Completion of Territorial Consolidation in 2020

In January 2019, policymakers in Kyiv announced the second phase of the decentralization reform.[25] Its main objective was to speed up the pace of the local amalgamation process to get it completed prior to the next regular round of nationwide local council elections on 25 October 2020. The key instrument to achieve this goal was speeding up the approval of "prospect plans" for creating ATCs in all *oblasts*, covering 100% of Ukraine's territory, and thus enabling completion of the amalgamation process throughout the country. To assist this process, the parliament was to approve a law that allowed the Cabinet of Ministers to approve ATC "prospect plans" without prior approval from regional councils, as had been the rule until then.

Additionally, the second phase of the reform included a fundamental change of administrative and territorial division at the level of *rayons*. Local amalgamation had considerably shifted responsibilities from *rayons* to the municipal level. According to the 1996 Constitution, directly elected subregional councils were responsible for representing the interests of the localities in their respective *rayons*. The amalgamation and gradual empowerment of ATCs often resulted in the establishment of relatively large and

---

25 The Cabinet of Minister's Decree "On Approving the Action Plan of a New Phase of Reforming Local Self-Government and the Territorial Division of Power in Ukraine in 2019-2021" issued on 23 January 2019 (№ 77-p). https://www.kmu.gov.ua/ua/npas/pro-zatverdzhennya-planu-zahodiv-z-realizaciyi-novogo-etapu-reformuvannya-miscevogo-samovryaduvannya-ta-teritorialnoyi-organizaciyi-vladi-v-ukrayini-na-20192021-roki

powerful ATCs that no longer required administrative help from the upper subregional councils and executives on the *rayon* level. Thus, many *rayons* devolved considerable responsibilities and financial resources on the newly established ATCs. Another reason for introducing bigger *rayons* was a certain "economy of scale", i.e., to reduce public administration expenditures.[26]

At the start of the second stage of the reform, there were 490 subregional districts, with an average population of approximately 25,000 residents. The government planned to establish new — bigger and stronger — *rayons*, in line with the requirements of the Nomenclature of Units for Territorial Statistics (NUTS) applied in the EU. Old *rayons* were expected to merge administratively.[27] Their new territorial boundaries would be guided by the modified functions of the new subregional branches of the central government.[28]

The legal framework for merging old *rayons* into new *rayons* was drafted by the government in the first stage of the decentralization reform, and parliament was expected to pass it into law. However, the draft laws clarifying the new responsibilities of subregional executives and councils in "new" *rayons* were still being prepared by the working group of the *Minregion*. As a consequence, it was impossible to specify the precise functions that would be allocated to the subregional executives in the new *rayons*. The government-established working group was conducting fieldwork in a number of regions and subregions and collecting evidence to define the final set of criteria for establishing the new amalgamated *rayons*.

---

26 However, this issue was not as straightforward as some Ukrainian reformers assumed. See Felix Roesel, "Do Mergers of Large Local Governments Reduce Expenditures? Evidence from Germany Using the Synthetic Control Method", *European Journal of Political Economy* 50 (2017): 22-36.
27 Natal'ya Shutka, "Yu. Ganushchak o detsentralizatsii: Yesli gosudarstvo vozglavit avtoritarshchik, budet popytka vse vernut' nazad [Yu. Hanushchak about decentralization: If the state is run by an authoritarian leader, there will be an attempt to turn everything back]", *ZIK*, 29 October 2018. https://zik.ua/r u/news/2018/10/29/yuganushchak_o_detsentralyzatsyy_esly_gosudarstvo_ vozglavyt_avtorytarshchyk_budet_1436531.
28 Anatoliy Tkachuk and Yuriy Hanushchak, "Transformatsiya rayoniv v protsesi ta za pidsumkamy detsentralizatsii [The transformation of *rayons* in the process and as a result of decentralization]", *Ukrainskyy kryzovyy media-tsentr*, 10 May 2017. http://decentralization.uacrisis.org/.

The key law concerning the enlarged *rayons*, prepared by *Minregion* for parliament's consideration (the Law Draft No. 8051 "On the Basics of the Administrative-Territorial Structure of Ukraine"), identified the key principles and procedures for changing the boundaries of administrative-territorial entities, including the *rayons*. In line with these principles, the 490 existing *rayons* could be consolidated into approximately 100 without a constitutional amendment. The new *rayons* would have a population of approximately 150,000 residents each — corresponding to the EU's so-called NUTS-3 level. The government submitted the draft law to the Supreme Council (*Verkhovna Rada*) in February 2018; however, some stakeholders in the national parliament seemed to have hindered the adoption of this law in its first reading.

Finally, the new stage of the decentralization reform included a partial renewal of subnational self-government at the *oblast* and *rayon* levels, namely constitutional amendments to introduce executive committees into regional and subregional councils. As early as 2015, parliament attempted to adopt these amendments (Law Draft No. 2217a).[29] Shortly before being submitted, the amendments had been linked to a controversial clause imposed by the widely disliked Minsk Agreements signed with Russia in September 2014 and February 2015. The clause allowed granting a "special status" to the currently non-government-controlled territories in the Donetsk and Luhansk *oblasts*. Because of public discontent, violent clashes in the center of Kyiv, and the opposition of key stakeholders at the crucial vote on 31 August 2015, parliament failed to proceed beyond passing the draft law on its first reading.

During his 2019 presidential re-election campaign, Petro Poroshenko reminded policymakers and voters of the need to introduce executive committees into regional and subregional councils. In reply, some MPs claimed that giving additional powers to regional authorities in *oblasts* could be risky at a time when the territorial integrity of the state was threatened. Volodymyr Zelenskyy's

---

29 "Proekt Zakonu pro vnesennya zmin do Konstytutsii Ukrainy (shchodo detsentralizatsii vlady)", *Verkhovna Rada Ukrainy: ofitsiynyy veb-portal*, 1 July 2015. http://w1.c1.rada.gov.ua/pls/zweb2/webproc4_1?pf3511=55812.

official position on this issue was not announced until he won the 2019 presidential election.

This altogether threefold agenda of the second phase of the decentralization reform encountered a peculiar challenge in the electoral calendar. First, getting it on track was complicated by the fact that 2019 was marked by three rounds of nationwide voting in presidential and parliamentary elections. Second, it was difficult to implement the reform in advance of the 2020 local elections, as this involved establishing enlarged *rayons* and quickly unifying the remaining unamalgamated local communities. It was naïve to believe that parliament, which did not make the time to approve Draft Law No. 8051 "On the Basics of the Administrative-Territorial Structure of Ukraine" in 2018, would gather enough political will to pass the law before the 2019 parliamentary elections. There was the onerous task of establishing sustainable and roughly equal basic self-government bodies — via amalgamation — for nearly two-thirds of the remaining small basic communities. Approximately 900 out of the nearly 1,200 planned ATCs had been established by May 2019. A total of 6,774 villages and towns were expected to merge into approximately 300 ATCs in a period of about 12 months.[30]

There was a plan B: some of the smaller already existing ATCs could "annex" many of the remaining unamalgamated basic communities. Clearly, it was impossible to achieve these tasks without administrative pressure from above. The success of the speedy amalgamation of territorial communities thus depended on the central state's willingness and ability to push through further multidimensional decentralization.

After the announcement of the second phase of the decentralization reform in January 2019, there was little progress in implementing the reform because most policymakers — in Kyiv and, notably, at substate scales — were preoccupied by the upcoming 2019 presidential elections. Once the incumbent president lost, many domestic decentralization experts expected the reform to be abandoned as the newly elected president did not appear to be a

---

30 See also the section "Main Directions of Securing a Continuously Effective Advancement of Decentralization", in: Zhalilo et al., *Detsentralizatsiya vlady* (2018), 19-20.

proponent of local government. However, soon after winning the presidency and securing a one-party majority in the 2019 parliamentary election, President Volodymyr Zelenskyy announced his intention to pursue decentralization.[31] Moreover, he speedily initiated changes in accordance with the 2014 Concept and with the action plan, approved by the government in January 2019, designed for the second stage of the reform.[32]

On 19 September 2019, *Minregion* was tasked with preparing a draft law on the administrative details of local amalgamation, in line with the above-mentioned action plan. The objective was to exclude regional councils from the procedure of establishing ATCs, thus enabling regional executives to approve ATC designs in the regions and submit them to the central government for final approval. The draft law was completed quickly: it was a revised version of the draft law proposed in the first phase of the reform. Simultaneously, *Minregion* supplied regional executives with revised methodological recommendations for assessing the capacities of ATCs to carry out their functions. In May 2020, the government made final decisions on the "prospect plans" of all ATCs in Ukraine, and on 12 June 2020, it approved 1,469 ATCs across Ukraine (excluding Crimea, for obvious reasons).

The process of consolidating *rayons* was more complicated but not less urgent. On 20 September 2019, the government was asked to prepare and submit to parliament a draft law on the principles of administrative-territorial organization of Ukraine by 1 January 2020. *Minregion* quickly prepared, and the government approved, the requested draft law, which was strikingly similar to Draft Law

---

31 "Prezident Okreslyv Pershocherhovi Zavdannia u Sferi Decentralizatsii ta Regionalnoi Polityky [The President Highlighted the Priority Tasks with respect to Decentralization and Regional Policy]". www.president.gov.ua, 2 September, 2019. https://www.president.gov.ua/news/prezident-okresliv-pershochergovi-zavdannya-u-sferi-decentra-57089.

32 The Cabinet of Minister's Decree "On Approving the Action Plan of a New Phase of Reforming Local Self-Government and the Territorial Division of Power in Ukraine in 2019-2021" issued on 23 January 2019 (№ 77-p). https://www.kmu.gov.ua/ua/npas/pro-zatverdzhennya-planu-zahodiv-z-realizaciyi-novogo-etapu-reformuvannya-miscevogo-samovryaduvannya-ta-teritorialnoy i-organizaciyi-vladi-v-ukrayini-na-20192021-roki (accessed 9 July 2020)

No. 8051 "On the Basics of the Administrative-Territorial Structure of Ukraine".

However, the newly elected parliament, despite a pro-presidential one-party majority, proved hesitant about redesigning *rayons*. As mentioned, the *Verkhovna Rada* had earlier already failed to approve a law on administrative-territorial divisions in Ukraine previously — in 2018–2019. To avoid similar failure, the MPs in 2019 developed a plan B: they deferred approval of the law but approved a parliamentary decree, thus making it possible to elect substate councils in new territorial units in the upcoming local elections. On 17 July 2020, the *Verkhovna Rada* adopted parliamentary *decree* No. 3650 "On the Establishment and Dissolution of Subregions", which approved a list of 136 *rayons* (in place of the existing 490) and 1,469 ATCs. Only 238 MPs supported this decree, most of them from or aligned with the pro-presidential party. All other factions gave "zero votes to support the decree".[33]

The design approved for the remaining ATCs and new *rayons* was not perfect, and arguably reflected the special interests of local stakeholders. It represented a compromise between central policymakers and local actors. Apparently, this compromise was more important than defining the functions of subregional authorities. Once the decision was made, territorial consolidation at the local and subregional levels was complete. This all happened in advance of the 2020 regular local elections. Thus, on 25 October 2020 voters elected local and subregional authorities for new administrative-territorial units - in ATCs and new *rayons* all over Ukraine.

Conclusions

This chapter illustrated that territorial consolidation of Ukraine on the local and subregional (*rayon*) levels was the paramount achievement of the two initial phases of decentralization that had started in 2014. It happened despite the great challenge that faced the

---

33 Valentyna Matsuzato, "Ukraine's Subregions in Transition: Misalignment of Funding and Mandates", *Kennan Institute: Focus Ukraine*, 3 November 2020. https://www.wilsoncenter.org/blog-post/ukraines-subregions-transition-misalignment-funding-and-mandates.

reform—the well-known gap between capability and expectation, i.e., the difference between an ambitious reform agenda, on the one hand, and the limited capacity to make and implement policy decisions in the time available, on the other.

In the first stage of the reform, fiscal decentralization and voluntary local amalgamation significantly contributed to the territorial consolidation of the country, from the bottom up. Regional, subregional, and local authorities and their interactions made a crucial impact on the amalgamation of territorial communities. On the one hand, their input was positive. Many of them actively participated in voluntary local amalgamation for the benefit of territorial communities and taking into account local and regional interests. As a result, the speed of voluntary local amalgamation was impressive. On the other hand, there were cases when regional and subregional authorities were not eager to devolve their responsibilities to their local counterparts, and some local authorities in territorial communities were hesitant to merge and did not want new duties.

In the second stage of the decentralization reform, in 2019-20, two simultaneous policy changes were introduced: local amalgamation was finalized, and *rayons* were merged via administrative means. In this case, the input of regional, subregional, and local authorities into reform implementation was limited. The key decision-makers were in Kyiv. Regional councils had fewer opportunities for lobbyism and clientelism once they lost the power to design ATCs in the *oblasts*. Territorial consolidation at the level of *rayons* was completed although the division of responsibilities remained blurred. The subregional *rayon* councils were left few responsibilities and finances.

Once local amalgamation was completed, municipal authorities were significantly strengthened, especially in relation to subregional authorities, who lost a considerable amount of their prerogatives and struggled to obtain new duties within the amended territorial boundaries. Direct inter-budgetary relations between the central budget and local budgets proved beneficial for Ukraine's center-periphery relations. Localities grew closer to Kyiv than they were prior to the start of the post-2014 decentralization reform.

In 2019-2020, the major reason to speed up reform implementation was the need to complete it before regular local elections scheduled for 25 October 2020. A couple of years later, it is clear that this fast pace had another dimension. The timely completion of local amalgamation and redesign of the territorial composition of *rayons* helped advance Ukraine's territorial consolidation and internal cohesion in advance of Russia's full-fledged military invasion in February of 2022.

3. Fiscal Decentralization in Ukraine, 2014-17 Prospects and Challenges for Amalgamated Territorial Communities

Maryna Rabinovych

Introduction

Since the early 1980s, a range of countries in Southeast Asia, Latin America, Africa, and the former Communist Bloc have undergone profound political and economic transformations. Many states in these regions converted their regimes from authoritarianism to (at least formal) liberal democracies, adopted the foundations of a market economy, and promoted the decentralization of power. In addressing the different modes of transformation across the world, the World Bank stressed that the decentralization of power and responsibilities from the center to lower levels of authority represented a common — although generally not the most visible — aspect of democratic transition.[1]

Bird and Villancourt state that decentralization informs the agenda of almost every country and looks like "either panacea, or a plague".[2] If local budgets do not cover public needs and the subnational governments have a low institutional capacity, the decentralization-driven "plague" reduces the quality of public services and leads to increased macroeconomic instability. However, numerous decentralization success stories[3] have inspired scholars to identify the following virtues of decentralization.

---

1   *Administrative Decentralization* (The World Bank Group, 2001). http://www1.w orldbank.org/publicsector/decentralization/admin.htm.
2   Richard Miller Bird and Francois Villancourt, *Fiscal Decentralization in Developing Countries* (Cambridge: Cambridge University Press, 2008), 1.
3   For examples of decentralization success stories (Uganda, Senegal, Gambia), see *Decentralization and Poverty Reduction. Africa and Asia Experience* (UN, 2003). http://ww w.unpan.org/Portals/0/60yrhistory/documents/Publications/Decentralization%
20-%20Africa%20and%20Asia%20Experience.2003.pdf.

First, decentralization brings governments closer to the people and represents a crucial tool for promoting democratization through enhanced accountability, citizen participation, and civil society development.[4] Second, greater public engagement in self-government and local democracy "result in more popular support for government, and presumably in improved political stability".[5] (This virtue especially benefits states that experience frequent changes in government and/or face the need to manage diversity.) Third, as demonstrated by the empirical research conducted by *KfW Entwicklungsbank*, successful decentralization is directly associated with the achievement of sustainable development goals, such as poverty reduction and bridging income inequality gaps within and between countries.[6]

Given the sheer number of its positive and empirically proven political and economic development-related benefits (especially the potential to mitigate the effects of diversity),[7] decentralization has become a top priority on Ukraine's post-Euromaidan reform agenda. Fiscal decentralization has revealed itself to be a crucial prerequisite for strengthening regional and local authorities, since stable sources of funding are necessary to delegate power to self-government authorities.

---

4 For a detailed overview of decentralization's impact on democratization and accountability, see Harry Blair, "Participation and Accountability at the Periphery: Democratic Local Governance in Six Countries", *World Development*, no. 28:1 (2000): 21-39; Jean-Paul Faguet, "Decentralization and Governance", *World Development*, no. 53 (2014): 2-13; Marcelin Joanis, "Shared Accountability and Partial Decentralization in Local Public Goods Provision", *World Development*, no. 107 (2014): 28-37.
5 Richard Miller Bird and Francois Villancourt, *Fiscal Decentralization in Developing Countries* (Cambridge: Cambridge University Press, 2008); *Decentralization and Poverty Reduction. Africa and Asia Experience* (New York: UN, 2003). http://www.unpan.org/Portals/0/60yrhistory/documents/Publications/Decentralization%20-%20Africa%20and%20Asia%20Experience.2003.pdf.
6 *Decentralization: Bringing Government Closer to the People* (Berlin: KfW Entwicklungsbank, 2014). https://www.kfw-entwicklungsbank.de/PDF/Entwicklungsfinanzierung/Themen-NEU/Governance-Dezentralisierung-EN-2014.pdf.
7 Local Governance and Decentralization Assessment: Implications of Proposed Reforms in Ukraine (Washington, DC: USAID, 2014). http://pdf.usaid.gov/pdf_docs/pa00k59f.pdf.

This chapter aims to identify the extent to which Ukraine's fiscal decentralization meets the conditions for successful decentralization proposed by the scholarship. It discusses the conceptual foundations of fiscal decentralization, outlines its major modes, and highlights the conditions that are necessary for its success. The chapter then presents the background to Ukraine's efforts to decentralize and the objectives of the ongoing reform. It outlines the dynamics of domestic politics and the legislature from 1991-2013 (i.e., from Ukraine gaining independence until the Revolution of Dignity, which led to the appointment of the government that introduced fiscal decentralization). The chapter proceeds to analyze the degree to which Ukraine's fiscal decentralization in 2014-2017 met the conditions identified in the scholarship as the prerequisites for successful reform. Finally, the chapter summarizes Ukraine's efforts at fiscal decentralization with reference to the scholarship-recognized conditions for fiscal decentralization.

Conceptual Foundations of Fiscal Decentralization

The definition and the components of fiscal decentralization

Decentralization is a multifaceted concept that refers to various political, administrative, and fiscal aspects.[8] It means "a transfer of authority and responsibility of public function to intermediate and local governments or quasi-independent government institutions".[9]

First, it is necessary to distinguish between the concepts of fiscal federalism and fiscal decentralization. Fiscal federalism implies the preexisting sharing of competences between the federation and its subjects, while fiscal decentralization is associated with the process of transferring particular responsibilities and/or powers to

---

[8] Daniel Mullins, Accountability and Coordination in a Decentralized Context: Institutional, Fiscal and Governance Issues (Washington, DC: American University, 2003), 73-75.
[9] *Decentralization and Subnational Regional Economies: What? Why? Where?* (Washington, DC: The World Bank Group, 2001). http://www1.worldbank.org/pub licsector/decentralization/what.htm.

subnational authorities to improve the management of local interests.[10] Fiscal decentralization does not necessarily mean the transfer of competencies from the central to the regional and local levels, as deconcentration and delegation modes of fiscal decentralization imply. In contrast to fiscal federalism, fiscal deconcentration and delegation mean that subnational governments do not receive extra competencies, despite the broadening scope of their responsibilities and respective financial assignments. Fiscal devolution—the third mode of fiscal decentralization—is most closely linked to fiscal federalism because it presupposes the transfer of responsibilities and the redesign of the ways competencies are shared between different levels of government.[11]

In transition studies, fiscal decentralization connects to the concept of multilevel governance and the wider "libertarian reform agenda", including, inter alia, privatization and deregulation.[12] Like fiscal devolution, multilevel governance goes beyond the introduction of precise divisions of competencies between the different levels of government. Multilevel governance means that authorities belonging to different levels of governance are responsible for the management of a single policy domain. Multilevel governance respects the principles of subsidiarity[13] and proportionality.[14] Fiscal devolution represents an important component of the transition agenda, and its starting point addresses sharing competencies between different levels of governance (a "political component" of fiscal decentralization).

---

10 For an in-depth analysis of the concept of "fiscal federalism", see: Richard Miller Bird and François Villancourt, eds., *Perspectives on Fiscal Decentralization* (Washington, DC: World Bank Institute, 2006), 247-250.
11 *Decentralization and Subnational Regional Economies.*
12 For an analysis of the interplay between fiscal decentralization and multilevel governance, see: *Multilevel Governance Reforms: Overview of OECD Countries Experiences* (Paris: OECD, 2017).
13 The definition of the principle of subsidiarity is found in Art. 5 of the Treaty of the European Union. This principle states that the EU will not take action (apart from cases falling within the area of its exclusive competencies), if action taken at the national, regional or local level is more effective.
14 The definition of the principle of proportionality is provided in Art. 5 of the Treaty of the European Union. According to this principle, EU action is limited to the minimum necessary for the achievement of the Treaty's objectives.

There are four major components of fiscal devolution:[15]

- First, expenditure assignment is a necessary follow-up tool for providing subnational self-government bodies with any new decision-making competencies. The mode of fiscal decentralization depends on the extent to which local and regional self-government bodies enjoy autonomy in allocating their expenditures. In federations and in decentralized unitary states, expenditure assignment is exercised according to the principle of subsidiarity.
- Second, effective revenue assignment is possible when a tax-transfer system secures tax revenues for subnational self-government bodies. Along with revenue assignment measures, fiscal devolution facilitates the revenue-generating capacity of local and regional self-government bodies.
- Third, the crucial source of revenue for subnational self-government bodies is intergovernmental transfers. Intergovernmental transfers can account for up to 46 percent of regional and local self-government revenue.[16] There are "vertical" and "horizontal" transfers,[17] as well as general grants and specific-purpose transfers.
- Finally, fiscal devolution helps provide subnational self-government bodies with access to financial markets.[18] According to the World Bank, providing subnational tiers of government with direct borrowing powers represents a "strong political push" to the development of local capital markets.[19]

Thus, successful fiscal devolution implies *a jigsaw puzzle*, where expenditure assignment, revenue assignment, intergovernmental

---

15 *Intergovernmental Fiscal Relations* (Washington, DC: The World Bank Group, 2011). h ttp://www1.worldbank.org/publicsector/decentralization/fiscal.htm.
16 Robin Boadway and Anwar Shah, eds., *Intergovernmental Fiscal Transfers: Principles and Practices* (Washington, DC: The World Bank, 2007), 1.
17 Ibid., 3-6.
18 "Decentralizing Borrowing Powers", *World Bank: PremNotes*, no. 15 (January, 1999). http://www1.worldbank.org/prem/PREMNotes/premnote15.pdf.
19 Ibid.

transfers and borrowing powers of subnational governments need to form a comprehensive development-oriented system.

Fiscal decentralization, economic growth and poverty reduction: What makes fiscal decentralization successful?

A review of the literature reveals that the success of fiscal decentralization is often linked to economic growth.[20] Although the relation between fiscal decentralization and economic growth has been examined since the 1980s, scholars still address it as an "open-ended question".[21] Empirical studies of fiscal decentralization reforms across the globe can be divided into three major research strains.

The first strain gathers together contributions that prove the positive relation between fiscal decentralization and economic growth. Fiscal decentralization can contribute to economic growth in three ways. According to the traditional "allocative efficiency" argument, fiscal decentralization brings the government closer to the people and thereby improves the quality of decisions and the delivery of public services.[22] Scholars have established a positive relation between fiscal decentralization, the improved quality of decisions and public service delivery.[23] For example, the Chinese development model that combines political centralization and

---

20 Apart from poverty reduction and economic growth, fiscal decentralization is linked to democracy, democratization, good governance and accountability. See, for example, *Decentralization and Subnational Regional Economies*.
21 Andres Rodriguez-Pose and Anne Kroijer, "Fiscal Decentralization and Economic Growth in Central and Eastern Europe", *LSE: Europe in Question*, no. 12, 2009. http://www.lse.ac.uk/europeanInstitute/LEQS%20Discussion%20Paper%20Series/LEQSPaper12.pdf.
22 Friedrich Hayek, "The Use of Knowledge in Society", *American Economic Review* 35 (1945): 519-531; Richard Musgrave, "Who Should Tax, Where and What?", in: C. E. McLure (ed.), *Tax Assignment in Federal Countries* (Canberra: Australian National University Press, 1983), 2-19.
23 Wallace Oates, "An Essay on Fiscal Federalism", *Journal of Economic Literature* 37 (1999): 1120-1149; Luiz Mello, "Fiscal Decentralization and Intergovernmental Fiscal Relations: a Cross-Country Analysis", *World Development* 28, no. 2 (2000): 365-380; Pranab Bardhan, "Decentralization of Governance and Development", *The Journal of Economic Perspectives* 16, no. 4 (2002): 185-205.

economic decentralization demonstrates a positive relation between fiscal decentralization and the promotion of local markets and local business development, leading to growth.[24] Second, academic studies that investigate fiscal decentralization and multilevel governance argue that fiscal decentralization contributes to economic growth via better-coordinated, coherent, and inclusive policies.[25] Finally, there are researchers who claim that fiscal decentralization promotes "competition among local jurisdictions for mobile citizen-consumers and investment and increased accountability for performance".[26]

Notably, the literature on development studies assesses the extent to which fiscal decentralization contributes to poverty reduction. Analyzing data from a large number of countries, it finds that fiscal decentralization promotes poverty reduction through reducing income inequality.[27] However, some recent studies identify a negative correlation between fiscal decentralization and economic growth and poverty alleviation. Research finds that fiscal devolution under the UK's New Labour negatively affected economic growth by boosting economic inequalities between regions and undermining territorial justice.[28]

Numerous case studies in Latin America demonstrate that decentralization can even harm the economic and political evolution

---

[24] Xiaobo Zhang, "Fiscal Decentralization and Political Centralization in China: Implications for Growth and Inequality", *Journal of Comparative Economics* 34, no. 4 (2006): 713-726.

[25] Liesbet Hooghe and Gary Marks, "Unraveling the Central State, but How? Types of Mutilevel Governance", *American Political Science Review* 97, no. 2 (2003): 233-243.

[26] Charles M. Tiebout, "A Pure Theory of Local Expenditures", *Journal of Political Economy* 64, no. 5 (1956): 416-424; *Decentralization and Subnational Regional Economies*.

[27] Christian F. Sepulveda and Jorge Martinez-Vazquez, "The Consequences of Fiscal Decentralization on Poverty and Income Inequality", *Environment and Planning C: Politics and Space* 29, no. 2 (2011); Govinda M Rao, Richard M. Bird, Jennie I Litvack, "Fiscal Decentralization and Poverty Alleviation in a Transitional Economy: the Case of Vietnam", *Asian Economic Journal* 12, no. 4 (1998): 353-378; Richard Bird, Edgar R Rodriguez, "Decentralization and Poverty Alleviation. International Experience and the Case of Philippines", *PublicAdministration and Development* 19, no. 3 (1999): 299-319.

[28] Kevin Morgan, "Devolution and Development: Territorial Justice and the North-South Divide", *Publius* 36, no. 1 (2006): 189-206.

of a developing state.²⁹ Academics have found a negative correlation between fiscal decentralization reform and the implementation of poverty reduction strategies in developing countries,³⁰ while also revealing a negative correlation between expenditure assignment and transfers and economic growth in the CEE and OECD states.³¹ The above-mentioned studies find that only tax assignment can generate economic growth.

Third, scholars seek to identify the conditions that determine successful fiscal decentralization. Their findings are presented in the table below. This chapter will use them as benchmarks for the study of Ukraine's decentralization reforms.

Table 3.1. The Conditions of Successful Fiscal Decentralization.

No	Factor	Source	Relation to fiscal decentralization
1.	Political stability and the stability of legislation	Norris, Martinez-Vasquez and Norregaard (2000); Martinez-Vasquez and McNab (2003)³²	Political stability is necessary to continue decentralization reforms once started
2.	Clear division of power between	Huther and Shah (1998);	Clear horizontal and vertical division of power helps

---

29 Jonathan Rodden, "The Dilemma of Fiscal Federalism: Grants and Fiscal Performance around the World", *American Journal of Political Science* 46, no. 3 (2002): 670-687.
30 David Craig and Dough Porter, "Poverty Reduction Strategy Papers: a New Convergence", *World Development* 31, no. 1 (2003): 53-69; Gordon Crawford, "Decentralization and the Limits to Poverty Reduction: Findings from Ghana", *Oxford Development Studies* 36, no. 2 (2008): 235-258.
31 Andres Rodriguez-Pose and Anne Kroijer, "Fiscal Decentralization and Economic Growth in Central and Eastern Europe", *LSE: Europe in Question*, no. 12 (2009). http://www.lse.ac.uk/europeanInstitute/LEQS%20Discussion%20Paper%20Series/LEQSPaper12.pdf; Andres Rodriguez-Pose and Roberto Ezcurra, "Is Fiscal Decentralization Harmful for EconomicGrowth. Evidence from the OECD Countries", *SERC Discussion Paper*, no. 51 (2010).
32 Era-Dabla Norris, Jorge Martinez-Vasquez, and John Norregaard, "Making Decentralization Work: the Case of Russia, Ukraine and Kazakhstan, Conference on Post-Election Strategy", Moscow, April 5-7 2000. https://www.imf.org/external/pubs/ft/seminar/2000/fiscal/norris.pdf; Jorge Martinez-Vasquez, Robert McNab, "Fiscal Decentralization and Economic Growth", *World Development* 31, no. 9 (2003), 1597-1616.

	different levels of government and between subnational self-government bodies	Norris, Martinez-Vasquez and Norregaard (2000); Dabla-Norris (2006)[33]	streamline expenditure and revenue assignment, as well as fiscal equalization
3.	Legal assignment of expenditure responsibilities, based on a clear and stable decentralization strategy	McLure and Martinez-Vasquez (n.d); Bahl (1999)[34]	Clear and stable expenditure assignment is necessary to avoid overlaps in the activities of subnational governments. Additionally, it is necessary in regard to applying the key rule of fiscal decentralization: "money follows responsibilities"
4.	Revenue assignment: increasing local self-government taxing powers and income-generating capacities	Bahl (1999); Pycroft (2000)[35]	The responsibilities of subnational self-government bodies have mandatory funding sources, due to assigning particular tax revenue sources to the respective subnational self-government; their fiscal autonomy promotes local development
5.	Administrative and technical capacity of	Bahl (1999); Smoke (1996); Francis and James (2003)[36]	Decentralization reforms in developing countries often fail due to the insufficient administrative and technical

---

33 Jeff Huther, Anwar Shah, *Applying a Simple Measure of Good Governance to the Debate on Fiscal Decentralization* (Washington, DC: World Bank Publications, 1998); Norris, Martinez-Vasquez and Norregaard, "Making Decentralization Work"; Era Dabla-Norris, "The Challenge of Fiscal Decentralization in Transition Countries", *Comparative Economic Studies* 48, no. 1 (2006), 100-131.

34 Charles. E McLure, Jorge Martinez-Vasquez, *The Assignment of Revenues and Expenditures in Intergovernmental Fiscal Relations* (Washington, DC: World Bank, 1999). http://www1.worldbank.org/publicsector/pe/PEAMMarch2005/AssignmentRevenues.pdf; Roy Bahl, "Implementation Rules for Fiscal Decentralization", International Seminar on Land Policy and Economic Development, Land Reform Training Institute, Taiwan, 17 November, 1998. http://citeseerx.ist.psu.edu/viewdoc/download?doi=10.1.1.200.7474&rep=rep1&type=pdf.

35 Ibid; Christopher Pycroft, "Democracy and Delivery: the Rationalization of Local Government in South Africa", *International Review of Administrative Science* 66 , no. 1 (2000): 143-159.

36 Ibid; Paul Smoke, "Fiscal Decentralization in Indonesia: a New Approach to an Old Idea", *World Development* 24, no. 8 (1996): 1281-1299; Paul Francis, Robert James, "Balancing Rural Poverty Reduction and Citizen Participation: the

	subnational self-government bodies		capacities of the subnational self-government bodies to exercise their increased fiscal autonomy
6.	Development-oriented nature of the fiscal equalization schemes utilized	Bahl (1999); Bahl and Linn (1994)[37]	Intergovernmental transfers are the crucial instrument for development, including poverty reduction. However, they should not be used solely to fill the gaps in subnational budgets
7.	Viable domestic subnational debt market, guaranteed by the elaborate risk management system	World Bank (2008)[38]	A viable domestic subnational debt market is an important illustration of the fiscal autonomy of local and regional self-governments and a crucial development tool (e.g. with regard to covering the needs of infrastructure investment)

Thus, an overview of the literature on decentralization reforms in different parts of the world reveals that fiscal decentralization is not necessarily a "panacea" for boosting economic growth and regional development. It is necessary to consider state-wide political and economic conditions and to ensure that fiscal decentralization reforms are tailored to the needs of the country. A review of the literature does demonstrate that fiscal decentralization reform needs to fulfill certain conditions to promote economic growth and reduce poverty. Seven conditions of successful fiscal decentralization serve as benchmarks for the study of the path of post-Euromaidan fiscal decentralization in Ukraine.

Contradictions of Uganda's Decentralization Program", *World Development* 3, no. 2 (2003): 325-337.

37 Ibid; Roy Bahl, Linn Johannes, "Fiscal Decentralization and Intergovernmental Transfers in Less Developed Countries", *Publius* 24, no. 1 (1994): 1-19.

38 Lili Liu, "Creating a Regulatory Framework for Managing Subnational Borrowing", in: J. Lou and S. Wang, eds., *Public Finance in China: Reform and Growth for a Harmonious Society* (Washington, DC: The World Bank, 2008), 171-190.

The Decentralization Reform in Ukraine: Background and Objectives

The core legal framework regarding center-periphery relations in Ukraine was in place by the end of the 1990s. Art. 140 of the 1996 Constitution of Ukraine grants the right to local self-governance,[39] while Arts. 141-146 clarify the election procedure for the local self-government bodies, their responsibilities, and funding.[40] At the same time, Art. 118 of the Constitution adds that executive power in *oblasts*, *rayons* and the cities of Kyiv and Sevastopol is exercised by regional and subregional state administrations.[41] The 1997 Law "On Local Self-Government in Ukraine" and the 1999 Law "On Local State Administrations" detail the nuances of the legal status of local self-government bodies and state administrations.[42] The Budgetary Code of Ukraine and the Law of Ukraine "On the State Budget of Ukraine" (adopted annually) deal with financial matters.[43]

A number of scholars claim that Ukraine suffered from centralization, which represented the major obstacle to Ukraine's democratic transition and economic growth.[44] Transition scholars (e.g. Iwasaki, Wolczuk) explained that independent Ukraine's centralization was due to the Soviet legacy of governance, outdated

---

39 Konstytutsiia Ukraïny, Art.140. http://zakon2.rada.gov.ua/laws/show/254%D0%BA/96-%D0%B2%D1%80.
40 Ibid., Art. 141-146.
41 Ibid, Art.118.
42 Zakon Ukraïny "Pro Mistseve Samovriaduvannia v Ukraïni", 21 May 1997. http://zakon0.rada.gov.ua/laws/show/280/97-%D0%B2%D1%80/page6; Zakon Ukraïny "Pro Mistsevi Derzhavni Administratsiï," 9 April 1999. http://zakon3.rada.gov.ua/laws/show/586-14.
43 Biudzhetny Kodeks Ukraïny, 8 July 2010. http://zakon2.rada.gov.ua/laws/show/2456-17/; ZakonUkraïny "Pro Derzhavnyi Biudzhet Ukraïny na 2017 Rik", 21 December 2016. http://zakon.rada.gov.ua/laws/show/1801-19.
44 Charles Wise, Trevor Brown, "The Separation of Powers in Ukraine", *Communist and Post-Communist Studies* 32, no. 1 (1999): 23-44; Anders Aslund, "Why Has Ukraine Returned to Economic Growth?" *Working Paper of the Institute for Economic Research and Policy Consulting*, no. 15 (2002); Ichiro Iwasaki, "Evolution of the Government-Business Relationship and Economic Performance in the Former Soviet States—Order State, Rescue State, Punish State", *Economics of Planning* 36, no. 3 (2003): 223-257.

administrative and fiscal structures, and corruption at different levels of government.[45] The system of governance in Ukraine did not anticipate the principles and mechanisms of the division of power between different levels or between local self-government bodies and state administrations.[46] In addition, it was difficult to promote local self-government given the fragmented nature of the administrative-territorial system of Ukraine, which had too many small territorial communities with insufficient institutional and financial capacities to exercise power. Moreover, in the early 2000s, there was a lack of legislation on intermunicipal cooperation. Finally, scholars have identified excessive fiscal centralization, the lack of appropriate division between public and communal property, and ineffective intergovernmental transfers.[47] Even after the Orange Revolution, centralization persisted. Viktor Yushchenko's presidency did little to contribute to the progress of decentralization.[48] Under President Viktor Yanukovych, power was increasingly centralized in Ukraine.

A number of domestic policy documents set out the objectives of the post-Euromaidan decentralization reform. Parliament committed itself to decentralization in the Coalition Agreement negotiated in November 2014. The Coalition Agreement called, on the one hand, for the effective delimitation of competencies between the different levels of self-government bodies, and between the local self-government bodies and state administrations. On the other hand, it called for strengthening the financial capacities of local self-government; the formation of self-sufficient communities; and for

---

45 Ibid; Kataryna Wolczuk, "Catching up with 'Europe'? Constitutional Debates on the Territorial-Administrative Model in Independent Ukraine", *Regional and Federal Studies* 12, no. 2 (2010): 65-88.
46 *Local Governance and Decentralization Assessment: Implications of Proposed Reforms in Ukraine* (USAID, 2014), 13-14. http://pdf.usaid.gov/pdf_docs/pa00k59f.pdf
47 Halyna Minaeva, "Mekhanizmy pidvyschchennya efektyvnosti diyalnosti organiv mistsevoho samovryaduvannya shchodo stalogo rozvytku", in: *Napryamy reformuvannya systemy mistsevogo samovryaduvannya v Ukraïni* (Kharkiv, 2011). http://www.kbuapa.kharkov.ua/e-book/tpdu/2011-2/doc/3/07.pdf; *Udoskonalennya Konstytutsiinykh zasad mistsevoho samovryaduvannia v Ukraïni: Analitychna zapyska* (Kyiv: NISD, 2012). http://www.niss.gov.ua/articles/672.
48 Aleksandr Libman, "Cycles of Decentralization in the Post-Soviet Space", *Russian Politics and Law* 48, no.1 (2010): 8-20.

improving the territorial organization of power at the regional level.[49]

The President committed himself to decentralization in the "Ukraine 2020" Sustainable Development Strategy, which mentions decentralization reform in the section titled "The Responsibility Vector".[50] "Ukraine 2020" calls for departing from a centralized model of government; ensuring capable local self-government; creating an effective system for the territorial organization of power; implementing the provisions of the European Charter of Local Self-Government as well as the principles of subsidiarity, comprehensiveness and local self-government financial self-sufficiency.

Furthermore, the government associated decentralization with an improved quality of public services and with strengthening regional competitiveness, which implied the creation of stronger legal prerequisites for interregional cooperation and sustainable regional development.[51]

Analysis of the goals and the initial conception of the scope of the decentralization reform demonstrates that full implementation would require amendments to constitutional, budget, tax and administrative laws. Moreover, successful decentralization entailed not only amendments to legislation but also "changes in political and administrative culture among elected officials and public servants" that would enable them to adapt to the changed policy-making environment,[52] including an emphasis on local and regional development.

---

49 Verkhovna Rada Ukraïny III sklykannia, Ugoda pro Koalitsiiu peputats'kykh fraktsiï "Yevropeïs'ka Ukraïna", 27 November 2014, http://zakon0.rada.gov.ua/laws/show/n0001001-15.
50 President Ukraïny, Ukaz "Pro Stratehiyu staloho rozvytku 'Ukraïna 2020'", 12 January 2015, http://zakon0.rada.gov.ua/laws/show/5/2015.
51 National Reform Council, "Decentralization" (2014), https://decentralization.gov.ua/about.
52 European Commission, "Commission Implementing Decision on the Special Measure 2015 for Decentralization Reform in Favor of Ukraine to be Financed from the General Budget of the European Union", 12 December 2015, https://ec.europa.eu/neighbourhood-enlargement/sites/near/files/neighbourhood/pdf/key-documents/ukraine/20160407-special-measure-2015-for-decentralization.pdf.

Fiscal Decentralization in Ukraine: Assessing Key Aspects of Change

Now it is time to assess Ukraine's fiscal decentralization reform in 2014-2017 in relation to the seven conditions of successful fiscal decentralization. Political and legislative stability represents an important dimension of governance. The World Bank defines this indicator as "the likelihood of political instability and/or politically motivated violence, including terrorism".[53] Given that political stability forms the basis for a clear interinstitutional distribution of the roles in reform efforts, and of their continuity, it is the framework for implementing fiscal decentralization reform and ensuring the sustainability of its results.

Russia's annexation of Crimea in 2014 and the subsequent occupation of Eastern Ukraine by Russian and pro-Russian forces led to a continual decrease of political stability in Ukraine. While Ukraine's political stability indicator was -0.1 in 2012 (the range runs from -2.5 to 2.5), in 2013 and 2014, it was -2.0 and -1.9, respectively.[54] From 2015 to 2017, the value of this indicator registered insignificant improvement, rising from -1.96 to -1.89.[55] The failure of the Minsk I and Minsk II agreements to enact a ceasefire regime meant that some Eastern Ukrainian territories were beyond the control of the central government.

At the same time, it is worth noting that the post-Euromaidan rise of separatism in the Donetsk and Lugansk *oblasts*, supported by the Russian Federation both politically and militarily, made regionalism and decentralization the key prerequisites for conflict resolution and for preserving the territorial integrity of Ukraine. According to the 2015 Minsk II Agreement, constitutional reform, with a focus on decentralization and "a dialogue on the modalities of local elections in accordance with Ukrainian legislation", represented a

---

53 *Political Stability and Absence of Violence/Terrorism* (Washington, DC: World Bank Group, 2001), http://info.worldbank.org/governance/wgi/pdf/pv.pdf.
54 *Worldwide Governance Indicators Databank* (Washington, DC: World Bank Group, 2018), http://databank.worldbank.org/data/reports.aspx?source=Worldwide-Governance-Indicators.
55 Ibid.

condition of the ceasefire. However, the constitutional amendments related to decentralization were not approved by the parliament. Thus, the lack of political stability in Ukraine formed a barrier to successful decentralization reform.

A clear division of power between different levels of government and between subnational self-government bodies is another important dimension. Norris, Martinuez-Vazquez and Norregaard argue that "clarity, transparency, and stability are paramount for achieving the accountability at the administrative, as well as political levels that efficient governance requires".[56] In Ukraine, achieving a sustainable clarity of roles in local self-government domain requires three actions:[57]

1. The division of responsibilities between local councils, subregional councils, and regional councils, according to the principle of subsidiarity.
2. Redesigning the territorial organization of power, with the purpose of ensuring accessible public services.
3. The division of responsibilities between local self-government bodies and state administrations is necessary to prevent duplication of responsibilities.

"The Concept of Reforming Local Self-Government and the Territorial Division of Power" approved by the government on 1 April 2014 introduced a clear division of responsibilities between local councils, subregional councils, and regional councils. Subregional councils were in charge of the "upbringing and education of children in general-profile boarding schools" and of "providing medical services at the secondary level".[58] Regional councils were responsible for regional development, environmental protection, the development of *oblast* infrastructure, professional education, the provision of highly specialized medical services, and the

---

56 Norris, Martinez-Vasquez, and Norregaard, "Making Decentralization Work".
57 *Local Governance and Decentralization Assessment: Implications of Proposed Reforms in Ukraine* (Washington, DC: USAID, 2014), 5.
58 Kabinet Ministriv Ukraïny, Rozporiadzhennia No 33p "Pro Skhvalennia Kotseptsiï reformuvannia mistsevoho savovryaduvannya ta terytorial'noï organizatsiï vlady v Ukraïni", 01 April 2014. http://zakon.rada.gov.ua/laws/show/333-2014-%D1%80.

development of culture, sports and tourism. Importantly, the Concept highlighted the key role of the principle of subsidiarity with regard to the reform of local self-government and the territorial organization of power.[59] However, the 1997 Law "On Local Self-Government" did not even mention the principle of subsidiarity.[60]

As entailed by the Concept, one of the key tasks of the decentralization reform was to ensure access to public services (i.e. that individuals can receive similar services at the community level). Fulfilling this requirement meant redesigning the Ukrainian territorial organization of power. The 2015 Law "On the Voluntary Amalgamation of Communities" aimed to boost communities' capacities through the amalgamation of weak territorial communities.[61] By the end of 2017, 366 amalgamated territorial communities (ATCs) were established.[62] Optimizing the territorial organization of power was facilitated by the 2017 Law "On Amending Some Laws of Ukraine Regarding the Voluntary Accession of Territorial Communities", which allowed communities to voluntarily join an ATC.[63] An ATC obtained state funding for public service delivery, local development and other matters.[64] However, without adopting the Law "On the Foundations of the Administrative-Territorial Division of Power in Ukraine", the territorial organization of power remained incomplete on the subregional level.[65]

The division of responsibilities between local self-government bodies and state administrations was another key task of the

---

59 Ibid.
60 Zakon Ukraïny "Pro Mistseve Samovriaduvannia v Ukraïni", 21 May 1997. http://zakon5.rada.gov.ua/laws/show/280/97-%D0%B2%D1%80, Art.43.
61 Zakon Ukraïny "Pro dobrovilne ob'ednannya terytorialnykh hromad", 5 February 2017. http://zakon3.rada.gov.ua/laws/show/157-19.
62 "Try roky detsentralisatsiï v Ukraïni: Naïvazhlyvishchi tsyfry", *Detsentralizatsiya*, 29 March 2017. http://decentralization.gov.ua/infographics/item/id/37.
63 Zakon Ukraïny "Pro vnesennya zmin do deyakykh zakoniv Ukraïny shchodo dobrovilnoho pryednannya terytorial'nykh hromad", 09 February 2017. http://zakon2.rada.gov.ua/laws/show/1851-19.
64 For an analysis of the funding-related benefits to merged communities, see "Detsentralizatsiya pid mikroskopom: Ekspertnyï analiz", *Detsentralizatsiya*, 28 January 2016. http://decentralization.gov.ua/news/item/id/1453.
65 For the reflection on these issues in the Draft Law, see Verkhovna Rada Ukraïny, Proekt Zakonu Ukraïny "Pro administratyvno-terytorialnyï ustriï", 18 October 2013. http://w1.c1.rada.gov.ua/pls/zweb2/webproc4_1?pf3511=48586.

decentralization reform. To avoid inconsistencies, overlap in responsibilities and double spending, the Concept proposed abolishing regional and subregional state administrations and introducing prefects in their place. According to the 2015 Draft Law "On Prefects", the major tasks of prefects would include oversight to ensure the observance of the Constitution of Ukraine and the laws of Ukraine by local self-government authorities and officials; coordinating the activities of ministries' territorial bodies and other central executive bodies, while ensuring their observance of the Constitution and laws of Ukraine; the implementation of state programs; streamlining and organizing the activities of the central executive's territorial bodies and their coordination with local self-government authorities in conditions of war or in emergency situations.[66]

In contrast to regional and subregional state administrations,[67] the prefects' proposed tasks would not duplicate the competencies of local self-government bodies. Yet, despite the fact that, in order to ensure transparency in expenditure assignment, the lack of a clear division of power between local self-government bodies and state administrations remained the key issue to be resolved, a number of concerns prevented the Law "On Prefects" from being adopted.[68] To cite a single example, the broad oversight and control functions of prefects, who would be accountable to the President of Ukraine, were viewed by both MPs and civil society activists as leading to excessive presidential influence over local affairs.[69] In consequence, the problem of drawing a clear line between the

---

66 Verkhovna Rada Ukraïny: Proekt Zakonu: "Pro prefektiv". http://www.min region.gov.ua/attachments/content-attachments/4851/Prefectu.pdf; Zakon Ukraïny: "Pro mistsevi derzhavni administratsiï", 9 April 1999. http://zakon3.rada.gov.ua/laws/show/586-14.
67 Zakon Ukraïny: "Pro mistsevi derzhavni administratsiï", 9 April 1999. http://zakon3.rada.gov.ua/laws/show/586-14.
68 For a criticism of the Law "On Prefects", see: Yuiry Ganushchak, "Yakym buty ukraïns'komu prefektu?" ZN.UA, 18 December 2015. http://gazeta.dt.ua/inter nal/yakim-buti-ukrayinskomu-prefektu-_.html.
69 Ibid.; Oksana Syroïd, "Never Ever", 1 July 2015. https://www.facebook.com/o ksana.syroyid/posts/1009049622453533.

authorities of the above-mentioned bodies remains unresolved, and new solutions have been sought.

In summary, due to political instability and the lack of constitutional provisions regarding decentralization, a stable and clear division of power at the local level remained a task to be fulfilled. This section has highlighted significant difficulties in redesigning the territorial organization of power, required to ensure access to public services and the division of responsibilities between local self-government bodies and state administrations, and necessary to prevent the duplication of responsibilities. The above issues are likely to exert a negative influence on the quality and sustainability of expenditure and revenue assignment, as well as on the design of the interbudgetary transfers.

The next important dimension is the legal assignment of expenditure responsibilities based on a clear and stable decentralization strategy. Several studies of fiscal decentralization in the post-Soviet space in the early 2000s claimed that the lack of clear expenditure assignment was a key concern.[70] A major requirement was the need to distinguish between expenditure stemming from the execution of "own" and "delegated" responsibilities.[71] Moreover, since the mid-2000s, the assignment of expenditures to subnational budgets has repeatedly been associated with "capital decumulation" rather than with promoting development. The reason for this, besides the lack of respective revenue assignment, was the absence of a strategic approach to regional development and to strengthening the capacities of local self-government.

In 2014-2015, amendments were introduced to Chapter 14 of the Budgetary Code of Ukraine, "The Delimitation of Expenditures

---

70 Norris, Martinez-Vasquez, and Norregaard, "Making Decentralization Work"; Lucan Way, "The Dilemmas of Reform in Weak States: The Case of Post-Soviet Fiscal Decentralization", *Political Theory* 30, no. 4 (2002); Lev Freinkman, Alexander Plekhanov, "Fiscal Decentralization in Rentier Regions: Evidence from Russia", *World Development* 37, no. 2 (2009): 503-512.

71 Local self-government authorities' "own" and "delegated" authorities are distinguished in the 1997 Law "On Local Self-Government" (Zakon Ukraïny "Pro mistseve samovryaduvannya v Ukraini", 21 May 1997. http://zakon0.rad a.gov.ua/laws/show/280/97-%D0%B2%D1%80/page6).

between Budgets".[72] They included clear lists of the expenditures to be financed from the budgets of different government levels, allegedly aligned with the authorities of these levels. Yet the simultaneous review of local self-government authorities, provided by the Concept of "Reforming Local Self-Government" and the Law "On Local Self-Government", reveals striking differences between these authorities and the expenditures assigned to local budgets.[73] As with the situation in 2000, the Budgetary Code of Ukraine did not distinguish between expenditures related to the exercise of "own" and "delegated" responsibilities.[74] Thus, omitted by the annually adopted Law "On the State Budget of Ukraine",[75] the source of financing for subnational government bodies' exercise of "delegated" responsibilities remained unclear. Such a situation erased the difference between "own" and "delegated" responsibilities, simultaneously undermining the quality of the execution of delegated responsibilities. The major areas of mismatch between the responsibilities to be exercised by particular levels of subnational governments dealt with social security, the environment, culture and sports.

Another problematic issue regarding expenditure assignment at the start of the implementation of the local amalgamation reform was the line between the expenditures to be assigned to amalgamated communities and to those that did not participate in the amalgamation procedure, provided by Art. 89 and 90 of the Budgetary Code. While the Budgetary Code of Ukraine mentioned ATC budgets, the budgets of the cities of *oblast* and *rayon* significance, and *rayons* in terms of expenditure, neither the Constitution of Ukraine nor the Law "On Local Self-Government" drew a clear line

---

72 Byudzhetny Kodeks Ukraïny, 8 July 2010, http://zakon2.rada.gov.ua/laws/show/2456-17/, Chapter 14.
73 Zakon Ukraïny "Pro Mistseve Samovriaduvannia v Ukraïni", 21 May 1997. http://zakon0.rada.gov.ua/laws/show/280/97-%D0%B2%D1%80/.
74 Verkhovna Rada Ukraïny: Proekt zakonu: "Pro prefektiv". http://www.minregion.gov.ua/attachments/content-attachments/4851/Prefectu.pdf; Zakon Ukraïny: "Pro mistsevi derzhavni administratsiï", 9 April 1999. http://zakon3.rada.gov.ua/laws/show/586-14.
75 Zakon Ukraïny "Pro derzhavnyï byudzhet Ukraïny na 2017 rik", 21 December 2016. http://zakon0.rada.gov.ua/laws/show/1801-19.

between them. This created additional uncertainties regarding the delimitation of authorities and expenditures between the governments of different levels.

Finally, in contrast to the revenue assignment regulations, Chapter 14 of the Budgetary Code did not distinguish between the expenditures for the daily life of communities and those directed to the communities' development. Along with a broad range of subsidies and other social benefits to be financed from local budgets, this lack of categorization regarding expenditures contributed to the local budgets' remaining "budgets of decumulation" until 2017. This issue was especially vital to communities that did not participate in the voluntary amalgamation, given that they had no access to funding from the State Regional Development Fund.

As can be seen, expenditure assignment regulations contained a number of crucial controversies. Notably, the emergence of the issues highlighted above was closely related to the lack of constitutional provisions regarding decentralization and the status of ATCs, and to the unclear delimitation of authorities between self-government bodies at different levels.

The next dimension concerns revenue assignment, namely expanding local self-government taxing powers and income-generating capacities. Ensuring adequate funding for local self-government authorities to execute their tasks represents a crucial requirement of fiscal decentralization. Several amendments to the Budgetary and Tax Codes of Ukraine,[76] in 2014 and 2015, addressed the creation of new sources of revenue for local self-government, thus supporting its expanded decision-making autonomy. The experience of fiscal decentralization reforms in foreign countries allows us to distinguish three major channels to change the revenue assignment to local self-government bodies: (1) creating a legal basis for the stable assignment of revenues from state-wide taxes to subnational budgets, (2) expanding the taxing powers of subnational

---

76 Zakon Ukraïny "Pro vnesennia zmin do byudzhetnogo kodeksu Ukraïny shchodo reformy mizhbyudzhetnykh vidnosyn", 28 December 2014. http://zakon3.rada.go v.ua/laws/show/79-19/page3; Zakon Ukraïny "Pro vnesennya zmin do podatkovogo kodeksu Ukraïny shchodo hranychnogo rozmiru orendnoï platy", 30 June 2015. http://zakon2.rada.gov.ua/laws/show/557-19/paran2#n2.

government bodies, and (3) boosting the income-generating capacities of local and regional governments through liberalizing legislation on community land and immovable property.

The 2014 Law "On Amending the Budgetary Code of Ukraine with regard to the Reform of Interbudgetary Relations" provided for the direct assigning of revenue from a range of state-based taxes to subnational budgets. The changes are presented in the table below.

Table 3.2. Subnational budgets' tax revenue before and after fiscal decentralization.[77]

Subnational budgets' revenue from state-wide taxes prior to 2015		Subnational budgets' revenue from state-wide taxes after 2015	
Income Tax	50%	Income Tax paid on a respective territory (apart from Kyiv and Sevastopol)	60%
Duty on special use of forest resources (with regard to wood acquired through general lumbering)	50%	Rent duty on the special use of forests	50%
Duty on the special use of water	50%	Rent duty on the special use of water	50%
Duty on the use of subsoil for the extraction of mineral resources of state significance (apart from oil and natural gas)	50%	Duty on the use of subsoil for the extraction of mineral resources of state significance	25%
State duty	100%	Duty on the use of subsoil for the extraction of mineral resources of local significance	100%
		State duty (in accordance with the location of actions conducted and the issuance of documents)	100%
		Excise tax on the retail sale of goods, subject to excise tax	5%
		Tax on the income of enterprises	10%

---

[77] Zakon Ukraïny "Pro vnesennya zmin do byudzhetnoho kodeksu Ukraïny shchodo reformy mizhbyudzhetnykh vidnosyn", 28 December 2014. http://zakon3.rada.gov.ua/laws/show/79-19/page3.

| | | Tax on the income of communal enterprises and financial establishments | 100% |
| | | Ecological tax (in part unrelated to the use of radioactive substances) | 80% |

In addition to an increase in the assignment of revenue from statewide taxes to subnational budgets, fiscal decentralization provided for the expansion of the taxation powers of subnational government bodies and for the direct assignment of revenue from local taxes to local budgets. In particular, subnational self-government bodies acquired the right to determine the rate of two local taxes (on real estate, other than land; unified tax) and three duties (on the exercise of particular entrepreneurial activities; on parking spots for means of transport; and tourism [Art. 10 of the Tax Code of Ukraine]).[78] The revenues from these taxes and duties were all directly transferred to subnational budgets. This novelty helped Ukraine's budgetary system solve the eternal problem of local tax revenue not serving local needs, and to reset the role of the central budget. The success of the revised tax assignment is made clear by the fact that, following the introduction of the relevant amendments in 2015, the revenue of subnational budgets grew by 42.1 percent. In January-September 2016, the growth in subnational budgets' revenues (in general fund terms) accounted for 47.5 percent (or UAH146.6 billion), demonstrating increased gains from all taxes. The overall growth of subnational budgets' revenues from 2014 to 2016 is estimated to amount to more than UAH100 billion.[79] Compared to 2016, in 2017 the growth of subnational budgets' revenues accounted for 31% (UAH45.3 billion), with an overall yearly revenue of UAH192 billion.[80]

---

78   Podatkovyï Kodeks Ukraïny, 2 December 2010. http://zakon2.rada.gov.ua/laws/show/2755-17/page55.
79   "Resul'tat detsentralizatsiï — ponad 100 mlrd hrn dodatkovykh resursiv na mistyakh, - Volodymyr Hroïsman", *Detsentralizatsiya*, 31 March 2017, http://decentralization.gov.ua/news/item/id/4993.
80   D "U 2017-mu Dohody Mistzevyh B'udzhetiv Zrosly do 192 mlrd grn — Zubko", *Detsentralizatsiya dae mozhlyvosti*, 10 January 2018. https://decentralizationn.gov.ua/news/7990.

Despite the 2014-2015 fiscal decentralization efforts to improve the fiscal autonomy of subnational budgets, two major problematic concerns need to be addressed in this regard. First, the reform did not provide any measures aimed at increasing subnational governments' own capacities to generate nontax income (e.g. through liberalizing legislation regarding the rent of communally owned property or the right of local communities to run a business). In general, in contrast to many European countries, Ukraine's legislation on local self-government tends to ignore subnational governments' nontax revenue as a crucial source of their income. Moreover, the new guarantees for subnational governments' fiscal autonomy were not added to the Constitution of Ukraine (as with the other aspects of decentralization), making the reform's achievements easily reversible.

The next dimension concerns the administrative and technical capacity of subnational self-government bodies. The literature that associates fiscal decentralization with poverty eradication[81] claims that the administrative and technical capacities of subnational governments largely determine the success of the reform. Ukraine's decentralization and regional policy reforms were accompanied by three major arrays of activities meant to enhance the administrative and technical capacities of local, subregional, and regional self-government bodies. First, strengthening subnational governments' capacities was ensured through the continuing voluntary process of local amalgamation, which was tightly linked to a range of financial benefits. These benefits can be summarized as follows:

- Despite the lack of a clear legal delimitation of the legal status of ATCs and of unmerged communities, amalgamated communities were granted direct interbudgetary relations

---

[81] Paul Francis, Robert James, "Balancing Rural Poverty Reduction and Citizen Participation: The Contradictions of Uganda's Decentralization Program", *World Development* 31, no. 2 (2003): 325-337; Govinda M Rao, Richard M. Bird, Jennie I Litvack, "Fiscal Decentralization and Poverty Alleviation in a Transitional Economy: the Case of Vietnam", *Asian Economic Journal* 12, no.4 (1998): 353-378; Johannes Juetting, Celine Kauffman, Ida McDonell, Holger Osterrieder, Nikolas Pinaud, Lucia Wegner, *Decentralization and Poverty Reduction in Developing Countries: Exploring the Impact* (Paris: OECD, 2004).

with the State Budget (similar to cities of *oblast* significance).
- Only ATCs had access to state infrastructure subvention. In 2017, that subvention amounted to UAH1.5 billion and was distributed among the budgets of 366 ATCs proportionate to the size and population of the merged communities.[82]
- ATCs obtained the architectural-construction inspections that were expected to simplify the infrastructural and, thus, economic development of communities.
- ATCs had a broader authority regarding the determination of the land tax rates compared to unmerged communities.[83]

In 2016, there were 159 ATCs in Ukraine, and the above financial benefits (along with the revised tax assignment system) allowed them to increase their own revenue by UAH48.5 billion (three times the 2015 amount).[84] Overall, from 2014 to 2017, the own revenue of the 366 merged communities' budgets grew by UAH124 billion compared to 2013.[85] Furthermore, in 2017, for the first time, the overall amount of financial resources at the disposal of local self-government bodies (of both merged and unmerged communities) exceeded half of the total consolidated State Budget of Ukraine.[86]

Nevertheless, experts drew attention to several important obstacles that prevented assessing the voluntary local amalgamation as ultimately a success. First, despite being initially positioned as a voluntary process, in practice local amalgamation often took the

---

82 "Opublikovano postanovu pro rozpodil derzhavnoyi infrastrukturnoyi subventsii ob'ednanym hromadam", *Detsentralizatsiya*, 13 June 2017. https://de centralization.gov.ua/news/5869.
83 For a detailed analysis of these benefits, see: Olena Sas, "Detsentralizatsiya pid mikroskopom: Analiz plyusiv ta minusiv dlya ob'iednanykh hromad", *Detsentralizatsiya*, 28 January 2016. http://decentralization.gov.ua/news/item/id/1453.
84 The financial results of fiscal decentralization are highlighted by Yanina Kaziuk, "Dokhody 159 ob'iednanykh hromad zrosly bil'she nizh u 7 raziv - ekspert pro rezultaty finansovoï detsentralizatsiï 2016 Roku", *Detsentralizatsiya*, 17 January 2017. http://decentralization.gov.ua/news/item/id/4013.
85 "Vlasni dohody miszevyh byudzhetiv Ukrainy zrosly na 124 mil'ardy", *Ukrinform*, 16 March 2018. https://www.ukrinform.ua/rubric-regions/2423255-vlasni-dohodi-miscevih-budzetiv-ukraini-zrosli-na-124-milardi.html.
86 Ibid.

form of a "coercive" attachment of small communities to amalgamated ones. Such situations were repeatedly witnessed in the Lviv, Kyiv, Odesa and Kherson *oblasts*.[87] The lack of consideration of the interests and visions of particular communities in the local amalgamation process represented a crucial deficiency regarding the democratic aspect of decentralization. Another issue related to participation was the lack of involvement of all the relevant stakeholders in local amalgamation (the population of the territorial community, local self-government bodies, last councils, representatives of ethnic minorities, etc.).

Second, the ATCs' low institutional capacity was a crucial concern for development-oriented projects financed by the State Fund for Regional Development. The latter aimed to facilitate local development; however, the majority of project proposals submitted in 2016 were confined to the fragmentary improvement of infrastructure. Yet it is necessary to stress that capacity development is a continuous process, and the recovery of isolated elements of local infrastructure may be viewed as an intermediate step to on the way to launching true development projects.

The successful transition from the post-Soviet legacy of administrative-command to modern managerial approaches to local development projects also required "external" capacity-building measures provided by international donors. The most important project dedicated to the development of subnational government staff is the "U-LEAD" project, which is mostly funded by the European Commission and serves as a hub for projects implemented by the German Gesselschaft für Internationale Zusammenarbeit (GIZ), USAID and the Canadian development cooperation.[88] Along with

---

[87] For examples of the "coercive-voluntary" merger of communities, see Tetyana Kostyuk, "Detsentralizatsiya po-l'vovski: Dobrovol'no-prinuditel'nyï protses", *RIA-Novosti Ukraina*, 17 October 2016. http://rian.com.ua/story/20161017/1017815231.html; Halyna Studennikova, "Bunt sel'sovetov: Gromady ne khot'iat ob'edineniya", *Strana.UA*, 23 March 2016. https://strana.ua/articles/analysis/5338-bunt-selsovetov-gromady-ne-hotyat-obedineniya.html.

[88] For more detailed information about "U-LEAD", see Gennadiy Zubko, "Zapusk proektu U-LEAD—"HUB Dezentralizatsiï", *Detsentralizatsiya*, 14 September 2016. http://www.segodnya.ua/opinion/zybkocolumn/zapusk-proektu-u-lead-hub-decentralzac-751735.html.

sectoral decentralization, and its task of communicating the reform to citizens, "U-LEAD" encompasses educational programs for local self-government officials with an emphasis on the development of project management skills. The project also increases the administrative capacities of local self-government by supporting the launch of administrative services centers under "U-LEAD". The consolidation of donors' efforts into a single hub is a positive development, allowing a new scale of capacity-building projects.

The next dimension concerns the development-oriented nature of fiscal equalization schemes. Interbudgetary relations represent a crucial aspect of fiscal decentralization. Petchey and Levtchenkova argue that interbudgetary transfers need to balance the needs of communities' daily lives and emphasize development-related needs and approaches.[89] Ukraine's reform of interbudgetary transfers under the fiscal decentralization reform comprises three major elements:

- An overall change in the fiscal equalization scheme from one based on expenditures to one based on revenue;
- Introducing new subventions from the Central Budget to subnational ones for the fulfillment of particular goals (and to support the newly formed amalgamated communities);
- Reforming the State Fund for Regional Development to finance development projects (in 2016 there were 498 projects so funded; in 2017 the number rose to 767).[90]

As emphasized by the Reanimation Package of Reforms, the transfer from expenditure-based fiscal equalization schemes to revenue-based ones decreased the dependence of subnational budgets on subsidies by 22 percent (from 96 to 74 percent).[91] The number of donor budgets increased by 3.7% in 2014 and by 15.2% in 2015.

---

89 Sophia Levtchenkova and Jeffrey Petchey, "A Model for Public Infrastructure Equalization in Transitional Economies", in: Jorge Martinez-Vasquez and Bob Searle, eds., *Fiscal Equalization* (Berlin: Springer, 2007), 345-362.
90 "GROMadna Reforma: Shcho Dala Dezentralizatsiia?" *Ekonomichna Pravda*, 4 August 2017, https://www.epravda.com.ua/columns/2017/08/4/627740/.
91 Reanimation Package of Reforms, "Detsentralizatsiya: Zdobutky reformy mizhbyudzhetnykh vidnosyn", http://2.auc.org.ua/sites/default/files/present_zdobutki.pdf.

Moreover, the above transfer served development needs by withdrawing only 50 percent of the excess revenue of communities that received more expenditure than they required (provided that the index exceeded 1.1). However, the "basic subsidy" for subnational budgets lacking revenues constituted only 80 percent.[92] But the above changes stimulated their income-generating capacities of communities of both types.

Another crucial step is the abolition of the "supplementary subsidy for fiscal equalization of subnational budgets' funding" and the introduction of a broad range of new subventions.

The subventions were as follows:

- subvention for the implementation of state social protection programs;
- subvention for the implementation of investment programs (projects);
- education subvention;
- subvention for the preparation of the regular labor force;
- medical subvention (until summer 2018);
- subvention for the implementation of the medical measures of state programs;
- subvention for financing socioeconomic compensation measures for the risks of populations living in territories with possible radioactive emissions;
- subvention for projects for the liquidation of carbon and peat enterprises and for securing the maintenance of drainage complexes (50%, based on co-financing).[93]

The purpose of replacing subsidies by subventions was to promote the so-called goal-oriented application of public funds.

However, there were some shortcomings:

---

92 Ibid.
93 For more detailed information regarding the existing forms of intergovernmental transfers, see: Byudzhetny kodeks Ukraïny, 8 July 2010. http://zakon2.rada.gov.ua/laws/show/2456-17/, Chapter 16.

- First, funds that were transferred via subvention depended on the annually adopted Law "On the State Budget of Ukraine".
- Second, the funds could even diminish, as in the case of the so-called "infrastructure subvention for ATCs". The amount of this subvention remained the same, but the number of ATCs grew each year; thus, each ATC received less money from the central budget annually. This subvention expired by 2021.
- Third, given the lack of clarity regarding the status of the "subvention for the implementation of measures for the socioeconomic development of particular territories", and the procedures related to it, ensuring the fair distribution and goal-oriented use of this subvention remained problematic.[94]
- Fourth, since the education subvention did not cover all the costs related to the exercise of the relevant functions, there was a risk that the quality of public services would be reduced because of the unequal financing of communities. The education subvention did not address the wages of the technical and support staff. The key concern of the "medical subvention" remained the financing of utilities.
- Fifth, there was a lack of practical delimitation between application of the "infrastructure subvention" and the funding available from the State Fund for Regional Development.

The trend was to decrease the subsidy dependence of subnational budgets, promoting goal-oriented interbudgetary transfers, and strengthening the support for local development. Nevertheless, both the legal regulation and practical implementation of the above innovations encountered several barriers, including regional and local inequalities, a lack of subnational governments' institutional capacities, and persistent legislative controversies.

---

94 Anatoliy Tkachuk, "Pro detsentralizatsiyu, uspikhy, ryzyky i rol' parlamentu", *ZN.UA*, 13 January 2017. http://gazeta.dt.ua/internal/pro-decentralizaciyu-u spihi-riziki-i-rol-parlamentu-_.html.

The next dimension concerns a viable domestic subnational debt market, guaranteed by the elaborate risk management system. A subnational self-government body's right to borrow funds from external sources constitutes a necessary aspect of fiscal autonomy and serves as a means of development for self-government. The 2010 World Bank Report highlighted that the underdevelopment of the subnational debt market was crucial challenge to local development, and proposed a number of recommendations for the development of the public debt market in Ukraine, including the adoption of the Law "On Public Debt".[95]

Despite the move toward fiscal decentralization, only a few steps were taken by the *Verkhovna Rada* to promote subnational borrowing. In particular, the cities of *oblast* significance received the right to borrow money from external sources, raising the number of cities exercising such a right from 16 to 182.[96] Moreover, the expenditures related to subnational debt were granted the status of "protected budget expenditures" in accordance with Art. 55 of the Budgetary Code of Ukraine. Art.55 (1) defines "protected budget expenditures" as "expenditures of the general fund of a budget whose volume cannot be changed in case of the shortening of respective budgetary assignments".[97] The status of protected budget expenditures provides investors with a legislative guarantee regarding costs. However, no other guarantees of investors' rights were introduced. The limits of the change are reflected in the low number of subnational debts and related guarantees reported by the Ministry of Finance of Ukraine.[98]

---

[95] *Developing the Domestic Subnational Debt Market in Ukraine: Key Challenges and Proposed Action Plan* (Washington, DC: World Bank, 2010), http://documents.w orldbank.org/curated/en/206171468316445931/Developing-the-domestic-su b-national-debt-market-in-Ukraine-key-challenges-and-proposed-action-plan.

[96] Podatkovyï kodeks Ukraïny, 2 December 2010. http://zakon2.rada.gov.ua/la ws/show/2755-17/page55.

[97] For more detailed information regarding the existing forms of intergovernmental transfers, see: Byudzhetny kodeks Ukraïny vid 8.07.2010. http://zakon2.rad a.gov.ua/laws/show/2456-17/, Art.55.

[98] Ministerstvo finansiv Ukraïny, "Reestr mistsevykh zapozychen' za 2016 rik", 2016. http://www.minfin.gov.ua/news/view/reiestr-mistsevykh-zapozyche n-stanom-z--po-?category=borg&subcategory=mistsevyi-borh.

In summary, with regard to the 2006 World Bank recommendations, the creation of a viable subnational debt market is still a task to be completed.

Conclusions

As opposed to previous governments' attempts to decentralize the budgetary and tax systems of Ukraine, the 2014-2015 fiscal decentralization led to tangible achievements and the creation of new opportunities for both ATCs and communities that did not amalgamate. The major achievements of the reform lie in the domains of tax assignment, the development of territorial communities' capacities, and interbudgetary relations.

First, the revised assignment of taxes and the broadening of local self-government authorities' taxing powers helped increase subnational budget revenues by more than UAH100 billion from 2014 to 2017. The direct transfer of tax-related revenues to subnational budgets made subnational governments independent of the State Treasury of Ukraine. Along with the changes to the fiscal equalization schemes, the above changes contributed to the fiscal autonomy of subnational budgets.

Second, territorial community amalgamation represents a crucial means for raising communities' administrative and technical capacities. The financial benefits of ATCs (e.g. direct interbudgetary relations with the State Budget; "infrastructure" subvention) strengthened their financial capacities and enabled the implementation of a broad range of infrastructure projects. The launch of "U-LEAD", a hub for multiple international decentralization support initiatives, is a positive development in the domain of communities' capacity-building.

Third, the reform of the fiscal equalization schemes led to a decrease in the subsidy dependence of subnational budgets and promoted goal-oriented intergovernmental transfers.

While the changes in the above domains evidently contributed to increasing the autonomy of subnational budgets and the implementation of the reform goals, the reform as conducted cannot be described as a true fiscal devolution, because of the lack of constitutional provisions, the division of responsibilities between subnational self-governments and state administrations, and the assignment of particular revenue sources to subnational budgets. This situation made all the legislative measures adopted regarding fiscal decentralization unsustainable and easily reversible, especially in times of political instability. The key obstacles to moving from the fiscal deconcentration to true devolution were the mismatch between the norms of competencies and expenditure assignment, contained in different laws, and the broad authorities of substate administrations. A special concern was the uncertain legal status of ATCs vis-à-vis old communities, and the legally undetermined changes to the administrative-territorial system of Ukraine. Finally, subnational debt market regulations were barely addressed by the reform.

4. Decentralization Reform in Ukraine
Political Context, Key Results, Public Attitudes

Oleksii Sydorchuk

Introduction

On 31 August 2015, the *Verkhovna Rada* (Ukraine's unicameral parliament) approved the constitutional bill "On changes to the Constitution of Ukraine on the Decentralization of Power" on the first reading, with 265 votes for and 87 against. Meanwhile, outside of the parliament, a peaceful public protest against these constitutional changes turned into a violent confrontation, resulting in the death of four law enforcement officers. The violence on the streets, however, had nothing to do with the decentralization reform: the protests were against a single provision, which proposed the "specific conduct of local government in the several regions of the Donetsk and Luhansk *oblasts*", popularly known as a "special status" for territories in Donbas (which includes the Donetsk and Luhansk *oblasts*) controlled by Russian proxies. This provision was later included in the constitutional changes regarding decentralization, and was connected to the controversial Minsk process aimed at resolving the military conflict in Donbas.

The preliminary vote on the constitutional bill on decentralization, although formally successful, deeply divided Ukrainian MPs and society. Opponents of the "special status" of occupied Donbas were able to block further deliberation of the bill, and the government failed to convince the critical mass of ordinary Ukrainians of the need to adopt the changes to the constitution that included such a provision. As a result, the final vote on the constitutional package was postponed indefinitely. Furthermore, since no changes to the constitutional project were made after August 2015, issues of decentralization and the regulation of the Donbas conflict were still bundled together both in public opinion and in the perception of many foreign observers. Why this happened and how it influenced the decentralization reform will be investigated in detail below.

Origins of the Decentralization Reform

In a nutshell, decentralization means the transfer of powers and resources from the central government to local authorities directly representing the interests of community members. In Ukraine, the need for such redistribution was especially pronounced, given several significant problems that characterized various regions of the country.

First, the state was often unable to provide citizens with high-quality and affordable services, including healthcare, education, social welfare, transportation, infrastructure, etc. For instance, more than half of the approximately 11,500 territorial communities that existed in Ukraine before the start of decentralization lacked funds to maintain kindergartens in their territories.[1] Public opinion polls confirmed the poor quality of services. In November 2014, before the start of the implementation of key decentralization measures, 72 percent of Ukrainians were not satisfied with the quality of healthcare; the figures of those not satisfied with social welfare and the work of community services were 70 percent and 66 percent, respectively.[2] Table 4.1 summarizes public assessment of the quality of various public services.

---

1 Yurii Hanushchak, "Polityky dumayut', shcho detsentralizatsiya—proklyata reforma", *Platforma*, 7 April 2015. http://reforms.platfor.ma/yurii-ganushchak/.
2 Oleksii Sydorchuk, "Stavlennya zhyteliv mist do ideï detsentralizatsiï", *Hromadska dumka*, no. 3 (December 2014). http://dif.org.ua/article/stavlennya-zhiteliv-mist-do-idei-detsentralizatsii.

Table 4.1. How would you evaluate the following issues in your city (town)? (%, November 2014)

	Positively	Negatively	Difficult to answer
Creating jobs, fighting unemployment	4.1	77.1	18.8
Providing social welfare for the poor	6.4	63.4	30.2
Providing social care for vulnerable groups	6.8	70.5	22.7
Fighting crime	8	64.2	27.8
Creating a favorable business environment	8.3	43.8	47.9
Providing housing	9.2	71.5	19.3
Improving ecology	10.5	54.9	34.6
Improving healthcare	10.5	72.1	17.4
Improving communal services	10.9	66.3	21.8
Fighting illegal construction works	12.6	39.7	47.7
Improving school education	16.3	38.9	44.8
Improving the state of sanitation around buildings	27.8	52.2	20.0
Fighting traffic congestion	34.4	31.2	34.4
Improving public transportation	47.2	32.3	20.6

Second, a lack of effective feedback between citizens and local authorities was also evident, preventing ordinary Ukrainians from influencing decisions made at the local level or holding local public officials accountable. Again, public polls provide convincing data on this issue. In November 2014, 74 percent of Ukrainians were not satisfied with their ability to influence the decisions of local authorities. Furthermore, citizens were not happy with the activities of local government bodies, both the state-appointed and elected ones. Only 33 percent were satisfied with their mayors, 27 percent with their local councils, and 26 percent with their local state administrations (Table 4.2).

Table 4.2. Are you satisfied with the activities of the following government bodies? (%, November 2014)

	Yes	No	Difficult to answer
Local courts	16.9	57.8	25.3
Local prosecutor's office	18.3	56.5	25.3
Local police	21.8	61.1	17.2
Local state administration	26.1	57.8	16.1
Local council	27.3	54.2	18.5
Local mayor	33	49.9	17.1

The reasons for the poor conditions of public services and for popular discontent can be found in the system of distribution of power and resources in the country. According to the constitution, subnational public administration is de facto divided into three levels: basic (city, town, village), district (*rayon*), and region (*oblast*). On each of these levels, deficiencies in the allocation of competencies and resources were apparent and contributed unfavorably to the weak ability of the state and local self-government bodies to perform their basic functions.

The lack of resources was most evident at the basic level. The division of the country into many small communities dispersed funds and human resources. More than 10,000 out of the 11,500 existing communities were concentrated in villages, 92 percent with less than 3,000 inhabitants and 47 percent with less than 1,000 inhabitants.[3] Naturally, these communities struggled to generate enough funds not only to provide high-quality public services but, in some cases, even to maintain their own administrative apparatus. In many, a major share of the budget expense (up to 90 percent in some cases) covered the salaries of administrative staff. As a result, local authorities lacked funds for other vitally important functions, and their communities grew highly dependent on

---

3 "Prezentatsiya zakonoproektiv shchodo ob'iednannia ta spivrobitnytstva terytorial'nykh hromad", *Detsentralizatsiya*, September 2014. http://decentraliz ation.gov.ua/infographics/item/id/5.

subsidies from the central budget. In 2014, 96 percent of local communities required budget support to cover all of their expenses.[4]

However, even receiving such needed state support could often involve problems. Most communities (except the so-called cities of *oblast* significance) received subsidies from the state budget not directly, but through district and regional state administrations, which created additional difficulties and produced bureaucratic bottlenecks. Moreover, local self-government bodies were legally responsible to provide services in a number of areas, such as healthcare and education, often without having enough funds to cover the related expenses. To meet these demands, many were forced to use money allocated for other purposes, such as infrastructure or road repairs. As a result, the funds available were insufficient to fully cover any of the above-mentioned expenses.

Deficiencies were also present at the district and regional levels, where elected bodies represented the common interests of territorial communities by implementing regional development projects. To finance these projects, the government created the State Fund for Regional Development, through which it distributed money to different regions. Before the start of the post-Euromaidan decentralization, the government allocated funds in a nontransparent way and often for specific political motives. This led to the disproportionate support for regions where the ruling party had the strongest presence, while other *oblasts* were almost entirely without state funds. During the Viktor Yanukovych's presidency (2010-2014), the government clearly favored the Donetsk region, the birthplace of Yanukovych's Party of Regions, and the Autonomous Republic of Crimea, equally important to the Party of Regions. In 2011, for instance, Crimea received UAH900 million and Donetsk UAH343 million, while the total sum for the 27 regions of Ukraine amounted to a little more than UAH2.9 billion.[5]

Public administration at the district and regional level was also overly centralized. Unlike the basic level local councils, district

---

[4] V. Miskyi and O. Halushka, eds., *Reforms under the Microscope – 2015* (Kyiv: Rodovid, 2015), 18.

[5] Anatolii Tkachuk, *Derzhavna rehionalna polityka: vid asymetriï do solidarnosti (robochyi zoshyt)* (Kyiv: Lehalnyi status, 2013), 45.

and regional councils lacked executive bodies, and all executive powers were concentrated in the hands of district and regional state administrations, whose heads were nominated by the cabinet and appointed by the president. The concentration of competencies, especially the power to draft and manage budgets, in the hands of public officials appointed by Kyiv prevented the development of genuine self-government and restricted the ability of citizens to influence the decision-making process in their regions.

Decentralization or Federalization?

Despite long-running problems connected with the excessive centralization of power, all previous attempts to implement decentralization reforms failed. The first comprehensive effort to decentralize Ukraine was made under the presidency of Viktor Yushchenko (2005–2010), but all such plans were abandoned after Yanukovych came to power in 2010. Eventually, the Euromaidan revolution of late 2013-early 2014 triggered the launch of a full-fledged decentralization reform. On 1 April 2014, the Cabinet of Ministers of Ukraine led by Prime Minister Arseniy Yatsenyuk adopted the Concept of "Reforming Local Self-Government and the Territorial Organization of Power in Ukraine", which outlined the key aims, principles, and elements of the reform. The adoption of the Concept signaled the start of decentralization in Ukraine.

The timing of this legal act clearly demonstrates that decentralization began long before the start of the Minsk Process, as the first Minsk agreements, aimed at resolving the military conflict in Donbas, were signed only in September 2014. More specifically, the start of decentralization preceded the beginning of the active phase of the military clashes in Donbas. The Ukrainian government officially announced the Anti-Terror Operation directed against the Russian-backed separatists on 14 April 2014. This makes it clear that Ukraine's decentralization reform had altogether different objectives than appeasing Donbas separatists. Its authors sought first and foremost to improve the quality of life of Ukrainians in all the regions of the country.

On the other hand, the very idea of empowering local self-government bodies was exploited by Russian President Vladimir Putin during the pro-Russian upheavals in the Eastern and Southern regions of Ukraine from March–April 2014. However, the purpose of Putin's rhetoric was not the decentralization but the federalization of Ukraine, which meant changing the Ukrainian territorial regime from a unitary to a federal one. It was clear that Putin's idea had nothing to do with genuine decentralization and at times even contradicted it. The federalization he promoted entailed the significant empowerment of regional authorities by granting them extensive competencies in taxation, financial, economic, cultural, and even foreign policies. During the period when the Ukrainian state was in limbo, after the old government had collapsed and the new one was not yet completely formed, federalization could have escalated centrifugal tendencies and prompted the disintegration of the country.[6] Most likely, Russian attempts to impose federalization on Ukraine were meant to further weaken the central government and increase Moscow's influence on Ukraine's regional elites.[7]

Decentralization of the Ukrainian type, on the contrary, had other tasks and different instruments for achieving them. At its core, decentralization aimed to empower the lowest level of administration—that of cities, towns, and villages—where most public services are delivered to citizens. Moreover, the increased significance of local self-government at the basic level could restrain separatist tendencies, which were most visible at the higher subnational level of *oblasts*. Ukraine's regional councils were notorious for their propensity to pursue autonomous policies and overstep legal boundaries in their decisions, most likely deriving from the lack of real administrative functions at their disposal. In contrast, local councils were directly responsible for providing services to their residents and were thus not interested in exploiting politically

---

6   Vladimir Ryzhkov, "Putin's Federalization Card in Ukraine", *The Moscow Times*, 7 April 2014. https://themoscowtimes.com/articles/putins-federalizati on-card-in-ukraine-33715.
7   Anatoliy Tkachuk, *Pro detsentralizatsiyu, federalizatsiyu, separatystiv ta ul'tymatumy (zapytannya ta vidpovidi)* (Kyiv: Lehalnyi status, 2014), 8–9.

sensitive issues.[8] Unlike federalization, decentralization was partly aimed at limiting the power of regions and strengthening the state. Therefore, decentralization, although planned long before the start of the Russian aggression, became an asymmetric response to Russia's hybrid aggression.

The idea of federalization did not gain support in Ukrainian society, even in its Eastern and Southern regions, where pro-Russian sentiments were traditionally more common. According to the public opinion poll held by the Kyiv International Institute of Sociology in April 2014, only 25 percent of the inhabitants of eight Eastern and Southern *oblasts* supported the transformation of Ukraine into a federal state. Only in the Luhansk *oblast*—one of the two where Russian-backed separatists would later form a quasi-state—did a relative majority of citizens (42 percent) favor federalization over any other form of territorial organization of power. Moreover, 45 percent of all respondents in Eastern and Southern Ukraine supported the decentralization of the country, and 19 percent preferred no change to the territorial arrangements at all (detailed results are presented in Table 3). Similarly, when asked what measures could keep the country together in a time of increased violence in a number of regions, only 12 percent of respondents from the East and the South chose federalization. These results clearly point to the fact that the idea of federalization was alien to most Ukrainians, as it was imported from outside and lacked strong roots within society.

---

8   Oleksii Sydorchuk and Marharyta Chabanna, "Detsentralizatsiya vlady v Ukraïni: dosyahnennya i zahrozy", in: Oleksii Haran, ed., *Transformatsiï suspil'nykh nastroïv v umovakh protydiï ahresiï Rosiï na Donbasi: rehional'nyi vymir* (Kyiv: Stylos, 2017), 149–150.

Table 4.3. The territorial regime of Ukraine should be ... (%, April 2014)[9]

	Unitary, the same as now	Unitary, but decentralized	Federal	Difficult to answer
Dnipropetrovsk oblast	19.6	51	11.4	11.6
Donetsk oblast	10.6	41.1	38.4	8.7
Zaporizska oblast	19.8	51.4	15.3	13.6
Luhansk oblast	12.4	34.2	41.9	7.9
Mykolaïv oblast	17.9	63	10.7	8.4
Odesa oblast	29.1	44.2	17.5	8.1
Kharkiv oblast	23.3	39.1	32.2	5.2
Kherson oblast	32.9	54.5	6.9	5
East and South combined	<u>19.1</u>	<u>45.2</u>	<u>24.8</u>	<u>8.8</u>

Importantly, key political actors, including the leadership of the once dominant Party of Regions, which struggled to keep its grip on the electorate in the East and the South of Ukraine, also rejected the idea of federalization, most likely out of fear of it leading to the country's possible disintegration. As a result, no major candidate in the May 2014 presidential elections embraced the introduction of the federal model into Ukraine, while most explicitly supported at least some decentralization of power. The victory of Petro Poroshenko, who devoted special attention to decentralization in his electoral program, created a favorable ground for the launch of the reform.

Achievements and Challenges of the Decentralization Reform

Although decentralization officially started in April 2014, the first significant legal changes triggering the redistribution of power and

---

[9] Inna Vedernikova, "Pivdennyi Skhid: hilka dereva nashoho", *Dzerkalo tyzhnya*, 18 April 2014. http://gazeta.dt.ua/internal/pivdenniy-shid-gilka-dereva-nashogo-_.html.

resources to local governments occurred later that year. In June 2014, the *Verkhovna Rada* passed the law on the cooperation of territorial communities, aimed at encouraging small communities to pool their resources to implement common projects. However, the law was clearly ahead of its time, and the new instruments for cooperation between communities have rarely been used. The most plausible explanation is that communities simply lacked freely available funds to engage in cooperation with their neighbors. The lack of official guidelines, and any supporting communication about the opportunities for intercommunal or intermunicipal cooperation, contributed to the virtual absence of any meaningful cooperation projects in almost all the regions of the country.[10]

In December 2014, parliament added provisions for fiscal decentralization to the Budget Code and the Tax Code. The amendments had several important aspects. First, revenues from several taxes, including personal income tax, were redistributed in favor of local budgets. In accordance with the decentralization Concept, however, only the new amalgamated territorial communities (ATCs) (which were not yet created, as explained below) would benefit from such an increase. Second, local councils gained more freedom in establishing the rates of local taxes. Third, the financing of expenses connected with education and healthcare, for which local communities often lacked funds, was officially assigned to the line ministries, which became responsible for providing the necessary subsidies to local budgets.

Finally, the changes introduced a new system of interbudgetary transfers. Previously, the central government tried to mitigate the differences in the abilities of local communities to cover their expenses by transferring funds from richer communities to poorer ones. For obvious reasons, this system did not create incentives for economic competition between the regions, as most of the communities expected the state to address all their financial needs. The new model proposed that communities that earned more than the country average would transfer only half of this additional income

---

10 Oleksii Sydorchuk, *Decentralization: Results, Challenges and Prospects* (Kyiv: Ilko Kucheriv Democratic Initiatives Foundation, 2017), 9.

to the state budget. Similarly, communities that earned less would be provided only 80 percent of the missing funds.[11] By introducing such changes, the government hoped to stimulate economic competition between communities and encourage them to make themselves more attractive to domestic and foreign investors.

Given the scarcity of resources in most territorial communities, the initiators of the reform created opportunities for the amalgamation of territorial communities. The law on amalgamation of territorial communities was passed in February 2015. According to its provisions, communities eager to obtain new financial resources could merge with their neighbors into amalgamated territorial communities (ATCs). To streamline this process, regional authorities were made responsible for drafting plans for all the ATCs to be created in their *oblasts*. According to these plans, ATCs could then negotiate with each other about the details of amalgamation and proceed to obtain approval for conducting elections from the Central Election Commission (CEC). Newly created ATCs would switch to direct budget relations with the central government, obtain new tax revenues and budget subsidies, and gain new competencies. Notably, Ukrainian legislators intentionally made the process of amalgamation voluntary, allowing communities that did not want to amalgamate with others to exempt themselves.

Taken together, these legal changes created favorable conditions for a relatively quick process of enriching local budgets and the amalgamation of territorial communities. In 2015, local budgets increased their revenues by 42 percent compared to 2014, from UAH70.2 billion in 2014 to UAH99.8 billion in 2015. Furthermore, the resulting income exceeded forecast revenues by 16 percent.[12] This progress continued in 2016: local budgets further increased their revenues by 49 percent to UAH146.6 billion, which again exceeded the expected amount by 16 percent (Figure 1 summarizes

---

11 Miskyi and Halushka, *Reforms under the Microscope*, 17.
12 "Dovidka shchodo stanu vykonannia misttsevykh biudzhetiv. Vykonannia dohodiv misttsevykh biudzhetiv za 2015 rik", *Ministerstvo finansiv Ukraïny*, last modified January 12, 2016. http://www.minfin.gov.ua/uploads/redactor/files/56969ae43ec34.docx.

the dynamics of local budget increases in 2014–2016).[13] If such a significant increase could be explained at least in part by the considerable devaluation of Ukrainian currency and related inflation in 2015, the continued rise in local budgets' revenues in 2016 indicated the significant potential of financial decentralization. This trend was expected to continue in the future.

Figure 4.1. Total amounts of local budgets in 2014–2016 (excluding the non-government-controlled territories in Crimea and Donbas, UAH bn)

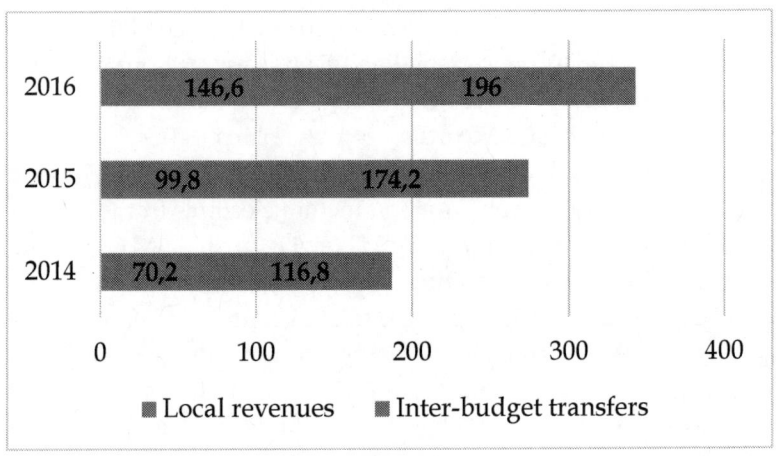

Due to the considerable increase in funds available to local authorities, their revenues notably exceeded their expenses in both 2015 and 2016. In total, local budget revenues (including state subsidies) surpassed expenses by UAH6 billion in 2014;[14] in 2015, the

---

13 "Dovidka shchodo stanu vykonannia misttsevykh biudzhetiv. Vykonannia dohodiv misttsevykh biudzhetiv za sichen'–hruden' 2016 roku", *Ministerstvo finansiv Ukraïny*, last modified December 20, 2016. http://www.minfin.gov.ua/uploads/redactor/files/%D0%94%D0%9E%D0%92%D0%86%D0%94%D0%9A%D0%90%20(%D1%81%D1%96%D1%87%D0%B5%D0%BD%D1%8C-%D0%B3%D1%80%D1%83%D0%B4%D0%B5%D0%BD%D1%8C).docx.

14 "Dovidka pro vykonannya misttsevykh byudzhetiv za dohodamy stanom na 01.01.2015", *Derzhavna kaznacheis'ka sluzhba Ukraïny*, last modified January 26, 2015. http://www.treasury.gov.ua/main/file/link/245416/file/Mb_12_14.xls; "Dovidka pro vykonannya misttsevykh byudzhetiv za vydatkamy stanom na 01.01.2015", *Derzhavna kaznacheis'ka sluzhba Ukraïny*, last modified January

difference increased to UAH42 billion,[15] and to almost UAH56 billion in 2016 (see Figure 4.2).[16] While such growth points to the significant enrichment of local communities, it also signals the inability of local authorities to fully cope with the considerable increase of funds at their disposal. Two factors could perhaps explain this outcome. On the one hand, many established ATCs had a shortage of qualified personnel, as local public officials often had little experience managing large funds and implementing complex projects. On the other hand, local councils were still in the process of mastering their new competencies — a problem complicated by the lack of a clearly defined division of power between elected councils and state administrations in the law.

26, 2015. http://www.treasury.gov.ua/main/file/link/245416/file/Mb_12_1 4.xls.

15 "Dovidka pro vykonannya misttsevykh byudzhetiv za dohodamy stanom na 01.01.2016", Derzhavna kaznacheis'ka sluzhba Ukraïny, last modified January 27, 2016. http://www.treasury.gov.ua/main/file/link/305326/file/Mb_12_15.xls; "Dovidka pro vykonannya misttsevykh byudzhetiv za vudatkamy stanom na 01.01.2016", Derzhavna kaznacheis'ka sluzhba Ukraïny, last modified January 27, 2016. http://www.treasury.gov.ua/main/file/link/305333/file/Mb_12_1 5_1.xls.

16 "Dovidka pro vykonannya misttsevykh byudzhetiv za dohodamy stanom na 01.01.2017", Derzhavna kaznacheis'ka sluzhba Ukraïny, last modified January 26, 2017. http://www.treasury.gov.ua/main/file/link/349856/file/Mb_12_16.xls; "Dovidka pro vykonannya misttsevykh byudzhetiv za vudatkamy stanom na 01.01.2017", Derzhavna kaznacheis'ka sluzhba Ukraïny, last modified January 26, 2017. http://www.treasury.gov.ua/main/file/link/349863/file/Mb_12_1 6_1.xls.

Figure 4.2. Revenues and expenses of local budgets in 2014–2016 (excluding the non-government-controlled territories in Crimea and Donbas, UAH bn)

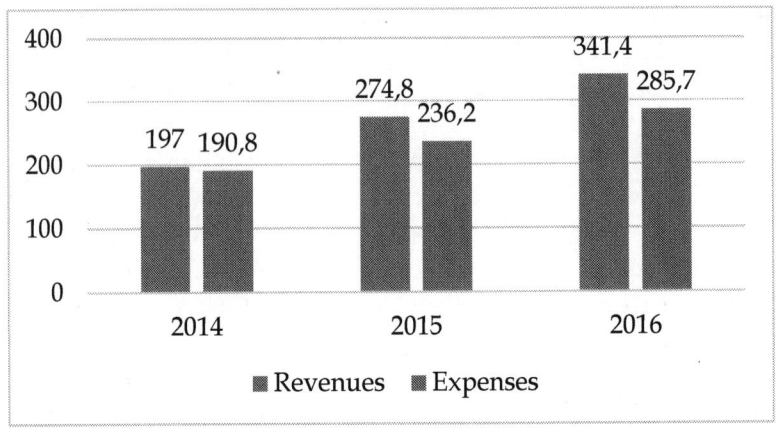

Ukraine achieved considerable success in community amalgamation. By the end of 2015, approximately 800 communities merged into 159 ATCs, which were able to conduct their first elections in October 2015.[17] In 2016, the process slowed down, mostly due to resistance from the CEC, which repeatedly delayed the announcement of elections in new ATCs, and to the inability of the parliament to pass several laws that would have accelerated amalgamation. Nevertheless, another 208 ATCs were created in 2016 and started to function properly in early 2017. In terms of pace, this result clearly put Ukraine ahead of many European countries that experienced similar processes of local amalgamation.[18]

In early 2017, after more than a year of unsuccessful attempts, the parliament finally adopted laws aimed at facilitating the process of creating new ATCs. The first package of laws simplified the process for ordinary communities to join already existing ATCs,

---

17 "Monitorynh prohresu reform. Zvit za 9 misyatsiv 2015", *Natsional'na rada reform*, 6 November 2015. http://reforms.in.ua/sites/default/files/upload/nationalreform_broshura4.pdf.
18 Analolii Tkachuk, "Pro detsentralizatsiyu, uspikhy, ryzyky i rol' parlamentu", *Dzerkalo tyzhnia*, 13 January 2017. http://gazeta.dt.ua/internal/pro-decentralizaciyu-uspihi-riziki-i-rol-parlamentu-_.html.

without the need to conduct new local elections. Another law paved the way for the creation of ATCs around the cities of *oblast* significance and from communities located in different districts. According to expert estimates, as a result of the adoption of these laws, up to 60 percent of the planned number of ATCs could be created in Ukraine by the end of 2017.[19] Overall, the government expected to decrease the number of communities from 11,500 to approximately 1,500 through the process of local amalgamation.

ATCs that were established in 2015 demonstrated considerable success. In 2016, they increased their budgets more than sixfold compared to the budgets of the previously existing communities in 2015.[20] ATCs used most of their newly obtained funds for infrastructure projects, willing both to address long-standing problems in their communities and to show their electorates the quick benefits of their new status. Widespread reconstruction of roads was probably the most visible result of decentralization. In 2016, more than twice the amount of road surface was laid than in the two previous years.[21] Local authorities also used additional funds for the reconstruction and repair of educational and healthcare facilities and public works.

A clear majority of the projects implemented by ATCs during the first year of their existence were short-term and addressed the most immediate needs of their communities. On the other hand, the practice of using the newly available funds for long-term projects, creating new sources of revenue, was clearly uncommon. Most ATCs avoided using their financial resources for profit-generating activities, such as opening new enterprises or improving the

---

19 Yuriy Hanushchak, Oleksii Sydorchuk, and Andreas Umland, "Ukraine's most underreported reform", *New Eastern Europe*, 13 April 2017. http://www.neweasterneurope.eu/articles-and-commentary/2328-ukraine-s-most-underreported-reform-decentralization-after-the-euromaidan-revolution.
20 "Decentralization of local budget revenues in 2016", *Cabinet of Ministers of Ukraine*, 18 April 2017. http://decentralization.gov.ua/pics/attachments/Viikonannya_OTG_(ang_versiya).pdf.
21 Ivan Lukerya and Olena Halushka, "10 ways decentralization is changing Ukraine", *Kyiv Post*, 7 December 2016. https://www.kyivpost.com/article/opinion/op-ed/ivan-lukerya-olena-halushka-10-ways-decentralization-changing-ukraine.html.

investment climate of their communities. There were several reasons for this state of affairs. First, ATC authorities usually needed time to cope with the new resources and powers and, thus, started with simpler and less demanding activities. Second, the lack of qualified personnel was evident in many of the newly created communities, and this posed another obstacle to the development and implementation of investment projects. Third, many of the newly elected heads and councils of ATCs intentionally started their work with activities that would provide quick results to fulfill their electoral promises.[22]

The predominance of short-term infrastructure projects was not a critical problem for ATCs, as they continued to benefit from an increase in tax revenues and additional state support. With time, however, local self-government bodies were expected to manage a growing number of competencies, transferred to them by the state, as financial support from the central government was expected to gradually decrease. To cover the expenses connected with these new competencies, ATCs were expected to create sustainable sources of revenue. Therefore, even though the transition to development projects posed a challenge for many ATCs, the inability to undertake them could threaten their economic sustainability in the future.

The discrepancy between available funds and the amount needed to cover all expenses was especially evident in many unamalgamated communities. Over the past two decades, many of these communities were poor, but, in the past, their budget deficits were (at least partly) covered by funds from district budgets. With the creation of ATCs, district authorities lost many of their funds to ATCs, and were increasingly unable to support impoverished communities within their territories. The growing gap between communities that were able to merge and those that failed to do so represented the other, albeit no less important, side of the amalgamation process. That is why so much attention was concentrated on creating the most favorable conditions for expanding the amalgamation process. Over time, more experts and practitioners argued for the

---

22 Sydorchuk, *Decentralization*, 7.

need to make amalgamation mandatory and to compel all communities to merge by some specific future date.

The Unfinished Constitutional Reform

Most likely, the amalgamation of communities would have happened faster, and the relations between elected councils and state administration would have had fewer problems, if parliament had adopted the changes on decentralization in the constitution. The conflict that prevented passage of the constitutional amendments in the final reading was related to the 18th provision of the bill, which proposed special conditions for local self-government in specific territories of the Donetsk and Luhansk *oblasts*. Opponents of that provision argued that its inclusion would grant the Russian proxies in control of some parts of Donbas enhanced rights and competencies, beyond those available to other local self-government bodies in Ukraine. In addition, they pointed to the law on the specific conduct of local self-government in some territories of the Donetsk and Luhansk *oblasts*, which parliament adopted in September 2014 but never implemented. The law proposed to increase the autonomy of local governments in the non-government-controlled Donbas territories, including new competencies in the areas of appointing a "people's militia", judges, and prosecutors, and granting additional funds from the state budget. Critics of the constitutional bill feared that, if adopted, it would prompt the practical implementation of these norms.

Supporters of the constitutional changes denied that they would endow any "special status" to the occupied territories in Donbas. According to them, the "specific conduct of local self-government" would only give the state additional leverage to change the competencies of local government in the non-government-controlled Donbas region, for instance, by reducing their scope. Arguably, President Poroshenko's intention was to demonstrate Ukraine's commitment to the Minsk agreements while preserving room to maneuver for dealing with the rebel-held territories in Donbas. The president believed that the *Verkhovna Rada* would be more inclined to support the controversial provision if it were included in the decentralization package.[23] However, staunch opposition on the part of several parliamentary factions derailed Poroshenko's plan.

That said, much the greater part of the constitutional bill dealt not with the Minsk agreements but with decentralization. If adopted, it would have introduced several important changes. First, it would have harmonized the administrative-territorial regime of the country, which was rather chaotic and inconsistent. To this end, the constitutional amendments explicitly arranged a three-tier territorial division of Ukraine: communities (*hromadas*), districts (*rayons*), and regions (the latter category including 24 *oblasts* and the Autonomous Republic of Crimea).

Second, the constitutional changes would have created a new model of relations between the elected councils and the centrally appointed heads of state administrations at the district and regional levels. According to the proposed constitutional provisions, district and regional state administrations, which performed executive functions, would have been abolished, while their competencies would have been transferred to executive bodies established by directly elected district and regional councils.

Third, to balance the increased powers of local elected bodies and officials, the constitutional project would have introduced prefects who would represent the state and ensure the legality of local self-government bodies' acts. To exercise such control, prefects would have the power to suspend the decisions of local councils or mayors, simultaneously referring these decisions to the courts. The courts would then decide whether or not to repeal the local self-government's decisions. Furthermore, if the local self-government body's decision threatened the state's sovereignty, territorial integrity, or national security, the president would have the right to dismiss this body and refer the case to the constitutional court.

---

23 Serhiy Rakhmanin, "Koma, krapka, krapka: Pro prykhovani osoblyvosti konstytutsiinoho protsesu", *Dzerkalo Tyzhnya*, 17 July 2015. http://gazeta.dt.ua /internal/koma-krapka-krapka-pro-prihovani-osoblivosti-konstituciynogo-pr ocesu-_.html.

The Venice Commission of the Council of Europe assessed the draft of the constitutional amendments positively,[24] as did many Ukrainian experts. Adoption of the constitutional amendments would have allowed several important objectives of the decentralization reform to be reached.

First, it would have facilitated the amalgamation of communities and the enlargement of districts necessary to complete the reform of the territorial arrangements of the country.

Second, the transfer of executive functions from state-appointed to elected bodies at the district and regional levels would probably have increased the influence of ordinary citizens on the decision-making processes in their regions. Furthermore, elected councils would not only have obtained new competencies but would have been more accountable to their voters.

Third, the introduction of prefects would have re-established state oversight over the legality of local self-government decisions, which was lost with the reform of the prosecutor's office (which had performed a similar function). Such oversight would have been important, given that local authorities obtained enhanced powers without any new checks on their activities.[25]

The position and powers of prefects, however, raised considerable controversy. On the one hand, since prefects would have lacked the extensive executive functions that local state administrations enjoyed, the danger of them gaining undue influence over elected bodies would be limited. However, the complicated mechanism of appointing prefects had the potential to backfire. According to the constitutional amendments, the cabinet would have nominated candidates for prefects, and the president would have appointed them. Furthermore, both the president and the cabinet would have had the right to repeal certain of the prefects' acts. Obviously, such procedures could have generated conflicts between

---

24 "Preliminary Opinion on the Proposed Constitutional Changes regarding the Territorial Structure and Local Administration of Ukraine", *European Commission for Democracy through Law (Venice Commission)*, June 24, 2015. http://venice.coe.int/files/CDL-PI(2015)008-e.pdf.

25 Oleksii Sydorchuk, *Decentralization Reform in Ukraine: Prospects and Challenges* (Kyiv: Ilko Kucheriv Democratic Initiatives Foundation, 2015), 6.

the president and the cabinet over control of the prefects. On the other hand, the president could have used the prefects to preserve his political influence over regional governments, and this could have undermined some of the positive effects of the reform. To address these issues, parliament should have considered introducing transparent and open competition procedures for selecting prefects, shielding them from political influence, in case the constitutional bill would have been passed.

Finally, the constitutional amendments would explicitly obligate the central government to provide local authorities with the financial resources needed for the latter to perform their functions. Although declarative, this norm could relieve the financial burden on many communities and prevent the state from unjustifiably declining to provide funds for local governments, using budget limitations as a reason.

After the Pyrrhic victory of approving the constitutional amendments on first reading, the *Verkhovna Rada* planned to start final deliberations during its third session, scheduled to start in September 2015. However, with insufficient votes for the reform, President Poroshenko decided to indefinitely postpone the final vote. Since the constitution required parliament to follow the first reading of the constitutional bill with a second reading at the next session, a group of Petro Poroshenko Bloc deputies referred the case to the Constitutional court. In its decision, which was widely seen heavy influenced by the Presidential Administration, the Constitutional court allowed parliament to begin the second reading of the decentralization bill at any session prior to the conclusion of the parliament's tenure. Since then, there have been no attempts to bring the constitutional project into session during Poroshenko's presidency.

After the collapse of the ruling parliamentary coalition in early 2016, and the intensifying confrontations between the government and the opposition inside the *Verkhovna Rada*, the prospects of adopting the constitutional changes were close to none. Although not being included in the constitution hinders the decentralization reform, it did not fully prevent its implementation. Both financial decentralization and the amalgamation of territorial communities continued despite the failed efforts to change the constitution. At the same time, the absence of constitutional changes complicated administrative-territorial reform and unbalances the distribution of powers and resources between ATCs, unamalgamated territorial communities, and district authorities, leading to a shortage of resources in and increasing income gaps between sometimes neighboring communities. While several legislative acts to harmonize the existing territorial arrangements were drafted, they lacked the necessary support from either the government or the parliament. The inability of the *Verkhovna Rada* to improve the administrative-territorial structure of the country could also pose a problem for the implementation of important sectoral reforms connected with decentralization, such as educational and healthcare reform.

Controversies in the Public Perception of Decentralization

As with any other reform that is underway, the effectiveness of decentralization can and should be measured not only by objective data but also by the subjective attitudes and evaluations of ordinary citizens. Given the highly complex nature of the reform—involving not only public administration and the territorial organization of power, but also education, healthcare, social welfare, etc.—public opinion should be treated with care. Sociological surveys point to several important results of decentralization for the public.

First, while Ukrainians were mostly in favor of empowering local self-government bodies, the core of the decentralization reform, their attitudes to government decentralization efforts were mixed. In November 2014, 58 percent of Ukrainians supported extending the competencies of local elected authorities, while only 13 percent opposed this idea.[26] Even more pronounced was support for the transfer of powers and resources to local authorities and communities in July 2015, according to a poll by the "Rating" Sociological Group: 67 percent supported this initiative, and 14 percent

---

26 Sydorchuk, "Stavlennya zhyteliv mist", 7.

opposed it.[27] The general popularity of the idea of decentralization was rather self-evident, as most citizens were in favor of bringing the power closer to them.

Although generally supportive of decentralization, Ukrainians also foresaw several risks. For instance, 18 percent of the population expected decentralization to improve the quality of public services, and another 24 percent expected decentralization to provide citizens with new instruments of influencing local authorities. However, many respondents also pointed to possible negative repercussions of the reform. According to 27 percent of Ukrainians, decentralization could lead to the empowerment of "local barons", and in the view of 15 percent, it could result in the devastation of villages and small towns.[28] The latter danger could be alleviated, however, if the reform were implemented according to the 2014 Concept. In such cases, villages would in fact receive new incentives to develop both as independent centers of economic growth and as parts of large communities that generate profit by providing necessary resources and infrastructure to their larger neighbors.

Meanwhile, the threat of the excessive concentration of power and resources in the hands of elected mayors and the heads of communities could indeed be genuine, especially after the central government lost its right to supervise the legality of the acts of local elected authorities. The ability of the government to effectively address this danger to a great extent hinged, again, on the willingness of parliament to adopt the constitutional changes on decentralization, as they would create preventive mechanisms through the institution of the prefect. As the constitutional changes on decentralization remained in limbo, however, some experts had advocated entrusting local state administrations with powers similar to those proposed for prefects. However, such initiatives had drawn criticism, as many feared that such an increase in the competency of

---

27 "Dynamika suspil'no-politychnykh pohlyadiv v Ukraïni, July 2015", *Sotsiolohichna hrupa "Reitynh"*, August 26, 2015. http://ratinggroup.ua/research/ukraine/dinamika_obschestvenno-politicheskih_vzglyadov_v_ukraine.html.

28 "Hromads'ka dumka naselennya shchodo reform detsentralizatsiï", *Fond "Demokratychni Initsiatyvy" imeni Il'ka Kucheriva*, July 24, 2017. http://dif.org.ua/article/gromadska-dumka-naselennya-shchodo-reformi-detsentralizatsii

regional and district state administrations would have repressed the empowerment of local self-government.

Meanwhile, other polls showed the different attitudes of Ukrainians to the measures adopted by the government regarding decentralization. In August 2016, according to the poll of the Ilko Kucheriv Democratic Initiatives Foundation (DIF), 43 percent of Ukrainians supported the reform, while 32 percent opposed it. In June 2017, the number remained virtually the same: 42 percent and 27 percent, respectively (Figure 3 presents the results).[29] At the same time, the polls by the "Rating" Group painted a rather different picture. When asked, in 2016, whether the governmental decentralization policy was successful, only 22 percent of Ukrainians answered "yes", while 62 percent answered "no".[30] Notably, the share of negative responses was even greater at the end of 2015—67 percent.[31]

One possible explanation for such seemingly paradoxical numbers was the general political and socioeconomic context of Ukraine's post-Maidan development. On the one hand, most Ukrainians sincerely supported empowering local authorities and local communities and even viewed government efforts in this direction in quite a positive way. At the same time, given the Ukrainian government's general lack of success in meeting public expectations for quick and efficient reforms, and the poor quality of life of the majority of Ukrainians, decentralization was often perceived through the lens of one's attitude to the government and one's assessment of one's own personal socioeconomic well-being. Clearly, the same person could generally support the government's decentralization efforts but at the same time criticize them for not improving her quality of life.

---

29 Ibid.
30 "Otsinka podii 2016 roku ta suspil'no politychni nastroï naselennya", *Sotsiolohichna hrupa "Reitynh"*, December 23, 2016. http://ratinggroup.ua/research/ukraine/ocenka_sobytiy_2016_i_obschestvenno-politicheskie_nastroeniya_naseleniya.html.
31 "Elektoral'ni ta suspil'ni nastroï naselennya", *Sotsiolohichna hrupa "Reitynh"*, February 4, 2016. http://ratinggroup.ua/research/ukraine/elektoralnye_i_obschestvennye_nastroeniya_naseleniya.html.

In addition, Ukrainians are traditionally skeptical about any reforms initiated by the government. In most cases, the population generally has a negative view of government reform efforts. For example, the public consistently pointed to the deteriorating situation in all areas of state responsibility (except the defense sector).[32] Rather notably, the poll cited by the "Rating" Group named decentralization as one of the top three reforms (the others being improvements in defense and police reform), according to the public's own assessment, even though government actions were evaluated negatively in all areas.

Figure 4.3. Do you support the measures implemented by the government in the framework of the decentralization of power? (%)

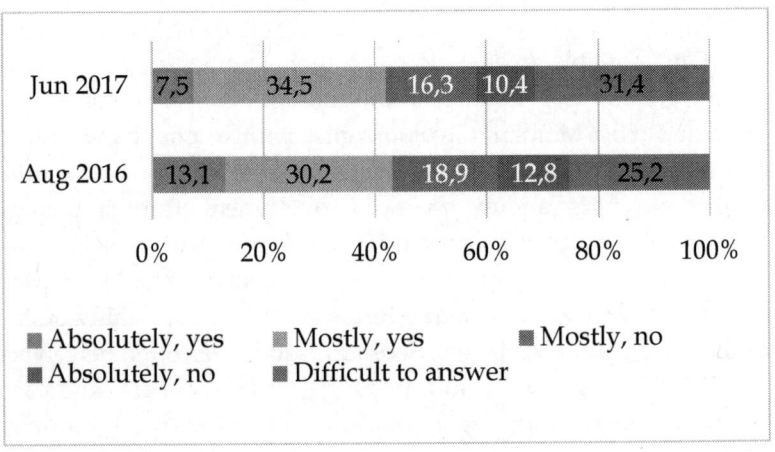

A related trend revealed by sociological surveys was the view of the majority of citizens that decentralization had brought no significant changes. When, in August 2016, the DIF survey asked Ukrainians if they noticed any results from new funds acquired by local budgets, a clear majority—67 percent—answered that they did not, while 16 percent recorded feeling positive results and 8 percent

---

32 "2016-i: politychni pidsumky—zahal'nonatsional'ne opytuvannya", *Fond "Demokratychni Initsiatyvy" imeni Il'ka Kucheriva*, December 28, 2016. http://dif.org.ua/article/2016-y-politychni-pidsumki-zagalnonatsionalne-opituvannya.

recorded feeling negative results.[33] Furthermore, in June 2017, even more Ukrainians—16 percent—answered that they thought the changes for the worse, while the number of those who saw positive changes remained the same. As before, a clear majority of citizens (55 percent) did not notice any change.

Paradoxically, these results did not match the ones obtained by the Kyiv International Institute of Sociology (KIIS), which held a public opinion poll in November 2016. According to this survey, 46 percent of Ukrainians felt some improvements from the larger local budgets as opposed to 43 percent who perceived no changes, and 5 percent who felt the changes were for the worse (Graph 4 presents the detailed results).[34] Such discrepancies could be explained by differences in the wording of the questions. The KIIS poll asked about improvements in infrastructure and public works, which were visible to many Ukrainians from the start of decentralization, while the DIF survey also inquired about changes in the quality of social services, an area in which the great majority of the population had not yet seen any considerable improvement.

Nevertheless, additional results provide better insight into public sentiments regarding the results of decentralization. Both in November 2016 and June 2017, among those who felt that the changes were for the better, a large majority (70 percent and 64 percent, respectively) saw improvement in the roads, while a significant share of these respondents also noticed improvements in the sanitation around buildings, communal services, and infrastructure. On the other hand, the respondents who felt the changes were for the worse indicated a decline in the quality of medical services (63 percent in August 2016 and 53 percent in June 2017), a high level of unemployment (57 percent and 39 percent, respectively), inadequate care for socially vulnerable groups (53 percent and 44 percent), and even an unsuccessful fight against corruption (46 percent

---

33 "Hromads'ka dumka naselennya shchodo reform detsentralizatsiï", Fond "Demokratychni Initsiatyvy".
34 "Detsentralizatsiya ta reforma misttsevoho samovryaduvannya: rezul'taty druhoï khvyli sotsiolohichnoho doslidzhennya", Kyïvs'kyi mizhnarodnyi instytut sotsiolohiï, December 27, 2016. http://www.slg-coe.org.ua/wp-content/uploads/2016/12/Analitychnyi_zvit_Detsentralizatsia_2-Khvylia.pdf

and 38 percent).³⁵ Interestingly, none of these areas was directly connected with decentralization reform, as they required government effort in other policy spheres. These results also corresponded to the above-mentioned survey of heads of ATCs, and served as additional evidence that local authorities had used most of the newly obtained funds on short-term infrastructure projects.

One could draw the conclusion that Ukrainians did in fact see some changes as a result of decentralization, but these changes were not sufficient to overcome a general skepticism to the Ukrainian government's reform efforts or their negative assessment of the country's socioeconomic situation. While Ukrainians noticed improvements in infrastructure across the regions, they did not perceive any significant changes (or even see the situation getting worse) in crucial areas such as medicine and social welfare. Furthermore, interpretation of these results should take into account the rather short span of the new realities of financial decentralization, which started only in 2015. The experience of other countries that undertook similar reforms presents strong evidence that the process not only takes a long time to complete (up to 10 years, and even, in some cases, decades), but also that it fails to immediately generate a clear response from the public.³⁶ Indeed, changes in both legislation and policy require time to make an impact on the daily life of ordinary citizens.

---

35 Ibid., 19.
36 Grigorij Mesežnikov, "Reforms and Euro-Integration in Slovakia: Lessons for Ukraine", in: *European integration of Ukraine: experience of neighbors and prospects of consolidation of society* (Kyiv: Ilko Kucheriv Democratic Initiatives Foundation), 30.

Figure 4.4. In 2015–2016, the revenues of local budgets significantly increased. Have you seen any results of use of these funds?[37] (%)

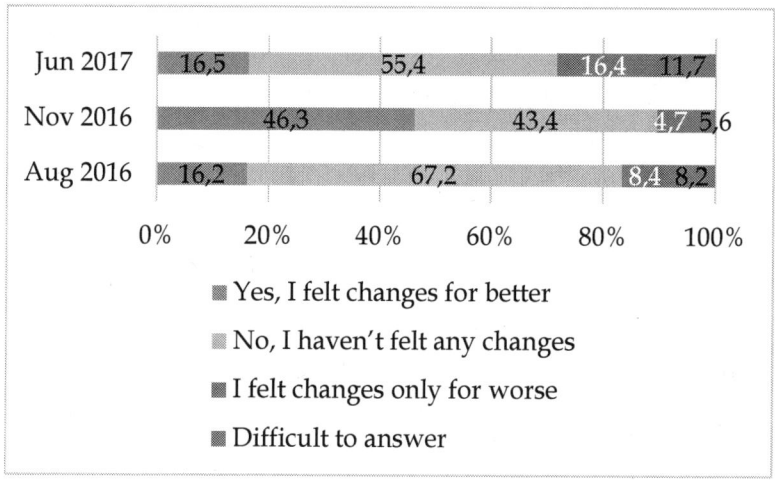

Public opinion polls painted a very similar picture about the attitude to amalgamating communities, one of the most important elements of the reform. As with decentralization in general, slightly more Ukrainians supported the amalgamation of communities (31 percent in August 2016 and 38 percent in June 2017) than not (28 percent and 26 percent, respectively). Similarly, in August 2016, the majority of ATC inhabitants (66 percent) perceived no changes from the enrichment of their budgets, and only 16 percent saw positive changes;[38] in June 2017, only 11 percent experienced positive

---

[37] The exact wording of the questionnaires used in these public opinion polls differed. The DIF surveys of August 2016 and June 2017 asked: "Throughout 2015-2016, revenues of local budgets have significantly increased. Have you noticed any results from the use of these funds (improved quality of services, public works, social welfare) compared with previous years?" The November 2016 KIIS survey asked: "This year, according to State Statistics data, revenues of local budgets have significantly increased due to the reform. Do you see any results from the use of these funds in your city/town/village, for instance in an increased number of public works (gardening, lighting, roadworks) or any improvement in their quality compared with previous years?"

[38] "Detsentralizatsiya", *Kyïvs'kyi mizhnarodnyi instytut sotsiolohiï*.

changes, and 63 percent noticed no change (see Graph 5).[39] Again, the improvements made in ATCs had mostly to do with better infrastructure, while more tectonic shifts in a number of social areas were still lacking.

Figure 4.5. Has the amalgamation of communities changed the conditions of life in your community? (*those who already live in ATCs, %*)

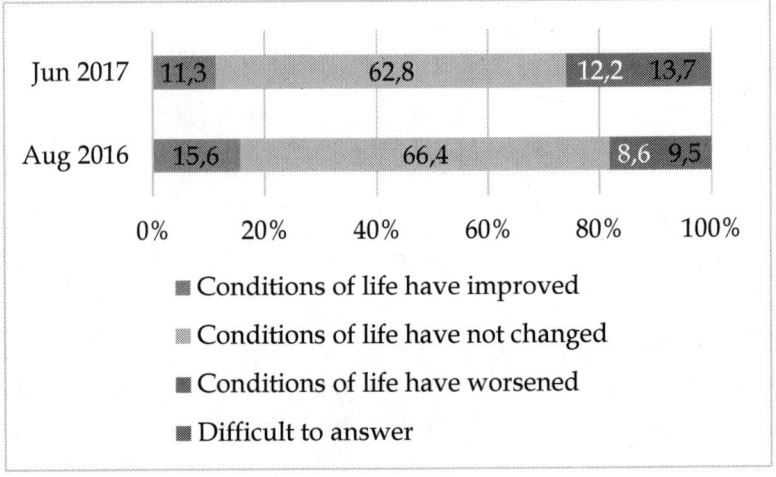

Finally, the success of decentralization also hinged on the willingness and readiness of citizens to become more involved in decision-making processes in their communities. Public opinion was ambivalent on this issue. On the one hand, the majority of Ukrainians (63 percent) remained dissatisfied with their influence on the decisions made by their local authorities. At the same time, even where there was a significant empowerment of local elected bodies, only 37 percent were willing to increase their participation in managing their communal affairs. This is surprising, given that, because of decentralization, an increasing number of problems could be solved at the local level. Moreover, of those who stated their willingness to engage more in local affairs, the relative majority opted for passive measures, such as participation in local elections (42 percent), while

---

39 "Hromads'ka dumka naselennya shchodo reform detsentralizatsii".

more direct forms of influence over local authorities were far less popular.⁴⁰

However, some anecdotal evidence pointed to a different situation in the newly created ATCs, where citizens tended to be more active in their attempts to have a say in managing their communities by participating in public hearings or local meetings.⁴¹ Such results demonstrated the importance of clearly communicating the new possibilities and instruments that decentralization could deliver to ordinary community members. If the state and local authorities succeeded in explaining to the public that decentralization improved their ability to influence decision-making at the local level, the prospects of successful implementing the reform would be greatly enhanced. Otherwise, local authorities, gaining more resources and more discretion in their own activities, could become unaccountable to their electorates and feel no incentives to prioritize the public good over their particularistic interests.

Conclusions

Decentralization proved a rather unique reform in post-Euromaidan Ukraine. On the one hand, it was one of the few of the government's reform initiatives that brought tangible results, at least partly reflected in public opinion, and enjoyed support from different stakeholders across the government/opposition divide. On the other hand, due to external factors, it became something of a hostage to the Minsk process aimed at resolving the conflict in Donbas. As a consequence, both Ukrainian society and Ukraine's Western partners had a significantly distorted perspective of decentralization and its seeming link to the "special status" of the non-government-controlled territories in Donbas.

After parliament finally adopted several laws facilitating the further amalgamation of communities, the reform was irreversible,

---

40   Ibid.
41   Balázs Jarábik and Yulia Yesmukhanova, "Ukraine's Slow Struggle for Decentralization", *Carnegie Endowment for International Peace*, 8 March 2017. http://carnegieendowment.org/2017/03/08/ukraine-s-slow-struggle-for-decentralizati on-pub-68219.

all the more so as an increasing number of communities were accustomed to living in the new reality. The flow of the reform would have been smoother if parliament had incorporated the changes on decentralization into the constitution. However, as long as the constitutional bill contained the controversial provision on the "specific conduct of local government" in the rebel-held Donbas territories, this simply could not happen.

Finally, effective communication was the key to ensuring that the initial reform successes remain sustainable. The government would be well advised not only to clearly explain the benefits the population will receive from the implementation of the reform, but also to provide information on how citizens could increase their involvement in local decision-making processes and effectively control their newly empowered and enriched local elected bodies. At the end of the day, decentralization will not work without the active and responsible engagement of the public at the lowest level.

5. State Fragility and the Risks of Decentralization in Ukraine

Max Bader

One of Ukraine's most prominent reforms since the Euromaidan Revolution has been the devolution of authority and resources to newly formed Amalgamated Territorial Communities as part of a wider decentralization undertaking. During the initial years of the implementation of the reform, 2014-2016, Ukraine was by most standards a weak state. Drawing on academic literature about the risks of decentralization, this chapter considers the relationship between state fragility and the decentralization reform. It argues that state fragility has negatively affected the implementation of the reform and that the reform has aggravated the problem of state fragility in some areas.

Introduction

Following the Euromaidan Revolution in 2014, the Ukrainian government embarked on an ambitious reform program. One of the reforms that has since led to real change is the decentralization of local government through the formation of amalgamated territorial communities (ATCs). Within a few years of the start of the reform, hundreds of such ATCs, each merging a number of former municipalities, have been formed. These new ATCs make the effects of the reform noticeable, as they control larger budgets and have significantly greater decision-making powers than the municipalities that they replaced.

The reform of local self-government is not without risks. Among other things, the formation of new ATCs may provoke local conflicts, create opportunities for the capture of power and resources by local elites, and impair the quality of public administration. The reform, moreover, was launched during an extraordinarily difficult time for the Ukrainian state. As key legislation was being adopted and the first ATC were formed, the government was sorting out a severe economic crisis and faced Russia's illegal annexation of Crimea, armed conflict in parts of Donbas, political tensions, and the challenges of gaining legitimacy. By most standards, the Ukrainian state was a weak state during the initial years of the implementation of the reform.

This chapter considers the relationship between decentralization reform and state fragility and advances two arguments. First, the weakness of the Ukrainian state has negatively affected the implementation of the reform. Due to a lack of oversight and coordination, in three years after the launch of the reform, the landscape of local government presented a chaotic patchwork. Second, the reform aggravated the problem of state fragility in some areas, as it sparked different types of local conflicts and led to the creation of communities whose capacity and accountability were to some degree questionable.

This chapter applies insights from academic research on decentralization to the recent decentralization reform in Ukraine. Data have been collected through extensive fieldwork in the Odesa *oblast* and from the analysis of reports in (mostly) local Ukrainian media outlets. In the Odesa *oblast*, 83 interviews were conducted with representatives of the newly formed ATC, as well as with local civic activists. The insights gained from this fieldwork illuminate broader phenomena regarding decentralization in Ukraine. The chapter's first section discusses the reform of local self-government in Ukraine since 2014. In the second section, we review the scholarship on decentralization and outline the main risks associated with decentralization reform. The third and main section finally discusses whether Ukraine has succeeded in avoiding these risks.

Decentralization reform in Ukraine since the Euromaidan Revolution

The decentralization reform set in motion in 2014 was highly anticipated for a number of reasons. One was that existing legislation was seen as flawed and at points contradictory, leading to conflicts between local self-government bodies and local state administrations.[1] Another reason was that the subnational government system was seen as constraining economic development in rural areas.[2] Finally, Ukraine's form of subnational government was incompatible with international norms, such as subsidiarity. [3] Ukraine is a unitary state with three levels of subnational self-government: regional (*oblast*), district (*rayon*), and local. At the local level, until the recent decentralization reform, there were three different types of municipalities: city (*misto*), town (*selishche*), and village (*selo*). The 1996 Constitution and several subsequent laws, such as the 1997 Law "Local Self-Government in Ukraine", afforded significant rights to self-government, including in so-called territorial communities (*hromady*). For the most part, however, these rights have not been exercised.[4] Under the presidencies of Leonid Kuchma and Viktor Yanukovych, there was a tendency to further centralize state power and weaken local self-government. During the presidency of Viktor Yushchenko, on the other hand, there were several attempts to draft and pass laws that would decentralize the state. Because of political conflicts and the change of presidency in 2010, however, these plans were not carried out.

The Euromaidan Revolution gave a strong new impetus to the decentralization reform. On 1 April 2014, barely a month after the concluding events of the revolution, the government adopted an order on the approval of the Reform Concept on "Local Self-Government and the Territorial Organization of Power in Ukraine", which spelled out the basic principles of the subsequent

---

1   Viktor Chumak and Ihor Shevliakov, *Local Government Functioning and Reform in Ukraine: An Overview of Analytical Studies of Local Government System and Local Services Provision in Ukraine* (Oslo: Norwegian Institute for Urban and Regional Research, 2009), 21; Aston Centre for Europe, *Local and Regional Government in Ukraine and the Development of Cooperation between Ukraine and the EU* (Brussels: European Union, 2011), 9.
2   Yurii Hanushchak, *Reforma teritorial'noi orhanizatsii vlady* (Kyiv: DESPRO, 2013), 12.
3   Anatolii Tkachuk, *Mistseve samovryaduvannya ta detsentralizatsiya* (Kyiv: DESPRO, 2012), 7.
4   Tkachuk, *Mistseve samovryaduvannya ta detsentralizatsiya*, 46; *Local Governance and Decentralization Assessment: Implications of Proposed Reforms in Ukraine* (USAID, 2014), 5-6.

decentralization reform.[5] According to this document, decentralization reform effectively would follow two tracks. The first track concerned the comprehensive overhaul of subnational self-government, which would be adopted through constitutional amendments.[6] According to the planned amendments, only three types of subnational administrative entities would remain: regions, districts, and communities. State administrations at the regional and district levels, whose heads are appointed by the president, would be abolished, while district and regional councils would form their own executive bodies. Prefects, appointed by the president, would monitor the compliance of their decisions with the constitution and coordinate the work of central state institutions in the regions, districts, and communities. The proposed constitutional amendments were highly controversial because they included mention of a separate law that would stipulate special provisions (a so-called "special status") for the temporarily occupied territories of the Donetsk and Luhansk *oblasts*. In addition, several factions in parliament (the *Verkhovna Rada*) opposed the idea of the new institution of prefects.[7] Because of the controversy, the constitutional amendments were not adopted, and the first track of decentralization reform has stopped at this obstacle.

The second track of the decentralization reform, which is the subject of this study, concerns the amalgamation of municipalities into so-called ATCs, coupled with the devolution of powers and resources from upper scales on the newly formed ATCs. There was a broad consensus about the need for such a reform. There were two main problems. The first was that the existing system of local self-government left municipalities unable to generate sufficient revenue to cover local needs. Generally speaking, more than 90 percent of municipal budgets consisted of transfers from the central budget,

---

5 The text of Concept can be found at http://zakon5.rada.gov.ua/laws/show/33 3-2014-%D1%80.
6 The proposed constitutional amendments can be consulted at http://w1.c1.rad a.gov.ua/pls/zweb2/webproc4_1?pf3511=55812.
7 Balázs Jarábik and Yulia Yesmukhanova, "Ukraine's Slow Struggle for Decentralization", *Carnegie Endowment for International Peace*, 8 March 2017. http://carnegieendowment.org/2017/03/08/ukraine-s-slow-struggle-for-decentrali zation-pub-68219.

managed via higher-level state administrations.[8] Local councils could not decide how to spend those funds and thus lacked financial autonomy.[9] In large part because of this limited financial autonomy and the general lack of resources, the quality of public service delivery in municipalities was widely regarded as poor.[10] The second main problem was a shortage of qualified professional staff in the executive committees of the local councils.[11] This shortage was the result of migration from rural areas to urban areas and of the small size of many municipalities, among other factors. Of the more than 10,000 rural municipalities that existed before the start of the decentralization reform, 92 percent had fewer than 3,000 residents, and of those, roughly half had fewer than 1,000 residents.[12] Each of these rural municipalities, however, had its own local council and executive committee.

When the government and the *Verkhovna Rada* revived the idea of decentralization reform after the Euromaidan Revolution, they accepted most of the elements of the reform that had originally been proposed by Deputy Prime Minister Bezsmertnyi in 2005, which was largely inspired by the Polish model of local self-government.[13] Two pieces of legislation in particular shaped the reform on the new modalities of local self-government.

First, in December 2014, amendments to the Tax and Budget Codes of Ukraine were adopted, which strongly favored local self-government. Because of these amendments, a larger share of taxes is transferred to local budgets. In addition, the amendments give ATCs greater powers to levy their own taxes, and include the promise of larger state subsidies.[14] Once a new ATC is recognized by the respective regional authorities as "capable" (*spromozhnyi*), it receives powers, responsibilities, and resources similar to those of the

---

8   Chumak and Shevliakov, *Local Government Functioning and Reform in Ukraine*, 8.
9   Oleksii Sydorchuk, *Decentralization Reform in Ukraine: Prospects and Challenges* (Kyiv: Ilko Kucheriv Democratic Initiatives Charitable Foundation, 2015), 2.
10 Chumak and Shevliakov, *Local Government Functioning and Reform in Ukraine*, 6.
11 Ibid., 21.
12 Sydorchuk, *Decentralization Reform in Ukraine*, 2.
13 *Local Governance and Decentralization Assessment: Implications of Proposed Reforms in Ukraine* (Washington, DC: USAID, 2014), 7.
14 Sydorchuk, *Decentralization Reform in Ukraine*, 3.

cities of *oblast* significance.[15] The main benefit to municipalities that amalgamate into ATCs is that they control a larger budget and enjoy more freedom to decide on how their income is spent.

Second, the Law "On the Voluntary Amalgamation of Territorial Communities", adopted in February 2015, allowed for the formation of ATCs. A separate decree, issued in April 2015, contained additional instructions about the process of ATC formation.[16] According to the law, ATCs must include at least two contiguous municipalities. Because of new local elections, a single ATC legislative council and a single ATC executive committee would replace the legislative councils and executive committees of the municipalities that chose to merge into the ATC. The newly elected ATC council and executive committee would operate in the ATC administrative center. All other settlements within the ATC, which previously had their own councils and executive committees, would be represented in the ATC executive committee by an elected village elder (*starosta*). The formation of an ATC had to follow a number of fixed, mandatory steps. These included public hearings in all municipalities that chose to merge into an ATC; a vote in the relevant municipality councils; the proposal of plans for the formation of the ATC by a working group; and a decision by regional authorities on whether the formation of the ATC met the legal requirements. A crucial element of ATC formation is that the process must be voluntary: the municipal councils of all the municipalities involved must agree to amalgamation. The initiative for the formation of an ATC, according to the law, must come from one of the municipalities of the future ATC. The regional authorities, however, would draw up a "prospect plan" (*perspektyvnyi plan*) of the prospective ATCs in their region, listing which ATCs are expected to meet the legal requirements set out by the government. The "prospect plan" is considered a blueprint and cannot be imposed on the municipalities.

---

15 *Praktichnyi posibnyk z pytan' formuvannya spromozhnykh terytorial'nykh hromad* (Kyiv: USAID, 2016), 3.
16 The law can be consulted here: http://zakon5.rada.gov.ua/laws/show/157-19/print1457728359241365; the decree can be consulted here: http//zakon3.rada.gov.ua/laws/show/214-2015-% DO%BF/print1492097154387858.

Scholars distinguish between political (or democratic), administrative, and fiscal forms of decentralization.[17] Political decentralization "presupposes the transfer of functions or authority from central levels of government to subnational institutions based on local political representation".[18] In the case of administrative decentralization, tasks that were previously carried out directly by the central government would be carried out by local branches of the central government, which are not accountable to or checked by local councils. Finally, fiscal decentralization implies a shift of decision-making authority on financial matters from the higher levels of government to lower levels of government. With fiscal decentralization, local authorities have more opportunities to generate income and a greater degree of autonomy over how they spend their income, whether self-generated or received through transfers. According to this basic classification, the reform of local self-government in Ukraine related to ATCs constitutes political and fiscal, but not administrative, decentralization.

According to another classification scheme, decentralization can be divided into three types: deconcentration, delegation, and devolution.[19] Devolution, which is sometimes called democratic decentralization, "refers to a situation in which not only implementation but also the authority to decide what is done is in the hands of local governments",[20] and is the most far-reaching of the three types. The reform of local self-government in Ukraine is a clear example of devolution.

Going back to the constitutional amendments of the first track of the decentralization reform, they stipulated that, on completion

---

17 Diana Conyers, "Decentralization: The Latest Fashion in Development Administration?" *Public Administration & Development* 3, no.2 (1983): 97; *Democratic Decentralization Programming Handbook* (Washington, DC: USAID, 2009).
18 Conyers, "Decentralization".
19 James Manor, *The Political Economy of Decentralization* (Washington, DC: The World Bank, 1996); Dennis Rondinelli, James S. McCullough, and Ronald W. Johnson, "Analyzing decentralization policies in developing countries: A political-economy framework", *Development and Change* 20, no. 1 (1989): 57-87.
20 Richard M. Bird and François Vaillancourt, "Fiscal decentralization in developing countries: an overview", in: Richard M. Bird and François Vaillancourt, eds., *Fiscal Decentralization in Developing Countries* (Cambridge: Cambridge University Press, 1998), 3.

of the reform, the lowest level of self-government would be composed of ATCs exclusively. The forecast was that between 1,000 and 1,500 ATCs would be formed in total. By the end of 2016, 367 ATCs had been formed. Although this may suggest that approximately one-third of the prospective number had been reached, it is important to remind that only about 14 percent of municipalities amalgamated by that time.[21] Most of the ATCs in fact comprised fewer municipalities than anticipated in the prospect plans.

Why have more ATCs not been formed, and why do the ATCs that have been formed comprise relatively few (former) municipalities? Stakeholders at various levels, from rural municipalities to *Verkhovna Rada* deputies, resisted the formation of ATCs. The heads of municipalities that would not become the administrative center of an ATC, and the staff on the executive committees of their local councils, resisted because they were likely to lose their jobs once the ATC was established. Another reason why municipal authorities had not rushed to form ATCs was the lack of information about the process of ATC formation, and a sense of unease about the potential consequences.[22] In addition, district authorities, who faced an uncertain future because of decentralization reform, also resisted the process as it would mean devolving significant powers and resources on ATCs. Furthermore, one of the goals of decentralization was the significant reduction of the number of districts. Some district authorities promoted the formation of large ATCs, whose borders would coincide with those of their own districts, anticipating that they could reposition themselves as ATC authorities.[23] The third set of actors resistant to ATCs were decision-makers in regional councils and lawmakers in the *Verkhovna Rada*. Driven by a wide array of motives, many lawmakers representing a single-

---

21 Calculations made on the basis of data from http://gromada.info/.
22 Oleksii Sydorchuk, *Detsentralizatsiya: Rezul'taty, vyklyky i perspektyvy* (Kyiv: Ilko Kucheriv Democratic Initiatives Charitable Foundation, 2016), 5-6.
23 For example, see http://chernyakhiv-rda.gov.ua/2016/05/23/один-район-одна-громада/.

mandate electoral district seek to influence either the formation or non-formation of ATCs in their respective districts.[24]

All in all, many different actors seek in one way or another to influence the formation of ATCs. According to one noted expert on the decentralization reform, the process suffered from a lack of central oversight and direction.[25] There was a great variety in the number of ATCs formed by the end of 2016 across Ukraine — from only one in Kyiv *oblast* to 36 in Ternopil *oblast*. This can be explained in part by the regional authorities' attitude toward the reform. But it is worth noting that the ATCs that were formed were also highly diverse. Many comprised only two or three municipalities, and some had fewer than 2,000 residents. At the other extreme, there were ATCs that comprised over 20 former municipalities and had a population of nearly 50,000.

The Promise and Risks of Decentralization

Supporters of decentralization put forward a broad range of arguments about its purported merits. These arguments fall into two categories: (1) normative arguments related to the input of citizens into self-government and (2) arguments about increased security.

Does decentralization deliver?

Normative arguments in favor of decentralization point to greater opportunities for citizen participation and to the greater accountability of government officials to citizens. Decentralization empowers citizens by giving them a bigger stake in issues of local self-government. Citizens will use their newly acquired opportunities to

---

24 Elena Dospekhova, "Anatolyi Tkachuk: Vtoraya volna dobrovol'nogo ob"edineniya obshchin nachnetsya vo vtorom polugodii 2016 g., nezavisimo ot togo, khochet etogo politikum ili net", *Dilova Stolytsya*, 5 June 2016. http://www.dsnews.ua/temy_nomerov/anatoliy-tkachuk-vtoraya-volna-dobrovolnogo-obediyneniya-05062016212800.

25 Anatolii Tkachuk, "Pro detsentralizatsiyu, uspikhy, ryzyky i rol' parlamentu", *Dzerkalo Tyzhnya*, 13 January 2017. http://gazeta.dt.ua/internal/pro-decentralizaciyu-uspihi-riziki-i-rol-parlamentu-_.html.

become more active in public affairs.[26] A positive side effect of increased citizen participation in public affairs is the strengthening of social capital.[27] A more politically and socially engaged citizenry would demand greater accountability from government officials and elected representatives. In the absence of democratic decentralization, government officials are primarily accountable "upward", to higher-level authorities or the central government. Democratic decentralization, by contrast, makes government officials at the subnational level more accountable "downward", to citizens.[28] In sum, decentralization deepens democracy: it increases the number of issues that can be influenced by active democratic citizen involvement while making officials at the local level more accountable.

The purported beneficial outcomes of decentralization include higher-quality self-governance. Perhaps the most common argument made in favor of decentralization is that local authorities are better informed than higher-tier authorities about peoples' preferences on issues of local import.[29] Local authorities can respond more adequately and more quickly to changes in demand.[30] Leaving questions of local import to be decided by authorities at the corresponding level should therefore lead to higher-quality governance. One example of an area where the higher quality of

---

26 Richard C. Crook and James Manor, *Democracy and Decentralization in South Asia and West Africa: Participation, Accountability and Performance* (Cambridge: Cambridge University Press, 1998).
27 Luiz R. De Mello Jr, "Can fiscal decentralization strengthen social capital?" *Public Finance Review* 32, no. 1 (2004): 4-35.
28 Derick W. Brinkerhoff and Omar Azfar, *Decentralization and Community Empowerment: Does Community Empowerment Deepen Democracy and Improve Service Delivery?* (Washington, DC: USAID, 2006).
29 Wallace Oates, *Fiscal Federalism* (New York: Harcourt Brace Jovanovich, 1972); Anwah Shah, *The Reform of Intergovernmental Fiscal Relations in Developing and Emerging Market Economies* (Washington, DC: The World Bank); Barry R. Weingast, 'The economic role of political institutions: Market-preserving federalism and economic growth", *Journal of Law, Economics and Organization* 11 (1995): 1–31.
30 Omar Azfar, Satu Kähkönen and Patrick Meagher, *Conditions for Effective Decentralized Governance: A Synthesis of Research Findings* (Maryland: Center for Institutional Reform and the Informal Sector, 2001); Syed Mansoob Murshed and Mohammad Zulfan Tadjoeddin, "Revisiting the greed and grievance explanations for violent internal conflict", *Journal of International Development* 21 (2009): 87-111.

governance at the local level should be particularly noticeable is the provision of public services.[31] Higher-quality governance, it is also believed, contributes to stronger economic development at the local level.[32]

Another beneficial outcome associated with decentralization is increased security. There are several ways that decentralization can reduce the potential of armed conflict and secessionism. First, when local governments acquire more powers, minority groups who felt that their interests had been disregarded would find opportunities to gain representation and thus become more involved politically.[33] This is especially true when measures are actively taken to include minorities in the political process. If different social or ethnic groups interact in local politics and work toward common goals, this may result in greater trust between them.[34] In addition, since decentralization entails an increase in local government expenditure, minorities may have fewer reasons to resent the central authorities.[35] Finally, increased participation, greater accountability, higher-quality governance, and better service delivery — among other purported benefits of decentralization — can all increase state legitimacy, which in turn reduces the likelihood of conflict.[36]

---

31   Derick W. Brinkerhoff and Ronald Johnson, "Good enough governance in fragile states: The role of center-periphery relations and local government", Paper prepared for the 4th International Specialized Conference on International Aid and Public Administration, International Institute of Administrative Sciences, 2008; *World Development Report 1999/2000: Entering the 21st Century* (New York: Oxford University Press, 1999).
32   *Local Governance and Decentralization Assessment: Implications of Proposed Reforms in Ukraine* (Washington, DC: USAID, 2014).
33   Gary Bland, "Decentralization, local governance, and conflict mitigation in Latin America", in: Derick W. Brinkerhoff, ed., *Governance in Post-Conflict Societies: Rebuilding Fragile States* (Abingdon: Routledge, 2007); Paul Jackson and Zoe Scott, *Local Government in Post-Conflict Environments* (Oslo: United Nations Development Programme, 2007).
34   Arild Schou and Marit Haug, *Decentralization in Conflict and Post-Conflict Situations* (Oslo: NIBR, 2005).
35   Joseph Siegle and Patrick O'Mahony, *Assessing the Merits of Decentralization as a Conflict Mitigation Strategy* (Bethesda, MD: Development Alternatives, 2006).
36   Axel Hadenius, "General Outline of the Study", in: Axel Hadenius, ed., *Decentralization and Democratic Governance Experiences from India, Bolivia and South Africa* (Stockholm: Elanders Gotab, 2003); M. Oosterom, "Fragility at the Local Level: Challenges to Building Local State – Citizen Relations in Fragile

Are the effects of decentralization truly so positive in practice? The empirical record is mixed, and context matters: what works in one country may not work elsewhere. As local contexts also vary, decentralization has different outcomes when implemented in a single country. Some studies show that decentralization increases popular participation.[37] Other studies, however, question the effect of decentralization on popular participation.[38] As already mentioned, one of the most important purported benefits of decentralization is higher-quality governance, including service delivery. While the theoretical arguments linking decentralization with good governance are convincing, the empirical evidence is less strong. Many studies have in fact found that decentralization often fails to lead to either improved governance[39] or better service delivery.[40] In many cases, decentralization reforms are tied to efforts to combat poverty. There are studies that show that decentralization can indeed help to decrease inequality and contribute to economic development.[41] However, there are also studies that conclude that

---

Settings", Working paper prepared for "Local Governance in Fragile Settings: Strengthening Local Governments, Civic Action or Both?" 24 November 2009, The Hague.

37 See, for example: T. Campbell, *The Quiet Revolution: Decentralization and the Rise of Political Participation in Latin American Cities* (Pittsburgh: University of Pittsburgh Press, 2003); Paul S. Maro, "The impact of decentralization on spatial equity and rural development in Tanzania", *World Development* 18, no. 5 (1990): 673-693.

38 See, for example: Christina W. Andrews and Michiel S. de Vries, "High expectations, varying outcomes: Decentralization and participation in Brazil, Japan, Russia and Sweden", *International Review of Administrative Sciences* 73, no. 3 (2007): 424-451; Paul Francis and Robert James, "Balancing rural poverty reduction and citizen participation: The contradictions of Uganda's decentralization program", *World Development* 31, no. 2 (2003): 325-337.

39 L. Adamolekun, ed., *Public Administration in Africa: Main Issues and Selected Country Studies* (Boulder, CO: Westview Press, 1999); Richard C. Crook, "Decentralization and poverty reduction in Africa: The politics of local–central relations", *Public Administration and Development* 23, no. 1 (2003): 77-88.

40 Omar Azfar and Jeffrey Livingston, *Federalist Disciplines or Local Capture? An Empirical Analysis of Decentralization in Uganda* (Maryland: Center for Institutional Reform and the Informal Center, 2002); J. Eldon and D. Gunby, *States in Development: Statebuilding and Service Delivery* (London: HSLP, 2009).

41 See, for example: Trond Vedeld, "Democratic decentralization and poverty reduction: Exploring the linkages", *Forum for Development Studies* 30, no. 2 (2003): 159-203; Joachim von Braun and Ulrike Grote, "Does decentralization serve the

decentralization does not help to reduce poverty.[42] Another belief is that decentralization can contribute to overcoming conflict or to reducing the potential for conflict, and some studies corroborate this view.[43] Other studies, however, point out that decentralization has no effect on (the potential for) conflict or may even rekindle conflict.[44]

Decentralization evidently does not always have the effects that its proponents say it does and, in some cases, its consequences are decidedly negative. What are the "dangers of decentralization"?[45] Below, we focus on three risks that were especially relevant to decentralization reform in Ukraine.

The risks of decentralization in Ukraine and beyond

The first major risk is that, rather than enhancing downward accountability and citizen participation in public affairs, decentralization may be conducive to the establishment or entrenchment of illiberal and corrupt practices at the local level. As Brinkerhoff and Goldsmith remind us, "small is not necessarily beautiful in regard to government".[46] Many countries with a national democratic

---

poor?" International Monetary Fund Conference on Fiscal Decentralization, Washington, DC, November, 2000.

42   Crook, "Decentralization and poverty reduction in Africa"; Johannes Jütting, Céline Kauffmann, Ida McDonnell, Holger Osterrieder, Nicolas Pinaud and Lucia Wegner, *Decentralization and Poverty in Developing Countries: Exploring the Impact* (Issy-les-Moulineaux: OECD Development Centre, 2004).

43   See, for example: Nancy Bermeo, "Position paper for the working group on federalism, conflict prevention and settlement", Paper prepared for the International Conference on Federalism, 3-5 March 2005, Brussels; S. M. Saideman, D. J. Lanoue, M. Campenni and S. Stanton, "Democratization, political institutions, and ethnic conflict: A pooled time-series analysis, 1985-1998", *Comparative Political Studies* 35, no. 1 (2002): 103-129.

44   Dawn Brancati, "Decentralization: Fueling the fire or dampening the flames of ethnic conflict and secessionism?" *International Organization* 60, no. 3 (2006): 651-685; B. Posen, "The security dilemma and ethnic conflict", *Survival* 35 (1993): 27-47.

45   Remy Prud'Homme, "The dangers of decentralization", *The World Bank Research Observer* 10, no. 2 (1995): 201-220.

46   Derick W. Brinkerhoff and Arthur A. Goldsmith, "Good governance, clientelism, and patrimonialism: New perspectives on old problems", *International Public Management Journal* 7 (2004): 177.

politics have regions, districts, or municipalities where illiberal practices are common or where some form of subnational authoritarianism exists.[47] There is often less political pluralism in local communities than at higher levels of government. National political parties may be absent at the local level, or one political party may be dominant. Local political cultures may be characterized by weaker democratic norms, especially when there has been little prior experience of democracy. Citizens at the local level may have less access to independent media, and their officials and elected representatives may be less subject to press scrutiny than officials and elected representatives at higher levels of government.[48]

In local communities, people are more likely to be connected through kinship and other personal relations or to be employed in one of a small number of enterprises. Where this is the case, there is a greater risk that local elections may be influenced by clientelism and intimidation, and patronage may be a more common feature of local self-government.[49] To the extent that greater participation in local politics occurs when the government is decentralized, this could be the result of clientelist practices rather than of vibrant political pluralism.[50] Even in cases where decentralization generally contributes to greater accountability and citizen participation, stable authoritarian enclaves can still be occasionally found. In other words, it is unlikely that decentralization will have the same political consequences across all local communities: political and governance practices vary widely.[51]

---

[47] Jacqueline Behrend and Laurence Whitehead, "The struggle for subnational democracy", *Journal of Democracy* 27, no. 2 (2016): 155-169.

[48] C.B. Barrett, A.G. Mude and J.M. Omiti, "Decentralization and the Social Economics of Development: An Overview of Concepts and Evidence from Kenya", in: C.B. by Barrett, A.G. Mude and J.M. Omiti, eds., *Decentralization and the Social Economics of Development* (CAB International, 2007).

[49] Brinkerhoff and Goldsmith, "Good governance, clientelism, and patrimonialism".

[50] Øivind Hetland, "Decentralization and territorial reorganization in Mali: Power and the institutionalisation of local politics", *Norsk Geografisk Tidsskrift – Norwegian Journal of Geography* 62, no. 1 (2008): 23-35.

[51] Paul D. Hutchcroft, "Centralization and decentralization in administration and politics: Assessing territorial dimensions of authority and power", *Governance* 14, no. 1 (2001): 23-53.

Another risk of decentralization is the reduced capacity of local self-government. Decentralization may lead to this in two ways. First, there could be a shortage of qualified people with the necessary expertise to carry out the functions of public administration at local scales. As Bardhan notes, "[t]he decentralization literature typically assumes that different levels of government all have similar levels of technical and administrative capacity. This assumption is questionable for all countries".[52] It is common, especially in developing countries, for people with higher-than-average skills and means seek to move from rural to urban areas and from less developed to more developed areas. When this happens, remote areas may descend into a spiral of increasing underdevelopment. Local self-governments that acquire greater authority through decentralization may find it a struggle to execute their new powers. In a study of decentralization in rural Kenya, Barrett et al., for instance, find that the "dearth of well-trained, knowledgeable, open-minded managers capable of running successful institutions"[53] hampered the success of decentralization.

Decentralization may also reduce the capacity of local self-government by allowing it to be captured by elites who act in their own private interest rather than in that of citizens or of the country as a whole. A wide range of scholars warns against the risk of local elite capture.[54] Hadenius, for instance, argues that "efforts to decentralize decision-making competence and resources may easily result in 'local predatory capture', i.e., a strengthening of prevailing networks of corruption, patronage and the rule of local 'big men'. The latter tends to weaken state capacity and bar democratic development."[55] As already stated, in countries with democratic national

---

52 Pranab Bardhan, "Decentralization of governance and development", *The Journal of Economic Perspectives* 16, no. 4 (2002): 189.
53 Barrett, Mude and Omiti, "Decentralization and the Social Economics of Development", 10.
54 Peter Heller, "Moving the State: The Politics of Democratic Decentralization in Kerala, South Africa, and Porto Alegre", *Politics and Society* 29, no. 1 (2001): 131-163; Manor, *The Political Economy of Decentralization*; Joel Migdal, *Strong Societies and Weak States: State-Society Relations and Capabilities in the Third World* (Princeton: Princeton University Press, 1988).
55 Hadenius, "General Outline of the Study", 3.

politics, politics at subnational levels may be less pluralist, and officials may be less accountable to citizens. In a more centralized government, local officials' accountability to higher levels of government may serve as a check on their potential abuse of power. Decentralization weakens or eliminates that check of upward accountability.[56] This can be especially dangerous in places where the economy is dominated by a limited number of individuals who abuse their economic clout to influence political processes and governance. Some elites who capture local self-government may opt to work for the public good, but other elites may treat local self-government resources as a source of rents. Given that local elites are often less accountable to citizens and face less scrutiny from the press than higher-level officials, corruption at the local level is usually easier than it is in the national government.[57] Corruption by predatory local elites undermines the provision of public services. Decentralization also makes it difficult for the central authorities to implement and enforce top-down anti-corruption measures.[58]

A third major risk of decentralization is that it can undermine the legitimacy of the government and stir up conflict. Decentralization has the potential to unsettle power relations that have obtained for a long period of time, with unpredictable consequences. When administrative powers are altered or expanded, this can trigger a disorderly fight for economic resources and political power among local elites. If the decentralization reform is unpopular, or its outcomes less positive than anticipated, the legitimacy of the central government may take a hit. If local authorities do not cope with their new responsibilities well, their legitimacy could also suffer, potentially provoking unrest in an area that was stable.

The effects of decentralization can be particularly dangerous with respect to the position of ethnic and other minorities. Two

---

56 Brinkerhoff and Goldsmith, "Good governance, clientelism, and patrimonialism".
57 Anwah Shah, "Corruption and decentralized local governance", in: Ahmad Ehtisham and Giorgio Brosio, eds., *Handbook of Fiscal Federalism* (Cheltenham: Edward Elgar, 2006), 495; Prud'Homme, "The dangers of decentralization", 211.
58 Peter Nasuti, "Administrative Cohesion and Anti-Corruption Reforms in Georgia and Ukraine", *Europe-Asia Studies* 68, no. 5 (2016): 847-867.

situations can be distinguished in this regard. First, the possibility that, as a result of decentralization, a minority becomes a majority in a certain administrative area with a greater degree of self-government (or else gains the upper hand in the area despite remaining a minority in terms of population). Second, the possibility that a minority remains a minority, but is now governed by representatives of the local majority population rather than by the central authorities or other higher-level authorities. In the first case, there is the risk that decentralization reinforces regionally based ethnic identities, potentially giving rise to secessionism.[59] In the second situation, the minority enjoys less protection from the central government and may claim that it is repressed by the local authorities, provoking local conflict between minority and majority populations.[60]

Decentralization and State Fragility in Ukraine

The risks of decentralization identified in the academic and nonacademic literature should be taken into consideration by those responsible for drafting the decentralization reform and implementing it. To ensure that elected local officials are accountable once decentralization is complete, their administrative units should have a political culture already generally conducive to accountability. To ensure that local self-government has sufficient capacity, it should be of sufficient size and be able to attract qualified staff, and measures should be taken to avoid elite capture. Finally, to prevent decentralization from stirring up conflicts and increasing state fragility, the process must be underpinned by the broad consent of local residents. In the following, we ask to what extent these conditions were met in Ukraine's recent decentralization reform.

---

59 Robert Hardgrave, Jr., "India: the Dilemmas of Diversity", in: L. Diamond and M. F. Plattner, eds., *Nationalism, Ethnic Conflict and Democracy* (Baltimore: John Hopkins University Press, 1994); Will Kymlicka, "Is Federalism and alternative to secession?", in: Percy B. Lehning, ed., *Theories of Secession* (New York: Routledge, 1998).
60 Pranab Bardhan and Dilip Mookherjee, "Capture and governance at local and national levels", *The American Economic Review* 90, no. 2 (2000): 135.

Accountability

Although the Euromaidan Revolution may have strengthened the commitment to democratic development in Ukraine, the country remained a nonconsolidated democracy beset by intense political strife.[61] National politics continued to be plagued by a range of issues that undermined the quality of both democracy and public administration. The country was sometimes described as a neopatrimonial democracy, in which patrimonial organizing principles of "client-patron ties, personal loyalty, and clan 'membership' [persisted]".[62] Even after the Euromaidan Revolution, the so-called oligarchs continued to wield political influence and capture some elements of the state.[63] Political parties remained underinstitutionalized.[64]

Ukrainian politics at the subnational (inclusive of the local) level was often a microcosm of national politics. Wealthy entrepreneurs attempted to control political processes in local self-government bodies and let public administration work in their favor. Informal relations in local government were rife, facilitated by the more manageable size of smaller communities. In addition, in the absence of stable national political forces, alliances changed quickly and often. There was substantial diversity in local communities. Many featured a healthy degree of political pluralism, citizen involvement, and true accountability through elections, with functioning checks and balances in government. At the other extreme, there were communities that were described as fiefdoms, where one individual or one "clan" effectively ruled without much

---

61 Ukraine is classified as a "transitional government or hybrid regime" in the Freedom House Nations in Transit report. See https://freedomhouse.org/repo rt/nations-transit/2017/ukraine.
62 Oleksandr Fisun, "The Future of Ukraine's Neopatrimonial Democracy", *PONARS Eurasia Policy Memo*, no. 394 (2015). http://www.ponarseurasia.org/ memo/future-ukraine-neopatrimonial-democracy.
63 Heiko Pleines, "Oligarchs and politics in Ukraine", *Demokratizatsiya: The Journal of Post-Soviet Democratization* 24, no. 1 (2016): 105-127.
64 Max Bader, "Party politics in Georgia and Ukraine and the failure of Western assistance", *Democratization* 17, no. 6 (2010): 1085-1107; Kostyantyn Fedorenko, Olena Rybiy and Andreas Umland, "The Ukrainian Party System before and after the 2013–2014 Euromaidan", *Europe-Asia Studies* 68, no. 4 (2016): 609-630.

opposition or accountability. An alleged example of the latter was the Zarichansk village in the Zakarpattya *oblast*, which, according to one account, "reminds one of a separate principality, which exists outside the democratic state and acts according to its own laws", under the control of its autocratic village head.[65] Few cases were that extreme. However, it is certainly likely that many local communities, including ATCs, had elected officials who lacked accountability.

One reason for this was the existence of often sharp horizontal inequalities at the local level. Many ATCs were home to one or several comparatively wealthy entrepreneurs who, by virtue of their wealth, and in accordance with the practice at the national level, could wield significant political influence. Those local "oligarchs" could be powerful political brokers and could themselves seek election as ATC head, or else seek to exert influence through loyal individuals in the executive committee of the ATC's legislative council. A Ukrainian political slang expression often heard in the ATCs visited for this study was "pocket deputies" (*karmannye deputaty*); it was used to describe council members controlled by individuals with vested economic interests. Due to their small size, ATCs were susceptible to other patrimonial practices as well. Sixty-nine percent of the ATCs formed in 2015 and 2016 had a population of less than 10,000.[66] As Tanzi has argued, the often direct contact between officials and citizens in such small communities promotes personalism and reduces professionalism, creating fertile ground for corruption.[67] In addition to a community's small size being conducive to the prevalence of patrimonialism, the situation was exacerbated if municipal heads remained in power for a long period of time.[68] It was common for municipal heads in Ukraine to enjoy long tenures. In many of the ATCs formed in 2015 and 2016 the head had previously served as the head of the central village of the ATC for

---

65 See http://archive.mistovechirne.in.ua/content/archive/989-2010-08-05-08-04-19.
66 Calculations made on the basis of data from http://gromada.info.
67 Vito Tanzi, "Fiscal federalism and decentralization: A review of some efficiency and microeconomic aspects", in: Vtio Tanzi, *Policies, Institutions and the Dark Side of Economics* (Cheltenham and Northampton: Edward Elgar, 2000).
68 Prud'Homme, "The dangers of decentralization".

decades. Unlike the president of Ukraine, who cannot serve for more than two consecutive terms, there are no term limits on municipal heads. This allows municipal heads to cement their hold on power and increase their chances of re-election. The incumbency rate in municipal head elections was indeed high. Four out of five of the ATC heads elected in 2015 or 2016 had previously served as the head of the ATC's central village.[69]

Another factor conducive to patrimonialism and a lack of political accountability in ATCs concerned the electoral system of local council elections. Fifty ATCs created in 2015 or 2016 were formed around a city (*misto*). Elections to city councils — and to the councils of ATCs with a city as their administrative center — used a mixed electoral system, in which one half of the deputies were elected from single-member districts and the other half are elected from the party lists in a multimember district, which covered the entire municipality. However, most ATCs formed in 2015 and 2016 were formed around a town (*selishche*) or were comprised of several villages (*sela*). Elections to the ATC local council used the majoritarian principle, with the deputies typically being elected from single-member districts, with sometimes no more than a few hundred registered voters. Only a few council members in ATCs belonged to political parties. Instead, in many ATCs, all council members ran in the elections as self-nominated candidates.[70] When council members did represent a (statewide) political party, they tended to coordinate their actions with regional or national party organizations; if there were several deputies from one party in a council, they could form a faction. Council members with no political party affiliation, on the other hand, were more susceptible to being manipulated or controlled by powerful local individuals. In none of the rural ATCs that we visited there were ruling factions in the ATC council or a clearly identifiable opposition faction. To the extent that

---

69 Calculations made on the basis of the results of the 2015 local elections, available from the website of the Central Election Commission: http://www.cvk.gov.ua/pls/vm2015/wm001.

70 The affiliation of candidates in the 2015 and 2016 local legislative council elections can be found on the website of the Central Election Commission: http://www.cvk.gov.ua/pls/vm2015/wm001 a.

council members voted against majority positions, they did so as individuals, not as part of an organized opposition. In interviews with representatives of ATC executive committees and council members, respondents described the lack of a sustained opposition faction in the ATC council as positive.[71]

The lack of a true separation of powers, which is typical of executive-legislative relations at the local level in Ukraine, is the principal cause of the limited accountability of the elected officials in ATCs. The ATC head and local council members are elected simultaneously. After the local elections, the ATC head proposes a list of members for the executive committee, which is then approved (or rejected) by the local council. The head of the ATC personally chairs the executive committee and organizes the work of the local council, whose meetings the head also chairs. The local council does not propose legislation but supports or rejects the decisions of the executive committee. ATC executive-legislative relations are similar to those in unamalgamated communities and are still largely based on the Soviet model. Described in state terms, the ATC would have a presidential form of government. Taking the analogy further, we can say that ATCs are vulnerable to the "perils of presidentialism" identified by political scientists, including the winner-takes-all mentality and the personalization of power.[72]

These considerations make it clear that the decentralization implemented in Ukraine in 2015 and 2016 did not necessarily translate into democratization. A sizable proportion of Ukrainian municipalities lacked a political culture in which elected officials were held accountable. Granting these municipalities a greater degree of self-government could exacerbate the problem of a lack of accountability and its concomitant effects, including poor public service delivery.

---

71 Interviews with ATC heads, other executive committee members and legislative council members in Konoplyane ATC, Krasnosila ATC, Marazliivka ATC, Rozkvit ATC, Velyka Mykhaylivka ATC.
72 Juan J. Linz, "The perils of presidentialism", *Journal of Democracy* 1, no. 1 (1991): 51-69.

Capacity

The small size of many ATCs raised questions about their capacity to exercise their powers and to deliver the services that fell under their authority. There were no guidelines that explicitly stated how many municipal councils should merge to form a single ATC or the minimum population of a "capable" ATC. According to the model plan developed by one of the principal architects of the decentralization reform in Ukraine, the average ATC should comprise approximately eight municipality councils.[73] According to the "prospect plans" for the formation of ATCs drafted (and, in most cases, adopted) in each region, the average ATC should cover the territory of approximately ten former municipalities.

Most of the ATCs formed in 2015 and 2016, however, were much smaller. Thirty-one percent of the ATCs formed by the end of 2016 comprised only two former municipalities, and 19 percent comprised three former municipalities. The average number was 3.5 former municipalities per ATC. Twenty-eight percent of ATCs had a population of less than 5,000 inhabitants, 41 percent had a population of between 5,000 and 10,000 inhabitants, and 31 percent had a population of more than 10,000 inhabitants.[74] Most ATCs, then, were (much) smaller than they should have been according to the "prospect plans" and the ideas of the decentralization reform's proponents. It is true that the legislation allowed unamalgamated municipalities to join existing ATCs. As long as the mergers remained voluntary, however, it seemed unlikely that many current small ATCs would expand.

With its preponderance of small ATCs, the Odesa *oblast* presents a typical case. Eight out of the 11 ATCs, all formed prior to December 2016, comprised two or three former municipalities. In interviews conducted for this study, the representatives of almost all the ATCs indicated that they struggled to attract qualified

---

73 Yurii Hanushchak, "Modelyuvannya administrativno-teritorial'nykh odynyts' yak etap pidhotovky reformy administratyvno-teritorial'noho ustroyu", *Efektyvnist' Derzhavnoho Upravlinnya*, no. 38, 2014.
74 Data on the composition and size of the ATCs can be found at http://gromada.info/.

professionals to work in the ATC administration. This problem was particularly acute in rural ATCs, as most villages in Ukraine were losing their populations. Much of this decline is due to the fact that living standards in Ukrainian cities are significantly higher than in rural areas. Unemployment is less of a problem in cities, and average wages tend to be higher. Moreover, many villages are without running water or decent roads.[75]

The second issue related to the capacity of ATCs is the potential for elite capture. One of the risks of decentralization is that local elites would seek to monopolize the power gained by subnational administrative entities, and that they would have control over more resources. It is difficult to determine whether or not elite capture has taken place in a particular ATC. There are indications, however, that elite capture is a real problem in many cases. As noted in the previous section, many municipalities lack a separation of powers, and the municipal head often wields a great deal of power. Research on ATCs in six of Ukraine's southern regions found that in nearly three out of four cases, it was the municipal head—rather than the municipal council or civic activists, for instance—who took the initiative to form the ATC.[76] In a substantial majority of cases, these municipal heads were subsequently elected heads of the ATCs. As noted above, 80 percent of ATC heads now in office used to serve as the heads of municipalities that became the administrative centers of the newly formed ATCs. Indeed, many municipal heads have been accused of initiating ATC amalgamation for their own personal advantage or interests (*'pid sebe'*). One report about the mayor of Irpin, in the Kyiv *oblast*, for instance, described him wanting to "expand his dominion" with some surrounding villages.[77] The head of the Polyana municipality in the Zakarpattya *oblast* similarly faced accusations of rent-seeking through the formation of a large ATC, to "realize his lifelong dream of being a

---

75 Yu. L. Kohat'ko, Yu.L., "Bidnist' silskoho naselennya Ukrayiny", *Demography and Social Economy* 23, no. 1 (2015).
76 See http://samoorg.com.ua/blog/2016/11/08/15679/.
77 See http://mykyivregion.com.ua/2017/02/26/stali-vidomo-yak-mer-irpenya-karplyuk-hoche-rozshiriti-svoyi-volodinnya-do-zhitomirskoyi-trasi/.

high-ranking official with unlimited powers".⁷⁸ Some ATCs were described as a "fiefdom" or a "feudal estate". One example was the Shiryaivo ATC in the Odesa *oblast*. The head of this ATC was the son of an important businessman in the district, and his spouse was the head of the district local council. So it is not surprising that this ATC was called a feudal estate.⁷⁹ Another example was the Khrestivka ATC in the Kherson *oblast*. According to one report, the ATC head and 14-15 of the 22 members of the ATC council had ties to the largest agrarian enterprise in the ATC, and this ATC was considered the feudal estate of the owners of the enterprise.⁸⁰ The author of the report alleges that at least one out of ten ATCs in Ukraine had similar arrangements that served the interests of a large enterprise.

Consent and legitimacy

As one academic study notes, "decentralization can in some instances generate new tensions in communal, ethnic and religious relations".⁸¹ The formation of ATCs had provoked numerous conflicts between citizens, as well as between citizens and local authorities across Ukraine. In some cases, these conflicts were about whether or not to form (or be included in) an ATC. In other cases, where stakeholders broadly supported the idea of forming an ATC, conflicts could arise about choosing a potential partner municipality (or municipalities) with which to merge into an ATC.

The difficulty was that even if a significant number of residents were resistant to amalgamation, the process of amalgamation could still go ahead. The process of ATC formation required every municipality that amalgamated into an ATC to hold two public

---

78 See https://zakarpattya.net/Обєднана-територіальна-громада-чи-П/.
79 See http://7kanal.com.ua/2016/03/feodalnaya-volnitsa-normalno-otdel-rassl edovaniy-na-sedmom/.
80 Aleksey Kopyt'ko, "Knyazhestvo svoimi rukami: budni detsentralizatsii," *Sprotyv*, 17 March 2017. http://sprotyv.info/ru/news/kiev/knyazhestvo-svoi mi-rukami-budni-decentralizacii.
81 Rachael Diprose and Ukoha Ukiwo, *Decentralization and Conflict Management in Indonesia and Nigeria* (Oxford: University of Oxford Centre for Research on Inequality, Human Security and Ethnicity, 2008).

hearings. The purpose of the first hearing was to discuss whether or not the municipality should join an ATC. If, after this hearing, the municipal council accepted ATC formation, a working group was established to develop more detailed plans for the formation of the prospective ATC. Once the working group completed its work, a second hearing was convened to discuss the group's plans. This wass then followed by another vote in the municipal council. These hearings were not formal. There was, for instance, no voting procedure to determine whether those present were for or against ATC formation. Instead, the public hearings provided the initiators of ATC formation an opportunity to explain their plans, and residents could ask questions and express their opinions on the issues under discussion. Municipal councils could take into consideration the extent of public support for the ATC when they were making the relevant decisions in local councils, but they were not obliged to do so. ATC formation could go ahead, despite severe opposition in municipal councils. The decision to form an ATC required only a simple majority in local councils. Where a council was split between those in favor of and those opposed to ATC formation, conflicts could arise.

Since the reform started to be implemented, numerous ATCs have emerged despite the substantial opposition from the municipalities that finally amalgamated. The inhabitants of the village of Usteriki in the Verkhovinsky *rayon* of the Ivano-Frankivsk *oblast*, for instance, according to several reports, did not want to amalgamate into the Biloberizka ATC, but the amalgamation took place nevertheless.[82] There are also reports about municipalities joining an ATC despite evident procedural irregularities during its formation. In the Pustomyty district of the Lviv *oblast*, according to one report, the signatures of inhabitants of the village of Vydniki were forged to give the impression that they supported the inclusion of their village in the Pustomyty ATC.[83] In the Kyiv *oblast*, to take another example, there was the alleged attempt to include the village of Vorzel

---

82 See http://westnews.com.ua/skandal-navkolo-usterik-politsiya-vidkrila-krim inalne-provadzhennya-cherez-pidroblennya-dokumentiv/.
83 See http://dyvys.info/2016/09/17/detsentralizatsijnyj-skandal-na/.

in an ATC with the city of Bucha, although no proper public hearing had taken place within the mandated timeframe.[84]

There are also cases of the population of a municipality being split over which municipalities to amalgamate with to establish an ATC. One such discussion, for instance, created a rift in the village of Stara Lyshnya in the Volyn *oblast*. In a survey held in the village, 506 inhabitants were in favor of forming an ATC with Novovolynsk, against 407 who preferred forming an ATC with Litovezh.[85] The population and the municipal council members of Sychavka in the Odesa *oblast* experienced a similar division over the choice of which municipality they should form an ATC with. The situation in Sychavka turned especially tense after it was alleged that municipal council members had been bribed to vote to form an ATC with the municipality of Vyzyrka.[86]

Two years after the first introduction of the ATCs, a significant majority of municipalities had not formed or joined an ATC. As noted, there were great discrepancies across regions and districts in terms of the number of ATCs formed. Some regions largely remained untouched by the reform in the initial years of its implementation. It is noteworthy that ATC formation lagged behind in the Zakarpattya *oblast* and in Bessarabia (the southern half of the Odesa *oblast*), which were well-known for their diverse ethnic makeup. It was expected that in the next few years, regional authorities would continue to push municipalities to embrace ATC formation. Some feared that decentralization could upset the delicate balance and peaceful relations in places such as the Zakarpattya *oblast* and Bessarabia, and that the authorities' attempts to push through ATC formation could instigate conflicts among local populations or between citizens and local authorities.[87]

---

84 See http://kotsubynske.com.ua/2016/01/22/chomu-objednannya-vorzelya-z-bucheyu-nezakonne-analitychnyj-ohlyad/.
85 See http://bug.org.ua/news/ivanychi/scho-peremozhe-u-starij-lishni-ambitsiji-chy-myr-hromada-na-ivanychivschyni-objednujetsya-zi-skandalom-111030/.
86 See http://volnorez.com.ua/novosti/ocherednoj-skandal-pod-odessoj-na-neu godnyx-organizovali-travlyu.html.
87 See https://day.kyiv.ua/ru/article/podrobnosti/decentralizaciya-v-bessarabii-kakie-ugrozy.

Conflicts could also arise between municipalities in newly formed ATCs, when the central municipality exercised its dominant position at the expense of the peripheral municipalities in the ATC.[88] In one example, the villagers of Popovychy complained that the funds of the Holoby ATC, which they joined in 2015, were being spent overwhelmingly in Holoby's central municipality, leaving their village empty-handed.[89] This type of conflict was especially common in ATCs that were asymmetrical or resulted from the amalgamation of a city with one or two villages. An example of a highly asymmetrical ATC was the Merefyanska ATC in the Kharkiv *oblast*, which consisted of the city of Merefya, with 22,000 inhabitants, and the village of Utkivka, with just over 2,000 inhabitants. Since the peripheral villages in such asymmetrical ATCs had a much smaller number of council members than the central municipality, they could be effectively disenfranchised.

Conclusions

Self-government reform has a great potential to help overcome the numerous difficulties in Ukrainian politics and public administration at the local level. In theory, the reform should empower local communities, improve service delivery, and create opportunities for economic development. Numerous domestic reports covered the reform from its very beginnings and highlighted its presumed benefits and its early successes. Frequently, these reports specifically draw attention to the drastic increase in ATC budgets just a few years after amalgamation, and to the newly established ATCs' great degree of fiscal autonomy. Across Ukraine, ATCs used their newly acquired spending powers and increased budgets to restore public facilities and infrastructure that had lain in disrepair for many years.

---

88   Asotsiatsiya spriyannya samoorhanizatsii naselennya, "Periferiyni terytoriyi ob'ednanykh hromad: Mekhanizm zakhistu prav ta realizatsiyi interesiv (na prykladi Pivdnya Ukrayiny)", *Samoorg*, 7 July 2016. http://samoorg.com.ua/d emolib/2016/07/07/periferiyni-teritoriyi-ob-yednanih-gromad-mehanizmi-z ahistu-prav-ta-realizatsiyi-interesiv-na-prikladi-pivdnya-ukrayini/.
89   See https://www.volynnews.com/news/authority/u-holobskiy-oth-skandal-cherez-lyst-z-pidroblenymy-pidpysamy/.

The Ukrainian government, however, failed to mitigate some risks associated with the decentralization reform in 2015-2016. Some ATCs were established on the basis of true popular consent, with a pluralist political culture that held elected officials accountable, and with enough capacity to carry out their tasks. However, there were also ATCs whose formation caused conflicts, that were managed by unaccountable local elites, and that lacked the capacity to deliver public services. Moreover, the geography of ATCs presented a chaotic patchwork. In some regions, a large number of ATCs were formed within two years of the start of the reform; in other regions, however, the process stalled. Most ATCs were much smaller in size than anticipated by the reform's architects; a small number of ATCs, on the contrary, were larger than initially expected.

The reform was launched at a time when the Ukrainian state was by most standards a weak state. This fact was reflected in the laissez-faire approach to the implementation of the reform. The lack of central oversight and of comprehensive coordination has resulted in runaway decentralization, one in which many different actors have influenced the process, leading to a wide variety of outcomes. If the weakness of the Ukrainian state has been conspicuous in the implementation of decentralization, the implementation has also compounded the problem of state fragility in some parts of the country, by causing conflicts among citizens, as well as between citizens and local authorities. Besides this direct impact, the reform has also indirectly increased state fragility in some cases, where ATCs were established with little accountability from elected officials and with poor public administration, thus creating a significant potential for conflict. Sober assessment and substantial effort are needed to repair the flaws of the decentralization reform and to deliver on its promise.

6. The Effects of Decentralization on Party Politics in Ukraine

Melanie Mierzejewski-Voznyak

Since 2014, Ukraine has slowly increased the "localization" of party politics through decentralization reforms. This chapter explores the territorial dimension of party competition in Ukraine, as well as the multilevel dimension of party organization. Particular attention is given to the way parties organize, campaign and compete, as well as strategize across different tiers of government. Furthermore, this analysis considers how the devolution of power affects political parties as individual institutions along with the party system as a whole, and how parties are and continue to be instrumental to the success of institutional reforms brought by decentralization in Ukraine.

Introduction

While the expression "all politics is local" has famously been used in the context of American politics, it is particularly applicable to the situation in Ukraine. After the 2014 Revolution of Dignity, Ukraine needed to re-establish the relationship between state and society. It was necessary to relegitimize the state after the Yanukovych regime, which not only broke the "social contract" through its failure to protect citizens' rights and freedoms, but violated the constitutional order through its abuse of power, which ultimately led to its own collapse. Furthermore, the subsequent occupation and annexation of Crimea and the covert intervention in eastern Ukraine by Russian forces left Ukraine territorially redefined. The new governments under Interim President Oleksandr Turchynov and President Petro Poroshenko initiated and supported devolution of power as a political strategy that would both respond to societal demands for a more accountable state and ameliorate social tensions, which intensified because of Ukraine's regional divisions.

Established after the 2014 revolution, the new government made the administrative-territorial reform a priority, with the support of a number of Western institutions, notably the European Union. The implementation of several interconnected decentralization reforms was hampered by an array of related problems, including a party system that functioned poorly, and a highly centralized state, inherited from the Soviet Union, which was characterized by a variety of ethnic, linguistic, and socioeconomic divisions that weakened its governability.

The purpose of decentralization is to enact a series of structural changes in a state. Such reforms alter the institutional context by redistributing power and resources from the center to subnational or, more precisely, subregional levels of government. They thus impact all major government institutions and political parties, whose classical function is to mediate between the state and society.

Both domestic and foreign political observers and supporters of democracy, among others, will monitor how the process of decentralization will affect the Ukrainian party system. Decentralization reforms tend to trigger a certain "denationalization" of party politics, with the additional potential to decentralize power within parties. An examination of the effects of the changing institutional context of party organization will allow us to draw some tentative conclusions regarding the future of Ukraine's party system. This chapter analyzes the territorialization of party competition and the growing multilevel dimension of party politics in Ukraine, focusing on the ways that parties organize and strategize and on the impact the devolution of power may have. In particular, it asks in what way the relationship between institutional reforms and party organization is critical to our understanding of the process of decentralization in Ukraine.

This analysis is based on evidence from the October 2015 municipal elections, as well as on local government elections in the newly amalgamated territorial communities (ATCs) — or, in Ukrainian, *hromady* — between December 2016 and April 2018.[1]

---

1   The 2015 municipal elections were not held in the illegally annexed Autonomous Republic of Crimea and in the occupied territories of the Donetsk and

Data are drawn from election and campaign monitoring reports conducted by the OPORA Civil Network, the Committee of Voters of Ukraine (CVU) and the European Network of Election Monitoring Organizations (ENEMO), as well as from analyses and public opinion polls by the Razumkov Centre, USAID and the OSCE. Data were also collected from various Ukrainian media outlets, as well as from statements made by Ukrainian political parties themselves.

Historical Background

Decentralization had long been discussed by Ukrainian political parties, who included it in their campaign rhetoric; prior to the Euromaidan protests, however, attempts to carry out the reform were unsuccessful. Bat'kivshchyna (All-Ukrainian Union Fatherland) made promises to reform local self-government structures following the Orange Revolution, and, in 2005, a new law on administrative and territorial reform was drafted. In 2005-2006, the Party of Regions vowed to create a federal Ukraine once it was in office. In 2009, the Ukrainian government approved the Concept on "Local Self-Government Reform", only to see it halted once Viktor Yanukovych assumed the presidency.[2]

One of the specific demands of the 2014 Euromaidan protesters was greater accountability and authority for regional and local self-government: indeed, to make their point, protesters occupied regional self-government offices and targeted the regional

---

Luhansk *oblasts*. Further, no elections were held in the *rayons* of the Donetsk and Luhansk *oblasts*, through which the frontline in the conflict runs, and which are administered by Ukraine's military-civilian administration (see the Decision by the Central Electoral Committee of Ukraine, No. 209, 29 August 2015). Local government elections in the newly formed ATCs first took place on 25 October 2015 at the same time as state-wide local elections. Subsequent rounds of ATC elections took place in December 2016, in October and December 2017, and in April 2018.

2   Yuriy Hanushchak, Oleksii Sydorchuk, Andreas Umland, "Ukraine's most underreported reform", *New Eastern Europe*, 13 April 2017. http://neweasterneurope.eu/2017/04/13/ukraine-s-most-underreported-reform-decentralization-after-the-euromaidan-revolution/; Natalia Shapovalova, "The politics of regionalism and decentralization in Ukraine", *Eurasia Review*, 3 August 2014. http://fride.org/descarga/03.08.2014_Eurasia%20Review_USA_NS.pdf.

governors appointed by the President.[3] The goal was never separatism or regional autonomy but better governance, and to foster democracy by increasing the competencies of subnational authorities across Ukraine. Unsurprisingly, several parties reacted to popular demand by listing decentralization as one of the top priorities in their 2014 parliamentary election manifestos: the People's Front, the Petro Poroshenko Bloc—"Solidarity" (PPB-S), Samopomich (Self-reliance), the Opposition Bloc, the Radical Party of Oleh Lyashko, the Communist Party of Ukraine, Civic Position, the ZASTUP All-Ukrainian Agrarian Union. For their part, Bat'kivshchyna, Pravyi Sektor (the Right Sector), Svoboda (the "Freedom" All-Ukrainian Union), and Serhiy Tihipko's "Strong Ukraine" mentioned increasing local authority in their manifestos.

Since independence, Ukraine has needed to devolve resources and responsibilities on subnational governments, as this would increase political autonomy and accountability and thus, ideally, reduce the central state's (abuse of) power.[4] Decentralization shifts the locus of democratic politics by granting real authority and autonomy to local leadership. The process of decentralization entails the transfer of responsibilities and political power from the central government to local institutions, granting them administrative independence and political legitimacy. Thus, subnational tiers of government have "constitutionally entrenched independent decision-making authority".[5] Many important policy decisions are no longer confined to the national level, which should allow voters to hold local politicians more accountable for the quality of the public administration and economic management of their communities. The intent is to increase civic engagement and participation in self-governance. This empowers citizens by granting them greater political power, as their electoral choices have a real impact on matters

---

3 Ibid.
4 Christopher Sabatini, "Decentralization and political parties", *Journal of Democracy* 14, no. 2 (2003): 138-150.
5 David Lublin, "Dispersing Authority or deepening divisions? Decentralization and ethnoregional party success", *The Journal of Politics* 74, no. 4 (2012): 1080.

pertaining to local development.⁶ Furthermore, the devolution of power increases both the efficiency and effectiveness of the distribution of public resources.

An important question is the reaction of parties to the political consequences of decentralization, specifically regarding the increased territorialization of politics and party organizational development. In Ukraine, weak party organizations and centralized state authority have prevented regional and local authorities from developing fiscal independence and political autonomy. In 2014, when President Poroshenko first proposed decentralization reforms, the heads of *oblast* (region) and *rayon* (district) administrations were appointed and dismissed by the President on the recommendation of the Cabinet of Ministers. The two levels had directly elected assemblies. State administrations implemented the decisions of these assemblies, but they also represented the central government and were in charge of resource distribution.⁷

In April 2014, the Ukrainian government approved the principles of the decentralization reform. According to this proposed comprehensive reset of local self-government in Ukraine, *oblast* and *rayon* state administrations would be eliminated; instead, *oblasts* and *rayon* councils would establish their own executive committees. Newly introduced presidential appointees – the regional prefects – would not be responsible for resource distribution but would ensure that local authorities complied with the law and constitutional requirements; in addition, the prefects would coordinate the activities of regional state executive bodies (e.g. tax administrations).⁸ The president's direct appointment of prefects would mean that the problem of strong presidential influence at the subnational level would likely remain. Nevertheless, the proposed reforms offered the first significant step toward realizing local self-governance in

---

6   Jonathan Hopkin, "Political decentralization, electoral change and party organizational adaptation: A framework for analysis", *European Urban and Regional Studies* 10, no. 3 (2003): 227-237; Sabatini, "Decentralization"; Lublin, "Dispersing".
7   Shapovalova, "The politics".
8   Ibid.

Ukraine.[9] It should be noted that many of the proposed reforms have yet to be implemented due to incomplete constitutional amendments, stalled in parliament since 2015, among other reasons.[10]

The principal exogenous effect of the ambitious reform process was the emergence of important new subnational political offices.[11] The 2015 Law on the voluntary amalgamation of the *hromady* created a whole new arena of political decision-making and competition. Decentralization reforms in Ukraine projected 27 large administrative regions (*oblasts* and cities with a "special status"), approximately 120-150 intermediary districts (*rayony*), and approximately 1500-1800 amalgamated territorial communities (ATCs) (*obyednani terytorialni hromady*). This plan implied a considerable increase in the financial and institutional capacity of existing territorial units: the number of districts would be reduced by 60-75 percent, and 95 percent of all villages/towns would become part of the new ATCs.[12] By establishing ATCs, Ukraine was enacting a massive administrative-territorial reform at the local level and strengthening local self-governance. The purpose of these new ATCs was to lessen the bureaucratic burden on the population and to reduce the number of local officials responsible for the administration of villages and towns.[13] Voters in an ATC elected a local

---

9 *Local Governance and Decentralization Assessment: Implications of Proposed Reforms in Ukraine* (Washington, DC: USAID, 2014). http://pdf.usaid.gov/pdf_docs/pa00k59f.pdf.

10 The necessary amendments that would see the division of competencies between local self-government bodies at different levels failed to pass second reading in parliament. This was in part due to the inclusion of controversial provisions that would grant "a special status" to the occupied territories in the Donbas region (as per the Minsk-II Agreement), and also because of the inclusion of continued presidential oversight on local councils via "prefects".

11 Bonnie Meguid, "Multi-level elections and party fortunes: The electoral impact of decentralization in Western Europe", *Comparative Politics* 47, no. 4 (2015): 379-398.

12 David J. Smith and Mariana Semenyshyn, "Territorial-administrative decentralization and ethno-cultural diversity in Ukraine: addressing Hungarian autonomy claims in Zakarpattya", *European Centre for Minority Issues Working Papers*, no. 95 (2016), 6.

13 Tetiana Kornieieva, Jean-Francois Devemy, and Tetiana Zatonatska, "Nature and trends of decentralization and its dimensions: Challenges for Ukraine", *Kyiv National Economic University*, 2017. http://ir.kneu.edu.ua:8080/handle/2010/.

council that formed an executive committee, while some villages within the ATC also elected *starosty* (elders) who represented their interests in the ATC executive committee.

The devolution of power creates new political offices at the municipal level, held by directly elected individuals, enriching the relationship between political parties and civil society.[14] The reform's greater goal is to empower people, not just delegate responsibility to local governments. The public will be able to take more responsibility for decision making, as well as for directing authorities and their policies. However, direct elections of regional, district, and local officials bring increased competition both within and between parties, and this can overtax an already weak party system that typically sees power concentrated in the hands of the central party elite. If, as is the case in Ukraine, political parties have weak internal democracy, then the increased status and power of a new tier of political elites may disrupt traditional patterns of party recruitment and advancement.[15] At the same time, its internal organizational inertia will impact how each party confronts the enacting of the decentralization reforms.[16]

Decentralization and Party Organization

Most political parties are active at multiple levels of government. However, the way that parties organize and strategize at different levels varies. There are two traditional models of party organization: 1) centralized state-wide parties controlled by a national leadership and 2) decentralized state-wide parties in which subnational party leaders play an important role. When party member lack real

---

14 María Pilar García-Guadilla and Carlos Pérez, "Democracy, decentralization, and clientelism: New relationships and old practices", *Latin American Perspectives* 29, no. 5 (2002): 90-109.
15 Melanie Mierzejewski-Voznyak, "Political parties and the institution of membership in Ukraine", 2018, unpublished article.
16 Jonathan Hopkin, "Political decentralization, electoral change and party organizational adaptation: A framework for analysis", *European Urban and Regional Studies* 10, no. 3 (2003); Jonathan Hopkin, "Decentralization and party organizational change: The case of Italy" in: Wilfried Swenden and Bart Maddens, eds., *Territorial Party Politics in Western Europe* (Hampshire: Palgrave Macmillan, 2008), 86-101.

influence, as is the case in Ukraine, what develops is a top-down approach to intraparty relations between the national leadership and subnational branches.[17] Similar to the trends in other parts of Europe, Ukrainian political parties demonstrate substantial organizational weakness; moreover, their failure to become successful membership organizations disconnects them from civil society.[18]

Even modest attempts at the devolution of power in Ukraine are likely to involve some degree of the denationalization of party politics. As party structures are influenced by the structure of the state, the increased importance of subnational tiers of government will give rise to a new group of important political actors within parties.[19] Such regional and local leaders, holding real institutional power, will potentially play a key new role in internal party politics. Thus, power and authority will no longer be exclusively based in Kyiv. The increasing number of important actors within the party system—and within parties themselves—will force the higher-ups in the capital to take notice of the rising subnational political elite.

The primary effect on party structure will be a change in organizational dynamics, specifically concerning the delegation of power and authority. As van Houten asserts, this creates a principle-agent relation within party organizations, where subnational branches operate as agents of the national leadership.[20] By delegating tasks to the branches, the national leadership can extract benefits from their regional and local expertise. However, the party faces costs associated with relinquishing certain powers. Granting some autonomy to subnational branches will benefit the party electorally, allowing it to build a strong voter base that will carry over to

---

17 Pieter Van Houten, "Multi-level relations in political parties: A delegation approach", *Party Politics* 15, no. 2 (2009): 137-156.
18 Susan E. Scarrow, "Parties Without Members? Party Organisation in a Changing Electoral Environment", in: R. Dalton and M. Wattenberg, eds., *Parties Without Partisans: Political Change in Advanced Industrial Democracies* (Oxford: Oxford University Press, 2000), 79-101; Peter Mair and Ingrid Van Biezen, "Party Membership in Twenty European Democracies, 1980-2000", *Party Politics* 7, no. 1 (2001): 5-22; Hopkin, "Political;" Mierzejewski-Voznyak, "Political parties".
19 Jonathan Hopkin and Pieter van Houten, "Decentralization and state-wide parties: Introduction", *Party Politics* 15, no. 2 (2009): 131-135.
20 Van Houten, "Multi-level", 138.

national elections, but too much subnational discretion in electoral and governing strategy may lead to conflicts of interest between branches and the party.[21] Parties are multilevel organizations, and political success requires cooperation and the coordination of political strategy across different levels of government. The interaction between different actors and organizational tiers within parties is complex; different territorial levels face different voter demands and are confronted with different policy priorities. The ability of political parties to reconcile the dual imperative of representation and the aggregation of interests will be critical for the development of party politics in Ukraine.

Assessing how decentralization will impact Ukrainian party politics first requires analyzing the territorialization of party competition and the ethno-cultural cleavages that structure party politics. How parties adopt political strategies and cooperate across different territorial units in the context of multilevel electoral politics will affect how parties organize and compete, as well as their ability to govern effectively when in office. Particularly important are the extent to which parties will denationalize and their ability to cooperate and coordinate political strategy and candidate selection between the different levels of party organization. While decentralization reforms allow the possibility for the devolution of power within parties and, thus, greater internal democracy, it is also likely that they will create new internal party tensions. In addition, any transfer of power by a party's central leadership would likely be checked by party laws that act as control mechanisms restricting the actions of subnational branches, and preserve centralized, decision-making authority. Large-scale redistribution of power can be destabilizing to parties and the larger party system. Thus, the fate of Ukrainian party politics will depend on the ability of parties to adapt to the changing institutional context that decentralization brings.

---

21 Ibid.; Anoop Sadanandan, "Patronage and decentralization: The politics of poverty in India", *Comparative Politics* 44, no. 2 (2012): 211-228.

Territorialization of Party Politics

Although there is empirical evidence that decentralization leads to the fragmentation of the party system, in certain instances, the redistribution of important policy competencies to subnational tiers of government can act as a response to growing voter apathy.[22] In multinational states with a high degree of regionalization, the goal of decentralization is to "maintain the unity of the country".[23] In these situations, decentralization is recommended as a "palliative" for regional or ethnic conflict.[24] Such reforms have been enacted in several multinational states whose regions have heterogeneous preferences—Canada, Belgium, Great Britain, Italy, India, and Spain, for example. While redistributing power to regional and local governments will improve representation, there is the possibility that trading away efficiency and unity will weaken the links between subnational and national institutions, and in turn weaken democratic accountability.[25] Thus, even when decentralization is advanced as a political strategy to satisfy the policy preferences of culturally distinct groups, political parties must resist the centrifugal forces within their political system that may further fragment an already fragile state.

Ukraine is a highly regionalized country, reflecting historical and ethnolinguistic differences that include cultural traditions and religious beliefs. Some form of decentralization, it is argued, will ameliorate the East–West divide that plagues Ukrainian politics. It

---

22 Jonathan Hopkin, "Party matters: Devolution and party politics in Britain and Spain", *Party Politics* 15, no. 2 (2009): 179-198.
23 Alfred C. Stepan, *Arguing Comparative Politics* (Oxford: Oxford University Press, 2001), 321.
24 Nancy Gina Bermeo, "The Import of Institutions," *Journal of Democracy* 13, no. 2 (2002); Ivo D. Duchacek, *Comparative Federalism* (Lanham: University Press of America, 1987); Ted Robert Gurr, *People versus States: Minorities at Risk in the New Century* (Washington, DC: United States Institute of Peace Press, 2000); Michael Hechter, *Containing Nationalism* (New York: Oxford University Press, 2000); Arend Lijphart, "The Puzzle of Indian Democracy: A Consociational Interpretation," *American Political Science Review* 90, no. 2 (1996): 258-68; Lublin, "Dispersing"; James Manor, "Making Federalism Work," *Journal of Democracy* 9, no. 3 (1998): 21-35; John McGarry and Brendan O'Leary, "Must Pluri-National Federations Fail?", *Ethnopolitics* 8, no. 3 (2009): 5-25.
25 Sabatini, "Decentralization".

should be noted that despite a cultural divide in Ukraine, ethnic polarization is relatively low. The problem lies rather in divisions regarding national identity that undermine democratic governance, as both sides compete to monopolize power. The devolution of power may thus ease regional tensions by promoting the representation and local self-governance of communities that are not ethnically Ukrainian communities.[26] Although Crimea and Donbas have historically been the most noteworthy for their ethnic, linguistic, and regional cleavages, Zakarpattya, Ukraine's westernmost region, also has significant ethno-cultural diversity owing to its large Hungarian population.

A major shortcoming of Ukraine's party system is that parties have largely failed to ease regional tensions, often inciting conflict that elevates one set of voters over another by pitting one set of economic interests against another.[27] Thus, the winner of national elections controls resources and can disburse favors to their local "clients". As Hale and Orttung state, "persistent political cleavages centered on identity and history have consistently structured not only electoral competition [in Ukraine] but also political conflict".[28] States with a diverse ethnic population may opt to devolve power (at least in part) because of complications associated with the representation of conflicting identities through "uniform institutional structures".[29] Different electoral strategies are needed for different territorial realities. This requires transferring some autonomy and power to local political authorities better positioned to appeal to voters.

---

26 Lucan A. Way, "Democracy and Governance in Divided Societies", in: Henry E. Hale and Robert W. Orttung, eds., *Beyond the Euromaidan: Comparative Perspectives on Advancing Reform in Ukraine* (Stanford: Stanford University Press, 2016), 41-58.
27 Peter Ordeshook, "Mancur Olson, collective action and the design of a federal state: The case of Ukraine", *Decyzje*, no. 24 (2015).
28 Henry E. Hale and Robert W. Orttung, *Beyond the Euromaidan: Comparative Perspectives on Advancing Reform in Ukraine* (Stanford: Stanford University Press, 2016), ix.
29 Ingrid van Biezen and Jonathan Hopkin, "Party organization in multi-level contexts", in: Dan Hough and Charlie Jeffery, eds., *Devolution and Electoral Politics* (Manchester: Manchester University Press, 2006), 14-36.

Decentralization scholars have posited that the devolution of power in heterogeneous societies would result in the greater appeal and influence of regionally based parties.[30] These "ethno-regionalist" parties, it is argued, will challenge the ability of state-wide parties to credibly represent local groups and their interests. Ukraine presents a unique case. Although Ukraine is a highly regionalized society, with a pronounced ethnolinguistic cleavage, as Lucan Way states, its politically significant divisions regarding national identity are "evenly matched".[31] That is, there are state-wide political parties representing both sides of Ukraine's ethno-cultural cleavage, with sufficient support in their respective regions, equally capable of gaining power at the national level — by themselves or as an equal coalition partner.[32]

The importance of regional appeal has long been an important factor in Ukrainian politics. The most successful politicians and the most lasting political parties had clear bases and foundations of regional support:[33] for example, Rukh (the People's Movement of Ukraine) in western Ukraine, Svoboda in the Halychyna region, the Communist Party of Ukraine in southern Ukraine, and the Party of Regions in eastern Ukraine. The Ukrainian party system contained a division that reflected the ethno-cultural cleavage that separated Ukrainian-speaking Ukrainians in the West and Russian-speaking Ukrainians in the South and East. Parties thus represented these two distinct cultural orientations — ethnic Ukrainian vs. a Russian/Soviet identity — and had distinct core electorates grounded in specific territories.

Decentralization increases the power and autonomy of subnational governments. However, centralized, state-wide parties typically lack adequate territorial organizations.[34] Consequently, decentralization leads to the growth of local parties. The 2015 municipal elections saw just such a rise in small regional and local party

---

30   Hopkin, "Political".
31   Way, "Democracy", 41.
32   Ibid., 41.
33   Ibid., 54.
34   Hopkin, "Decentralization".

projects, which succeeded in entering local government.[35] For example, the Trust Actions party *(Doviryay Dilam)* gained the leadership of the Odesa City Council, the European Strategy of Vinnytsya *(Vinnyts'ka Yevropeys'ka Stratehiya)* gained the leadership of the Vinnytsya City Council, and the Party of Free Democrats *(Partiya Vil'nykh Demokrativ)* gained the leadership of the Cherkasy City Council.[36] Additionally, the Cherkasians party *(Cherkashchany)* won representation in the Cherkasy Oblast Council (winning second place), and the United Center *(Yedynyi Tsentr)* and For Concrete Deeds parties *(Za konkretni spravy)* formed the largest factions in the Zakarpattya and Khmelnytskyi *oblast* councils, respectively. Additionally, two ethno-regionalist parties had success in Zakarpattya — the Party of Hungarians of Ukraine (KMKS) and the Democratic Party of Hungarians of Ukraine (UMDS). Both targeted the Hungarian minority, nearly all of whom lived in Zakarpattya.[37] Together these parties won 8.6 percent of the vote in the last council, making cooperation with them necessary to form a governing coalition. The concern about the emergence and success of small, territorially based parties like those listed is that problems of governance can result from territorial divisions and become more salient at the national level, if national governing parties and local political projects fail to cooperate.[38]

Regional-national discord emerged in the spring of 2017 between the small Zakarpattya-based United Centre party and President Petro Poroshenko. Viktor Baloha, the leader of the United Centre party, made inflammatory and false claims that the two heads of district state administrations *(rayonna derzhavna administratsiya)* appointed by the President held dual Ukrainian-Hungarian

---

35 While there appears to be a link between decentralization and the growth of local party projects in Ukraine, the evidence remains limited. More election cycles would need to pass before a causal link can be established.
36 H.V. Makarov and Yu. B. Kaplan. "Mistsevi vybory 2015: Problemy orhanizatsiyi, pidsumky, tendentsiyi", *National Institute of Strategic Studies*, 2015. http://www.niss.gov.ua/content/articles/files/vuboru-f2365.pdf.
37 Ibid.
38 Sabatini, "Decentralization".

citizenship.[39] The controversy related to Hungarians being given high political office in an ethnically heterogeneous region, whose Hungarian community had proposed national-territorial autonomy.[40] Such appointments would be in conflict with the draft law proposed by the President himself on 13 March 2017, making dual citizenship in Ukraine illegal. Baloha's false claims were intended to discredit Poroshenko with Zakarpattya's ethnic Ukrainians, decreasing the popularity of the Petro Porsoshenko Bloc—Solidarity (PPB-S), United Centre's main electoral competitor, in the region.[41] Once the decentralization reforms are completed and powers have been devolved from the national level, such clashes may become much more uncommon, as presidential influence over subnational governance will be greatly diminished (although still present). On the other hand, clashes between regional and nationwide parties may intensify as the new politically powerful regional parties look to consolidate power in their territory.

Decentralization as a Strategy for National Governance

Meguid argues that governing parties often use decentralization not to pursue their subnational interests but as a strategy to increase their national popularity and electoral success.[42] The results of the 2014 parliamentary elections gave evidence of the ability of smaller party projects to develop as parties in the national electoral arena, overcoming the traditional "regionalization" of their support.[43] Such was the case with Samopomich, which got the third largest number of votes, winning 33 seats in the parliament. This party was

---

39 "Vin prosto triplo, - Moskal vidreahuvav na zayavu Balohy", *Dyvys.info*, 18 April 2017. http://dyvys.info/2017/04/18/vin-prosto-triplo-moskal-vidreaguvav-na-zayavu-balogy/.
40 Smith & Semenyshyn, "Territorial".
41 In the 2015 municipal elections in Zakarpattya, United Centre came first with 22.7 percent of the vote—winning 19 seats on the *oblast* council. The PPB-S came second with 18.05 percent of the votes—gaining 15 seats on the *oblast* council.
42 Meguid, "Multi-level", 380.
43 Razumkov Centre, "Party System of Ukraine Before and After Maidan: Changes, Trends, and Public Demand", *National Security and Defense*, no. 6-7 (2015): 23.

founded in the city of Lviv and led by its mayor, Andriy Sadovyi, marking its beginnings as a regional party project. The situation with the Radical Party of Oleh Lyashko was similar: the party came fifth in the 2014 parliamentary elections, despite previously having only a small base of popular support in the Chernihiv *oblast* northeast of Kyiv.

The PPB-S's promotion of decentralization was meant to entrench the idea that a regional party's natural sphere of influence was confined to the "the region", and would only operate in subnational government. The hope was that decentralization would prevent any further nationalization of regionally based parties.[44] In other words, in legitimizing the perceived need for greater self-governance and accountability at the subnational level, the PPB-S used decentralization as a cooptation strategy.

Even if parties do not attempt to increase their subnational reach, they still try to maximize the benefits from the actions of their regional and local party branches. The success of nonparliamentary parties in the 2015 municipal elections suggests that nationwide parties need to develop their local party organizations. Decentralization is altering the scope of the political arena in Ukraine. As power and the control over resources continue to devolve, electoral dynamics change, along with parties' electoral fortunes. Older, more established parties are likely to gain immediate benefits from organizational inertia, having already devoted resources to building up local party offices and possessing greater familiarity with municipal election regulations and processes. For instance, in 2016, Yulia Tymoshenko's Bat'kivshchyna party had 370 permanent party branches open to the public (*pryimal'nya*) and 16,862 registered local party offices (*oseredok*), surpassing all other major parties.[45] The PPB-S had 285 permanent party branches and only 1,786 registered local party offices.

---

44 Bonnie Meguid, "Institutional change as Strategy: The Role of Decentralization in Party Competition", 2008, 9. https://papers.ssrn.com/sol3/papers.cfm?abstract_id=1450911.

45 OPORA, "Pryimalni parlamentskykh partiy ta deputativ-mazhorytarnykiv: Yak vony pratsyuyut ta de yikh shukaty", *OPORA*, July 2016. https://www.oporaua.org/parlament/42940-zvit-pryymalni-parlamentskykh-partiy-ta-de

As more authority passes to the local level, parties stand to gain more from winning subnational elections. A significant part of nationwide parties' ability to successfully compete at the regional, district, and local levels will depend on their capacity to "denationalize" (i.e., build local party organizations) and tailor campaign messages and governing strategies to the local electorate. Hence, parties' territorial organization and their activities at the subnational level are important factors in the development of party systems in a decentralized state.[46]

"Denationalizing" Party Politics

The development of local party branches with independent manifestos and campaign strategies is a relatively new factor in Ukrainian political parties. The Ukrainian party system has long been plagued by a lack of activity at the local level. Opinion polls conducted prior to municipal elections have found that the average voter is unaware of any work being done by local party branches in their region (see Figure 6.1). Changes made to the electoral law at the municipal level, which took effect in October 2015, were designed to promote local party development by increasing the role of political parties at the subnational level.[47] This would then deepen the continuity between local and national authorities as well as strengthen the perpetually weak party system.[48] As political authority was devolved to local levels, the larger parliamentary parties would be further pressured into investing in local party

---

putativ-mazhorytarnykiv-yak-vony-pratsyuyut-ta-de-yikh-shukaty. However, it should be noted that, according to investigations carried out by the OPORA civic network in mid-2016, many of the officially registered permanent local party branches listed on the party website were not in operation.

46 Seymore M. Lipset and Stein Rokkan, eds., *Party Systems and Voter Alignments* (New York: The Free Press, 1967).

47 Specifically, the change from a mixed system (proportional and majoritarian representation) at the *oblast*, *rayon* and city council levels to strictly proportional representation, with a multimandate constituency, targeted independent candidates. See Melanie Mierzejewski-Voznyak, "Ukraine's Local Elections: New Law, Old Problems", *New Eastern Europe*, 22 October 2015. http://www.neweasterneurope.eu/articles-and-commentary/1757-ukraine-s-local-elections-new-law-old-problems.

48 Ibid.

operations to compete with territorially based parties and small party projects, which, as previously noted, were enjoying a period of popularity at the subnational level.

Figure 6.1. "Have you heard anything about any party's local offices' work in your region?" (in percentages)

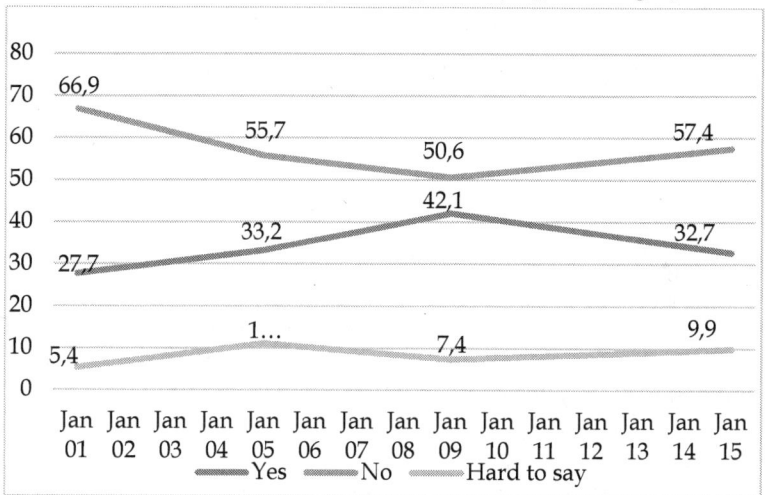

Source: Razumkov Center Report "Political parties and party system of Ukraine at present: Public opinion", *National Security and Defense*, nos. 6-7 (2015): 106-144.

Local party building

In late 2014 and 2015, a great deal of attention was paid to building and staffing local party organizations, selecting candidates to run in the 2015 elections, and forming political strategies responsive to the country's social, political and economic situation. Particularly notable were the efforts made by "new" parties to establish party structures across different regions in Ukraine (the PPB-S) and to develop properly managed party branches (the Lviv-based Samopomich). Before the 2015 municipal elections, only the PPB-S had established local party branches in all 24 *oblasts*.[49] Although it

---

49 Razumkov Centre, "Party System;" OPORA, "Local elections: campaign assessment one week before agitation ends", *OPORA*, October 2015. https://www.o

established local party branches in only nine *oblasts*, Samopomich persisted in excluding oligarchs and older, "seasoned" politicians from its party lists, as on its 2014 parliamentary candidate list, opting instead for medium-sized business owners, community organizers and journalists.[50]

The multilevel organization of the state directly impacts the organizational structures of political parties.[51] Centralized parties will need to establish and develop subnational branches, if only to maintain their political authority in regions where they have traditionally carried high levels of support. Depending on the party's roots and needs in a region, the type and degree of authority granted to subnational party organizations will vary.[52] Thus, the more a party is concerned with winning or maintaining political power in a particular region, the more time and resources will it devote to shoring up local party offices. The locations and number of permanent local party branches (*pryimal'nya*) opened and kept in operation by political parties across Ukraine is the evidence of this.[53]

For example, Andryi Sadovyi, the mayor of Lviv, had an interest in seeing his Samopomich party win a large share of the seats on the Lviv *oblast* and city councils. Thus, the party established a disproportionate amount of their party branches in Lviv — 17 percent.[54] The Opposition Bloc party established permanent party branches in only eight of Ukraine's 24 *oblasts*, but the party strategically chose the *oblasts* where they had won in the parliamentary

---

poraua.org/en/elections/40435-1267-1446984030-miscevi-vybory-ocinka-kam paniji-za-tyzhden-do-zavershennja-agitaciji.
50 Daisy Sindelar and Halyna Tereshchuk, "Can Lviv mayor change Ukrainian Politics once and for all?" *Radio Free Europe/Radio Liberty*, 31 October 2014. https://www.rferl.org/a/ukraine-reforms-elections-self-reliance-party-sadoviy-profile/26668300.html.
51 Hopkin and van Houten, "Decentralization", 133.
52 Van Houten, "Multi-level".
53 See OPORA monitoring report: OPORA, "Pryimalni parlamentskykh partiy ta deputativ-mazhorytarnykiv".
54 Ibid. In 2015 Samopomich had 23 (out of a total of 138) permanent party branches in the Lviv *oblast*. Its second largest number of party branches (10) were located in Kyiv. The average number of party branches Samopomich established in all other *oblasts* was 5.

elections.⁵⁵ As mentioned above, the 2014 parliamentary winner, PPB-S, was the only party that had local party branches in all 24 *oblasts*. This was likely an effort to transfer the widespread support it received at the national level to the local level.⁵⁶

Campaigning

Voter identification (and hence behavior) can differ depending on the level, as issues that are important at one level can lose their salience at another level. State-wide parties must tailor their campaign messages to the local electorate if they are to successfully compete with smaller, region-based party projects. While party branches largely continue to borrow from their party's national electoral program, some have begun to tailor their messages to the communities where they were campaigning in an attempt to engage local voters. Before the 2015 municipal elections, parties in Ternopil, for example, campaigned on local issues such as water pollution, while in Ivano-Frankivs'k party manifestos focused on regional safety and fighting increased crime.⁵⁷ However, the number of times that parties campaigned on policy agendas beyond the scope of local politics (e.g., creating a professional military or lowering taxes on utilities) highlights the general inexperience of Ukrainian political parties and politicians at the subnational level. Additionally, according to the Voters Committee of Ukraine (CVU) civic organization, 80 percent of political party and candidate manifestos and campaigns in the 2015 municipal elections were "without substance" as regards local government.⁵⁸ As the CVU analyst Denys Rybachok noted, a major electoral problem in municipal

---

55 Ibid. Opposition Bloc reported permanent party branches in the following oblasts in 2015: Dnipro, Donets'k, Zhytomyr, Zaporizhzhya, Kirovohrad, Odesa, Sumy, Chernihiv.
56 Ibid. It should be noted that subsequent to the 2015 local elections, not all local party offices continue to operate at the same level. For instance, the majority of branch locations in Chernivtsi work solely in an on-demand capacity.
57 ENEMO, "International election observation mission Ukraine local elections 2015, final report", *European Network of Election Monitoring Organizations*, 2015, http://iesc.lt/app/uploads/2016/05/Ukraine_Local_el_2015_EN.pdf.
58 Makarov and Kaplan, "*Mistsevi*".

elections are "populists who promise golden mountains", vowing to cancel the draft or put a moratorium on land sales; voters need to understand that the "heads of *hromady* should not be good orators but good municipal managers".[59]

Nevertheless, there was far more political activity at the regional and district levels in the run-up to the fall 2015 elections than in the municipal elections held in 2010. According to data from the OPORA civic network OPORA, 27 of the 132 parties running actively campaigned during the 2015 municipal elections.[60] However, only six of those parties were active in more than a third of Ukraine's *oblasts*: PPB-S in 24 *oblasts*, Bat'kivshchyna in 20 *oblasts*, Nash Kray (Our Land) in 12 *oblasts*, Opposition Bloc in 10 *oblasts*, UKROP (Ukrainian Union of Patriots) and Samopomich in nine *oblasts* each. Thus, the majority of the campaigning was targeted at specific regions and cities, deemed territorially important by individual parties.

Political and electoral strategy

When parties compete in multiple elections, they have multiple sources of legitimacy, which undermines the hierarchical power structures traditionally found within centralized parties.[61] There is a dual imperative: subnational party leaders must represent regional *and* national party interests.[62] In particular, voters will judge local party on their experience and performance, not just on their party loyalty. It is therefore difficult for the subnational party elite to prioritize national party needs at the expense of their local branches. Similarly, it is difficult for national and regional elites to support district or local policies and decisions that may potentially alienate general voters, simply because such policies are deemed

---

59 "Dva roky Verkhovnoyi Rady: yak fraktsiyi vykonuyut peredvyborchi prohramy", *VHO "Komitet vybortsiv Ukrayiny"*, 1 November 2016. http://www.cvu.org.ua/nodes/view/type:news/slug:Два%20роки%20Верховної%20Ради%3A%20як%20фракції%20виконують%20передвиборчі%20програми.
60 OPORA, "Local elections".
61 Van Biezen and Hopkin, "Party Organization".
62 Alfred Montero, "The politics of decentralization in a centralized party system: The case of democratic Spain", *Comparative Politics* 38, no. 1 (2005): 80.

important for local development. Such was the case on 16 May 2017, when the Bat'kivshchyna Zhytomyr *oblast* party branch expelled Oleh Soya, the head of the Korolov *rayon* party organization in the city of Zhytomyr, and removed him from his position. Soya's vote to increase public transport fares violated party discipline and ignored the decision of the Zhytomyr *oblast* party branch that Bat'kivshchyna would do nothing to worsen the situation of Zhytomyr inhabitants.[63] Such decisions are common when parties have a top-down organizational command structure.

Local leaders may act as agents of their party's central leadership, but they also have their own political ambitions and electoral concerns. Subnational party branches are more than just "franchises of the national party office".[64] Central leadership may incline to limit subnational autonomy to prevent branches from acting against the party's broader interests. Consequently, the devolution of power forces the central party leadership to make critical choices regarding party development. They can accept the new political reality and grant subnational party representatives greater autonomy, allowing them to pursue their own governing strategies and policies—although this may make the party appear divided—or else insist on the adoption of similar strategies at all levels, but with significant concessions to regional autonomy.[65] Political strategy will have to balance the needs of both the party branches and the central office.

Granting greater authority to party branches is particularly problematic for ideological parties, such as Svoboda, which have a concrete and coherent party program. On 7 April 2017, Svoboda's executive committee expelled three party members—Roman Navrotskyi, Ivan Sorokolita, Ihor Turskyi—for violating the party's

---

63 "Ofitsiyna zayava zhytomyrs'koho oblasnoho oseredku VO 'Bat'kivshchyna' pro vyklyuchennya Oleha Soya z lav partiyi", *Bat'kivshchyna*, 16 May 2017. http://Batkivshchyna.zt.ua/oficijna-zayava-zhitomirskogo-oblasnogo-oseredku-v o-batkivshhina-pro-viklyuchennya-olega-soya-z-lav-partii/.
64 Montero, "The Politics", 67.
65 Elisa Roller and Pieter van Houten, "National Parties in Regional Party Systems: The PSC-PSOE in Catalonia", Paper presented at the American Political Science Association annual meeting, Boston (August-1 September 2002); van Biezen and Hopkin, "Party Organization".

regulations when they served on the Ternopil city council between fall 2015 and spring 2017. After their election in October 2015, the three council members cast 100 votes that went against Svoboda's party program as outlined in the 2015 elections.[66] According to Svoboda's analysis, the deputies' votes instead aligned with the regional state administration's guidelines, and this was interpreted as a betrayal of Svoboda's voters.

Related to the issue of the various levels of party leadership cooperating over electoral and political strategy is the matter of the different political parties' governing strategy, particularly as concerns coalition building. With the increase in the number of important political offices due to decentralization, there is a greater potential for internal party discord over interparty alliances at the national and/or subnational level.[67] In the majority of Ukrainian subnational councils (including those at the *oblast* level), no one party typically obtains more than half the total seats, precluding a single-party majority and making it necessary to form a coalition to the elect council heads. The result is that in certain areas of Ukraine, subnational candidates have declared themselves willing to cooperate with candidates from other political parties although the parties may oppose each other either at the national level or in other regions of Ukraine.[68] For example, while campaigning in the 2015 municipal elections in the Kharkiv *oblast*, Vidrodzhennya candidates announced a possible partnership with Opposition Bloc despite relations between the two parties being particularly hostile in the neighboring Dnipropetrovsk *oblast*.[69]

---

66 "Ternopil's'ka 'Svoboda' vymahaye pozbavyty mandativ deputativ-zradnykiv Romana Navrotskoho, Ivana Sorokolita ta Ihorya Turskoho", *Svoboda*, April 24, 2017, http://svoboda.org.ua/news/events/00115155/.
67 Hopkin, "Political".
68 Makarov and Kaplan, "*Mistsevi*".
69 "Oliynyk: Yakshcho 'Vidrodzhennya' v Dnipropetrovs'ku ne zareyestruyut, vybory budut zirvani", *Informatsiyno-Analitychnyi Tsentr Natsionalnoyi Bezpeky Ukrayiny*, 7 October 2015. http://mediarnbo.org/2015/10/07/oliynik-yakshho-vidrodzhennya-v-dnipropetrovsku-ne-zareyestruyut-vibori-budut-zirvani/.

Party management and candidate nomination

In unitary states with centralized internal power structures, political parties tend to exhibit similar centralized control over candidate selection — even after the introduction of decentralization reforms.[70] The majority of Ukrainian political parties have a top-down structure; thus, the selection of party candidates often has little to do with who is the most qualified and more to do with who carries favor with the party heads.[71] Due to a lack of internal party democracy, important decisions tend to be made by the party elite, regardless of the opinions of rank and file members (or even of the electorate who successfully voted for certain officials). This was evidenced in February of 2016, when President Poroshenko signed bill #3700 into law, establishing the imperative mandate. The imperative mandate, first introduced in 2006, according to Article 81 of the Constitution of Ukraine, decrees that a deputy's absence or withdrawal from their party's parliamentary faction, after being elected to parliament as a party member, entitles the party leadership to relieve him of his status as a deputy.[72] The imperative mandate thus strictly enforces party discipline and grants the party leadership a monopoly over party seats.

Through elections citizens are able to influence public decision-making, selecting public officials. Elections thus establish public confidence in government institutions. The imperative mandate allows a disproportionate concentration of power in the hands of the party leadership, threatening responsible and democratic party building. In a system that lacks adequate internal democracy in political parties, it was therefore no surprise that this legislation was cosponsored by numerous party leaders, including Bat'kivshchyna's Yulia Tymoshenko, the Poroshenko Bloc Deputy Faction Leader Yuri Lutsenko, the Radical Party Head Oleh Lyashko, the Samopomich Faction Head Oleh Berezyuk, and the People's Front

---

70 van Biezen and Hopkin, "Party organization".
71 Mierzejewski-Voznyak, "Political parties".
72 Oleksiy Sydorchuk, *Nazad vid Yevropy: Nastup partiynoyi dyktatury v Ukrayini* (Kyiv: Democratic Initiatives Foundation, 2016). http://dif.org.ua/uploads/pdf/1463410310_4103.pdf.

Faction Head Maksym Burbak.[73] The centralization of power in political parties will inevitably form a point of contention between the central party, regional branches, and local voters. As power devolves to regional and local levels, subnational elites will need to gain control over the candidate selection and ratification process and be held accountable for the transparency of the nomination process.

Electoral engineering and centralized leadership

Ukrainian parties used closed electoral lists that empowered national party leaders.[74] The party elite not only nominated candidates. It also determined a candidate's chances of being elected to office by fixing the order of the candidates. The party leadership had a vested interest in controlling candidate selection, particularly at the national level, as this determined who represented the party in parliament and, potentially, in the government.[75] However, in the 2015 municipal elections, parties took more of an interest in candidate selection at the municipal level, since the enactment of decentralization reforms would allow the winners of these elections to capitalize from the devolution of power. The greater the power wielded by subnational levels of government, the more concerned the national leadership would be over which candidates occupy these offices.

Parties engaged in composing electoral lists — particularly at the last level — to attract as many votes as possible in a given region. A significant portion of party electoral lists — party candidates to city and *oblast* councils — often featured members of parliament (MPs) in the top positions. Predictably, the MPs' recognizability meant they enjoyed higher levels of electoral support than local

---

73 Brian Mefford, "Ukraine's New Political Law Privileges Party Bosses", *Atlantic Council*, 9 March 2016. http://www.atlanticcouncil.org/blogs/ukrainealert/tyrannical-tendencies-ukraine-s-new-january-16th-law.
74 Stephan Haggard and Steven B. Webb, "Political Incentives and Intergovernmental Fiscal Relations: Argentina, Brazil and Mexico Compared", in: Alfred Montero and David J. Samuels, eds., *Decentralization and Democracy in Latin America* (Notre Dame: University of Notre Dame, 2004).
75 van Biezen and Hopkin, "Party organization".

party branch members; however, MPs would almost always refuse positions on city councils as parliamentary seats offered them greater political and financial benefits.[76] By withdrawing themselves from consideration, the elected councilors were able to pass their seats to colleagues who performed worse and who may have not reached the number of votes required to win a seat on the council.[77]

This party practice discredited the validity of regional councils, as they ended up largely composed of individuals whom voters did not choose. For example, following the 2015 municipal elections in the Vinnytsya *oblast*, 52 Opposition Bloc candidates refused to accept their mandates.[78] This amounted to more than 80 percent of the party's list. In the Khmelnyts'kyi *oblast*, four city councilors in Kamyanets'-Podil's'kyi elected from the Ridne Misto (Hometown) list withdrew, passing their council seats to a local businessman and to former Party of Regions members who had themselves not received enough votes for a seat. The number of elected officials who gave up their positions only a month after taking office, so they could be filled by less popular local party colleagues, is a cause for concern. By the end of November 2015, 16 out of 64 officials in the Rivne *oblast* council left their elected positions (25 percent of the council's seats); in the Mykolayiv *oblast* council, eight officials out of 64 left (12.5 percent), in Zhytomyr the number was seven out of 64 (11%), and in Ternopil it was five out of 64 (7.8 percent).[79]

Candidate selection

Against the general trend of electoral engineering in the drafting of party lists and the nomination of candidates, at least one party – Samopomich – has made a genuine effort at local party development and to increase internal democratization. This Lviv-based

---

76 Makarov and Kaplan, "Mistsevi".
77 OSCE, "Ukraine: Local elections 25 October and 15 November 2015", *OSCE*, 2016, http://www.osce.org/odihr/elections/ukraine/223641?download=true.
78 Makarov and Kaplan, "Mistsevi".
79 Ibid.

party engaged in public discussions over candidate selection and became the first party to conduct true public primary elections for a mayoral candidate.[80] Between 15 June and 15 July 2015, the party held online primary elections to nominate a candidate for mayor of Ivano-Frankivs'k (voters could also call in to vote). The party advertised the primaries in local media and presented people with four candidates. While this marked significant progress for internal party democracy, at least in sentiment, it was flawed in practice and criticized by the media for a lack of transparency.[81]

Traditionally, parties' subnational activities have focused exclusively on campaigning for mayoral, and *oblast* and city council elections. With the creation of the ATCs, however, a new important level of self-government was introduced, requiring parties to organize and campaign. In this way, the local level of politics has the potential to improve representation by creating a new political arena for party competition. As more authority is handed down to the lowest community level, the selection of candidate for these positions becomes increasingly important. The first local ATC elections held on 30 April 2017 demonstrated greater competition. Whereas one or two candidates had run for a seat on a village council and three to four candidates had run for village elder in the local ATC elections of December 2016, five to eight candidates ran for the two positions in the April 2017 round.[82]

The ATC elections of 29 October 2017 and 24 December 2017 saw a rise in the number of political parties (50 in October and 42 in December) declaring their intention to participate.[83] Nevertheless, in the 2017 elections, independently nominated candidates

---

80 Makarov and Kaplan, "Mistsevi".
81 "Samopomich obmanyuye frankivtsiv?" *Versiyi.if.ua*, July 8, 2017. http://versii.if.ua/novunu/samopomich-obmanyuye-frankivtsiv/.
82 "30 kvitnya vybory v 47 OTH. Eksperty ta lidery hromad radyat', zayakykh kandydativ varto holosuvaty", *Detsentralizatsiya vlady*, May 28, 2017, http://decentralization.gov.ua/news/item/id/5405.
83 OPORA, "Promizhnyi zvit za resultatamy sposterezhennya na pershykh mistsevykh vyborakh u obyednanykh terytorialnykh hromadakh 24 hrudnia 2017 roku (04.11.2017−21.12.2017)", *OPORA*, December 2017. https://www.oporaua.org/vybory/45156-promizhnyi-zvit-za-rezultatamy-sposterezhennia-na-pershykh-mistsevykh-vyborakh-u-obiednanykh-terytorialnykh-hromadakh-24-hrudnia-2017-roku-04112017-21122017. Accessed February 21, 2018.

continued to make up the majority of those running for ATC heads. The October 2017 election saw 65 percent of candidates nominated independently and only 35 percent nominated by local party organizations. However, political parties nominated the vast majority of candidates running in local council elections, confirming parties' growing interest and involvement in local politics. According to OPORA's reports on the October and December 2017 elections for village and settlement council deputies, 70 percent and 80 percent of candidates, respectively, were nominated by local party branches, with only 30 percent and 20 percent being self-nominated candidates.[84] This contrasted with the elections of December 2016, when 51 percent of deputy candidates were self-nominated. The results of the April 2018 elections further attested to the growing interest (and popularity) of political parties in local politics. Candidates nominated by political parties won 88 percent of the deputy seats, with independent candidates taking only 12 percent.[85]

Activities and Electoral Rules Violations of Parties in ATC Elections

The continued increase in political parties' participation (and eventual success) in the first rounds of ATC elections between December 2016 and April 2018 was matched by a similarly slow yet steady increase in the development and activity of local party organizations, specifically in matters of staffing and campaigning. According to OPORA's monitoring reports, in the run-up to the ATC elections of 11 and 18 December 2016, the levels of campaign activity remained low among political parties' local organizations, and campaigning by party candidates only became noticeable in the last

---

84 "Interim report on observation results of the first local elections in united territorial communities on 29 October 2017 (19.10.2017 26.10.2017)", *OPORA*, October 2017. https://www.oporaua.org/en/news/45055-interim-report-on-observation-results-of-the-first-local-elections-in-united-territorial-communities-on-29-october-2017-19102017-26102017; OPORA, "Promizhnyi". Accessed 21 February 2018.
85 "Peremozhtsi i autsaydery vyboriv v OTH", *Informator*, May 6, 2018. https://informator.news/peremozhtsi-i-autsajdery-vyboriv-v-oth/

week of November 2016.[86] Furthermore, despite candidate nomination beginning on 7 and 14 November for the elections on 11 and 18 December, respectively, almost all candidate names were submitted to the territorial electoral commission only in a few days before the vote. This left little time for voters to learn about the candidates prior to the elections.

In contrast, campaigning intensified in the October and December 2017 elections, with the Bat'kivshchyna and PPB-S candidates and local party organizations conducting the most active campaigns in the ATCs monitored by OPORA. Bat'kivshchyna campaigned in 54 percent and 52 percent of ATCs in the two elections, respectively, and PPB-S actively campaigned in 42 percent and 66 percent of ATCs.[87] An overall increase in campaigning was in fact noticeable among all candidates, with 87 percent of those running for the position of deputy distributing some form of printed campaign material and 78 percent holding meetings with voters.[88]

The increased participation of parties in local politics resulted in increased reports of election-related violations. Such violations have been common in all ATC elections. In the December 2016 elections, a major issue was the transparency and legitimacy of candidate selection. Legislation required parties to inform the public about the date, time, and location of candidate nomination meetings and to make them accessible to media and other election observers. However, OPORA reported that some of the more popular state-wide parties violated these laws.[89] In Ternopil, Svoboda and UKROP failed to notify the Velyki Dederkaly and Borsuky village election commissions of their candidate nomination meetings. In the Dnipropetrovsk *oblast*, Bat'kivshchyna's Shyroke *rayon* party office held its candidate nomination conference the day prior to the announced date, making attendance impossible. Similar irregularities in the candidate nomination process occurred in the Mykolaiv region. The regional branch of PPB-S held its party conference to

---

86 OPORA, "Local elections".
87 OPORA, "Interim".
88 Ibid.
89 OPORA, "Local elections".

nominate candidates at a venue that OPORA observers could not access. The Svoboda district party branch in Mikolaiv's Bashtanka *rayon* started its party conference to nominate candidates two hours before the officially stated time, preventing observers and others from attending. Additionally, the Bat'kivshchyna party office in Berezan gave an unlocatable address in the official notification of its candidate nomination meeting.

In the week before the 29 October 2017 ATC elections, OPORA had recorded over 250 electoral violations of various kinds, the worst violation being the dissemination of campaign materials in places not allowed by law.[90] Additionally, the October 2017 elections saw an increase in indirect voter bribing by political parties. For example, the Poltava *oblast* branch of Nash Kray donated football equipment and equipped a children's playground in the village of Zchepylivka village in the Novosanzharska *hromada*.[91] The December 2017 elections saw similar violations. By February 2018, the police were investigating 20 criminal cases related to violations during the October and December elections.[92]

That said, according to Oleksiy Koshelev, the CVU Chairman, the 29 April 2018 elections presented the "dirtiest campaign" in the history of ATC elections.[93] Political parties and candidates set a "record" for the number and size of voter bribes. According to the CVU, 19 criminal cases were opened by the police following the elections, half of which related to allegations of voter bribery.[94] According to Koshelev, there was documentary evidence that Bat'kivshchyna, the Agrarian Party and Our Land purchased votes.[95] Furthermore, in the Lozno-Oleksandrivka *hromada* in the

---

90 OPORA, "Interim".
91 Ibid.
92 OPORA, "Final Report".
93 "CVU: vybory do OTH 29 kvitnya staly "naybrudnishoyu kampaniyeyu" z 2015 roku", *Radio Svoboda*, 30 April 2018. https://www.radiosvoboda.org/a/news/29200602.html.
94 "CVU sprostovuye informatsiyu pro pidkup vybortsiv kandydatamy vid 'Samopomochi'", *CVU*, 7 May 2018. http://www.cvu.org.ua/nodes/view/type:news/slug:kvu-sprostovuie-informatsiiu-pro-pidkup-vybortsiv-kandydatamy-vid-samopomochi. Accessed December 4, 2018.
95 Oleksiy Koshelev, 30 April 2018, In *Facebook* [Komitet vybortsiv Ukrayiny]. Retrieved November 27, 2018, from http://www.facebook.com/cvu.ngo/

Luhansk region, it was reported that two parties—Za zhyttya (For Life) and the Radical Party of Oleg Lyashko—provided transportation for voters to polling stations, which could be considered a form of voter bribery.[96] Illegal campaigning also occurred in the April 2018 elections. The CVU reported violations by Bat'kivshchyna in the Donetsk, Rivne, and Poltava *oblasts*, sending SMS messages calling for locals to vote and illegally circulating campaign materials at polling stations.[97]

A major challenge to decentralization in Ukraine is the malfunctioning of the election process in the newly formed ATCs. Specifically, there is a lack of professionalism among members of the local election commissions, and local politicians and candidates engage in illegal actions. A major concern emerged in the 24 December 2017 election with the presence of unauthorized persons using their official status or political authority to observe the voting process and interact with voters. In one instance, representatives of the Vinnytsia *oblast* Bat'kivshchyna branch were present in the election precincts of the Novohrebelska ATC.[98] The April 2018 elections gave evidence of the widespread failure of the election commissions to adequately perform their duties.[99] Polling stations in Oknyansky, Odesa and Zahvizdynsk, Ivano-Frankivs'k failed to open on time, resulting in long lines, preventing some voters from casting their ballots. In addition, in Zahvizdynsk, the commission secretary registered voters without checking if they had proper identification. In Pereshapinskaya, Dnipropetrovsk voters were marking ballots outside the polling stations; one person was filmed

---

[96] "Prodovzhuye fiksuvaty porushennya na vyborakh v OTH", Pro Komitet vybortsiv Ukrayiny, 28 April 2018. http://www.cvu.org.ua/nodes/view/type:news/slug:kvu-prodovzhuie-fiksuvaty-porushennia-na-vyborakh-v-oth. Accessed December 4, 2018.

[97] Ibid.

[98] "Statement of civil network OPORA on preliminary observation results of the first local elections in united territorial communities, held on 24 December 2017", *OPORA*, December 2017. https://www.oporaua.org/en/news/45210-statement-of-civil-network-opora-on-preliminary-observation-results-of-the-first-local-elections-in-united-territorial-communities-held-on-24-december-2017.

[99] "CVU zafiksuvav pershi porushennya na vyborakh v OTH", CVU, 29 April 2018. http://www.cvu.org.ua/nodes/view/type:news/slug:kvu-zafiksuvav-pershi-porushennia-na-vyborakh-v-oth. Accessed December 4, 2018.

filling out a ballot on the hood of a car. Indisputably, a major challenge to decentralization in Ukraine remained the "lack of human capital and capacity to effectively administer the duties of governance at the local level".[100]

Conclusion: Institutional Reforms and the Party System

We can draw some tentative conclusions concerning the relationship between the institutional reforms brought by decentralization and party politics in Ukraine. Increased party competition—and electoral success—has taken place at the municipal level since 2015 and, as a result of the newly formed ATCs, has penetrated to the local level. Additionally, now that the local level has real decision-making authority and control over resources, local governing bodies are more accountable to the citizenry. However, the failure of the Ukrainian parliament to pass constitutional amendments that would recognize ATCs as *the* basic unit of the territorial administrative system has left open numerous questions about the actual duties, the role, and the powers of the different subnational self-government tiers.[101] Furthermore, this lack of clarity, combined with the *oblast* and *rayon* authorities' reluctance to transfer certain responsibilities to the local level, has intensified the conflicts between self-government levels, as well as within parties. What then must be done to prevent the devolution of resources and responsibilities to local self-government from fragmenting the party system or injecting greater volatility?

First, Ukraine must pass the constitutional amendments necessary for the redistribution of powers from the state to subnational self-governments, allowing the abolition of substate state

---

100 Roberts and Fisun, "Local".
101 Roberts and Fisun, "Local;" Oleksii Sydorchuk, "Decentralization Reform In Ukraine: Prospects And Challenges", *Ilko Kucheriv Democratic Initiatives Foundation,* 3 December 2015, https://ukraine-office.eu/en/03-12-2015-policy-brief-decentralization-reform-in-ukraine-prospects-and-challenges/; Tomila Lankina, Claire Gordon, and Svitlana Slava, "Regional Development in Ukraine: Priority Actions in Terms of Decentralization", *European Union* 2017, http://cor.europa.eu/en/documentation/studies/Documents/Regional-Development-Ukraine.pdf.

administrations. Admittedly, this will remain a challenge as long as the issue of decentralization is closely linked to the approval of a "special status" designation for the occupied territories in the Donbas region. However, the failure to formally devolve powers, as the new ATCs' financial and institutional capacity continues to increase, will generate conflicts among the various tiers of authority.

Second, local election commissioners' lack of professionalism and awareness in the newly formed ATCs calls for greater education and training.[102] The Central Election Commission and NGOs need to provide hands-on, interactive training not only to the Precinct Election Commissions but also to the District Election Commissions to enhance their professional competencies and identify where technical assistance is necessary for the proper functioning of ATC elections. This would raise awareness of electoral legislation and interpretation, and better equip the commissioners with practical skills to deal with vote counting, an understanding of the rights and duties of all participants in the electoral process (including official observers), and allowing them to identify and classify electoral violations.[103] By increasing the knowledge of commissioners and improving the management of local elections, political parties and independent candidates will adhere to higher standards, injecting much needed legitimacy and transparency into the party system starting at the lowest government levels. In particular, this will better prepare the commissioners for dealing with violations, such as those related to the registration and nomination of candidates. Even if electoral commissioners are better able to perform their duties and identify violations, however, the absence of sanctions makes it likely that the infringement of electoral law will continue. Proper sanctions and penalties must be applied to electoral violations, and nationwide electoral laws at all levels of government must be applied uniformly to *all* political parties and candidates guilty of violation.

---

102 "Otsinka yakosti roboty DVK: vysnovky OPORY za resyltatamy sposterezhennya na pershykh mistevykh vyporakh v OTH", OPORA, 15 February 2016, https://www.oporaua.org/vybory/pershi-vybory-v-obiednanykh-hromadakh-2016/44117-otsinka-iakosti-roboty-dvk-vysnovky-opory-za-rezultatamy-sposterezhennia-na-pershykh-mistsevykh-vyborakh-v-oth.
103 Ibid.

Third, to counter the growing wave of populism and to check ineffective local governance, state-wide parties in Ukraine need to better coordinate their political and electoral strategies across the levels of self-government and build up their local party organizations. Given the current political climate, in which regional parties and small party projects are experiencing a period of popularity at the municipal level, state-wide parties will need to invest in local organizational development to strengthen their "brand", and not just superficially. This is particularly important as municipal politics continues to display high levels of participation by independent candidates. Although decentralization devolves power to the lowest level (ATC), parties have only begun to engage in true competition at this level. Thus, we return to the question of the kind of changes we can expect to see in internal party dynamics.

By reinforcing the massive reorganization of administrative capacities at the various subnational levels, political parties will be instrumental for the success of the decentralization reforms. However, whether parties will choose to decentralize their own organizations remains to be seen. Ideally, Ukrainian political parties would respond to the decentralization reforms by 1) decreasing centralized control within the parties, thus improving internal democracy, and 2) "denationalizing" the parties to develop durable local party organizations capable of responsible representation. This will not only alleviate the internal party conflict that will arise as subnational elites amass more power and authority, but will likely benefit the parties' overall electoral performance. By improving the quality of representation at all levels, a party will increase its credibility and extend its longevity in national office. Nevertheless, it will remain necessary for leaders at various levels of government to work with those above and below them in the political hierarchy, facilitating coordination and cooperation across the political spectrum.[104] Thus, not only do politicians and political parties have the potential to alter the political and administrative culture of Ukraine, but, by accepting and adopting subnational authorities' new roles and responsibilities, will strengthen the stability of the party system as a whole.

---

104 Ordeshook, "Mancur", 167.

7. Trends in Ukrainian Regions in 2015-17 Toward a Decentralized Model of Regional Development

Igor Dunayev

Introduction

In the past decade, regions in different countries around the world experienced unexpected macroeconomic, geopolitical and other changes, sluggish economic growth, a redistribution in the areas of influence of their largest economic centers, and so on.[1] In this context, the concept of the "new normal" has become a popular way of designating the new global macroeconomic reality.[2] The "new normal" describes an L-shaped development trajectory: "fast fall — long-lasting stagnation (recession) with an incremental 'reaching the bottom' — late and slow recovery".[3] The main point is that the global economy will never fully recover and return to the pre-crisis norm.

The global financial and economic crisis has had a negative effect on Ukraine. The economy of Ukraine has been deindustrializing. Prior to the launch of the 2014 decentralization reform, Ukraine's economic space was heavily polarized (see Appendix A). Economic differentiation between regions was increasing. In 2012, the wealthiest regions had a per capita gross regional product (GRP) 2.91 times higher than the poorest regions; in 2014, it was 2.97 times (see Appendix B). In 2012-2014, the relevant GRP

---

1 Fabrizio Barca, Philip McCann, Andrés Rodríguez-Pose, "The case for regional development intervention: Place-based versus place-neutral approaches", *Journal of Regional Science* 52, no. 1 (2012): 134-149; *How Regions Grow: Trends and Analysis* (Paris: OECD Publishing, 2009). https://www.oecd.org/cfe/regional-policy/howregionsgrowtrendsandanalysis.htm.
2 Mohamed A. El-Erian, "Navigation the New Normal in Industrial Countries Per Jacobsson Foundation Lecture", *IMF*, 10 October 2010. www.imf.org/en/News/Articles/2015/09/28/04/53/sp101010.
3 O. N. Voronkova, "'Novaya normal'nost'" mirokhozyaystvennoho razvitiya i strategiya rossiiskogo biznesa", *Finansovye issledovaniya* 3, no. 52 (2016): 119-23.

absolute values (in actual prices) of the group of regions with the highest value (the Dnipropetrovsk, Donetsk, Zaporizhzhia, Kharkiv regions and the City of Kyiv) were eight times higher than those of the group of regions with the lowest value (the Volyn, Zakarpattia, Ternopil, Kherson, Chernivtsi regions).

In late 2016 and early 2017, Ukraine managed to reverse the negative trend of its macroeconomic recession, but the "new normal" in Ukraine meant that "the discrepancy between the regions' economic potential and their social welfare and life quality indices"[4] was likely to be observed. In these circumstances, it was vital for Ukraine to promote local and regional development.

In reforming its local governance, regional policy, and administrative and territorial system, Ukraine transitioned from a centralized model of regional development to a decentralized one. To understand the factors that challenged this transition, I conducted an expert survey "Determining the ability of Ukraine's regional economic policy to change" in February-March 2017. I surveyed 44 experts from 14 regions and the City of Kyiv[5] and found that, to a considerable extent, the inertia of regional authorities' decision-making undermined Ukraine's transition. Based on data analysis of the expert survey, I identified the factors that could help overcome this inertia, increasing regional authorities' ability to problem-solve and accommodate public needs during the implementation of the decentralization reform, and thus foster regional development.

---

4 *Rehional'nyy rozvytok ta derzhavna rehional'na polityka v Ukrayini: Stan i perspektyvy zmin u konteksti hlobal'nykh vyklykiv ta yevropeys'kykh standartiv polityky* (Kyiv: EU SURDP, 2013).

5 A detailed description of the experts surveyed is presented in Appendix C. The survey was conducted anonymously online, using questionnaires designed with Google Form (https://docs.google.com/forms/d/1mXYQRgjMo1Q73w XLe3cHjgt7CkIdeDfdoZBZGGFRAA/); experts could not change their answers once they completed the questionnaire. The questionnaire contained four questions about the expert (their region, professional work area, education, and gender) and 43 questions about the matter under investigation.

Post-2014 Regional Development: Challenges and Opportunities

The post-Euromaidan decentralization reform had several objectives, including fostering Ukraine's spatial development. Local self-government, state regional policy, and administrative and territorial division reforms have shifted responsibilities from the statewide level to substate levels. Most significantly, strategic planning of the country's regional development has been institutionalized.

In 2014-2015, Ukraine approved the Law "On the Principles of State Regional Policy" and the State Strategy for Regional Development-2020 (SSRD-2020), thus establishing the legal framework for implementing Ukraine's regional policy. The SSRD-2020's priority was "territorial socioeconomic integration and spatial development".[6] The implementation of some regulatory acts critical for Ukraine's spatial development were delayed; however, the strategic planning system for regional development was established, and the sources for the financing of regional projects (through the mechanism of the State Fund for Regional Development [SFRD]) were identified. Starting in 2015-2016, regions were allocated funds to carry out regional development projects according to the formula (not based on bargaining or loyalty to the central authorities). Thus, SFRD had a positive impact on economic activities in the regions. However, its contribution should not be exaggerated. In 2015-2016, up to 25 percent of SFRD applications were rejected due to noncompliance with the government requirements. None of Ukraine's regions was able to use the full annual quota of the allocated funding. In 2015, the Zaporizhia region made use of only 56 percent of the available SFRD funding. In 2015, of the 876 projects initiated, only 532, or 60.7 percent, were fully implemented.[7] Moreover, the Law "On the State Budget of Ukraine for 2017" allocated UAH3.2 billion (see Appendix D) to implement SFRD programs and projects: UAH1 billion from the general fund and UAH2.5 billion from the

---

6 "Pro zatverdzhennya Derzhavnoyi stratehiyi rehional'noho rozvytku na period do 2020 roku", Postanova KMU vid 06.08.2014 № 385, *Uryadovyy kur'yer*, no. 160 (2014). http://zakon4.rada.gov.ua/laws/show/385-2014-%D0%BF.
7 Ibid.

special fund. In December 2016, when the State Budget of Ukraine was approved, Article 24-1 of the Budget Code of Ukraine was amended, opening the system of regional development planning and financing to question.

In 2014, intermunicipal cooperation was introduced. This mechanism gave municipalities additional opportunities to pool their resources to solve various socioeconomic problems. By summer 2016, approximately 50 intermunicipal cooperation agreements were signed: 20 in the Poltava region, 10 in the Ivano-Frankivsk region, five in the Chernihiv region, three in the Cherkassy region, two in the Khmelmytsk region, and one each in the Vinnytsia, Zhytomyr, and Dnipropetrovsk regions.[8]

Additionally, investment subventions contributed to economic activity in the regions (in accordance with the "subventions for fulfillment of programs [projects]" of the Budget Code of Ukraine). Economic activity was facilitated due to public procuremenst "since they facilitate the activity of enterprises that are system-forming for the regional economy and important for the functioning of all industry".[9]

International investment projects made an important positive difference. These included the International Bank for Reconstruction and Development's road-building and urban infrastructure projects, the European Investment Bank's support for the Program to upgrade Ukraine's municipal infrastructure, and the German KfW Development Bank's unbound financial loan to meet the needs of the power industry and infrastructure. In each case, the amount exceeded EUR300 million.[10] International technical aid increased over time (Figure 7.1).[11] In 2016, U-LEAD with Europe and the USAID-funded DOBRE were launched. They had a positive

---

8   Alla Pavlyuk, *Napryamy aktyvizatsiyi zaprovadzhenyan mekhanizmu spirobitnytstva terytorial'nykh hromad* (Kyiv: NISS, 2016). http://www.niss.gov.ua/content/articles/files/AZ-Sp-vrob-tnitstvo-TG-d2e37.pdf.
9   *Ekonomika rehioniv u 2015 rotsi: Novi realiyi i mozhlyvosti v umovakh zapochatkovanykh reform*, (Kyiv: NISS, 2015).
10 http://openaid.gov.ua/uk/
11 "Agreement on Financing of the Sector Policy Support—Support for Ukraine's Regional Policy (Contract for the Sector Reform)", *LigaZakon*, 27 November 2014. http://search.ligazakon.ua/l_doc2.nsf/link1/MU14212.html.

impact on local communities' economic development and on local amalgamation.

Figure 7.1. Total number of international technical assistance projects in Ukraine for years, pcs. (as of April 2017).

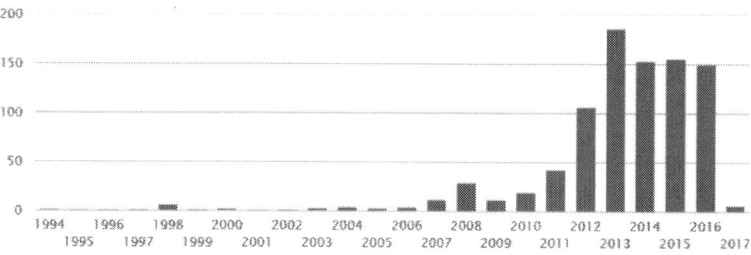

Source: Openaid.gov.ua, 2017.

Yet this positive input had its limits. In 2017, Ukraine displayed regional economic disparities. The post-2014 decentralization reform prioritized voluntary local amalgamation, also it emphasized local development rather than regional development.[12] The challenges that impaired regional development could be hidden from view in Ukraine' policy documents, because issues of local development could overshadow them. "A characteristic feature (maybe even the main line of Ukraine's regional developmental policy) is that disproportion between regions has been concealed behind the problem of local depression".[13] This was evidenced by the Law "On the Stimulation of Regional Development" (Art. 11) and the government's respective procedure.[14] In addition, post-decentralization reform led to the redistribution of tax revenues in favor of local budgets, and this had negative implications for regional budgets.

---

12 Ihor Dunayev, Publychna rehionalna ekonomichna polityka v Ukraini: Formuvannya mechnaizmov modernizatsii (Kharkiv: Magister, 2017).
13 *Podolannya dysproportsiy u rozvytku rehioniv v Ukrayini: Vyklyky ta mozhlyvosti* (Kyiv: EU SURDP, 2015).
14 "Pro zatverdzhennya Poryadku zdiysnennya monitorynhu sotsial'no-ekonomichnykh pokaznykiv rozvytku rehioniv, rayoniv ta mist oblasnoho, respublikans'koho v Avtonomniy Respublitsi Krym znachennya dlya vyznannya terytoriy depresyvnymy", Postanova KMU vid 02.03.2010 № 235, *Uryadovyy kur'yer*, no. 54 (2010).

The 2017 expert survey demonstrated that obtaining resources to achieve the goals declared in regional development strategies (regional socioeconomic development strategies) was challenging (36.4 percent), and regional authorities often made few efforts to engage and address this issue accordingly (38.6 percent) (Figure 7.2).

Figure 7.2. Experts' responses to the survey question: "What issues have the most negative impact on regional bodies' adaptation to their enhanced role and responsibilities in the course of decentralization?", in %.

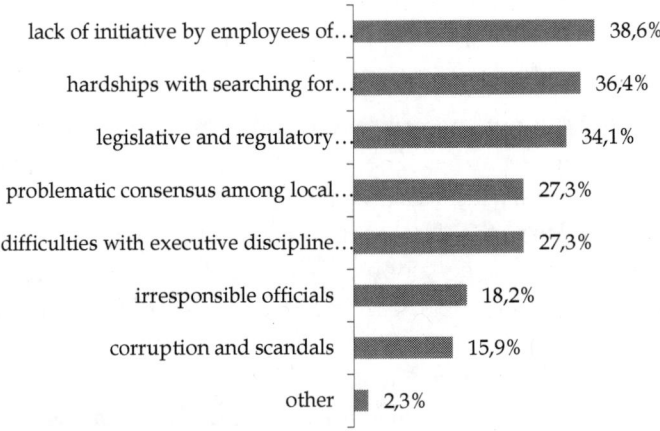

Issue	%
lack of initiative by employees of…	38,6%
hardships with searching for…	36,4%
legislative and regulatory…	34,1%
problematic consensus among local…	27,3%
difficulties with executive discipline…	27,3%
irresponsible officials	18,2%
corruption and scandals	15,9%
other	2,3%

Source: Dunayev, Publychna rehionalna ekonomichna polityka v Ukraini.

Most regional socioeconomic development strategies neglected the tasks of spatial integration and interregional cooperation. Often, regional development strategies prioritized "exclusively their own [regional] issues, without any attention to interregional cooperation".[15] According to the 2017 expert survey, interregional cooperation was often neglected due to regional authorities' low institutional capacity to adapt to changes (47.7 percent), a lack of understanding of the advantages of interregional cooperation (43.2

---

15 Olha Shevchenko, *Onovlennya rehional'nykh stratehiy zadlya zabezpechennya stabil'noho rozvytku* (Kyiv: NISS, 2016). https://niss.gov.ua/sites/default/files/2016-11/region_strategy-26d31.pdf.

percent), and contradictions between regional interest groups (40.9 percent) (Figure 7.3.).

Figure 7.3. Experts' responses to the survey question: "What prevents a region from benefiting from intraregional and interregional cooperation/integration?", in %.

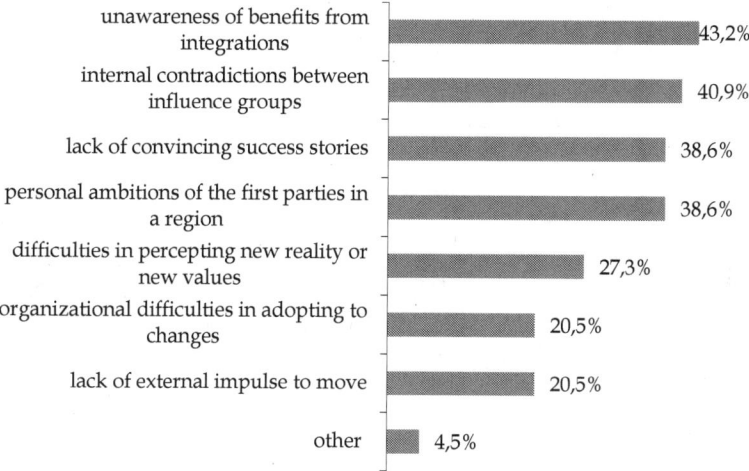

- unawareness of benefits from integrations — 43,2%
- internal contradictions between influence groups — 40,9%
- lack of convincing success stories — 38,6%
- personal ambitions of the first parties in a region — 38,6%
- difficulties in percepting new reality or new values — 27,3%
- organizational difficulties in adopting to changes — 20,5%
- lack of external impulse to move — 20,5%
- other — 4,5%

Source: Dunayev, Publychna rehionalna ekonomichna polityka v Ukraini.

Regional authorities rarely prioritized the promotion of regional development. The 2017 expert survey showed (Figure 7.4) that over half of the respondents (56.8 percent) said that only 15.9 percent of experts believed that "achievement of development goals, defined by regional strategies" were actually a priority for regional authorities. This is striking because, in 2014-2015, regional authorities in every region approved the regional development strategy, along with its operational plan. This was an official requirement; regional development strategies had to be synchronized, to some extent, with all Ukrainian regional development policy documents.

Regional socioeconomic development strategies were revised mostly as a result of growing pressure from the central executive authorities, who attempted to establish a unified system for the strategic planning and forecasting of regional and local development. This can be observed in the government's methodological recommendations regarding regional strategy implementation plans[16] and the information campaign directed at regional executives (regional state administrations) about how to implement these plans. While doing that, the central executive authorities were supported in this by international technical aid, including the EU-funded "Support to Ukraine's Regional Development Policy" project (2011-2017).

Figure 7.4. Experts' responses to the survey question: "What do regional authorities mostly incline to?", in %.

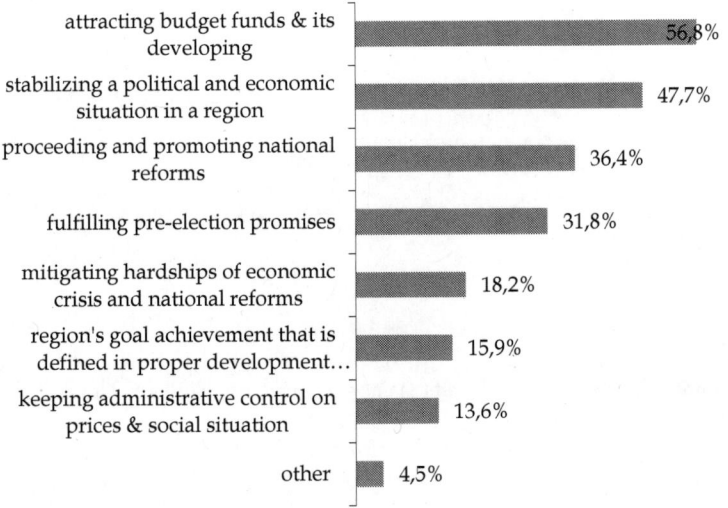

Source: The 2017 expert survey.

The 2017 expert survey revealed a lack of proactive decision-making at the regional level (Figure 7.5-A). Moreover, over half (56.8 percent) of the respondents believed that the solutions and/or decisions offered by regional authorities were designed to mitigate the consequences of various issues rather than to address the issues (Figure 7.5-B). This proved that achieving regional developmental

---

16 "Pro zatverdzhennya Metodiki rozroblennya, provedennya monitoringu ta otsinki rezul'tativnosti realizatsii regional'nikh strategiy rozvitku ta planiv zakhodiv z ih realizatsii", Nakaz Minregionu Ukrainy vid 31.03.2016 № 79, *Ofitsiyniy visnik Ukrainy, 17.05.2016.* - № 36, stor. 368, stattya 1422, kod aktu 81826/2016.

goals, as defined by regional strategies, was hardly a priority for regional authorities (see Figure 7.4).

Figure 7.5. Experts' responses to the survey questions:

A) "Do you think that the decisions of regional authorities are made on time or delayed?", in %.

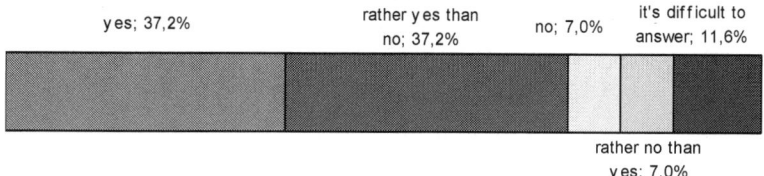

B) "Do you think that regional authorities' decisions are focused on mitigation more than on preventing negative phenomena?", in %.

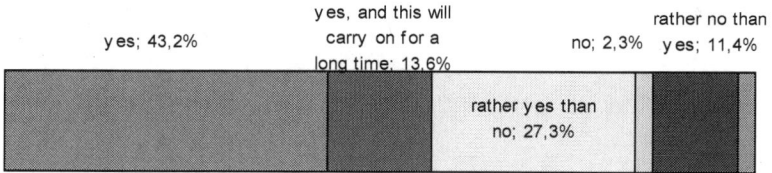

Source: The 2017 expert survey.

Regional purpose-oriented programs were frequently out of date and uncoordinated. For instance, the ones in the Kharkiv region were not based on up-to-date data and did not contain a middle- and long-term vision of the future of Ukraine and the region. There was no register of such programs, and no estimate was made of the expected consequences for Ukraine as a whole. This complicated the planning process and the implementation of the government's sectoral policies.

The lack of proactive decision-making at the regional level is explained by a variety of economic, political, communication, and sociocultural causes. According to the 2017 expert survey, giving regional councils more responsibilities and allowing them to establish their own executive committees could stimulate regional authorities to be more active in decision-making (in total, over 50 percent; points "5" and "4", Figure 7.6). Notably, the surveyed experts believed that the 2020 regional elections could have a positive effect on regional authorities' capacity to perform their duties (approximately 60 percent in total; Figure 7.6).

Figure 7.6. Aggregated results of experts' assessment of economic and political impact factors that could help overcome inertia in decision-making at the regional level, in %.

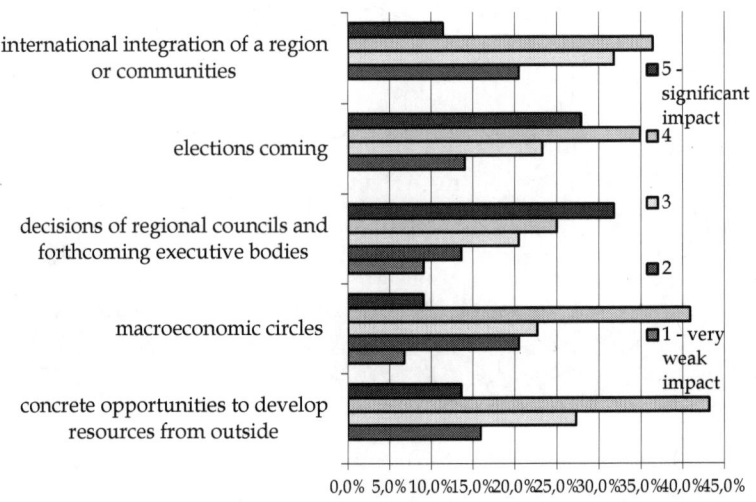

Source: The 2017 expert survey.

Additionally, the surveyed experts believed that striking the right balance between regional interest groups and fostering cooperation with international partners could help overcome inertia in decision-making at the regional level (Figure 7.7).

Figure 7.7. Aggregated results of experts' assessment of social and communication impact factors that could help overcome inertia in decision-making at the regional level, in %.

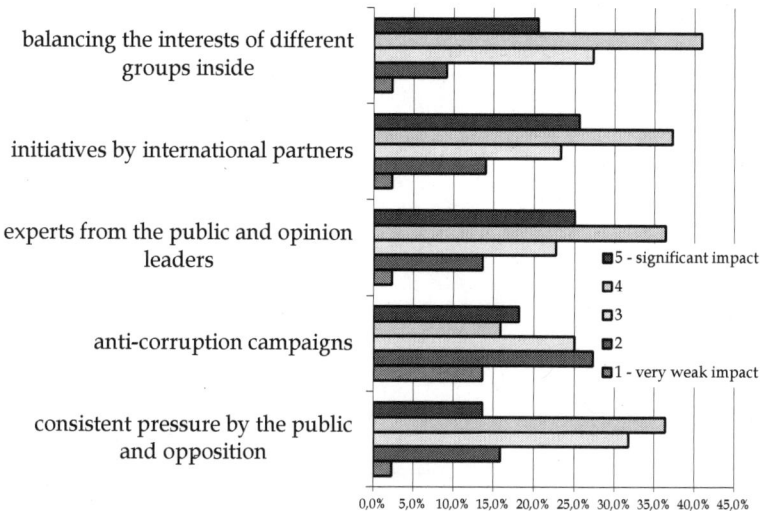

Source: The 2017 expert survey.

Decentralization lays bare the conflicts of interest among local elites and between the branches and levels of local power (state administrations and the councils of different levels). The majory of respondents to the 2017 expert survey supported this contention, specifically mentioning these types of conflicts (70.5 percent and 47.7 percent, respectively; Figure 7.8). These conflicts all have the same origin: competition for influence and power. Such competition erects a barrier to reaching elite consensus at the regional level.

Figure 7.8. Respondents' answers to the survey question: "What contradictions and conflicts are most evident at the regional level during the implementation of decentralization reforms?", in %.

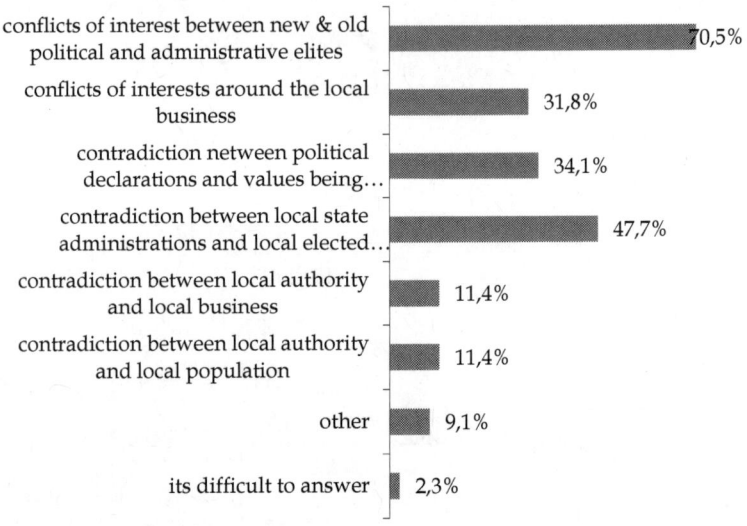

Source: The 2017 expert survey.

Yet, despite these concerns, the surveyed experts expected that regional authorities would make a greater effort to promote regional development, and that regions would increase their input into Ukraine's economy in the future (Figure 7.9). The majority of experts (95.5 percent) recognized that assuming responsibility over their own economic development was very important for regions; however, almost half of the respondents (45.5 percent) did not believe that regions would all be better off in the short run, primarily because of great regional disparities.

Figure 7.9. Experts' responses to the survey question: "In the next 3-5 years, can Ukrainian regions change their economic agenda so that they could realize their own potential to the full and become self-sufficient?", in %

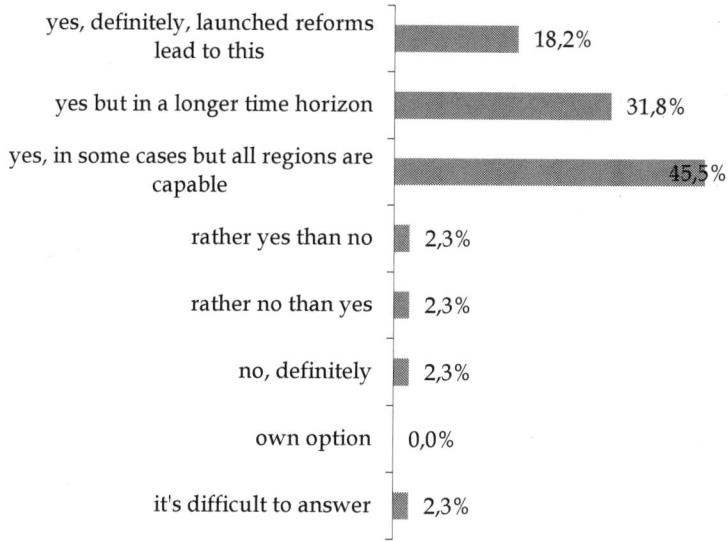

Source: The 2017 expert survey.

This implies that the central government and regional authorities should both make an effort to reduce regional disparities by fostering interregional cooperation.

Conclusions

This brief study has highlighted a number of challenges to Ukraine's transition to a decentralized model of regional development, but it has also identified several opportunities that could amplify its scope. Thus far, regional authorities have not made use of the institutional opportunities at their disposal (i.e., regional development strategies) to foster interregional cooperation and exploit their potential to boost regional development. Arguably, regional authorities tend to prioritize urgent issues rather than long-term development because of a lack of expertise and funding.

Starting in 2014-2015, the central government and the national parliament adopted the "State Strategy for Regional Development until 2020", the regulatory documents critical for Ukraine's spatial development, and significantly enhanced the operation of the State Fund for Regional Development. Regional authorities adopted regional development strategies and their corresponding performance plans; this was expected to contribute to the implementation of the State Strategy for Regional Development until 2020.

In practice, a decentralized model of regional development can function only when regional authorities perform their duties well. Until now, regional authorities have appeared to underperform, demonstrating a lack of engagement in fostering regional development and promoting interregional cooperation. Yet, to positively contribute to Ukraine's economic development, it is critical for regional authorities to proactively revise their regional development strategies so as to adapt to changing circumstances, identify adequate drivers of economic growth at the regional level, and foster interregional cooperation.

Appendix A

Table A-1. Gross regional product (GRP) in 2012-2014 (in actual prices, in UAH)

Region	Years					
	2012		2013		2014	
	GRP, mln UAH	GRP per capita, UAH	GRP, mln UAH	GRP per capita, UAH	GRP, mln UAH	GRP per capita, UAH
Ukraine	1 459 096	32 002	1 522 657	33 473	1 586 915	36 904
AR Crimea	44536	22675	46393	23595	...	...
Cherkasy	31265	24558	33087	26168	38466	30628
Chernihiv	23934	22096	24237	22603	28156	26530
Chernivtsy	13166	14529	13757	15154	15049	16552
Dnipropetrovsk	147970	44650	152905	46333	176540	53749
Donetsk	170775	38907	164926	37830	119983	27771
Ivano-Frankivsk	32286	23379	33196	24022	37643	27232
Kharkiv	82223	29972	85315	31128	96596	35328
Kherson	19357	17910	20767	19311	23250	21725
Khmelnitsky	26237	19920	26426	20165	32162	24662
Kyiv	69663	40483	68931	39988	79561	46058
Kyrovohrad	22056	22082	25313	25533	28758	29223
Luhansk	58767	25950	55108	24514	31393	14079
Lviv	61962	24387	63329	24937	72923	28731
Mykolaiv	29205	24838	32030	27355	35408	30357
Odesa	64743	27070	69760	29118	74934	31268
Poltava	56580	38424	58464	39962	69831	48040
Rivne	21795	18860	22004	19003	28724	24762
Sumy	24933	21722	26765	23517	30397	26943
Ternopil	17957	16644	18085	16819	21676	20228
Vinnytsya	33024	20253	36191	22303	43990	27249
Volyn	20005	19249	20622	19817	24195	23218

Region	Years					
	2012		2013		2014	
	GRP, mln UAH	GRP per capita, UAH	GRP, mln UAH	GRP per capita, UAH	GRP, mln UAH	GRP per capita, UAH
Zakarpatska	21404	17088	21400	17044	24120	19170
Zaporizhzhia	54828	30656	54352	30526	65968	37251
Zhytomyr	24849	19551	25676	20286	29815	23678
Kyiv city	275685	97429	312552	109402	357377	124163
Sevastopol city	9891	25872	11066	28765	...	...

Source: *Valovyy rehional'nyy produkt za 2014 rik. Statystychnyy zbirnyk,* State Committee of Statistics of Ukraine (K.: DSSU, 2016).

Appendix B

Table B-1. Comparative calculations of per capita GRP in the regions with the lowest and highest values before the commencement of the active phase of decentralization in Ukraine (in actual prices, in UAH)

Group A «Regions with the smallest GRP per capita»				Group B «Regions with the biggest GRP per capita»			
Region	2012	2013	2014	Region	2012	2013	2014
Volyn	19249	19817	23218	Dnipropetrovsk	44650	46333	53749
Zakarpatska	17088	17044	19170	Zaporizhzhia	30656	30526	37251
Rivne	18860	19003	24762	Kyiv	40483	39988	46058
Ternopil	16644	16819	20228	Poltava	38424	39962	48040
Chernivtsy	14529	15154	16552	Kyiv city	97429	109402	124163
Totally a year	86370	87837	103930	Totally a year	251642	266211	309261
Annual arithmetic mean	17274	17567,4	20786	Annual arithmetic mean	50328,4	53242,2	61852,2
Summarized share in total Ukraine's GRP per capita	0,5397	0,5248	0,5632	Summarized share in total Ukraine's GRP per capita	1,5726	1,5906	1,6760
Rate of change relatively to previous year	0	0,9722	1,0732	Rate of change relatively to previous year	0	1,0114	1,0537
Difference between groups B and A, times	-	-	-		2,91	3,03	2,97

Source: Author's calculations on the basis of 2014 GRP (See: Valovyy rehional'nyy produkt za 2014 rik. Statystychnyy zbirnyk, State Committee of Statistics of Ukraine [K.: DSSU, 2016]).

Appendix C

Figure. A-1. Geographical origins of the 44 experts surveyed.

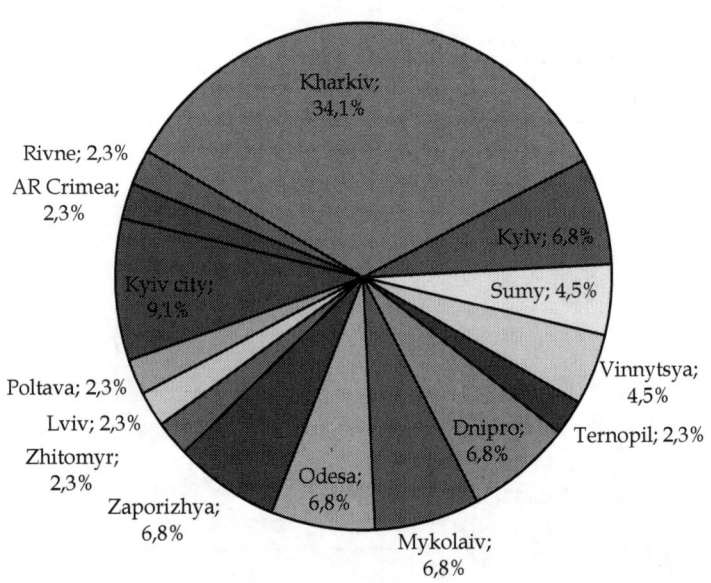

Figure. A-2. Occupations of the 44 experts surveyed.

Figure A-3.   Education and gender of the 44 experts surveyed.

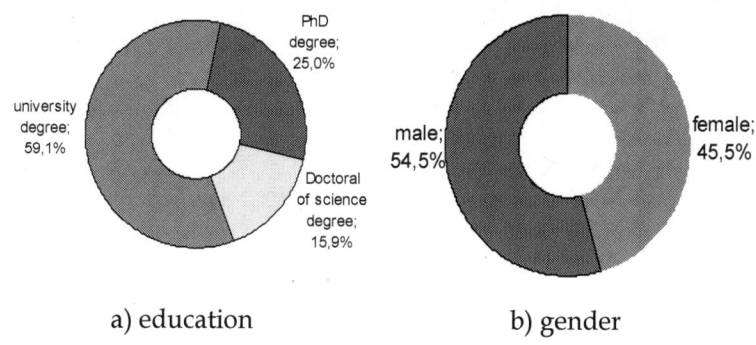

a) education   b) gender

Appendix D.

Table D-1. An indicative distribution of the 2015-2017 State Fund for Regional Development (SFRD) funds in the regions, in thousands, in UAH

Region	Total SFRD-2015	Total SFRD-2016	SFRD-2017		
			Total	Special fund	General fund
Cherkasy	67 882,397	69 814,668	81 135,275	57 953,768	23 181,507
Chernihiv	98 013,201	91 891,034	112 553,559	80 395,399	32 158,160
Chernivtsy	83 467,947	79 865,421	98 655,738	70 468,384	28 187,354
Dnipropetrovsk	177 385,503	182 776,081	212 628,496	151 877,497	60 750,999
Donetsk	234 034,273	239 472,083	279 137,355	199 383,825	79 753,530
Ivano-Frankivsk	126978,207	121 357,217	149 822,742	107 016,244	42 806,498
Kharkiv	147 473,721	152 580,074	177 708,126	126 934,376	50 773,750
Kherson	98 540,647	93 363,716	114 753,812	81 967,009	32 786,803
Khmelnitsky	120 078,128	113 751,317	139 812,459	99 866,042	39 946,417
Kyiv	92 963,158	97 127,050	113 932,914	81 380,653	32 552,261
Kyrovohrad	90 731,203	54 670,869	63 599,014	45 427,867	18 171,147
Luhansk	120 655,542	193 732,147	238 543,309	170 388,078	68 155,231
Lviv	136 762,698	222 523,776	166 561,277	118 972,341	47 588,936
Mykolaiv	62 948,094	65 042,205	75 692,949	54 066,392	21 626,557
Odesa	129 115,270	134 097,041	156 838,407	112 027,434	44 810,973
Poltava	78 563,356	80 805,895	93 889,333	67 063,809	26 825,524
Rivne	106 467,872	101986,188	126 104,588	90 074,706	36 029,882
Sumy	104 088,896	97 861,450	120 089,735	85 778,382	34 311,353

Region	Total SFRD-2015	Total SFRD-2016	SFRD-2017		
			Total	Special fund	General fund
Ternopil	98 610,470	93 602,434	115 198,292	82 284,494	32 913,798
Vinnytsya	148 675,639	140 797,317	172 989,068	123 563,620	49 425,448
Volyn	95 668,309	91 525,233	113 128,831	80 806,308	32 322,523
Zakarpatska	115 471,399	110 538,624	136 726,612	97 661,866	39 064,746
Zaporizhzhia	95 676,122	98 472,615	114 501,389	81 786,706	32 714,683
Zhytomyr	115991,588	109 637,111	134 971,054	96 407,896	38 563,158
Kyiv city	154 556,360	162 708,434	191 025,666	136 446,904	54 578,762
Total	2 900 800	3 000 000	3 500 000	2 500 000	1 000 000

8. Spatial Planning in Ukraine's Sustainable Development and European Integration*
The National, Regional, and Local Levels

Yuriy Palekha

This chapter explains how administrative-territorial reform and decentralization changed spatial planning in Ukraine. It examines the structure of spatial planning documentation, including the General Planning Scheme of the territory of Ukraine and a detailed plan of the territory. The Law "On Amendments to Certain Legislative Acts of Ukraine Regarding Land Use Planning", adopted in 2020, introduced a new type of documentation—a comprehensive plan for the spatial development of territorial community territory.[1] The newly established amalgamated territorial communities (ATCs) require spatial planning documentation at the central, regional, and local levels.

This chapter details the new types of urban planning documentation associated with the planning of functional regions, including cross-border regions. The development of these projects will create opportunities for local authorities to master the planning tools used in the European Union (EU) and will contribute to the sustainable development of territorial communities. This chapter argues that the urban planning documentation developed in Ukraine in recent years benefits from hierarchical interconnectedness, and the chapter claims that this advantage should be preserved during the implementation of the urban planning reform.

---

* An early version of this chapter was presented at the webinar "Local Government in Ukraine: Formation, Reforms, Geopolitical Implications and Postwar Recovery", *IGU Commission on Geography of Governance*, 6 June 2022. https://sites.google.com/view/lgukraine2022/home.

1 Zakon Ukrayiny, "Pro vnesennya zmin do deyakykh zakonodavchykh aktiv Ukrayiny shchodo planuvannya vykorystannya zemel", vid 17 serpnya 2020 r., *Verkhovna Rada Ukrainy*, 17 August 2020. https://zakon.rada.gov.ua/laws/show/711-20#Text.

The chapter outlines the institutional changes that can help Ukraine meet EU spatial planning standards and requirements.

Introduction

Ukraine's administrative-territorial system was formed in the time of the Soviet Union according to a centralized command-administrative principle. The system of spatial planning ("urban planning" or "urban planning documentation" was the term in Soviet times) reflected this centralized approach and was directed to the development of urban planning documentation for a period of five, 10, or 20 years.

We cannot say that the development of urban planning documentation in the Ukrainian Soviet Socialist Republic was ineffective. Its main positive features were a hierarchical and sequential implementation. First, planning documentation was developed and approved at the state level, then at the regional level, and finally at the local level. It was impossible to develop a detailed plan of the territory without a master plan of the city; and, before this master plan could be devised, it was necessary to develop a regional and district territorial planning scheme. The State Building Regulations were responsible for the normative issues regarding the development of urban planning documentation.[2]

After Ukraine regained its independence, it became necessary to change the system of spatial planning. This happened rather slowly. Although the *Verkhovna Rada*, Ukraine's parliament, adopted the necessary laws[3] and the Ministry responsible for spatial development approved the rules governing the planning and

---

2 "Mistobuduvannya: Planuvannya i zabudova mis'kykh i sil's'kykh poselen", *Minrehion Ukrainy*, 2002. https://dbn.co.ua/load/normativy/dbn/dbn_360_9 2_ua/1-1-0-116.
3 Zakon Ukrayiny "Pro osnovy mistobuduvannya" vid 16 lystopada 1992 r., *Verkhovna Rada Ukrainy*, 16 November 1992. https://zakon.rada.gov.ua/laws/show/2780-12#Text; Zakon Ukrayiny «Pro arkhitekturnu diyal'nist'» vid 20 travnya 1999 r., *Verkhovna Rada Ukrainy*, 20 May 1999. https://zakon.rada.gov.ua/laws/show/687-14#Text; Zakon Ukrayiny «Pro rehulyuvannya mistobudivnoyi diyal'nosti» vid 17 lyutoho 2011 r., *Verkhovna Rada Ukrainy*, 17 February 2011. https://zakon.rada.gov.ua/laws/show/3038-17#Text.

development of settlements and territories,[4] the core of spatial planning did not change much, remaining too centralized, insufficiently transparent and undemocratic. The interests of individual people and local communities were not sufficiently taken into account, and public discussions were largely lacking.

Spatial planning reform first required revolutionary changes to the system of state administration and to Ukraine's administrative-territorial organization. These changes were introduced after the 2013-2014 Revolution of Dignity. The Law "On Voluntary Amalgamation of Territorial Communities"[5] played an important part. The formation of new territorial units (ATCs) and the reorganization of administrative districts forced the Ukrainian leadership to reorganize spatial planning documentation, harmonizing the content with generally recognized European requirements, and ensuring the sustainable development of both regions and localities. At the same time, it was important to preserve the principle of hierarchy concerning urban planning documents.

Overview of the Spatial Planning System in Ukraine

According to the Law "On the Regulation of Urban Development",[6] Ukraine has three hierarchical levels of spatial planning documentation: national (the General Planning Scheme of the Territory of Ukraine and planning schemes of the parts of the country); regional (planning schemes for the territories of regions and districts) and local (master plans of settlements, detailed plans of territories,

---

4 "Planuvannya ta zabudova terytoriy": DBN B.2.2-12:2019, *Minregion Ukrainy*, Kyiv, 2019. https://dbn.co.ua/load/normativy/dbn/b_2_2_12/1-1-0-1802; "Sklad ta zmist mistobudivnoyi dokumentatsiyi na derzhavnomu ta rehional'nomu rivnyakh": DBN B.1.1-13:2012, *Minregion Ukrainy*, Kyiv, 2012. h ttps://dbn.co.ua/load/normativy/dbn/1-1-0-1025; "Sklad ta zmist heneral'noho planu naselenoho punktu": DBN B.1.1-15:2012, *Minregion Ukrainy*, Kyiv, 2012. https://dbn.co.ua/load/normativy/dbn/1-1-0-1040.
5 Zakon Ukrayiny "Pro dobrovil'ne ob'ednannya terytorial'nykh hromad" vid 05 lyutoho 2015 r. *Verkhovna Rada Ukrainy*, 20 February 2015. https://zakon.rada.g ov.ua/laws/show/157-19#Text.
6 Zakon Ukrayiny "Pro rehulyuvannya mistobudivnoyi diyal'nosti" vid 17 lyutoho 2011 r., *Verkhovna Rada Ukrainy*, 17 February 2011. https://zakon.rada. gov.ua/laws/show/3038-17#Text.

comprehensive plans for the spatial development of territories of territorial communities) (Figure 8.1.). This system allows for the formation of common standpoints and the integration of spatial planning at the national, regional, and local levels.

Figure 8.1. The hierarchical levels of spatial planning documentation in Ukraine.

At the national level, the main document is the General Planning Scheme of the Territory of Ukraine, approved by the 2002 Law.[7] This document defines conceptual decisions regarding the planning and rational use of Ukrainian territory, the creation and maintenance of a favorable living environment, the protection of the natural environment and of historical and cultural monuments, and sets out state priorities for the development of settlement systems and social and transportation infrastructure.

---

7   Zakon Ukrayiny "Pro Heneral'nu skhemu planuvannya terytoriyi Ukrayiny" vid 7 lyutoho 2002 r., *Verkhovna Rada Ukrainy*, 7 February 2002. https://zakon.rada.gov.ua/laws/show/3059-14#Text.

The General Scheme includes 27 individual schemes that cover various aspects of the spatial development of Ukraine. Of these, the perspective planning structure map that reflects the types of preferential use of certain territories, the map of settlement systems, the spatial organization of the national eco-network map, and the transport system map deserve special attention (Map 8.1.). The General Scheme has great importance for regional and local territorial community development. It establishes the requirements and priorities that must be taken into account when planning at the local level. This concerns first of all international transport corridor routes, integrated into the TIN system,[8] the location of the National Ecological Network (Emerald Network of Ukraine) objects,[9] integrated into the European NATURA 2000 system, the location of large energy and industrial enterprises, etc.

---

8   Yurii Palekha, "New edition of the General Scheme of planning of the territory of Ukraine – strategy of integration of Ukraine in the European space", *Ukrainian Geographical Journal*, no. 1 (2020): 7-15.
9   Zakon Ukrayiny "Pro ekomerezhu Ukrayiny" vid 24 chervnya 2004 r. *Verkhovna Rada Ukrainy*, 24 June 2004. https://zakon.rada.gov.ua/laws/show/1864-15#Text.

Map 8.1.   The General Planning Scheme of the Territory of Ukraine: The Transportation System.

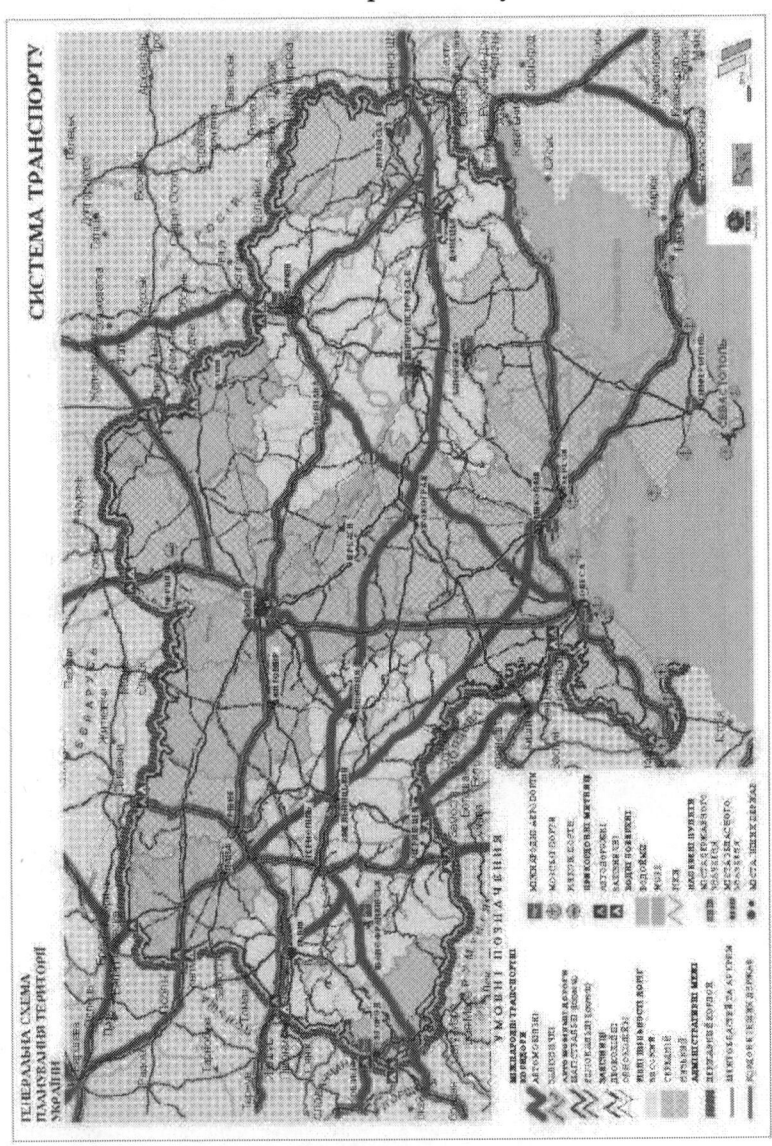

Note: International transport corridor routes are marked in purple.

The Russian Federation's military aggression against Ukraine requires the fastest possible approval of a new General Scheme, one which will present the principal measures to be taken for the spatial development of Ukraine after victory over the enemy. The major changes of the General Scheme should include:

- Determination of Ukraine's postwar spatial framework, taking into account integration into the European Union planning space;
- Development of a transport scheme, taking into account changes in the direction of transport corridors;
- Replacement of the energy supply system, taking into account the refusal to use Russian energy carriers and the active development of renewable energy technologies (green transition);
- Optimization of the economic complex structure and drafting proposals for the location of individual production enterprises, taking into account the partial relocation of production to the western region, as well as the need to renovate and diversify production in the eastern region;
- Optimization of the settlement system, taking into account the migration, displacement, and partial redistribution of the population in the territory of Ukraine;
- Development of measures to ensure ecological stabilization of the territory of Ukraine, and neutralization of the consequences of military operations;
- Determination of the the development strategies of large cities and urban agglomerations in new conditions.

The new (postwar) General Scheme should be developed as soon as possible on a new technological and methodological basis using modern Geographic Information System (GIS) technologies.

According to Ukrainian law, in addition to the General Scheme, planning schemes for individual parts of the territory of Ukraine are also developed at the state level; they fit into geographical rather than administrative criteria. These include planning schemes for the Black and Azov sea coasts; the mountainous territories of the Carpathians; territories that have suffered radioactive contamination from the Chernobyl disaster, as well as other territories with an increased technogenic load or at risk of emergencies; cross-border regions; and international transport corridor zones of influence. Planning issues affecting this type of regions will be discussed in the section on planning functional regions.

Territorial planning schemes (for the Autonomous Republic of Crimea and Ukraine's 24 regions) are developed at the regional level. There were 490 such schemes before the post-2014 administrative-territorial reform.

Regional planning schemes unite the General Planning Scheme of the Territory of Ukraine, the planning schemes of individual parts of the territory of Ukraine, and the planning of ATCs. Regional state administrations are in charge of the implementation of regional territorial planning schemes. Additionally, these must comply with urban planning requirements and restrictions regarding the location of individual production facilities, the construction of transport and engineering networks, and the development of recreational areas.

Between 2002 and 2020, planning schemes for all regions except for the Kyiv region were developed. DIPROMISTO developed the majority of planning schemes (23); the planning scheme of the sole remaining region (the Sumy region) was developed by the Research and Design Institute of Urban Planning. At present, due to changes in the legislative framework, the planning schemes of some regions need to be revised.

The main planning tools for regulating building construction outside of settlements are the area district planning schemes. Before the introduction of ATC territorial planning schemes, this type of documentation functioned as a connecting link between regional territorial planning schemes and settlement master plans. Over the past 25 years, only 82 district planning schemes (16.8 percent of the total)[10] were developed in Ukraine, indicating a lack of interest on the part of the district authorities.

---

10 "Dopovid' Kabinetu Ministriv Ukrayiny pro stan realizatsiyi Heneral'noyi skhemy planuvannya terytoriyi Ukrayiny za 2019 rik", *Minregion Ukrainy*, 2020. https://www.minregion.gov.ua/wp-content/uploads/2020/12/na_22_12_2020_dopovid-kmu.-monitoryng-gsptu-2019.pdf.

SPATIAL PLANNING AND EUROPEAN INTEGRATION   213

Decentralization led to the consolidation of district territories, approximately tripling the size of the districts, and reducing their number from 490 to 135. Some district functions were transferred to ATCs, others were transferred to the regional level.

The following three examples illustrate the importance of spatial planning documentation.

First, consider the Planning Scheme of the Transcarpathian Region, which defines the route of International Cretan Transport Corridor No. 5. The direction of this corridor is determined by the General Planning Scheme of the Territory of Ukraine. However, in the Territory Planning Scheme of the Transcarpathian region, this direction is defined on a greater scale, taking into account the location of individual settlements, elements of the nature reserve fund, and the locally important networks of roads. It forecasts that, in the future, a tunnel will be built through the Carpathian ridge. This transport highway will cross several European countries and positively affect the development of local communities in the Transcarpathian region. Notably, the master plans of the Transcarpathian cities of Mukacheve and Berehove developed their prospective planning structures taking into account Cretan Transport Corridor No. 5.

Second, consider the Planning Scheme of the territory of the Poltava region, where several new industrial iron ore extraction enterprises are planned. The location of these enterprises will impact the development of the surrounding territorial communities. Proposals for new residential areas, social service centers, roads and engineering infrastructure facilities had to locate them so that they had sufficient transport access to the enterprises. It was also necessary to guarantee the environmental safety of the population of the entire region. These factors were initially proposed during the development of the territory planning scheme of the Poltava region's Kremenchuk district and later in the master plans of the city of Kremenchuk and of rural settlements.

Third, consider the location of waste processing plants. This is first determined by the Oblast Territory Planning Scheme before subsequently being specified in the District Territory Planning Schemes. When no proposals are made, a waste processing crisis can affect the entire region; this happened in the city of Lviv a few years ago.[11]

The final stage in the hierarchical spatial planning documentation structure refers to the local level. This level includes three types of documents:

- a comprehensive plan for the spatial development of the territorial community territory;
- a master plan of the settlement;
- a detailed plan of the territory.

The territorial community territory's comprehensive spatial development plan is a new type of spatial planning documentation. It appeared in 2020 after the the Law "On the Regulation of Urban Development" was amended.[12] Decentralization reforms required the introduction of this type of documentation. The new comprehensive plan combines regional level elements (district planning scheme), as well as solutions traditionally included in the master plan of the settlement.

The Resolution of the Cabinet of Ministers of Ukraine "On the approval of the Procedure for the development, updating, amendment and approval of urban planning documentation" specifies the composition of the comprehensive plan; the relevant state building regulations are close to the approval stage.[13] The structure of the

---

11 For Ukrainian commentaries on this, see: Andriy Denisenko, "Samopomich i Bankova mayut sisty za syil peregovoriv", *DNIPROGRAD*, 22 June 2017. https://web.archive.org/web/20170626003130/http://dniprograd.org/2017/06/22/samopomich-i-bankova-mayut-viyti-z-rezhimu-piaru-i-sisti-za-stil-peregovoriv-denisenko_57837; Natalya Gorbal, "Velikiy smitteviy pererozpodil", *Lvivska ratusha*, 12 August 2017. http://ratusha.lviv.ua/index.php?dn=news&to=art&id=1578; "Sadovyj i Sinyutka vs Gribovytske smittyezvalyshe: 10 rokiv porozhnich obitsyanok", *Dyvys.info*, 1 June 2016. https://web.archive.org/web/20170312120232/http://dyvys.info/2016/06/01/sadovyj-vs-grybovytske-s mittyezvalyshhe-10-rokiv-pustyh-obitsyanok-i-zhodnyh-konkretnyh-dij/.
12 Zakon Ukrayiny "Pro rehulyuvannya mistobudivnoyi diyal'nosti" vid 17 lyutoho 2011 r., *Verkhovna Rada Ukrainy*, 17 February 2011. https://zakon.rada.gov.ua/laws/show/3038-17#Text.
13 Rezolyutsiya vid 1 Serpnya 2021 r. № 926 "Pro zatverdzhennya Poryadku rozroblennya, onovlennya, vnesennya zmin ta zatverdzhennya mistobudivnoyi dokumentatsiyi", *Kabinet ministriv Ukrainy*, 1 August 2021. http s://zakon.rada.gov.ua/laws/show/926-2021-%D0%BF#Text.

comprehensive plan makes it a rather complex document, combining strategic issues related to community development and operational issues. A comprehensive plan is a document that addresses architectural issues, land management issues, and landscape planning issues simultaneously. It remains to be seen how local authorities will make use of this document. To date, on the initiative of the USAID agency, comprehensive plans for the spatial development of the territory of the Kharkiv region's Pisochynska and Roganska ATCs have been developed[14] as pilot projects.

For a very long time, the master plan was the main document that determined a settlement's future development for a period of up to 20 years. This is still the case. The master plan's solutions primarily lay out the sustainable development of the settlement. The master plan determines the prospective population size and the social and engineering infrastructure needs, the solution of key urban conflicts, and the best direction for the future development of a city or village. Contemporary opinions regarding the master plan differ from Soviet times. Now, more attention is given to the development of a comfortable urban environment, as well as to participatory issues, and the procedures for public discussions of major development issues. The master plan determines the optimal functional and planning structure of the city and establishes conditions and restrictions for developers. Representatives of the local community influence the social focus of these decisions, taking into account local interests.

When developing a master plan, it is important to take into account the impact of planning decisions of urban planning documentation of a higher hierarchical level, such as the planning scheme of the territory of the region or district, as well as the comprehensive spatial development plan of the community territory (which refers to the same local level but gives more general proposals for the development of a separate settlement).

---

14 Yuliya Davydova, Vita Dubovyk, and Al'ona Ryazantseva, "Dvi gromadi harkivshchini otrimali finansuvannya SShA na rozvitok planu teritorii", *Suspil'ne. Novyny*, 19 September 2021. https://suspilne.media/164880-dvi-gromadi-harkivsini-otrimali-finansuvanna-ssa-na-rozvitok-planu-teritorij/.

The final local level planning stage is the development of the detailed plans of territories. On the basis of the requirements and restrictions defined by the master plan, these involve the configuration of the construction of individual city blocks and microdistricts, the determination of public spaces and green areas, and proposals for the location of individual buildings and structures. As in other cases, residents can actively participate in the development of detailed plans.

The hierarchical relationship of spatial planning is vertical: from the national level to the local level. We see higher-level requirements being incorporated into lower-level projects. Feedback is important: recommendations and opinions expressed at a lower level should be included in higher level planning documentation. This principle resembles the principle of subsidiarity.

Planning and the Development of Functional Areas

Modern spatial planning development in Ukraine is based on the principles of the European Union's Sustainable Development Strategy and on the documents and resolutions of the CEMAT conferences.[15] Let us dwell on the important resolution of the CEMAT conference held in Bucharest in 2017. This conference focused on the development of functional areas and their importance for local authorities. The conference resolution declared that functional areas, represented the capitalization of local potential in territorial development policies across the European continent.

The resolution stated:

> "At [the] European level, there is a variety of functional areas. These can be structured according to the concerned territorial levels. One category is constituted by transnational cooperation or cooperation in macro-regions (including regions from different countries as well as entire national territories, geographically circumscribed areas which in turn convey a certain structure of economic activities). Other categories include regional or local level cooperation areas, functional urban areas (the areas of influence encompassing cities), functional rural areas, cross-border areas (involving a limited number of neighbouring regions from at least two countries with adjacent boundaries), areas sharing specific geographical, natural and/or cultural

---

15 *Kerivni pryntsypy staloho prostorovoho rozvytku Yevropeys'koho kontynentu* (Kyiv, 2017).

features as well as clusters (geographic concentrations of interconnected institutions and companies in a particular field)".[16]

Thus, European states focus on the development of functional, rather than administrative, regions. In addition, this development should be directed to revealing the potential of local communities.

In the legal acts adopted in Ukraine, some regional functional types have already been defined, corresponding to the decisions of the 17th CEMAT Conference. In particular, as described above, the Law "On the Regulation of Urban Development"[17] provides that "territorial planning at the state level is carried out by developing, in accordance with the law, the General Planning Scheme of the Territory of Ukraine, planning schemes of individual parts of the territory of Ukraine, as well as any changes to them".

The State Regional Development Strategy for 2021-2027 introduced new approaches to Ukraine's state regional policy, namely, a "transition to a territorially oriented development policy based on stimulating the use of territories' own potential, providing support to certain territories characterized by special socioeconomic development problems, high historical and cultural potential, ecological conditions and environmental protection needs".[18] The strategy defines the functional types of regions that require "special attention from the state and the use of special mechanisms and tools to stimulate their development: agglomerations, monofunctional cities, rural territorial communities in unfavorable conditions, the mountainous parts of the Ukrainian Carpathians, the Azov-Black Sea macro-region, border territories, the temporarily occupied

---

16 The Council of Europe Conference of Ministers responsible for Spatial/Regional Planning (CEMAT). Resolution no.1 – Functional areas – Capitalisation of local potential in territorial development policies over the European continent. https://rm.c oe.int/the-17th-session-of-the-council-of-europe-conference-of-ministers-resp/168 07670ac.
17 Zakon Ukrayiny "Pro rehulyuvannya mistobudivnoyi diyal'nosti" vid 17 lyutoho 2011 r., *Verkhovna Rada Ukrainy*, 17 February 2011. https://zakon.rada. gov.ua/laws/show/3038-17#Text.
18 Rezolyutsiya vid 5 Serpnya 2020 r. "Pro zatverdzhennya Derzhavnoyi stratehiyi rehional'noho rozvytku na 2021-2027 roky", *Cabinet of Ministers of Ukraine*, 1 August 2020. https://zakon.rada.gov.ua/laws/show/695-2020-%D 0%BF#Text.

territories of Ukraine, natural conservation territories and objects, as well as other types of functional regions".

Increasing the role and importance of the development of functional areas is important for ensuring the sustainable development of Ukraine and of Ukraine's local communities on the path of European integration.[19] For this reason, it is necessary to pay attention to the development of the separate types of spatial planning documentation connected to the functional regional areas.

Planning and the Development of Cross-Border Regions

Cross-border regions that are formed on the borders of several states are functional regions. The formation of such regions and the development of interregional cooperation strengthen the links between European territorial communities and states. In the case of Ukraine, this also stimulates European integration.

There are dozens of cross-border regions in Europe. Starting in the early 1990s, thanks to the efforts of the European Community, long-term programs to integrate the countries of Eastern Europe into the European Union were introduced. Spatial development in the countries of Eastern Europe was supported through special TACIS, MEDA, and PHARE programs.

Ukraine joined seven cross-border regions: Ukraine-Poland, Ukraine-Slovakia, Ukraine-Hungary, Ukraine-Romania, Ukraine-Belarus, Ukraine-Russia and Ukraine-Moldova. In Ukraine, 19 of the 24 regions can participate in cross-border cooperation.

Ukraine started to prepare for cross-border cooperation in the mid-1990s. In 2002, the Government of Ukraine's resolution "On Ensuring the Implementation of the Law of Ukraine on the General Planning Scheme of the Territory of Ukraine"[20] highlighted the need to develop joint projects for the urban development of cross-

---

19 Tsili staloho rozvytku: Ukrayina. Natsional'na dopovid (Kyiv: UNDP, 2017).
20 Rezolyutsiya vid 29 serpnya 2002 r. "Pro zabezpechennya realizatsiyi Zakonu Ukrayiny «Pro Heneral'nu skhemu planuvannya terytoriyi Ukrayiny", *Cabinet of Ministers of Ukraine*, 29 August, 2002. https://zakon.rada.gov.ua/laws/show/1291-2002-%D0%BF#Text.

border regions by 2020. The DIPROMISTO institute was in charge of developing these projects on the Ukrainian side.

The Ukraine-Poland cross-border region

This project was initiated in 1993, following the Agreement signed between the State Committee for Construction and Architecture of Ukraine and the Ministry of Territorial Planning and Construction of the Republic of Poland. Since then, the project has frequently been revised and extended.

The Ukraine-Poland region paid special attention to the development of transport infrastructure, arranging new border crossing points and developing ecological protection and recreational infrastructure. There are three especially important nodes in the region. The Zahidno-Polyskyi, Roztochanskyi and Uzhansko-Beschadskyi. Zahidno-Polysky and Uzhansko-Bieszczady nodes are trilateral, i.e., established on the border of three states (Ukraine, Poland and Belarus in the first case; Ukraine, Poland and Slovakia in the second case).

The Ukraine-Slovakia cross-border region

As in the case of Poland, the formation and development of the Ukrainian-Slovak cross-border region was stipulated by Ukraine's policy of strengthening economic, social, trade, cultural, scientific, religious and other ties with Slovakia.

The joint urban development project of the Ukraine-Slovakia cross-border region was undertaken in 2002-2007. As part of the project, more than 20 thematic and synthetic maps were made, the most important of which make promising proposals for the development of the settlement system, transport infrastructure and environmental protection. Within the region, two important nodes stand out: Uzhansko-Beschadskyi and Tyskyi. Both are trilateral.

The Ukraine-Hungary cross-border region

This project was finalized in 2012. On the Ukrainian, the border region was defined as the entire territory of the Transcarpathian Region. The project identified the main directions of further development of the Ukrainian-Hungarian cross-border region:

- Adapting to integrated management of water resources;
- Cooperation on cultural activities and strengthening of identity;
- Promotion of international and local transport connections;
- Use of safe, renewable energy sources;
- Limiting the impact of dangerous natural phenomena by preventive measures;
- Reducing negative impacts on the natural environment;
- Protection and improvement of natural resources, and of the natural and cultural heritage.

The Ukraine-Belarus cross-border region

Work on the development of a joint Ukraine-Belarus project was carried out in 2002-2010 on the basis of the Agreement signed between Ukraine and Belarus at the ministerial level.

A preliminary analysis of the urban planning situation of this cross-border region made it clear that its territorial and urban development is connected to the solution of three interdependent problems:

- the protection and rational use of the natural and cultural environment;
- the issues connected to the territories affected by the Chernobyl nuclear accident;
- improvement of the production field system and population resettlement.

In addition, as I mentioned above, there is the need to develop international, state-wide and regional transport infrastructure.

The Ukraine-Russia cross-border region

The development of cross-border projects with the Russian Federation deserves special attention. In 2012, efforts were made by the Ministry of Regional Development of Ukraine and the Ministry of the State Building of the Russian Federation to develop a cross-border Ukraine-Russia project. This development was terminated in 2014 due to Russia's annexation of the territory of Crimea and the occupation of parts of the Donetsk and Luhansk regions.

The group of cross-border projects includes the 2009-2013 Tisza Catchment Development Project (TICAD), in which five countries (Ukraine, Slovakia, Hungary, Romania and Serbia) were involved.[21] The TICAD project was developed as a consequence of the environmental disasters that occurred in the Tisza River basin in 2002, requiring joint measures to prevent future disasters. DIPROMISTO was the Ukrainian participant. Among other aspects of the project, a functional zoning of the region's territory was carried out. Certain categories of territories were determined, providing the methodological basis for the further spatial development of individual local communities (Map 8.2).

---

21 *Tisa Catchment Area Development: Transnational Strategy and Policy Recommendations* (Szeged, 2013).

Map 8.2. TICAD: Territorial Categories.

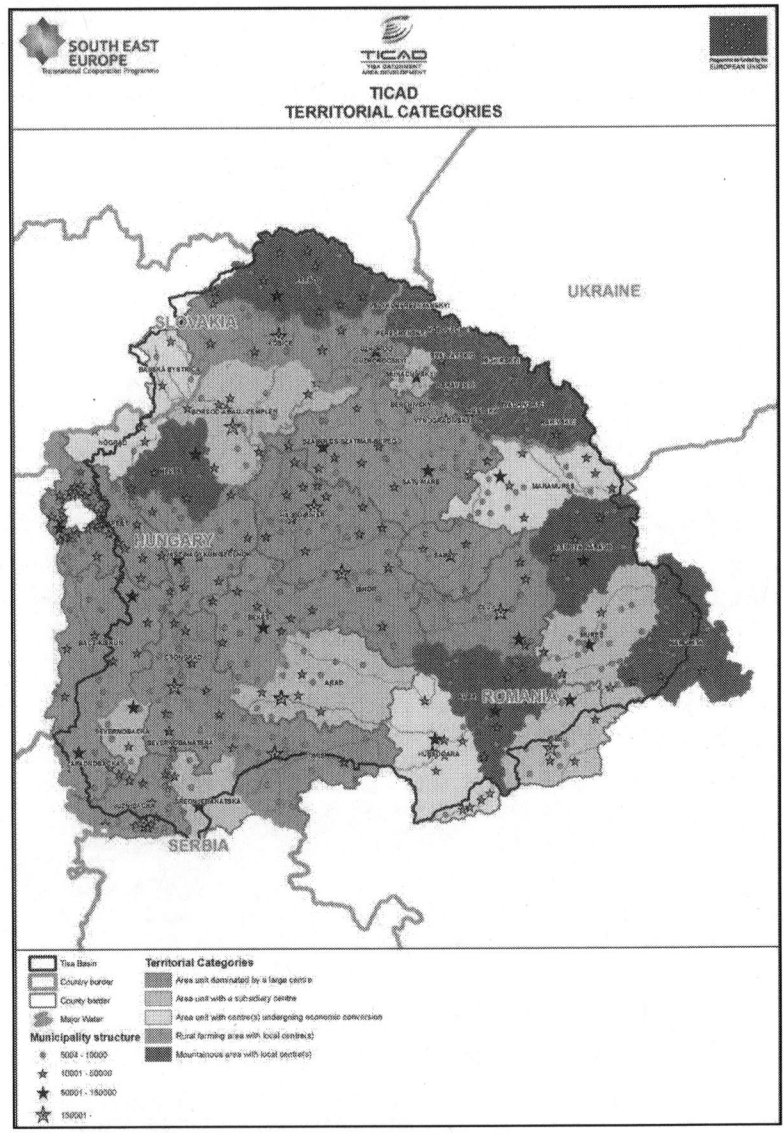

Note: Orange indicates an area unit dominated by a large center. Dark yellow indicates an area unit with a large subsidiary center. Light yellow indicates an area unit with center(s) undergoing economic conversion. Green indicates a rural farming area with local center(s). Brown indicates mountainous areas with local center(s).

The spatial development of cross-border regions brings Ukrainian planning integration closer to the planning systems of the countries of the European Union (Poland, Hungary, Slovakia). This makes it possible to use methodological tools that meet EU requirements and which can be used in the implementation of similar joint programs with different countries.

Conclusions

This chapter analyzed Ukraine's spatial planning tools in the context of sustainable development and European integration. Ukrainian spatial planning reform was delayed for almost 25 years after regaining independence. It began as part of the decentralization reform and benefited from close coordination with European partners.

Spatial planning reform involves, first, the introduction of new types of urban planning documentation, such as a comprehensive plan for the spatial development of ATC territory. The composition and content of already existing types of urban planning documentation are changing, becoming more open and transparent. This is facilitated by the active digitization of urban planning documentation and the creation of geoportals to represent project materials. The development of urban planning projects makes use of GIS technologies and spatial images.

However, there are concerns regarding the slow implementation of spatial planning, especially with respect to comprehensive plans for the spatial development of territorial communities' territories. In 2019, the World Bank was expected to assist Ukraine with the implementation of comprehensive plans for almost 500 territorial communities (a third of the total number) over the course of several years. Unfortunately, these ambitious plans were not carried out.

We can draw the following conclusions regarding the further development of spatial planning tools in Ukraine:

First, after victory in the war with the Russian Federation, it will be imperative to develop a new version of the General Planning Scheme of the Territory of Ukraine in a very short period of time. It should determine the key aspects of territorial reconstruction and the gradual integration of Ukraine into the European planning framework.[22] The idea that Ukraine would not need a General Scheme in this period is doubtful, even though most European countries do not have such a document. Ukraine is not yet a member of the European Union, but is now a candidate for EU membership. Preparation for entry requires the development of a "road map" for spatial development, and this significantly strengthens the importance of a General Scheme approved at the state level. Funds from nonstate sources could be used to finance this development.

Second, in the postwar period, there will be an urgent need to rebuild not only individual residential quarters, cities and towns but also entire districts and regions. This presupposes the adjustment of individual regions' territorial planning schemes, as well as the development of territorial planning schemes in newly formed administrative districts.

Third, the composition of the spatial planning documentation at the local level will change drastically. Eventually, it should combine aspects of architecture and planning, land management and landscape, the organic components of a single planning document in European practice. This will require active work toward the convergence of the urban planning sphere and the land management sphere, which have been developed in parallel and under the management of different ministries in Ukraine for decades.

Fourth, the development of new types of spatial planning documentation for functional areas not limited by administrative boundaries should be avoided at all costs. As noted in Resolution 17 of the CEMAT conference,[23] this would prevent the development of the potential of local territorial communities and thus the

---

[22] Yurii Palekha, "Planning framework of Ukraine as a basis for ensuring its sustainable spatial development", *Approach and Prospects of Development of the Cities of Ukraine*, no. 29 (2015): 48-56.

[23] The Council of Europe Conference of Ministers responsible for Spatial/Regional Planning (CEMAT). Resolution no.1 — Functional areas — Capitalisation of local potential in territorial development policies over the European continent. https://rm.coe.int/the-17th-session-of-the-council-of-europe-conference-of-ministers-resp/16807670ac.

acquisition of additional profits through the capitalization of local potential. One type of functional area planning is the development of cross-border region development projects. Ukraine has accumulated 25 years' worth of experience in this regard.

In summary, the spatial planning tools that were developed in Ukraine can contribute to the sustainable development of regions and settlements and help their smooth European integration in the future, if the requirements listed above are met. This should be facilitated by the standardization of legislation and design methodology. It will be vital to preserve the hierarchical principle of spatial planning, complemented by the principle of subsidiarity. Finally, ensuring the interaction of integrated and sectoral planning is crucial.

9. From Decentralization to Wartime Resistance
Building a Cohesive Ukraine*

Oleksandra Deineko and Aadne Aasland

This chapter focuses on the implementation of the Ukrainian decentralization reform and its impacts on social cohesion since the Russian invasion. Drawing on quantitative and qualitative data, the authors investigate how the reform has contributed to reinforcing social cohesion in conditions of war. They conceptualize the war as a trigger for social cohesion on the national level as both a "common threat" (Russian invasion) and a "common good" (Ukrainian victory) and consider how they intertwine. Previously gained social capital at the local level made wartime cooperation between the citizenry and the authorities more coordinated and more visible. The authors show how the relative boundaries between the state and its citizens, their relationships, and vertical and horizontal social ties have become blurred under military conditions, rapidly strengthening civil resistance.

Introduction

Russia's full-fledged military invasion of Ukraine, in the very heart of Europe, has dramatic humanitarian and social consequences for both the state and the world community. On 11 July 2022, the Office of the United Nations High Commissioner for Human Rights (OHCHR) confirmed a total of 5,024 civilian deaths and more than 6,520 injured.[1] However, these are only the officially verified

---

* An early version of this chapter was presented at the webinar "Local Government in Ukraine: Formation, Reforms, Geopolitical Implications and Post-war Recovery", *IGU Commission on the Geography of Governance*, 6 June 2022. https://sites.google.com/view/lgukraine2022/home. The chapter has also been published as a paper by the *Journal of Soviet and Post-Soviet Politics and Society* in 2024.

numbers: the actual figures are much higher, as confirmed by the OHCHR itself. Moreover, this massive humanitarian catastrophe has involved incessant military attacks, massive infrastructural damage, and a severe economic downturn.

In times of active warfare, society is built on a renewed system of social norms and patterns of behavior, with a key emphasis on the need for survival. Before the war, people's lives were organized according to daily routines with clear and established norms and social practices. Russia's invasion created three main goals for all social actors: to survive, to defend, and to hasten victory.

These normative goals created the basis for Ukraine's unexpectedly strong military and civil resistance, with mass volunteering, mutual support, high interpersonal and institutional trust evident from the very first days of the war. There have been accounts of Ukrainians who opened their homes to strangers, and treated them as family members;[2] who made their cars available for the military;[3] and who donated their savings to support the Ukrainian Army.[4] Ukrainian society has demonstrated profound unity against the common threat. Mayors declared their readiness to defend their cities, weapons in hand, standing side by side with the local territorial defense forces.[5]

---

[1] "Number of civilian casualties in Ukraine during Russia's invasion verified by OHCHR", https://www.statista.com/statistics/1293492/ukraine-war-casualties/. Accessed 11 July 2022.

[2] "Valery Shevchuk a resident of Horodyshchensk amalgamated territorial *hromada* in Volyn sheltered three families in his home", *Suspilne*, 14 May 2022. https://suspilne.media/238946-hotiv-dopomogti-ditam-volinanin-prihistiv-rodinu-z-kiivsini/

[3] "Dmytro Komarov sold a rare car and handed over a million *hryvnias* to our defenders", *Ukrainian Reporter*, 12 July 2022. https://ukrreporter.com.ua/war/dmytro-komarov-prodav-ridkisne-avto-i-peredav-nashym-zahysnykam-miljon-gryven.html.

[4] "83-year-old pensioner from Bukovina transferred 100,000 hryvnias and 10,000 dollars to support the Armed Forces", *Suspilne*, 2 March 2022. https://suspilne.media/212995-na-bukovini-83-ricnij-pensioner-pererahuvav-na-pidtrimku-zsu-100-tisac-griven-ta-10-tisac-dolariv/.

[5] "Klitschko: This is already a bloody war. I have no choice. I will fight!", *Unian*, 25 February 2022, https://www.unian.ua/war/klichko-ce-vzhe-krivava-viyna-v-mene-nemaye-viboru-ya-budu-borotisya-novini-kiyeva-11718019.html.

The way in which people have voluntarily pooled their efforts and promoted self-initiatives demonstrates the relevance of the concept of *social cohesion* as a "sense of togetherness" or "social glue". Researchers use this concept to highlight the vulnerable, bottom–up and consensual nature of the attitudes and actions that bind society together "through the action of specific attitudes, behaviors, rules, and institutions, which rely on consensus rather than pure coercion".[6]

Previously, studies devoted to social cohesion never considered Ukraine a socially cohesive society. In a study of 47 European countries in the European Value Survey, Dickes et al. (2008) found Ukraine characterized by low levels of behavioral and substantial attitudinal levels of social cohesion.[7] Using the results of the 2012–2013 European Social Survey and comparing Ukraine with the other Eastern and Central European countries, Bondarenko et al. (2017) found low scores on select indicators of social cohesion, and rather high levels of interpersonal trust.[8] However, these studies were conducted before Ukraine's 2014 Revolution of Dignity launched comprehensive political reforms aimed at promoting democracy and European integration.

The decentralization reform is especially important here. Initiated in 2014, it aimed at forming a new basic level of local self-government in Ukraine—amalgamated territorial communities (ATCs). These would create and maintain a fully-developed living environment for the citizenry, with high-quality, accessible public services and direct democracy institutions.[9] The pre-history, initial achievements and current challenges of the decentralization reform

---

[6] Andry Green Janmaat, Jan Germen & Christine Han, *Regimes of Social Cohesion* (London: Centre for Learning and Life Chances in Knowledge Economies and Societies, 2009).

[7] Dickes & M. Valentova, "Construction, validation and application of the measurement of social cohesion in 47 European countries and regions", *Social Indicators Research*, no. 113 (2013): 3.

[8] M. Bondarenko, S. Babenko & O. Borovskiy, "Sotsial'na zhurtovanist' v Ukraini" [Social cohesion in Ukraine], *Visnyk Kyivskoho natsional'noho universitetu imeni Tarasa Shevchenka, Sotsiologiya*, no. 8 (2017): 58–65.

[9] Order of the Cabinet of Ministers of Ukraine "On Approval of the Concept of Reforming Local Self-Government and Territorial Organization of Power in Ukraine", 2014. https://zakon5.rada.gov.ua/laws/show/333-2014-%D1%80.

have been analyzed in previous chapters of this book (e.g., Romanova, Umland); in this chapter, we emphasize the social specifics and effects of the implementation of this reform on Ukrainian society.

Although not referred to as such in legislative acts, the goals and procedures of decentralization meant that it was planned as a socially cohesive reform. Romanova and Umland highlight the political and geopolitical dimensions of this cohesiveness.[10] Reflecting on the sociopolitical context of decentralization, researchers have noted that it emerged in opposition to federalization and separatism, and served as a mechanism for strengthening national unity after the Russian annexation of Crimea and the occupation of Donbas in 2014. Shelest and Rabinovych[11] have examined the implications of decentralization for the process of Ukrainian democratization and European integration, emphasizing its potential as a tool for conflict resolution. While their study finds both positive and negative correlations between decentralization and conflict resolution, one of their contributors sees the reform in general as a "vehicle for modernization",[12] aimed at uniting Ukrainian regions by giving more power and financial opportunities to the new self-government bodies, the ATCs, or *hromadas*. Other scholars[13] have observed that successfully implemented territorial development projects at the ATC level have had significant positive effects on state cohesion. One study of 169 EU regions found the quality of local self-government to be the key factor in the efficiency of cohesion policy and the use of EU structural funds.[14]

---

10 Romanova Valentyna and Andreas Umland, "Decentralising Ukraine: Geopolitical Implications", *Survival* 61, no. 5 (2019): 99–112.
11 Hanna Shelest and Maryna Rabinovych, eds., *Decentralization, Regional Diversity, and Conflict: The Case of Ukraine* (Basingstoke: Palgrave Macmillan, 2020).
12 Olga Oleinekova "Decentralization Reform: An Effective Vehicle for Modernization and Democratization in Ukraine?", in: Shelest and Rabinovych, *Decentralization, Regional Diversity, and Conflict*, 311–338.
13 Y.A. Zhalilo, O.V. Shevchenko & V.V. Romanova, *Decentralization of Power: Agenda for the Medium Term* (Kyiv: National Institute for Strategic Studies, 2019).
14 A. Rodriguez-Pose & E. Garcilazo, *Quality of Government and the Returns on Investment: Examining the Impact of Cohesion Expenditure in European Regions* (Paris: OECD, 2013).

Two other aspects of Ukraine's decentralization reform have contributed to reinforcing social cohesion at the local level. First, according to the nationwide survey "Decentralization and the reform of local self-government: the fifth wave of sociological research results", among those who stated that they were well acquainted with the decentralization reform, 81 percent recognized it as necessary for Ukraine.[15] Unlike other legislative amendments (e.g., land reform, the privatization of state enterprises), which polarized opinion, the decentralization reform has demonstrated a powerful potential for social consolidation around a common idea.

Second, decentralization's contribution to social cohesion is connected to the specifics of the amalgamation procedure, which is based on interactions among various local actors, the authorities as well as the citizenry. The amalgamation process involves different stages: public hearings on the proposal to merge, adoption of the recommendation by the local councils, and the formation of a working group to draft the decision regarding amalgamation.[16] Viewed from a sociological perspective, the amalgamation procedure activated interactions within and between territorial units, building and strengthening social ties, thus promoting bridging and the bonding of social capital[17] between the social actors of the future amalgamated *hromada*.

Previous studies have analyzed the social impact of amalgamation on social cohesion in border regions of Ukraine. Within the framework of the ARDU project,[18] we focused on the quantitative links between decentralization and social cohesion,[19] as well as on

---

15 "Decentralization and reform of local self-government: Results of the fifth wave of sociological research among the population of Ukraine", *Detsentralizatsiya*, 2020, https://decentralization.gov.ua/uploads/library/file/633/2020Report_UKR_ukr.pdf.
16 "On the Voluntary Amalgamation of Territorial Hromadas", *Verkhovna Rada*, 2015. https://zakon.rada.gov.ua/laws/show/157-19#Text.
17 Robert D. Putnam, *Bowling Alone: The Collapse and Revival of American Community* (New York: Simon and Schuster, 2000).
18 https://uni.oslomet.no/ardu/
19 Aadne Aasland, Oleksandra Deineko, Olga Filippova and Sabine Kropp, "Citizens' Perspectives: Reform and Social Cohesion in Ukraine's Border Regions", in: A. Aasland and S. Kropp, eds., *The Accommodation of Regional and Ethno-cultural Diversity in Ukraine* (Basingstoke: Palgrave Macmillan, 2021), 237–272.

the qualitative transformations at the local level, as a result of decentralization in two Ukrainian border regions: Kharkiv[20] and Chernivtsi.[21] Despite the promising shifts seen from the qualitative angle, the quantitative data showed the scores on the social cohesion indices to be rather mixed, with low trust in state institutions but a strong sense of belonging at all levels—local, regional, and national. Amalgamation was found to result in higher levels of participation compared with non-amalgamated rural communities.[22] We documented a strengthening of social cohesion as a result of the decentralization reform — but it should be noted that data collection for the ARDU project was completed by the end of 2020 (the fieldwork in 2019; the survey in 2020), a little more than a year before the Russian invasion of Ukraine.

Bearing in mind the new "sense of togetherness" demonstrated by Ukrainians from the very beginning of the war, we ask:

- how has the decentralization reform contributed to reinforcing social cohesion in Ukrainian society during the war?
- what are the essential wartime transformations of social cohesion?
- in what way could the war change the conceptual framework of social cohesion theorizing developed in peacetime?

Decentralization, Social Cohesion, and War: The Theoretical Framework

Studying social cohesion requires theoretical concretization, given the range of definitions and models of empirical measurement in scientific discourse. Since "social cohesion" is sometimes seen as a "quasi-concept" or an ill-defined term, it is a challenge to propose

---

20 Aadne Aasland, Olga Filippova, Oleksandra Deineko and Ruslan Zaporozhchenko, "Decentralization, Social Cohesion and Ethno-cultural Diversity in Ukraine's Border Regions", in: Aasland and Kropp, *The Accommodation of Regional and Ethno-cultural Diversity in Ukraine*, 143–170.
21 O. O. Deineko, "Social Cohesion in Decentralized Ukraine: From Old Practices to New Order", *Studia Socjologiczne*, no. 1(240) (2021): 117–138.
22 Aasland et al., "Citizens' Perspectives", 237–272.

and justify an appropriate theoretical framework.[23] Social cohesion is a relatively new concept in quality-of-life research.[24] But its roots can be traced back to Durkheim's theorizing on social solidarity.[25] Tönnies's concepts of *Gemeinschaft* and *Gesellschaft* illustrated the dialectical changes in social interaction in the context of the early development of capitalism.[26] These (proto-)concepts of social cohesion defined its core identity as an attribute of social interaction and a characteristic of social groups, communities and societies. However, globalized postmodernity, which has sometimes provoked a decline of social cohesion, throws up multiple new challenges to the contemporary "sense of togetherness".[27]

Social cohesion is commonly viewed as a feature of society as a whole and used as the basis for constructing empirical models of cross-cultural measurement.[28] At the meso-social level, social cohesion is studied as a property of territorial communities, such as neighborhoods and local communities.[29] Some researchers employ a broader approach, insisting on the relevance of studying social cohesion at all group levels, regardless of their size.[30] This chapter

---

23 Jane Jenson, *Mapping Social Cohesion: The State of Canadian Research* (Ottawa: Canadian Policy Research Networks, 1998).
24 H. Noll, "Towards a European System of Social Indicators: Theoretical Framework and System Architecture", *Social Indicators Research* 58 (2000): 1-3.
25 Emile Durkheim, *The Division of Labour in Society* (New York: Free Press, 1933).
26 Ferdinand Tönnies, *Community and Association (Gemeinschaft und Gesellschaft)* (London: Routledge & Kegan Paul, 1955).
27 R. Eckersley, "Whatever Happened to Western Civilization? The Cultural Crisis, 20 Years Later". *The Futurist* (2011): 16–22.
28 J. Delhey, K. Boehnke, G. Dragolov, Z.S. Ignácz, M. Larsen, J. Lorenz, & M. Koch, "Social Cohesion and its Correlates: A Comparison of Western and Asian Societies", *Comparative Sociology* 17, nos. 3-4 (2018): 426–455.
29 F. Rajulton, Z.R., Ravanera, &. R. Beaujot, "Measuring Social Cohesion: An Experiment Using the Canadian National Survey of Giving, Volunteering, and Participating", *Social Indicators Research* 80, no. 3 (2007): 461–492; A. Kearns & R. Forres, "Social Cohesion and Multilevel Urban Governance", *Urban Studies* 37, nos. 5-6 (2000): 995–1017.
30 C. Whelan & B. Maître, "Economic Vulnerability, Multidimensional Deprivation and Social Cohesion in an Enlarged European Community", *International Journal of Comparative Sociology* 46, no. 3 (2005): 215–239.

modifies Joseph Chan's methodological framework to combine macro- and meso-social levels of social cohesion.[31]

Joseph Chan and his colleagues define social cohesion as "a state of affairs concerning both the vertical and the horizontal interactions among members of society as characterized by a set of attitudes and norms that includes trust, a sense of belonging and the willingness to participate and help, as well as their behavioural manifestations".[32] This definition operates in two dimensions (horizontal and vertical) and with two components (objective and subjective). The horizontal dimension concerns social bonds (relationships among individuals and groups within society); the vertical one designates relationships between the state and the citizenry. These dimensions are viewed according to subjective (state of mind) and objective (behavioral manifestations) components. Social cohesion is measured by several indicators: political participation; trust in public figures; confidence in political and major social institutions; willingness to cooperate and help; general trust in fellow citizens; social participation and the vibrancy of civil society; voluntarism and donations; the sense of belonging; and the presence or absence of major inter-group alliances or cleavages.

Chan et al. present a fairly static mode of social cohesion; other scholars pay more attention to how social cohesion is (re)produced and maintained in societies. For instance, Andy Green and his colleagues acknowledge the "embeddedness" of social cohesion in historical, political, social, and cultural contexts, proposing a separate category: regimes of social cohesion.[33] They distinguish three such regimes: a) liberal regimes (with emphasis on civil society initiatives, tolerance, acceptance of diversity); b) social market regimes (a leading role played by the state, whose institutions ensure welfare and social protection; the importance of common values, a sense of belonging and institutional trust); c) social democratic regimes (similar to social market regimes, but with greater emphasis

---

31 Joseph Chan, Ho-Pong To, and Elaine Chan, "Reconsidering social cohesion: Developing a definition and analytical framework for empirical research", *Social Indicators Research* 75, no. 2 (2006): 273–302.
32 Ibid., 290.
33 Andy Green, Janmaat, and Han, *Regimes of Social Cohesion*.

on equality and social partnership). Drawing on this approach, we can see that Ukraine's decentralization reform employed elements of all three regimes of social cohesion—civil initiatives; welfare, in the devolution from the state to the *hromadas*; the principles of equality and social partnership. However, Green et al.'s conceptualization remains insufficiently clear for our purposes. Moreover, it offers no understanding of the core that prompts the building and rebuilding of social cohesion; it also mixes the components and factors of social cohesion—for instance, welfare and common values are viewed as factors, whereas civil initiatives are presented as a component.

Martial law as the new normative regime of Ukrainian society prompts reflection on the specifics of social cohesion and its regimes under conditions of war. According to Yarskaya-Smirnova, the emergence of social cohesion may be adduced as the "adherence to a common good" and as "social closure in response to a common threat".[34] Ukraine's decentralization reform has been presented as a "common good": new financial capacities and decision-making procedures on the local level contribute to quality of life and open new perspectives for local development.

In wartime, both the "common good" and "common threat" regimes of social cohesion seem relevant to Ukrainian realities. The classic German sociologist Georg Simmel linked the acuteness of a conflict to the internal cohesion of the groups in conflict: the more acute the conflict, the stronger their internal consolidation.[35] Members of a certain social group perceive a common external threat, thereby triggering individual and collective actions. If we can say that the "common threat" was recognized and articulated in Ukrainian society with the annexation of Crimea and the occupation of Donbas in 2014, recognition and articulation of the "common good" was prompted on 24 February 2022, with the start of a full-

---

[34] E. R. Yarskaya-Smirnova and V. N. Yarskaya, "Sotsial'naya splochennost': Napravleniya teoreticheskoi diskussii i perspektivy sotsial'noi politiki [Social Cohesion: Directions of Theoretical Discussion and Perspectives for Social Policy]". http://www.jourssa.ru/sites/all/files/volumes/2014_4/Iarskaya_Yarskaya_2014_4.pdf.

[35] Georg Simmel "The Sociology of Conflict", *American Journal of Sociology* 9, no. 4 (1904): 490–525.

scale military invasion. The "common good" has now become "Victory for Ukraine", as a new nation-building idea, one that can be accomplished by individual actions and group solidarity. The "common threat" remains the enemy invasion, and ongoing warfare.

Data and Methods

This chapter draws on research results gathered within the framework of the Ukrainian-Norwegian Accommodation of Regional Diversity in Ukraine (ARDU) (2018-2021) research project, and during the war in Ukraine (March-June 2022). Drawing on the ARDU project we present new analyses of the results of a nationwide representative survey conducted by the Dnipro-based opinion poll agency Operatyvna Sociologia on behalf of Oslo Metropolitan University in December 2020 (sample size: 2100; method used: telephone interviews). The population surveyed was largely representative in terms of geographical distribution across the country, type of settlement, gender, and age. The aim of the survey was to capture social cohesion dimensions at the local level among Ukrainians, based on Chan's methodological approach. The survey results are used to study the decentralization reform's perceived effects on the work of local government with the help of logistic regressions.

In the framework of the ARDU project, we modified Chan et al.'s measurement scheme, placing the main emphasis on the local community level as the most indicative for assessing the impact of the decentralization reform. Instead of asking about "people in this country ...", in several questions we changed the wording to "people in this local community ...". Further, we altered "relations between local residents and immigrants" to "relations with persons internally displaced from Crimea and Donbas". The "belonging and identity" indicator was enlarged by adding different types of identification (local community, regional, national, and European). Concerning "trust in public figures" and "confidence in political and other major social institutions" we measured the levels of trust in the President, the Parliament of Ukraine, judges, local authorities, NGOs, and the mass media.

To study the degree to which decentralization has enhanced local cooperation, we employed 26 semi-structured interviews in October 2019 with decentralization experts, representatives of civil society, cultural experts, local elected officials and local authorities in the amalgamated *hromadas* of the Kharkiv and Chernivtsi regions. The interview guide was developed in collaboration with Ukrainian and Norwegian ARDU project participants, and focused on how the decentralization reform had affected social cohesion. When interviewing local elected officials, representatives from various political parties were selected, to balance local authorities' possibly conformist views of the implementation of decentralization.

In a subchapter studying resistance during the military invasion of Ukraine, we use the results of the nationwide survey, "War in Ukraine: A sociological survey", conducted by the Dnipro-based Ukrainian company *Operatyvna Sotsiologiya* at the request of the Norwegian Institute of Regional and Urban Research (NIBR) on the general population in mid-March 2022 (sample size: 3007; method used: telephone interviews). The questionnaire covered the issues of relocation and damage, current humanitarian needs, resistance practices, the psychological and emotional condition of the populace, and other challenges faced by Ukrainians in conditions of active warfare.[36] We also partially draw on survey data gathered by *Operatyvna Sotsiologiya* (27–30 July 2022) using the Computer Assisted Web Interview (CAWI) method on the OpeSo mobile app. The sample (received questionnaires: 1,507) is representative in terms of gender, age, and region of residence.

Because of the lack of sociological surveys conducted in Ukraine during the war we have also undertaken a secondary analysis of the nationwide survey results gathered by the Rating Sociological Group (March–June 2022).

---

36 Oleksandra Deineko, *War in Ukraine: A Sociological Study* (Oslo: Norwegian Institute for Urban and Regional Research, 2022), 21.

Pre-war Survey Results on Decentralization and Social Cohesion

In the 2020 ARDU survey—i.e., just over a year before the Russian invasion—we asked the respondents: "Since 2015, Ukraine has been undergoing a comprehensive decentralization reform. In your opinion, during this period, has the work of local governments become ...", giving them seven options.[37] Their answers gave an indication of the success of the decentralization reform as perceived by ordinary citizens. The options and results are shown in Figure 9.1. Even though a large proportion did not see big changes, and a considerable proportion was undecided (one in ten even saying that they did not know anything about the reform), among those with an opinion, more people (32 percent) tilted towards a positive than a negative (20 percent) assessment. It should be noted that the survey was conducted when the Covid-19 pandemic was at its height and many were experiencing uncertainty and economic difficulties; the assessment was probably more negative than that shown by the pre-pandemic figures.[38]

To better understand which population groups were most likely to show satisfaction with the reform at the local level, we performed logistic regressions with the perceived effects of the decentralization reform on the work of local government as the dependent variable. Those answering that the work had become better (including slightly better) were given a score of 1, those saying that nothing had changed or had gotten worse were given a score of 0 (respondents who did not know about the reform or found it hard

---

37 Responses to this question do not necessarily correspond to respondents' attitudes to the reform itself. However, a survey conducted in 2017 showed a relatively high correlation between responses to this question and support for the decentralization reform (r=0.3). See: Aadne Aasland and Oleksii Lyska, "Signs of Progress: Local Democracy Developments in Ukrainian Cities", in: Shelest and Rabinovych, *Decentralization, Regional Diversity, and Conflict*, 283-310.

38 When the same question was asked in a local democracy survey conducted by Operatyvna Sociologiya in the fall of 2017, 11 percent of the responses were negative ("local government work had become slightly worse or worse"), 35 percent said nothing had changed, while 42 per cent said it had become slightly better or better (and 11 percent said they "do not know"). See also Aasland and Lyska, "Signs of Progress".

to answer were removed from the analysis). Two models were tested: in the first model we included socioeconomic and socio-demographic variables (gender, age, self-reported ethnic identity, educational level, financial situation, geographical location in Ukraine [see map], and type of settlement). Descriptive statistics and the wording of the questions can be found in Appendix 1.

Figure 9.1. Perceived effects of the decentralization reform on the work of local government, in % (N=2,103) a nationwide sample.

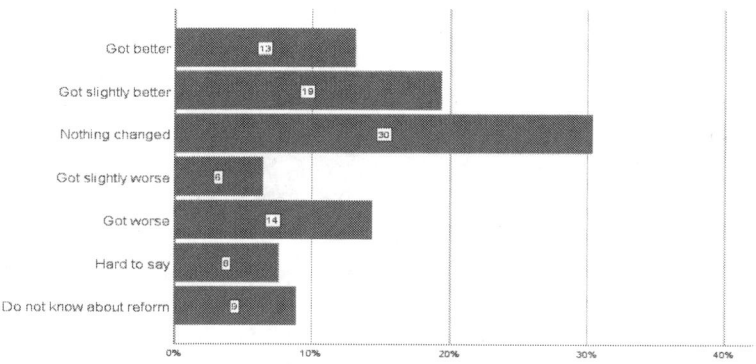

The results are presented in Tables 9.1. and 9.2. Model 1 shows that age, gender and Ukrainian vs other ethnic identity do not have statistically significant effects on the perceived success of the decentralization reform on the work of local government. The largest effect concerns *economic status*: the more financially secure the respondent, the more positive is the assessment of the reform on the work of local government. This might indicate that the better-off segments of the population have benefited more from the reform than those less well-off. The statistically significant effect of *education* on the dependent variable could indicate that those who know more about the reform (assuming that persons with higher education are more likely to be informed) have a more positive view.

There is a large body of literature on how the views of people in Ukraine's various regions differ on Ukrainian politics and reform. For a long time, Mykola Ryabchuk's concept of "two

Ukraines"[39] was used by foreign scholars to explain the political orientations and linguistic preferences of Ukrainians living in the eastern and western parts of the country. Studies, conducted after the Revolution of Dignity, however, have indicated that this approach oversimplifies and exaggerates the case.[40] Moreover, Rabinovych and Shelest conclude that the occupation of Donbas was "marked by an intense yet "hybrid" foreign support of separatists, promoting narratives based on the securitization of diversity".[41] Thus, the unproven discourse of diversity became a justification for foreign intervention.

Map 9.1: Geographical regions of Ukraine.

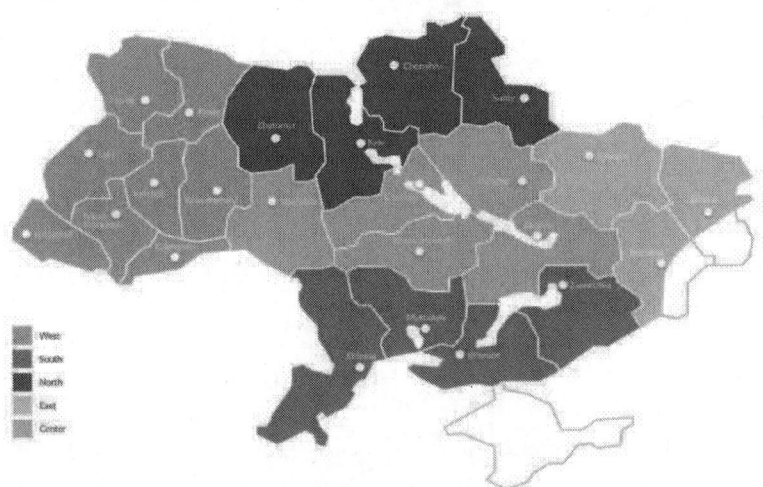

Our data refute Ryabchuk's framing. As regards assessment of local government performance, we find no East-West divide. The greatest number of positive assessments were given by respondents in the east (see Fig. 1), followed by the west, and then the south. The respondents in the central and northern parts of the country were

---

39   Mykola Ryabczuk, "Two Ukraines?", *East European Reporter* 5, no. 4 (1999).
40   J. Fomina, "Language, Identity, Politics: The Myth of Two Ukraines", *Bertelsman Policy Brief*. April 2014. http://aei.pitt.edu/74064/1/Language_Identity_P olitics_the_Myth_of_Two_Ukraines.pdf.
41   Shelest and Rabinovych, *Decentralization, Regional Diversity, and Conflict*, 366.

less positive. The responses from the east could be explained by the government policy's on rebuilding the controlled territories of Donbass.[42] However, only the differences between the most negative (north) and most positive (east) responses are statistically significant.

An important aspect of the decentralization reform has been the amalgamation of smaller rural communities into ATCs. However, our findings show that the most positive post-decentralization assessments of local government come from city dwellers, especially those living in *oblast* centers. It would seem that the reform has given the resource-endowed urban centers even more resources, and more independence on how to spend them.

In line with Chan et al.'s framework, in Model 2 we introduced the following social cohesion indicators: trust in institutions, interpersonal trust, organizational participation, the sense of belonging to Ukraine and to the local community, organizational membership, local activism, self-declared humanitarian aid and donations, and perceived local disunity (see the Appendix for the wording of the questions and the descriptive statistics).

As shown in Table 9.1, the statistically significant variables in Model 1 remained significant in Model 2. In the latter, the indicator with the greatest effect on the dependent variable was the level of institutional trust: the greater the trust in institutions (the President, the Parliament, local government, media, the judicial system), the more likely the respondent was to see improvements in local government after decentralization. Interestingly, interpersonal trust was also associated with a positive assessment of local government performance, demonstrating the close connection between trust in its various dimensions and perceptions of the reform.

Although identifying as ethnically Ukrainian had no effect on perceptions of the decentralization reform, the sense of belonging to Ukraine had a statistically significant and positive effect, as shown in Model 2: the more the respondent identified as a citizen

---

42 "Derzhavna tsilova prohrama vidnovlennia ta rozbudovy myru v skhidnykh rehionakh Ukrainy", *Minregion*, 2020. https://minre.gov.ua/project/derzhavna-cilova-programa-vidnovlennya-ta-rozbudovy-myru-v-shidnyh-regionah-ukrayiny.

of Ukraine, the more likely that person was to positively assess the effect of the reform on the work of local government. That is, civic rather than ethnic identity correlates with assessment of the reform when controlling for all the other variables in the model. However, no similar effect was found about the sense of belonging to the local community.

None of the other independent variables had a statistically significant effect on the dependent variable, whether they concerned civic activism (organizational membership or other local activity), help and donations to those in need, or perceived disunity in the local community. Thus, although these indicators are likely to enhance local social cohesion, they do not appear to have affected perceptions of local government performance.

In summary, the survey results indicate rather positive views on the effect of the decentralization reform on local authorities' performance, and hence on the prospects for local social cohesion. Furthermore, we find that socioeconomic, rather than socio-demographic, indicators affect people's satisfaction with the reform; that the reform has produced benefits in all parts of Ukraine; and that perceptions are not influenced by ethnic affiliations. We also note the importance of institutional trust and the sense of belonging (key social cohesion components) as aspects that have a positive effect on perceptions of decentralization in Ukraine.

Decentralization and Local Cooperation: The Qualitative Angle of Social Cohesion

As noted above, interpersonal and institutional trust as well as civil identity had a statistically significant effect on the perceived success of the decentralization reform on the work of local government. In Chan's theoretical framework, all these components are classified as indicators of the subjective dimension of social cohesion — and this dimension refers primarily to the attitudes and orientations rather than actual practices. Whereas regression analysis did not reveal significant correlations between the objective (practical) dimensions of social cohesion and positive assessments of decentralization, our qualitative interviews with *hromada* representatives and local residents gave a different picture.

Here it should be recalled that *hromada* amalgamation was based on a set of interactions among various local actors, involving both the authorities and the citizenry. Viewed in sociological terms, amalgamation prompted interactions within and between the territorial units to be merged, building and reinforcing social ties, thus enhancing bridging and the bonding of social capital among the social actors of the future amalgamated *hromada*.

The qualitative data obtained through the ARDU project indicate that cooperation between the new *hromada* authorities and local citizens was improved by greater democratization, mutual responsibility and an increase in the citizenry's active participation. At least at the declarative level, practical transparency was promoted in statements from the representatives of the *hromada* authorities in both regions studied: "People should have an influence on all of us because we are here to work for people. We are 'hired workers'. Let's say, the people voted for us, so we are accountable to them" (ATC *starosta*, Chernivtsi region).

Local ATC authorities also noted new mechanisms for more active civic participation in *hromadas* in comparison with pre-amalgamation times. *Hromada* officials improved the institutional basis for more intensive and fruitful communication and cooperation with the local population: "And always, any decisions ... we publish all this on the website, and everyone can come, listen, influence" (ATC administration representative, Kharkiv region).

Participatory budgeting was introduced into decision-making. Both the local population and the authorities emphasized decentralization's indisputable advantage in allowing people to "be heard". Positive evaluations came also from local critics of the decentralization reform: "In the Novovodolazhska ATC, they launched a participatory budgeting project. Such mechanisms really help to increase local participation in ATC activities" (local council deputy, Kharkiv region).

Such attitudes were expressed not only by local officials, but also by the citizenry in both the regions studied: "All these changes and reforms also provide a chance to feel that something depends on you. That you are a member of a community. Not merely a simple cog—you are a member of this community, you can say something, you can be heard, they can react, you will get results" (local activist, Chernivtsi region).

Some interviewees contrasted participatory budgeting with Soviet paternalism, as revealing major changes in local residents' awareness of new practices of active citizenship:

> "The inertia had become even greater, because for almost 70 years we lived in a structure that said that someone else would think and decide for me. But after seeing the real cases, using participatory budgeting as one example ... this showed that people can manage resources, take part in hromada life, identify the most problematic issues and request the necessary funding" (ATC administration representative, Kharkiv region).

The greater funding released by financial decentralization has strengthened the ability to solve local problems. This has contributed to the intensification of common local practices. Interviewees shared their experiences of using donations to solve local issues and promote initiatives supported by others in the *hromada*:

> "There are many people who are not indifferent. For example, the director of *** company. He gave us 400 Crimean pine seedlings. They needed to be watered every day. And I gathered people, distributed the seedlings. And they planted them in school areas, near the churches and across all our *hromada*..." (ATC *starosta*, Kharkiv region).

Similar assessments of the impacts of decentralization were expressed even by those who were generally critical of the reform:

> "The ability to solve local problems has become much better. There are more tools for local authorities to solve these issues. The most prosaic tool is money. Earlier, the villages were alone with their problems: but now, having a larger number of these villages in the *hromada* has made it much easier to solve the problems together" (local council deputy, Kharkiv region).

The last remark relates to the phenomenon of the "common good" often noted in research on social cohesion and civil society. Edward Shils links the common good with the behavioral ethos of the civil society—the concept of civility.[43] He sees civility as a component of social cohesion, which helps transcend class, ethnic, and professional characteristics in conflict situations and allows people to work for the common good. Our qualitative research data show that territorial *hromada* amalgamation—accompanied by local budget increases, the expansion of local authorities' powers, and stronger social ties between local actors—has created an image of the "common good". This "common good", perceived as new life chances for *hromada* members and offering perspectives for enhancing the quality-of-life demands of local civil activism, has helped to strengthen social cohesion at the local *hromada* level.

From Decentralization to War: Resistance to Military Invasion

Since the beginning of the war, new images of the "common good" and the "common threat" have come to the fore. The previously underestimated threat of a Russian invasion—according to a representative survey conducted in January 2022 by the New Image Group, only 33 percent of Ukrainian respondents felt that there was a real and serious danger of an attack by Russia[44]—turned real and affected every family. The Russian invasion of Ukraine (as a "common threat") determined the formation of a new "common good" in citizens' perceptions: Ukrainian victory in the war. Both social cohesion formulas ("common good" and "common threat") were mobilized, empowering each other in citizens' attitudes and practices.

Ukrainian politicians took important steps towards "common good" achievements. President Zelensky's call for political consolidation was supported by representatives of most political parties, uniting forces to achieve a single common goal: victory for Ukraine. Formerly antagonistic political actors (at least temporarily)

---

43 Edward Shils, *The Virtue of Civility: Selected Essays on Liberalism, Tradition, and Civil Society* (Indianapolis, IN: Liberty Fund, 1997).
44 "Are Ukrainians ready for a large-scale war? Results of a sociological research", *Ukrainian Institute for the Future*, 27 January 2022. https://uifuture.org/publications/are-ukrainians-ready-for-a-large-scale-war-results-of-a-sociological-research/.

changed their conduct from criticizing to assisting. Under martial law, the Ukrainian Parliament and government worked with fewer disputes, rapidly establishing new legal norms: an extremely important undertaking on the part of the political elite, establishing and spreading the discourse of unity in Ukrainian society. Indeed, the 1 March 2022 survey by the Rating sociological group showed that President Zelensky enjoyed an absolute level of support of 93 percent.[45] The change is striking. According to survey results from 14-16 December 2021, only 38 percent of Ukrainians trusted the President; 61 percent did not.[46] President Zelensky's refusal to desert Ukraine and spearhead the national resistance established a model of wartime behavior that won unprecedent levels of trust and support from Ukrainians. Levels of trust in state institutions have also increased rapidly. At the end of 2021, only 5 percent believed that the central authorities successfully met their commitments;[47] by contrast, in May 2022, 54 percent of those surveyed expressed their support.[48] We interpret these results as evidence that Ukrainians are keen to show that, despite the multiple weaknesses of state policies and the past activities of the authorities, they deeply value their country as an independent and sovereign state. In the course of the war, citizens' assessments of Ukrainian state effectiveness have improved significantly. Indeed, 84 percent of Ukrainians surveyed expressed support for local authorities' wartime actions: as many as 98 percent have voiced their support for the Armed Forces of Ukraine.[49]

From the very first days of the war, Ukrainians demonstrated unprecedented military and civil resistance to the Russian invasion.

---

45 "Zahalnonatsionalne opytuvannia: Ukraina v umovakh viiny (1 bereznia 2022)", *Reytinh*, March 2022. https://ratinggroup.ua/research/ukraine/obschenacionalnyy_opros_ukraina_v_usloviyah_voyny_1_marta_2022.html.

46 "Suspilno-politychni nastroi naselennia (14-16 hrudnia 2021)", *Reytinh*, December 2022. https://ratinggroup.ua/research/ukraine/obschestvenno-politicheskie_nastroeniya_naseleniya_14-16_dekabrya_2021.html.

47 Ibid.

48 "Dvanadtsiate zahalnonatsionalne opytuvannia: Dynamika otsinky obrazu derzhavy (18-19 travnia 2022)", *Reytinh*, May 2022. https://ratinggroup.ua/research/ukraine/dvenadcatyy_obschenacionalnyy_opros_dinamika_ocenki_obraza_gosudarstva_18-19_maya_20.

49 "Zahalnonatsionalne opytuvannia".

Ukrainian media and civil video reports broadcast accounts of how ordinary unarmed civilians halted tanks, prepared and used Molotov cocktails against the enemy to assist the Ukrainian army, and participated in building neighborhood defense systems. People were eager to engage military and civil resistance, standing in extremely long draft-board queues and launching a range of volunteering initiatives. Since the beginning of the war, the vast majority of Ukrainians — more than 80 percent — have become volunteers.[50]

According to a nationwide survey conducted by *Operatyvna Sotsiologiya* — at the request of the Norwegian Institute for Urban and Regional Research (March 13-23, N: 3007) — Ukrainians wanted to help not only their friends and relatives (38 percent), but also other people in need (34 percent). One in every three respondents reported giving money to support the Ukrainian army and people in need (see Table 3). *Informal* volunteering has become much more prevalent (as shown by responses to the option "I'm a volunteer (work in volunteer centers; provide financial assistance with things like food)", marked by only 19 percent of respondents). This shows the power of bottom-up self-motivated capacities enabled by the war. According to a survey by the same agency, conducted in July 2022, Ukrainians' volunteer activities had not diminished by the fifth month of the war. Moreover, monetary donations increased from 29 percent in March to 36 percent in July. Formal volunteering has grown less widespread (dropping from 18.7 percent to 14.1 percent in the same period) but there have been no significant changes in helping those in one's closest surroundings and other persons in need. Despite war fatigue, people continue to demonstrate a clear trend to mass volunteering and horizontal bonding. This indicates that the strengthening of social cohesion seems set to become a long-term tendency, and not merely a short-term effect of the war.

---

50 "Vosme zahalnonatsionalne opytuvannia: Ukraina v umovakh viiny (6 kvitnia 2022)", *Reytinh*, April 2022. https://ratinggroup.ua/research/ukraine/vosmoy_ob schenacionalnyy_opros_ukraina_v_usloviyah_voyny_6_aprelya_2022.html.

Table 9.3: Types of volunteering during the war (in %)

Types of volunteering	March 2022 N=3007	July 2022 N=1507
I help relatives / friends / acquaintances	381	36
I help other people in need	33.5	33.5
I make monetary donations	29.3	36.3
I'm a volunteer (work in volunteer centers; provide financial assistance with things, food)	18.7	14.1
Joined a cyberattack, cyber defense, or online resistance	8.1	5.4
I belong to the Territorial Defense or a volunteer battalion	(no data on security goals)	
I'm in the military		
Other	1.8	0.7
None of the above	15.9	15.6
Difficult to answer	2.3	2.2
I do not wish to answer	1.7	0.2

The recognized need to help others has given rise to new forms of interaction and communication between everyone, from complete strangers to close relatives and friends. The flourishing of volunteer practices has led to the formation of new horizontal bonds, enhancing both bridging and the bonding of social capital. This cooperation is particularly evident at local levels—neighborhoods, districts and *hromadas*—driven by the need to ensure local protection, with visible local support. The recent *hromada* amalgamation has become an important aspect of the decentralization reform, with enhanced trust and stronger social ties between social actors stimulating local cooperation. Acts of war occurring throughout the country have made Ukrainians more horizontally bonded, enhancing horizontal social capital. In summary, the war has significantly reinforced the horizontal dimension of social cohesion (relationships between individuals and groups within society) on both the attitudinal and the practical levels.

Since the beginning of the war, significant transformations have also occurred in the dimension of vertical social cohesion at the local level, in the relations between the state and citizens.

Importantly, all social actors' political and civil efforts in the war have been directed to achieving the common goal of victory for Ukraine, and against the common threat of the Russians invasion. Political actors as well as ordinary citizens have joined the Ukrainian military forces, arranged monetary donations, assisted people in need and participated in institutional volunteering.

The special role of city mayors and other local authorities should also be noted. Mayors, as the authorities closest to the people, have played a vital role in military and civil resistance, steering the citizenry in through the uncertainty of war: what to do, how to survive, where to go. During the first days of the war, Vitali Klitschko, the Mayor of Kyiv, announced that together with his brother Volodymyr, he would defend Ukraine, with weapons in their hands.[51] Vitali personally visited sites destroyed by shelling, and kept the people informed of the situation in the city. The Mayor of Kharkiv, Ihor Terekhov, ensured vital aid under massive shelling and spent much of his time in the Kharkiv Metro, together with the large numbers of local people who had sought refuge there in the first months of the war.[52] Oleksandr Lusenko, the Mayor of Sumi, organized provisions for the local territorial defense and personally gave information about the location of enemy troops.[53] Even under Russian occupation, brave leaders continued to govern their cities under the Ukrainian flag. Ivan Fedorov, the Mayor of Melitopol, was captured on the eleventh day of the city's occupation by Russian forces, and was tortured. A further example: at the end of March, another well-known official, Vadym Boichenko, the mayor of Mariupol, who had spearheaded the city's heroic resistance, was forced to leave the city, but retained control of all information.[54]

The example of such actions from the very first days of the war has influenced citizens' general attitudes. Respondents now say they are somewhat more satisfied with the actions of city mayors

---

51 "Top 10 most famous mayors during the war", *Glavkom*, 23 May 2022. https://glavcom.ua/country/politics/top-10-meriv-pro-yakih-naybilshe-govoryat-pid-chas-viyni-847039.html.
52 Ibid.
53 Ibid.
54 Ibid.

and the heads of *hromadas* than with the heads of regional military-civilian administrations, whom they do not know well (see Table 4).

Table 9.4: Satisfaction with activities of mayors/*hromada* heads, and heads of regional military-civilian administrations (in %, July 2022, N=1507)

Levels of satisfaction	Activities of the heads of regional military-civilian administrations	Activities of city mayors /hromada heads)
Fully dissatisfied	5.5%	13.8%
Rather dissatisfied	6.3%	15.4%
Rather satisfied	18.4%	29.5%
Fully satisfied	15.1%	23.9%
I do not know about his/her activity	22.4%	8.6%
I do not know him/her	19.0%	1.8%
Difficult to answer	12.8%	6.6%
I do not want to answer	0.4%	0.4%

These data also demonstrate a "decentralization trace" — how the social bonds formed and maintained during the amalgamation process have contributed to enhancing local awareness and trust during the war. According to annual monitoring by the Institute of Sociology of the National Academy of Sciences of Ukraine, in 2020, 17 percent of Ukrainians said they completely distrusted the local authorities, 28 percent partially distrusted them and only 2 percent fully trusted them. The war has led to both greater trust in and greater satisfaction with local authorities.

The decentralization reform enhanced institutional trust and prompted new models of cooperation between local actors, in this way contributing to the loyal and locally focused actions of Ukrainian mayors in the war. The above-mentioned examples of mayors' resistance show that the relative boundaries between the state and citizens, and vertical and horizontal social ties, have become blurred in conditions of war, rapidly strengthening civil resistance.

Concluding Remarks

Our study has shown that civic initiatives and the increased institutional and interpersonal trust prompted by the decentralization reform have built social capital among *hromada* members and strengthened civic identity. This has further contributed to the widespread and massive military and civil resistance of Ukrainian society since the beginning of the war. Greater trust in ATC heads and city mayors has fostered greater responsibility and the local attachment of local leaders, who have proven their leadership skills by personally supporting and participating in military and civil resistance in all parts of Ukraine. Social capital previously built at the local level made wartime cooperation more vital and coordinated, as local residents were able to draw on the experience gained during the amalgamation procedure.

Further, the war has demonstrated the enhancement of social cohesion in terms of the "common threat" (Russian invasion) and the "common good" (Ukrainian victory), as well as their intertwining. The previously underestimated threat of a Russian invasion became a reality, leading to the deepening of a negative social identity and a discourse of separation ("Ukrainians are not the same as Russians"). The "common good" has boosted individual and collective practical contributions aimed at hastening a Ukrainian victory: mass volunteering, mass donations, widespread support for the state and state institutions.

The specifics of the normative regime under martial law also make clear the importance of reviewing peacetime notions of how to measure social cohesion. Our case study could not identify precise distinctions between the various social cohesion indicators offered by Chan et al.'s measurement scheme. For instance, it is not obvious why "help neighbors or friends" should be an indicator of "voluntarism and donations" (horizontal dimension, objective component) and not "social participation". There are no criteria for distinguishing such interrelated indicators as "social participation" and "political participation". Instead, all these indicators should be seen as dimensions of the "vibrancy of civil society", which is more in line with Viktoriya Sereda's holistic approach.[55] Drawing on her results in "Region, nation and others: interdisciplinary and transcultural rethinking of Ukraine", Sereda shows the variety of civil activism in involvement in state decision-making (Chan's "political participation"), participation in NGOs (social participation), and assistance to other people (volunteering; donations). This situation arises due to terminological uncertainty regarding the concept of "civil activism", which is a key element of Chan's empirical model. We can see that the interplay of these indicators fails to show how to make precise distinctions between horizontal and vertical social cohesion dimensions.

Such distinctions become even more blurred under wartime conditions. Many new "cohesive practices" have appeared since the beginning of the war in Ukraine. For instance, it is hard to find in Chan's framework the practice of joining the army or the territorial defense (should this be considered political or social participation?). The political and civic efforts of all social actors during the war have been directed to achieving the common good of Ukrainian victory against the threat posed by the Russian invasion—erasing horizontal and vertical differences.

The examples of mayors' resistance have shown that the relative boundaries between the state and citizens, and the vertical and horizontal social ties postulated in the social sciences, have become blurred under wartime conditions, rapidly strengthening civil resistance in Ukraine.

As a consequence, peacetime indicators of social cohesion should be re-examined in view of the specifics of the martial law regime. The latter has made it impossible to rely on voting, participation in demonstrations or the signing of petitions as indicators of political participation, since they are prohibited under martial law. Going beyond the distinction of horizontal and vertical dimensions of social cohesion will enable greater room for maneuver.

---

55 Viktoriya Sereda, "Pereosmyslyuyuchy ukrainskyi identyfikatsiinyi prostir: Hromadskyi aktyvizm v Ukraini pislya Yevromaidanu", in: *Fenomen Maidanu v ukrainskomu suspilstvi: Sotsiolohichni interpretatsii* (Kyiv: Instytut sotsiolohii NAN Ukrainy, 2014), 58–78.

Appendix

Logistic regression analysis. Dependent variable: Assessment of performance of local government after decentralization reform (1 = improved, 0 = the same or worse). Coefficient, Standard error, Odds ratio, and Significance. (N=1,710).

Table 9.1 Regression analysis results

	Model 1			Model 2		
	B	SE	Exp(B)	B	SE	Exp(B)
Female gender (vs. male)	0.02	0.11	1.03	-0.08	0.11	0.92
Age (5 groups)	-0.01	0.04	0.99	-0.01	0.05	0.99
Ukrainian ethnicity (vs any other)	0.11	0.15	1.12	-0.01	0.16	0.99
Educational level (6 categories)	0.14**	0.04	1.15	0.12**	0.05	1.12
Financial situation (5 categories)	0.36**	0.06	1.43	0.28**	0.06	1.32
Type of settlement (vs. rural)						
Oblast center	0.58**	0.22	1.79	0.79**	0.23	2.20
Other city	0.46*	0.23	1.58	0.59*	0.24	1.81
Amalgamated territorial community	0.16	0.23	1.18	0.16	0.24	1.18
Geographical location (vs. West)						
North	-0.39*	0.16	0.68	-0.39*	0.17	1.73
Central	-0.16	0.16	0.86	-0.21	0.16	1.20
East	0.17	0.18	1.19	0.16	0.19	1.23
South	-0.05	0.16	0.95	-0.03	0.17	0.88
Trust in institutions (multiple index)				0.55**	0.07	1.73
Interpersonal trust (scale 1-5)				0.19**	0.04	1.20
Belonging to Ukraine (scale 1-4)				0.21*	0.10	1.23
Local belonging (scale 1-4)				-0.12	0.09	0.88
Organisational membership (vs. not)				-0.11	0.18	0.89
Local activism (scale 1-5)				0.06	0.04	1.07
Donations and help (multiple index)				-0.05	0.06	0.96
Disunity scale (multiple index)				-0.06	0.05	0.94
Constant	-2.352**	0.36	0.10	-4.09**	0.59	0.02
Cox & Snell R squared	0.06			0.12		

**Significant at 0.01 level.   *Significant at 0.05 level

Table 9.2. Univariate distribution of variables used in multiple logistic regression analyses

Socio-economic and sociodemographic variables	N	%
Gender		
Male	933	44.4
Female	1170	55.6
Age, years		
18-24	159	7.6
25-35	412	19.6
36-40	627	29.9
51-59	297	14.2
60+	603	28.7
Missing	5	
Ethnicity		
Ukrainian	1807	85.9
Other/not reported	296	14.1
Education		
Not completed secondary	50	2.4
Completed secondary	288	13.8
Specialised secondary / professional	792	37.9
Higher, not completed	177	8.5
Completed higher	670	32.0
Two or more higher	115	5.5
Missing/Hard to say	11	
Economic status		
Not enough for necessary products	307	15.0
Just enough for necessary products	515	25.1
Purchase of durable goods difficult	728	35.5
Some expensive goods difficult	457	22.3
Can afford anything	45	2.2
Missing/Do not know	51	
Geographical location		
West	443	21.1
North	447	21.3
Central	487	23.2
East	307	14.6
South	419	19.9
Settlement type		
Oblast centre	805	38.4
Other city	580	27.6
ATC	539	25.7
Other rural	174	8.3
Missing	5	

Social cohesion variables	N	Mean (St.dev)
Trust in institutions index[56][57]		
Mean index score (1=no trust; 5 = fully trust)	2085	2.5 (0.8)
Missing	18	
Interpersonal trust[58]		
Mean score (1=no trust; 5 = fully trust)	2103	2.8 (1.4)
Belonging to Ukraine[59]		
Mean score (1: not at all; 4: fully)	2103	3.7 (0.6)
Missing		
Belonging to local community[60]		
Mean score (1: not at all; 4: fully)	2103	3.7 (0.6)
Local activism[61]		
Mean score (1: very rarely; 5: very often)	2103	2.3 (1.3)
Donations and help index[62]		
Mean index score (1: very rarely; 5: very often)	2072	3.1 (1.0)
Missing	31	
Disunity index[63]		
Mean index score (1: no disunity; 5: very much disunity)	2065	2.3 (1.1)
Missing	38	
	N	%
Organisational participation		
Member of organisation	198	9.4
Not member / not reported	1905	90.6

---

56 All indices have been tested for internal consistency; Chronbach's Alpha exceeds 0.7.
57 To what extent do you trust the i) president; ii) parliament; iii) local government; iv) NGOs; v) media; vi) judiciary in Ukraine?
58 To what extent do you agree with the statement: It is hard to trust people in my villa ge/town/city. Scale 1= completely agree; 5 = completely disagree.
59 To what extent do you feel yourself to be a citizen of Ukraine?
60 To what extent do you feel yourself to be a resident of your city/ town /village?
61 How often do you participate in discussions of problems in your community /(city): signing petitions, public actions / hearings, etc.?
62 How often do you i) help other people (other than your family) with household chores, work, provide emotional support; ii) do charity work (provide material and financial assistance to those in need)?
63 Please state to what extent you agree that there is disunity between different groups in your community: i) between representatives of different ethnic groups; ii) between people speaking different languages; iii) between local residents and internally displaced persons.

10. Ukraine's Social Inclusion Policies Toward Internally Displaced Persons Has Local Amalgamation Made a Difference?*

Valentyna Romanova

Introduction

Since the Russian Federation started its full-fledged military invasion of Ukraine on 24 February 2022, many people have been displaced. Amalgamated territorial communities (ATCs) have provided support to internally displaced persons (IDPs) in the country. Yaroslav Zhalilo states that territorial communities have taken charge of humanitarian matters, hosting IDPs from the very first days of Russia's invasion.[1] Markiyan Datsyshyn and Sorin Ionitse add: "As local authorities acquired responsibilities and resources, territorial communities were able to carry out the new function of providing supplies to the Armed Forces of Ukraine (the Territorial Defense Forces) and hosting internally displaced persons (IDPs), as well as continuing to provide basic public services to their residents, even in the territorial communities that were badly affected by the war".[2]

The United Nations High Commissioner for Refugees (UN-HCR) *Handbook for the Protection of Internally Displaced Persons* recognizes that substate authorities affect domestic social inclusion policies on IDPs: "Regional and local governmental authorities are

---

* An early version of this chapter was presented at the conference "Evaluation of Policies on Social Inclusion, Migration", Inštitut pravnih znanosti, Maribor, 12-13 September 2022.
1 Yaroslav Zhalilo, "Samoorhanizovani hromady nadiino trymaut tyl", *Ukrainska Pravda*, 12 March 2022. https://www.epravda.com.ua/columns/2022/03/12/683841/.
2 Markiyan Datsyshyn and Sorin Ionitse, "Yak vidnovyty mistseve samovriaduvannia vid naslidkiv viiny?", *Ukrainska Pravda*, 5 August 2022. https://www.pravda.com.ua/columns/2022/08/5/7362004/.

likely to have closer contact with IDPs than the central government and, thus, a better understanding of the problems they face. While national policy decisions are made at the central level, the involvement of local government authorities is essential for the implementation and coordination of protection and assistance activities on the ground".[3] In its *Briefing Note* on Ukraine, the UNHCR stresses that "IDP integration primarily happens at the local level. For the last six years, there are several positive examples regarding implementation of the policies supporting IDP integration".[4]

In this chapter, I seek to analyze the contribution made by the post-2014 decentralization reform, specifically its local amalgamation policy, to Ukraine's social inclusion policies on IDPs. I compare the social policy provisions and their deliverables (i) since the Russian Federation annexed Ukraine's Autonomous Republic of Crimea in 2014 and fuelled the armed conflict in Donbas and (ii) since its military invasion of Ukraine on 24 February 2022. These dates roughly correspond to the launch and completion of the local amalgamation policy, which strengthened local authorities in line with the principle of subsidiarity. I employ two criteria to evaluate IDP social inclusion: housing, operationalized as access to communal accommodation; regular income, operationalized as access to pensions and social benefits.

My findings are that Ukraine's local amalgamation reform made some difference: While its contribution to ensuring a regular income for IDPs was moderate, it was crucial in providing IDPs with communal housing. In the former case, local self-government's direct engagement in IDP registration through the Centers for Administrative Service Provision played a positive role; however, the quality of IDP registration varied across Ukraine. In the case of housing, local authorities were significantly better prepared to host IDPs in 2022; moreover, they proactively used their increased financial capacities to meet the immediate needs of IDPs by providing temporary housing.

---

3   *Handbook for the Protection of Internally Displaced Persons* (Geneva: UNHCR, 2010), 69.
4   *Briefing Note: Inclusion of Internally Displaced Persons* (Kyiv: UNHCR Ukraine, 2022), 3.

The Analytical Framework

In order to identify the impact of Ukraine's local amalgamation on the social inclusion policy on IDPs, I apply a comparative method, the most similar system design, which explains difference or similarity by using similar cases that differ only in the key variable.

In 2014, the Russian Federation illegally annexed Ukraine's Autonomous Republic of Crimea and fuelled armed conflict in the Donetsk and Luhansk regions. Kyiv did not attempt to recover Crimea, but it undertook security operations in Donbas. Even so, the government of Ukraine lost de facto control of less than half of the territories of the Donetsk and Luhansk regions. Approximately 1.5 million people were displaced from these non-government controlled territories into other parts of Ukraine. "[T]here is no breakdown of the number of IDPs from Crimea and eastern Ukraine".[5] As of 30 June 2021, the highest numbers of IDPs were registered in the government-controlled parts of the Donetsk and Luhansk regions: 513,066 in the former and 284,245 in the latter.[6] "Areas with the highest shares of IDPs located further away from the mentioned oblasts included the city of Kyiv (160,036) and Kyiv Oblast (63,267), Kharkiv Oblast (134,335), Dnipropetrovsk Oblast (71,277) and Zaporizhia Oblast (56,107)".[7]

In the second period under study, the Russian Federation engaged in an open invasion of Ukraine and has been attacking both military and civilian infrastructure. As of 27 June 2022, the Office of the UN High Commissioner for Human Rights (OHCHR) recorded 10,631 civilian casualties in the country: 4,731 killed — including 330 children — and 5,900 injured. As of May 2022, the International Organization for Migration (IOM) estimates that a total of 13.7 million

---

5 Tania Bulakh, "Entangled in Social Safety Nets: Administrative Responses to and Lived Experiences of Internally Displaced Persons in Ukraine", *Europe-Asia Studies* 72, no. 3 (2020): 463.
6 "Strategy for Integration of Internally Displaced Persons and Implementation of the Mid-Term Solutions as to Internal Displacement until 2024", approved by Order of the Cabinet of Ministers of Ukraine No. 1364-p on 28 October 2021.
7 *Ukraine - National Monitoring System Report on the Situation of Internally Displaced Persons* (Kyiv: IOM, 2020).

people have been displaced within Ukraine and/or crossed into neighbouring countries; 8.02 million have become IDPs in Ukraine.[8]

As already mentioned, the two periods under study roughly correspond to the launch and completion of the local amalgamation reform in Ukraine. This reform led to the merging of local communities into amalgamated territorial communities (ATCs), granted greater authority in order to improve their capacity to provide public services, including administrative services and social protection. The local amalgamation policy was launched in early 2015 and completed in late 2020.[9] As a result, the number of local councils in Ukraine fell from 10,961 in 2014 to 1,470 in late 2020.

The local amalgamation reform involved devolving public service provision duties from regional and subregional authorities to local ATC authorities. Before the local amalgamation policy was launched, regional and subregional authorities were largely in charge of providing administrative services. After the reform was implemented, ATCs assumed the right to provide administrative services through so-called Centers for Administrative Service Provision or their territorial divisions. Often the Centers, run by local authorities, were established with international technical assistance (i.e., the EU-funded project U-LEAD with Europe). The government has been incrementally increasing the Centers' prerogatives in ATCs.[10] Fiscal decentralization was introduced to enable local authorities to perform their new functions. The 2014 amendments to the Budget Code and the Tax Code increased the ATC budgets' share of tax revenues—most importantly, Personal Income Tax—and assigned a range of subsidies, transfers and grants from the

---

8   *Ukraine Area Baseline Report Line 10: Internal Displacement Figures Recorded at Oblast and Raion Level* (Kyiv: IOM, 2022).
9   In 2015, 159 ATCs were established. In 2016, their number rose to 366. By the end of 2017, there were 665 ATCs in Ukraine. By the end of 2018, that number increased to 874. By July 2019, there were 925 ATCs in Ukraine.
10 Ya. A. Zhalilo et al., *Detsentralizatsiya vlady: Yak zberehty uspishnist' v umovakh novykh vyklykiv?* (Kyiv: NISD, 2018); Ya. A. Zhalilo et al., *Detsentralizatsiya vlady: Poriadok dennyy na sredn'ostrokovu perspektyvu* (Kyiv: NISD, 2019); Valentyna Romanova and Andreas Umland, *Ukraine's Decentralization Reforms Since 2014: Initial Achievements and Future Challenges* (London: Chatham House, 2019).

central budget to ATC budgets.[11] Nevertheless, there were instances when "numerous tasks [were] being transferred to the UTCs [i.e., ATCs] without a clear understanding of the impact in terms of charges and constraints. Apart from the fact that many small and/or under capacitated communities [were] ill-equipped to take on new responsibilities, the transfer of several functions to the local level is not always appropriate".[12]

In order to identify the relevant criteria to assessing and compare Ukraine's social inclusion policies on IDPs, I selected the following domestic policy documents:

- The Law "On Securing the Rights and Freedoms of Internally Displaced Persons" (№ 1706-VII) adopted on 20 October 2014 and amended on 12 December 2015. According to Article 2, its objective was twofold: "creating the conditions for IDPs to voluntarily return to their place of residence or integrate into their new location". Nieczypor claims that "when first drafted, this document only guaranteed displaced Ukrainian citizens the right to return to their place of residence once the causes due to which they left their place of residence ceased to exist. It was not until pressure was brought to bear by NGOs and international organisations that art. 2 of the act was amended on 12 December 2015".[13] Despite the policy document speaking of IDPs' integration, it does not specify any policy measures to achieve this objective.
- The Comprehensive State Program on Support, Social Adaptation, and Reintegration of the Citizens of Ukraine who Moved from the Temporarily Occupied Territories of Ukraine and the Areas where the Antiterrorist Operation is Held to Other Regions of Ukraine until 2017 (Resolution No. 1094 of the Cabinet of Ministers of Ukraine approved

---

11 Tony Levitas and Jasmina Djikic, *Caught Mid-Stream: "Decentralization", Local Government Finance Reform, and the Restructuring of Ukraine's Public Sector 2014 to 2016* (Kyiv: SIDA-SKL, 2017); *Maintaining the Momentum of Decentralisation in Ukraine* (Kyiv: OECD, 2018), 181.
12 *Maintaining the Momentum of Decentralisation in Ukraine*, 207.
13 Krzysztof Nieczypor, "In the shadow of war Ukraine's policy towards internally displaced persons", *OSW Commentary*, no. 290 (2019): 2.

on 16 December 2015) has the appearance of a relevant policy document. However, it lacked an action plan and suffered from a shortage of funding.[14] Additionally, it was in force only until 2017.
- The Strategy for Integration of Internally Displaced Persons and Implementation of the Mid-Term Solutions as to Internal Displacement until 2020 (Resolution No. 909-p approved of the Cabinet of Ministers of Ukraine approved on 15 November 2017) could serve as a relevant document for the purposes of this study. In 2018, it was supplemented with an action plan, but "financial support for the implementation remain[ed] challenging".[15] Notably, it was in force only until 2020.
- Finally, I selected the Strategy for Integration of Internally Displaced Persons and Implementation of the Mid-Term Solutions Regarding Internal Displacement until 2024, approved by Order of the Cabinet of Ministers of Ukraine No. 1364-p on 28 October 2021. The Strategy describes its purpose as facilitating IDPs' further integration by eliminating obstacles to the exercise of their rights and basic freedoms, ensuring their full access to public services, and creating the conditions for the development of their potential and the improvement of IDPs' capacities in their new host communities. Unlike the three policy documents listed above, the 2021 Strategy is supplemented by a detailed operational plan that contains specific policy measures for achieving its strategic objectives and suggests the criteria for evaluating the degree of integration of IDPs. However, the policy document was adopted in late 2021 and outlines the government's plans with respect to policy-making in 2022-2024.

---

14 Yuliya Kaplan, "Kluchovi zasady derzhavnoi polityky u sferi zabezpechennia prav i svobod vnutrishnyo peremishchenyh osib", *NISS*, 3 November 2016. https://niss.gov.ua/doslidzhennya/politika/klyuchovi-zasadi-derzhavnoi-politiki-u-sferi-zabezpechennya-prav-i-svobod.

15 "Humanitarian Needs Overview Ukraine", *OCHA*, 9 February 2021. https://www.humanitarianresponse.info/sites/www.humanitarianresponse.info/files/documents/files/hno_2021-eng_-_2021-02-09.pdf.

This limits my ability to make use of this policy document for the purposes of this study.

Having found that it was impossible to evaluate and compare Ukraine's social inclusion policies toward IDPs based on policy documents, I decided to use the evaluation criteria that IDPs themselves consider the most crucial to their social inclusion.

In the 2016 National Monitoring System Report on the Situation of Internally Displaced Persons, commissioned by IOM in cooperation with Ukraine's Ministry on Social Policy and the Ministry for Temporarily Occupied Territory and Internally Displaced Persons (MinTOT),[16] IDPs reported that housing and regular income (89 percent and 80 percent, respectively) were the most important conditions for their successful integration into their host communities.[17] Subsequent reports confirm that IDPs' perception of their successful integration did not change very much, and housing and regular income remained the top factors for their social inclusion.[18] "[L]ack of access to housing and predictable income are the main reasons why many, especially the elderly, are forced to return to the NGCA [non-government controlled areas] while preserving their IDP status to be able to receive pensions and other social payments in GCA [government-controlled areas]".[19]

For these reasons, I apply these two criteria to conduct my comparative analysis: IDPs' housing and regular income. I operationalize regular income as access to pensions and social benefits. IDPs report that pensions and welfare benefits constitute a considerable portion of their regular income. According to the National

---

16 The Ministry for Temporarily Occupied Territory and Internally Displaced Persons (MinTOT) was established in April 2016. The Minister was simultaneously assigned the position of Deputy Prime Minister.
17 *Ukraine - National Monitoring System Report on the Situation of Internally Displaced Persons* (Kyiv: IOM, 2016).
18 See, for example: *Ukraine - National Monitoring System Report on the Situation of Internally Displaced Persons* (Kyiv: IOM, 2020); *Ukraine Participatory Assessment* (Geneva: UNHCR, 2019).
19 *Briefing Note: After years of displacement aggravated by COVID-19, internally displaced persons from eastern Ukraine remain in need of housing solutions and predictable income* (Kyiv: OCHA, 2021). https://reports.unocha.org/en/country/ukraine/card/2bMBM0ECTo/.

Monitoring System Report on the Situation of Internally Displaced Persons issued in 2021, more than a half of IDPs (51 percent of the survey's respondents) relied on governmental support and more than a third (38 percent) relied on pensions.[20] Recent research on the situation since Russia's military invasion confirms that "[u]nemployment is linked with IDP status ... IDPs are twice as likely to search for a job than non-IDPs. The situation among IDPs who were forced to flee outside of their oblast of residence is the most drastic, with up to 64% of them looking for a job. The most in-demand sectors are service (17% of the sample of job-seeking IDPs), professional (16%), and IT (13%)".[21]

I operationalize IDP housing as access to communal accommodation. The latter includes accommodation in communal property, purchased by the state or local authorities for the benefit of IDPs, and compact temporary communal settlements for IDPs (like dormitories, module houses, etc.). By late 2021, approximately 7,000 IDPs resided in compact temporary communal settlements.[22] I recognize that there are other policy measures that refer to the issue of IDP housing: mortgages, compensation for destroyed housing, financial support for individuals who host IDPs.[23] Still, for the purposes of this study, I examine short-term and long-term communal housing for IDPs.

I acknowledge the limitations of this comparative study. It does not seek to prove that its independent variable explains dependent variables better than any other. For example, the input of

---

20 Taras Marshalok and Yuliya Markuts, "Mistsevi budzhety: yakyi stan sprav u rehionah?" *VoxUkraine*, 3 June 2022. https://voxukraine.org/mistsevi-byudzhety-yakyj-stan-sprav-u-regionah/.
21 *Displacement and Life in Ukraine During Russia's Full-Scale Military Aggression: Analysis of GeoPoll's Survey Results, April-May 2022* (Nicosia: Centre for Sustainable Peace and Democratic Development, 2022), 14.
22 *Protracted Temporality: How IDPs Live in Collective Centres* (Kyiv: R2P.org.ua, 2019). https://r2p.org.ua/wp-content/uploads/2019/10/R2P_CC_Report_ENG.pdf.
23 On 20 March 2022, the Cabinet of Ministers of Ukraine suggested compensation for utility fees for individuals who hosted IDPs (program "Prykhystok"); notably, the compensation would be provided from the central budget via local budgets. On 11 March 2022, the Cabinet of Ministers of Ukraine decided to compensate the utility fees paid by ATCs that hosted IDPs in community-owned buildings.

international stakeholders into Ukraine's social inclusion policies has significantly risen since February 2022. Also, the scope of Russia's aggression against Ukraine has changed dramatically since 24 February 2022, and the length of the two periods that I study is not the same.

Comparative Analysis of Ukraine's Social Inclusion Policies toward IDPs

Similarities

I find two core similarities in the social inclusion policy measures regarding IDPs during the two periods under study. The first similarity: IDP registration as a prerequisite for claiming benefits associated with the IDP status. IDP registration was introduced on 1 October 2014, when the Cabinet of Ministers of Ukraine adopted Decree 505 that requested displaced people officially register as IDPs and obtain official IDP status. Notably, the UN criticized Ukraine for this policy measure, stating: "According to international standards, internal displacement is described as a factual state and, unlike from International Refugee Law, there is nothing like a 'legal IDP status'".[24] On the other hand, this requirement understandable. It is difficult to collect official data on internal displacement, including the needs of IDPs, without registering them. Also, it is logical that the social benefits associated with the IDP status should go hand in hand with obtaining that status.

The second similarity: the state expects local authorities to contribute to the housing of IDPs. The Law "On Securing the Rights and Freedoms of Internally Displaced Persons" (№ 1706-VII), adopted on 20 October 2014 and amended on 12 December 2015, obligated local authorities to assist IDPs in finding a place of residence (Article 11). The Law was adopted long before the full implementation of the local amalgamation policy; nevertheless, the government declared that local government would be in charge of assisting IDPs. In order to provide some funding to local authorities

---

24 Briefing Note: Inclusion of Internally Displaced Persons, 3.

that would enable them to meet IDPs' housing needs, the Cabinet of Ministers of Ukraine approved Resolution № 769 on 4 October 2017, which introduced subventions from the state budget to local budgets, co-financing the local authorities' acquisition and conversion of housing to communal ownership, temporarily provide to IDPs. In line with Resolution № 769, the central budget would cover up to 50 percent of the costs; local budgets were expected to cover no less than 50 percent of the cost of purchasing flats or housing and converting them to communal property. IDPs were not expected to pay rent when residing in communal apartments. Notably, in 2021, the government permitted local authorities to cover 30 percent of the housing cost for IDPs, while the central budget was prepared to cover 70 percent.

On 11 March 2022, the Cabinet of Ministers of Ukraine decided to compensate the utility fees paid from the local budgets of ATCs that hosted IDPs in community-owned buildings. Resolution № 333 of the Cabinet of Ministers of Ukraine, adopted on 19 March 2022, highlighted that the costs for providing temporary accommodation to IDPs were to be covered by both central and local budgets (as well as other sources, like donor aid). Such accommodation was free of charge for IDPs. On 25 March 2022, the president announced an upcoming program aimed at building temporary accommodation for IDPs.[25] The government was in charge of designing and implementing the program across the whole country, and sub-state authorities would be in charge of implementing it on the ground.[26]

Differences

I identify three notable differences in Ukraine's social inclusion policies on IDPs in the two periods under study. The first difference:

---

[25] "U mezhah novoi programmy pidtrymky vnutrishnyo peremishchenyh osib peredbachaetsia budivnytstvo tymchasovoho zhytla—Volodymyr Zelenskyi", *Official Website of the President of Ukraine*, 25 March 2022. https://www.president.gov.ua/news/u-mezhah-novoyi-programi-pidtrimki-vnutrishno-peremishenih-o-73837.

[26] "Pereselentsi, yak i ekonomika, maut staty chastynou nashoi peremohy—vykonavchyi dyrektor AMU Oleksandr Slobozhan", *ZN.ua*, 2 April 2022. https://zn.ua/ukr/internal/pereselentsi-jak-i-ekonomika-majut-stati-chastinoju-nashoji-peremohi-vikonavchij-direktor-amu-oleksandr-slobozhan.html.

IDP registration during the two periods under consideration served different purposes. In contrast to 2022, in 2014 the government made IDP registration necessary to gain access to pensions and social welfare benefits. In late 2014, the government required displaced people to register as IDPs, in line with Resolution № 637 of the Cabinet of Ministers of Ukraine, if they wanted to keep receiving pensions and social welfare payments. Subsequently, to gain access to their payments, many people who were in fact resident in non-government controlled territories of Ukraine, started behaving as IDPs. They travelled to the government-controlled territories of Ukraine, registered as IDPs, and then returned to the non-government controlled territories. As a result, two groups of IDPs emerged: IDPs who in fact left the non-government controlled territories, and IDPs who did not want to leave their homes in the non-government controlled territories of Ukraine, but obtained IDP status in order to get access to pensions and social benefits. In 2021, the UN estimated that approximately 745,000 out of roughly 1.5 million IDPs resided in the government-controlled territories of Ukraine.[27]

Moreover, many IDPs faced obstacles when trying to get access to pensions and social benefits even after they obtained IDP status. "The payments are conducted through the single state bank, 'Oschadbank', which is authorised to issue and maintain the electronic pension certificates, as well as to conduct physical identification of pensioner-IDPs".[28] In 2016, the government introduced a special verification procedure that included regular physical identification at the bank (the state-owned Oshchadbank) and random home checks (IDPs could lose their access to payments if they were absent for more than 60 days from their declared place of residence in the government-controlled territories of Ukraine). In 2016, based on the advice of the Security Service of Ukraine, "the Ministry of

---

27 *Humanitarian Needs Overview Ukraine* (Kyiv: OCHA, 2021). https://www.humanitarianresponse.info/sites/www.humanitarianresponse.info/files/documents/files/hno_2021-eng_-_2021-02-09.pdf.

28 *Briefing Note: Protecting the rights of Ukraine's internally displaced people* (Oslo: Norwegian Refugee Council, 2017), 2.

Social Policy suspended 450,000 payments to displaced people".[29] In addition, "the number of persons residing in the non-government-controlled area and receiving pensions dropped from 1,278,200 in August 2014 to 956,000 in January 2016 and to 562,000 in December 2018".[30] In Spring 2020, due to the COVID-19-related quarantine, the government partially relaxed its strict policy measures and verification procedures. As a result, IDPs' access to pensions and social benefits was simplified.[31]

In contrast, in 2022, displaced persons required IDP registration to obtain social benefits specially intended to support IDPs, but did not require registration to gain access to their pensions and social benefits. In other words, they retained their access if they did not want to register as IDPs. Also in 2022, IDPs did not have to submit to any verification procedures by security services and banks. They could receive payments using the old means: in any bank or at the post office.[32] These policy measures ensured that IDPs continued to have access to their regular income.

The second difference: the administrative capacities of public service provisions for IDPs. In the first period under study, the state demonstrated a very poor ability to accommodate the needs of IDPs regarding registration in practice. As ethnographic research results demonstrate, the process of IDP registration at state agencies was both very lengthy and troublesome: a lot of time and effort was required to go through the various bureaucratic procedures and finally obtain IDP registration.[33]

---

29 Bulakh, "Entangled in Social Safety Nets", 468.
30 Natalia Shapovalova and Valentyna Romanova, "Second-class citizens? Kyiv's policy towards the residents of the conflict-torn eastern regions of Ukraine through the lens of citizenship", in: A. Filippov, N. Hayoz and J. Herlth, eds., *Centres and Peripheries in the Post-Soviet Space: Relevance and Meanings of a Classical Distinction* (Frankfurt am Main: Peter Lang, 2020), 213.
31 Anatoliy Bondarchuk and Oleksandr Kluzhev, "Okupovani. Sotsialni zobovyazannia derzhavy na staryh i novyh okupovanyh terytoriah. Platyty chy ne platyty?" *ZN.ua*, 19 July 2022. https://zn.ua/ukr/internal/okupovani-sotsialn i-zobovjazannja-derzhavi-na-starikh-i-novikh-timchasovo-okupovanikh-terito rijakh-platiti-chi-ne-platiti.html.
32 Ibid.
33 Bulakh, "Entangled in Social Safety Nets", 455-480.

In contrast, in line with Resolution № 269 of the Cabinet of Ministers of Ukraine issued on 13 March 2022, IDPs were allowed to register with local self-government, through territorial communities' executive authorities and the Centers for Administrative Service Provision. This was a very important change for IDPs, because the Centers' facilities, which had been often established with substantial international support during the implementation of the decentralization reform (most importantly—via the "U-LEAD" project, with active participation of Germany's GIZ and Sweden's SIDA), were often much easier to access than the state agencies that registered IDPs in 2014-2021.[34] According to a survey conducted by USAID in 2022, local authorities consulted IDPs regarding social welfare benefits very often.[35] One indicative example is the local authority of the Avanhardivska territorial community in the Odeska region in Southern Ukraine, which established a working group in charge of advising IDPs on this subject.[36]

That said, difficulties have to be acknowledged. Some IDPs temporarily resident in remote rural areas reported that they had received misleading guidance from the local authorities in their host communities and, as a result, did not receive IDP social benefits on time.[37] One IDP related their experience: "After 24 February [2022], we were displaced from Kharkiv to a village in the Kharkiv region. We filled in the application form to claim IDP welfare benefits. Now it is August [2022], and we still have not received anything".[38] The procedure required that displaced persons first

---

34 Also, on 19 April 2022 the government allowed IDP registration via the DIIA digital application launchedin 2020. This measure also simplified the IDP registration procedures.
35 "Za rezultatamy doslidzhennia potreb ta zapytiv hromad, povyazanyh z vyklykamy, yaki zyavylysia vnaslidok povnomashtabnoho vtorhnennia RF", *Decentralization.gov.ua*, 15 August 2022, https://decentralization.gov.ua/uploa ds/attachment/document/1096/%D0%B7%D0%B2%D1%96%D1%82-2022-ne w_08.08.pdf
36 "Vystoyaly u viini z 2014 roku—peremozhemo i zaraz", *Ukraine Crisis Media Centre*, 9 August 2022. https://uacrisis.org/uk/peremozhemo.
37 Phone interview conducted with an IDP on 18 September 2022.
38 "Scho rodyty, yaksho vynykly problem z dopomohou na prozhyvannia dlia VPO" [What should we do if there are issues with social benefits for IPDs], *Vchasno.UA*, 28 August 2022. https://vchasnoua.com/donbass/73556-shcho-r obyty-iakshcho-vynykly-problemy-z-dopomohoiu-na-prozhyvannia-dlia-vpo.

register as IDPs and only then submit an application form if they wanted to claim IDP welfare benefits. This two-part procedure was established because many IDPs did not want to claim benefits, but wanted to register the fact of their displacement. While most IDPs were informed of this two-part procedure, there were cases of local authorities failed to communicate that an additional step was required to claim IDP welfare benefits, or else did not provide enough guidance on how to complete the application form.[39]

This demonstrates that local authorities assumed the duty of public service provision for IDPs, but some of them apparently lacked the appropriate guidelines. That such important information was missing indicates insufficient cooperation between the central state authorities (the Ministry for Social Policy of Ukraine) and the regions (regional executives), on the one hand, and local self-government, on the other.

The third difference: the proactive action undertaken in 2022 by local authorities with respect to IDP housing; this contrasts with the previous period under consideration. The policy measures undertaken by the government in the first period under study did not help to solve problem, partly due to poor local budgets, but also to the lack of active engagement by the local authorities. "In 2016, the Ministry of Temporarily Occupied Territories and IDPs and UNHCR Ukraine launched the national Cities of Solidarity Initiative in Mariupol for cities hosting IDPs, followed by subsequent conferences in Kyiv in 2018 and in Kharkiv in 2019 that brought together representatives from 36 cities to identify further improvements for housing assistance for IDPs".[40] In 2017-2020, 340 flats were purchased for 1,100 IDPs across Ukraine. However, this number was too low to accommodate the displaced persons in need of accommodation. For example, there were approximately 4,700 IDPs in the Vinnytska region in Central Ukraine; only three communities made

---

39 Some who applied for IDP social benefits through the DIIA digital application "DIIA" also faced challenges.
40 *Briefing Ukraine: Adapting Pre-Existing Housing Schemes to Meet IDPs' Specific Needs* (Kyiv: OCHA, 2020). https://reliefweb.int/report/ukraine/ukraine-ada pting-pre-existing-housing-schemes-meet-idps-specific-needs.

use of the subventions for IDP housing, purchasing five flats for five displaced families.[41]

Notably, once the local amalgamation policy was completed, policy outputs changed dramatically. In 2021 alone, 325 flats were acquired for 850 IDPs.[42] This implies that additional financial resources available in the ATC budgets made a difference, but was still insufficient to solve the problem. "Affordable housing, social housing and compensation mechanisms for IDPs remain[ed] a priority need ... Over 500,000 IDPs across Ukraine continue[d] living in rented accommodation with no security of tenure".[43] The Strategy for Integration of Internally Displaced Persons and Implementation of the Mid-Term Solutions as to Internal Displacement until 2024 stated that, "[a]lthough the law provides for the internally displaced persons' right to social or temporary accommodation, social shared houses, practical exercise of this right is hindered by insufficient quantity or lack of respective housing in the settlements of the receiving territorial communities".[44]

Civil society has made efforts to address the issue. "With no infrastructure or process in place to facilitate IDP resettlement, a new breed of civil society organization has stepped in to provide IDPs assistance upon arrival and information on their new communities, and to advocate for local funding and support".[45] However, their input should not be overestimated. Despite the overwhelming majority of people in Ukraine claiming to have either positive or

---

41 "Na Vinnychyni vprovadzhuietsia derzhavna prohrama zabezpechennia zhytlom vnutrishnyo peremishenyh osib", *Official Website of Vinnytska Regional State Administration*, 27 October 2021. http://www.vin.gov.ua/news/ostanninovyny/40864-na-vinnychchyni-uspishno-vprovadzhuietsia-derzhavna-prohrama-zabezpechennia-zhytlom-vnutrishno-peremishchenykh-osib-4.
42 "Blyzko 850 IDP otrymayut tsyohorich zhytlo za programou 70/30", *Official Website of Ministry for Temporarily Occupied Territory and Internally Displaced Persons*, 3 June 2021, https://minre.gov.ua/news/blyzko-850-vpo-otrymayut-cogorich-zhytlo-za-programoyu-7030.
43 *Humanitarian Needs Overview Ukraine* (Kyiv: OCHA, 2021), 85-86.
44 "Strategy for Integration of Internally Displaced Persons and Implementation of the Mid-Term Solutions as to Internal Displacement until 2024", approved by Order of the Cabinet of Ministers of Ukraine No. 1364-p on 28 October 2021. https://www.kmu.gov.ua/npas/pro-shvalennya-strategiyi-integraciyi-v-a1364r.
45 Lauren Van Metre, Stephen E. Steiner and Melinda Haring, "Ukraine's Internally Displaced Persons Hold a Key to Peace", *Atlantic Council* (2017): 3.

neutral attitudes towards IDPs,[46] "in 2015 overall less than eight per cent of respondents acknowledged voluntarily helping the IDPs (compare that to 28.3 who helped the Ukrainian army) [...] Most claimed that they are either unable to help (from 11.5 per cent in Kyiv to 22.9 in Donetsk and Luhansk) or think that it is the state that should be responsible for such assistance (from 12.8 per cent in the west to 33.7 in Donbas)".[47]

In contrast, as early as 14-20 March 2022, "official channels of local government bodies and their representatives ... started sharing the information about the launch of additional locations for accommodating the displaced. For instance, Volyn will launch [an] additional 13,000 places, another 15,000 places will be launched in Zakarpattia; dormitories will be renovated in Ivano-Frankivsk".[48] In Spring 2022, 1,200 IDPs were registered in the Baikovetska territorial community in the Ternopilska region in Western Ukraine — an ATC with a population of 15,000 people. The Bilotserkivka territorial community in the Poltavska region in Central Ukraine accepted over 1,000 IDPs. This roughly corresponded to 12 per cent of its population. Like many other communities across Ukraine, they provided IDPs with temporary shelter in schools, summer camps, hotels/hostels, and other facilities at their disposal. The Kharkivska and Dnipropetrovska regions — the regions that have suffered from intense Russian's missile attacks from the first days of the war — hosted over 295,000 IDPs each. In the Dnipropetrovska

---

46 *Ukrainians' Attitudes Towards IDPs from Donbas and Crimea. Summary of Opinion Polls* (Geneva: UNHCR, 2016). http://unhcr.org.ua/attachments/article/1605/Public%20Survey%20Report_ENG.pdf; Tania Bulakh, "'Strangers Among Ours': State and Civil Responses to the Phenomenon of Internal Displacement in Ukraine", in: A. Pikulicka-Wilczewska and G. Uehling, eds., *Migration and the Ukraine Crisis: A Two-Country Perspective* (Bristol: E-International Relations, 2017), 49-61; Viktoriya Sereda, "'Social Distancing' and Hierarchies of Belonging: The Case of Displaced Population from Donbas and Crimea", *Europe-Asia Studies* 72, no. 3 (2020): 404-431.
47 Kateryna Ivashchenko-Stadnik, "The Social Challenge of Internal Displacement in Ukraine: The Host Community's Perspective", in: Pikulicka-Wilczewska and Uehling, *Migration and the Ukraine Crisis*, 33.
48 Anastasiia Bobrova, Valeriia Lazarenko, and Yelyzaveta Khassai, "Housing and War in Ukraine (February 24 — March 22, 2022)", *Cedos*, 22 March 2022. https://cedos.org.ua/wp-content/uploads/zhytlo-monitoryng-pdf-na-sajt-angl.docx.pdf.

region, in summer 2022, 273 settlements were actively hosting IDPs. By September 2022, the Kyivska region hosted 22,300 IDPs in communal accommodations.[49] The Avanhardivska territorial community in the Odeska region in Southern Ukraine provided temporary accommodation to a displaced family in one of the four flats that it purchased in late 2021, using a subvention from the central budget for accommodating IDPs.[50]

In 2022, local authorities reported that their priority was to support the Ukrainian Army and Ukraine's Territorial Defense, and that their next concern was taking care of IDPs, mainly addressing their accommodation needs.[51] In order to cope with these tasks, ATCs redistributed the funds available in local budgets and optimized their expenditures.[52] In addition, local authorities reorganized their staff members' responsibilities. The mayor of the Avanhardivska territorial community in the Odeska region in Southern Ukraine reported that five working groups were established in 2022, including one in charge of temporary accommodation for IDPs.[53]

Conclusions

I have compared Ukraine's social inclusion policies in the period of the Russian Federation's hybrid war against Ukraine in 2014 and since its military invasion of Ukraine in early 2022. This roughly corresponds to the launch of local amalgamation in late 2014 and early 2015 and its completion in 2021. I employed two criteria for evaluating IDP social inclusion: housing (operationalized as access

---

49 "Tymchasove zhytlo dlia pereselenciv: skilky vilnyh micts na Kyivshyni", *Suspilne.: Novyny*, 9 September 2022. https://suspilne.media/280212-timcasov e-zitlo-dla-pereselenciv-skilki-vilnih-misc-e-na-kiivsini/.
50 "Vystoyaly u viini z 2014 roku – peremozhemo i zaraz".
51 "Za rezultatamy doslidzhennia potreb ta zapytiv hromad, povyazanyh z vyklykamy, yaki zyavylysia vnaslidok povnomashtabnoho vtorhnennia RF", *Detsentralizatsiya*, 15 August 2022. https://decentralization.gov.ua/uploads/attachm ent/document/1096/%D0%B7%D0%B2%D1%96%D1%82-2022-new_08.08.pdf.
52 Ibid.
53 "Vystoyaly u viini z 2014 roku – peremozhemo i zaraz".

to communal accommodation) and regular income (operationalized as access to pensions and social benefits).

I conclude that local amalgamation reform had only a modest role in ensuring IDPs' regular income; however, its input into providing IDPs with communal housing was critical. The direct engagement of local self-government in IDP registration via the Centers for Administrative Service Provision in 2022-2023 made a positive difference. The Centers' facilities were better than those of the state agencies, making IDP registration less troublesome and protracted. This advance resulted from the fact that the facilities of the Centers for Administrative Service Provision had benefitted from international support during the implementation of the decentralization reform (via the "U-LEAD" project). However, some IDPs received misleading guidelines from local authorities when getting registered outside the Centers. This makes it imperative for the state (via the Ministry for Social Policy of Ukraine) to ensure that it provide accurate and comprehensive guidelines to local authorities so that they can carry out their delegated responsibilities. Since 2022, local authorities have been significantly better able to perform the duties of hosting IDPs assigned to them by the central government; they often acted on their own initiative and proactively used their financial capacities to benefit IDPs, specifically to provide IDPs with temporary housing. An important enabling factor was the receipt of urgent and substantial international aid, delivered via international organisations and projects, including ones that had actively cooperated with local authorities when the post-2014 decentralization reform was implemented.

The advance in IDPs' access to regular payments and housing in the second period under study resulted from a shift in government policy from "suspecting" IDPs to facilitating their social inclusion. In the first period under investigation, the government often suspected IDPs as potentially responsible for the armed conflict in Donbas. This perception was encouraged by the fact that the Russian Federation issued approximately 750,000 Russian passports to Ukrainians who resided in the non-government controlled territories of Ukraine.⁵⁴ This explains why the state would sometimes prevent rather than facilitate their social inclusion.⁵⁵ Since 24 February 2022, the Russian Federation has systematically threatened the lives of the citizens of Ukraine, disregarding their potential (pre-war) pro-Russian sentiments. After the launch of Russia's full-scale military invasion, the state adjusted its core policy measures to accommodate IDPs' urgent needs, and many policy measures have been directed to facilitating IDP's social inclusion by ensuring their access to regular income and housing.

---

54 Fabian Burkhardt, Cindy Wittke, Maryna Rabinovych, and Elia Bescotti, *Passportization, Diminished Citizenship Rights, and the Donbas Vote in Russia's 2021 Duma Elections* (Cambridge, MA: TCUP HURI, 2022).
55 Shapovalova and Romanova, "Second-class citizens?", 201-222.

11. Four Geopolitical Dimensions of Ukraine's Decentralization*

Andreas Umland and Valentyna Romanova

The rearrangement of political power and public finances in the Ukrainian state is often simply termed "decentralization". The unpretentiousness of the label, the largely technical character of the reform, and the provincial character of the transformation have meant that this fundamental restructuring of Ukrainian state-society relations has fallen below the radar of many Western journalists and analysts. Such inattention is hard to justify as the repercussions of Ukraine's decentralization extend beyond the country's borders and exert considerable influence on the geopolitics of Eastern Europe at large.

Introduction

As mentioned in previous chapters, the Western perception of Ukrainian decentralization sometimes sees it as something imposed by the West, prompted by the EU's Association Agreement with Kyiv, or even triggered by the conflict with Russia and the related Minsk Agreements (in which the term "decentralization" appears). Yet Ukraine's current administrative restructuring started before the ratification of the Association Agreement and the signing of the first Minsk documents in summer 2014. The reform's roots are national rather than foreign. Decentralization was attempted before the start of the Euromaidan Revolution in November 2013.[1]

The victory of the Euromaidan uprising in February 2014, the start of Russia's intervention in Ukraine, and the two subsequent

---

* Earlier versions of this chapter have appeared in different languages in *Survival, Dzerkalo tyzhnya, Vox Ukraine, Demokratizatsiya, Ukraine-Analysen* and other periodicals.
1 See, for example, Valentyna Romanova, "The Role of Centre–Periphery Relations in the 2004 Constitutional Reform in Ukraine", *Regional & Federal Studies* 21, no. 3 (2011): 321-339.

rounds of national—presidential and parliamentary—elections in 2014 changed the composition of the ruling elites of Ukraine. The unexpected and grave threat to Ukraine's territorial integrity demonstrated the vulnerability of the hitherto centralized, yet regionally diverse, state. Moreover, post-Euromaidan civil society continued to apply pressure to policymakers and demanded substantial rather than cosmetic reforms.

This chapter identifies four international dimensions of the Ukrainian local government reforms. These concern their support of the Ukrainian state's general resilience, internal cohesion, and ongoing Europeanization, as well as their growing role as reform templates for other former republics of the USSR. Ukraine's decentralization has geopolitical implications to the extent that it co-determines future stability and change not only in Ukraine, but also in other parts of the post-Soviet space.[2]

Why and How Decentralization Started

After 25 years of inconclusive reform attempts, Kyiv moved swiftly from declaring decentralization to its implementation by concrete policy-making. Some of the eagerness to finally start a genuine devolution of power to the local level, after the Euromaidan revolution, was due to many politicians' desire to avoid federalization. Remaking Ukraine into a federation was then (and partly still is) popular in both Russia and the West. These two parties are, of course, driven by different motives in promoting the empowerment of Ukrainian regions rather than municipalities.

Before the Russian Federation openly invaded Ukraine on 24 February 2022, Moscow saw federalization as an instrument to weaken, subvert or even dismember the Ukrainian state. Many in the West, in contrast, believed that a federation would result in a well-functioning Ukrainian state, similar to the US, Germany or

---

2   For instance, one recent report considers Ukraine's decentralization a potentially suitable model for local government reform in the UK: Anthony Breach and Stuart Bridgett, *Centralisation Nation: Britain's System of Local Government and Its Impact on the National Economy* (London: Centre for Cities, 2022), 55-58. https://www.centreforcities.org/publication/centralisation-nation/.

Switzerland. The latter federations, however, have the luxury of not sharing a long border with a militarily superior and "fraternal", irredentist, would-be empire. Many Ukrainians' categorical rejection of federalization has, therefore, little to do with the concept as such.[3] It is a preference driven by Ukrainian political caution, historic experiences of Tsarist, Soviet and Putin-era Russia, as well as a good sense of what "federalism" means within the Russian (so-called) Federation.

The Ukrainian decentralization reform today combines a number of separate transition processes that touch upon both the input and output aspects of rural and urban politics. So far, the reform has mostly affected local government and finance. Small local communities have been merged into larger, more sustainable and more powerful self-governing units. Additional budgetary and legal competencies have been devolved from regional bodies to the municipal level. Regional and subregional administrative agencies, whose staff is appointed by Kyiv, have been stripped of a share of their prerogatives to the benefit of the newly amalgamated territorial communities (ATCs). "[D]ecentralisation has resulted in a reallocation of spending responsibilities across subnational levels (particularly from the rayon to cities and the UTCs [i.e., ATCs]) instead of a reallocation of charges between the central (ministry) and subnational levels".[4] The share of local budgets' revenue increased from 5.1 percent of GDP in 2015 to 7.3 percent in 2021, while local budget revenues' share of Ukraine's consolidated budget increased from 18.5 percent in 2015 to 23.3 percent in 2021.[5] Notably, even during Russia's full-scale military invasion of Ukraine, which had significant consequences for Ukraine's economy, revenues to local

---

3   Mykola Rjabčuk, "Dezentralisierung und Subsidiarität: Wider die Föderalisierung à la russe", *Osteuropa* 64, nos. 5-6 (2014): 217-225.
4   *Maintaining the Momentum of Decentralisation in Ukraine* (Kyiv: OECD, 2018), 181. www.oecd.org/countries/ukraine/maintaining-the-momentum-of-decentralisation-in-ukraine-9789264301436-en.htm.
5   "Monitoring of the process of decentralisation of power and local government reform", *Detsentralizatsiya*, 2022. https://decentralization.gov.ua/uploads/library/file/800/10.01.2022.pdf.

budgets in the first half of 2022 were 10% higher compared to the same period in 2021.[6]

Cross-national comparative research finds that local amalgamation policies have both advantages and disadvantages, and Ukraine is no exception.[7] As the chapters of this volume demonstrate, the Ukrainian decentralization reform has not been flawless. The government of Ukraine plans to continue its implementation, despite the obvious wartime obstacles.

The decentralization reform has had notable positive outcomes and outputs. The implementation of the reform strengthened Ukraine's state-society relations, transparency of resource allocation increased, and opportunities for corruption were reduced.[8] Patriotic fervor has been deflected from mythologizing imagined communities to improving real ones. Civic activism has been encouraged and utilized for the public good.[9] Cities, towns and villages could cooperate with each other more easily, but also compete for direct investment, tourism, project funding, qualified personnel, and public resources. Such a situation generates stimuli for improving competitiveness.

Research results demonstrate that by improving public service delivery and strengthening local budgets, Ukraine's decentralization reform has contributed to resisting the Kremlin's hybrid aggression since 2014.[10] Local self-government has aided the Ukrainian state's capacity to provide life support to municipalities since

---

6   Taras Marshalok and Yuliya Markuts, "Mistsevi byudzhety: Yakyi stan sprav u rehionakh?", *VoxUkraine*, 3 June 2022. https://voxukraine.org/mistsevi-byudz hety-yakyj-stan-sprav-u-regionah/.
7   A detailed scholarly overview of the advantages and disadvantages of local amalgamation policies can be found in: Pawel Swianiewicz, "If territorial fragmentation is a problem, is amalgamation a solution? Ten years later", *Local Government Studies* 44, no. 1 (2018): 1-10.
8   Oesten Baller, "Korruptionsbekämpfung und Dezentralisierung auf dem Prüfstand des Reformbedarfs in der Ukraine", *Jahrbuch für Ostrecht*, no. 2 (2017): 235-268.
9   "Seventh Annual Ukrainian Municipal Survey. 12 May – 3 June 2021." *International Republican Institute*, May 2021. https://www.iri.org/sites/default/files/ wysiwyg/seventh_municipal_survey_may_2021_eng_-_v2.pdf.
10 Valentyna Romanova, "Ukraine's Resilience to Russia's Military Invasion in the Context of the Decentralisation Reform", *Stefan Batory Foundation: ideaForum*, January 2022. https://www.batory.org.pl/wp-content/uploads/2022/05/Ukr aines-resilience-to-Russias-military-invasion.pdf.

Russia's full-scale military invasion on 24 February 2022. After martial law was introduced, most directly elected substate councils continued to perform their principal duty: ensuring public service provision. Most city mayors and local councils have by and large resisted the Kremlin's pressure to collaborate and have instead protected people in accordance with Ukrainian law; democratically legitimate city and territorial administrations have actively participated in local defense efforts.

In addition, Ukraine's local governments have shown themselves ready to contribute to the multilevel system of national resilience. In line with the 2021 law on national resilience, local governments were tasked with taking charge of territorial defense (*teroborona*) and provide security for the regions and municipalities. Since martial law was declared on 24 February 2022, the mayors and substate councils of ATCs located in central and western Ukraine have taken care of people forced to evacuate their residences. Local councils approve programs to shelter internally displaced persons (IDPs) and cover their basic needs. To cope with these tasks, ATCs have redistributed the funds available in local budgets and optimized their expenditures.

In Ukraine, these and other positive effects of decentralization gain additional weight in view of the country's multiple significance: one of Europe's territorially largest nations, a civilizational frontier state, a crucial post-Soviet republic, and a geopolitically pivotal country. As a result of — among other reforms — decentralization, the Ukrainian state has become more robust and cohesive. This has broader implications for the spread and impact of European values across the Eurasian continent. Ukraine's decentralization has thus, at least, four geopolitical implications.

Decentralization Increases Resilience

First and foremost, decentralization makes Ukraine, as a state and nation, more resilient by reducing, suppressing or containing various post-Soviet pathologies of public administration and local development. This effect has not only municipal, regional or national relevance, but also an international dimension. To be sure, post-

Soviet Ukraine was significantly less centralized than the Russian (so-called) Federation or other authoritarian successor republics of the USSR, from the outset.[11]

In comparison to its western neighbors, Ukraine was more institutionally centralized than most countries in the European Union.[12] However, in terms of fiscal relations, Ukraine was, already before 2014, more decentralized than many other European countries: "at least in strictly fiscal terms, Ukraine has [long] been one of the most 'decentralized' countries in Europe".[13] That was because "local governments [in post-Soviet Ukraine] have had at least nominal control over almost 40% of public expenditures since independence".[14]

Before 2014, Ukraine had suffered from informal regionalization into semi-autonomous fiefdoms controlled by rent-extracting politico-economic magnates and their mafia-like structures. Behind the scenes, certain "oligarchs", bureaucrats or politicians functioned and still often continue to function as powerful patrons of clientelistic networks, which deeply subvert and partly control certain official governmental and non-governmental organizations, as well as many commercial enterprises.[15] The reach of this or that oligarchic clan could sometimes cover a macro-region, like the Donets Basin (Donbas), a particular *oblast* (region), or a larger city and its surroundings. In addition to regional diversity, Ukraine's unregulated regional crypto-regimes were and partly still are undermining the rule of law, hindering economic growth, and blocking political development.[16]

---

11 Cameron Ross and Petr Panov, "The range and limitation of sub-national regime variations under electoral authoritarianism: The case of Russia". *Regional and Federal Studies* 29, no. 3 (2019): 355-380.
12 *OECD Territorial Reviews: Ukraine 2013* (Paris: OECD, 2014).
13 Tony Levitas and Jasmina Djikic, *Caught Mid-Stream: "Decentralization", Local Government Finance Reform, and the Restructuring of Ukraine's Public Sector 2014 to 2016* (Kyiv: SIDA-SKL, 2017), 4.
14 Ibid.
15 Henry E. Hale, *Patronal Politics: Eurasian Regime Dynamics in Comparative Perspective* (Cambridge: Cambridge University Press, 2015).
16 *Integrity and Inclusiveness of the Democratic Process in Ukraine: Analysis of Interim Research Findings in the Regions* (Kyiv: UNDP, 2019).

The clear subregional focus of Ukraine's governance reform does not fully neutralize such clan-like structures. But it helps to weaken them, chase them away, or break them up. Ukrainian decentralization devolves power to a level lower, and to communities smaller, than those in which most of the old informal networks operate. This does not make state-capture by private interest impossible, but complicates the subversion of the public sphere by private interests.[17] It is true that decentralization sometimes simply transfers a corrupt network from the national or regional to the local level.[18] In some cases, it can even benefit clans that have been hitherto functioning within a municipal context.[19]

On the whole, however, decentralization in Ukraine — as elsewhere in the world — strengthens rather than weakens the rule of law and promotes economic development.[20] Newly empowered self-governing bodies are more responsible and exposed to public scrutiny by their local communities than the Byzantine administrations inherited from the Soviet system. When ambitious entrepreneurs encounter a local — rather than regional or national — political framework, their industry is more likely to turn into political and developmental rather than informal and extractive action.

On average, Ukraine's ATCs are thus less susceptible to subversion by semi-secretive networks and rapacious rent-seeking than the old *oblast* (regional) and *rayon* (district) administrations and councils. The new ATCs are — more than the older, less powerful and smaller communities — motivated to compete with other ATCs for investment, luring tourists, providing services, and gaining fame. This does not mean that all ATCs have proven capable of ensuring public service delivery across Ukraine. As a result, the government of Ukraine intends to assess the performance of each

---

17 *Decentralisation in Ukraine: Achievements, Expectations and Concerns* (Kyiv: UCIPR, 2017), 12.
18 William Dudley, "Ukraine's Decentralization Reform", *SWP Research Division Eastern Europe and Eurasia Working Papers*, no. 1 (2019): 28-30.
19 See Max Bader, "The Risk of Local Elite Capture in Ukraine's Decentralization Reform", *Vox Ukraine*, 25 January 2021. https://voxukraine.org/en/the-risk-of-local-elite-capture-in-ukraine-s-decentralization-reform/.
20 *Making Decentralisation Work: A Handbook for Policy-Makers* (Paris: OECD, 2019).

ATC and indicates that it might amend the geographical boundaries of those ATCs which demonstrate poor results.[21]

Decentralization thus makes the Ukrainian state more stable, functional, and effective. Ukraine's increased resilience and greater dynamism support its general modernization. By strengthening Ukraine's democracy and economy, decentralization can help — because of Ukraine's size and role in Eastern Europe — change the entire post-Soviet area for the better.

Decentralization Improves National Cohesion

Second, in addition to making Ukraine's state more solid in general, many Ukrainian politicians have also come to see decentralization as a potent antidote to Russia's hybrid warfare in particular. Not only does the deeper involvement of ordinary Ukrainians in government affairs, made possible by decentralization, support Ukrainian the civic spirit of its citizenry. As Andriy Parubiy, the Speaker of the national parliament, the *Verkhovna Rada* (Supreme Council), argued in the 2nd All-Ukrainian ATCs Forum in Kyiv in December 2017, that "[t]he path of decentralisation was an asymmetrical response to the aggressor [i.e., Russia]. In fact, the process of capable hromadas' [communities'] formation was a kind of sewing of the Ukrainian space".[22]

Moscow's tactic since 2014 has been to try to capture certain regions and their capitals using the Russian state's allies, proxies, and agents within Ukraine.[23] The general framework for these

---

21 Valentyna Romanova, "Ukraine: The first experiences with voting in the amalgamated territorial communities", in: Adam Gendźwiłł, Ulrik Kjaer, and Kristof Steyvers, eds., *Routledge Handbook of Local Elections and Voting in Europe* (Abingdon: Routledge, 2022).
22 "How European Ukraine is being sewn of amalgamated hromadas", *Detsentralizatsiya*, 5 December 2017. decentralization.gov.ua/en/news/7747.
23 Some early contributions to the heated debate about the relative weight of domestic versus foreign factors in the outbreak of the Donbas War — a discussion that is also relevant to some issues touched upon here — include, in chronological order: Nikolai Mitrokhin, "Infiltration, Instruktion, Invasion: Russlands Krieg in der Ukraine", *Osteuropa* 64, no. 8 (2014): 3-16; Sergiy Kudelia, "Domestic Sources of the Donbas Insurgency", *PONARS Eurasia Policy Memos*, no. 351 (2014). www.ponarseurasia.org/memo/domestic-sources-donbas-insurgency; Andreas Umland, "In Defense of

operations has been either the traditional *oblasts* and the Autonomous Republic of Crimea, or macro-regions like the above-mentioned Donets Basin and *Novorossiia* (New Russia), embracing the entirety of Ukraine's Russophone east and south. Russia is seen by Russians as consisting of *oblasts*, *krais* and republics, or of macro-regions (e.g., Siberia, the Urals, etc.). The Ukrainian state is also perceived by many Russian politicians in such terms. Until 2014, in Ukraine's mainly Russophone east and south, powerful regional clans and *oblast* administrations provided entry points for Russian operations designed to fan anti-centralist autonomism, pro-Russian separatism, and pan-Slavic nationalism.

The current devolution of power to the local level, in Ukraine, deprives Russia's various hybrid warriors of their customary institutional frameworks and blocks critical entry points for seditious action.[24] A decentralization that is not a federalization complicates

Conspirology: A Rejoinder to Serhiy Kudelia's Anti-Political Analysis of the Hybrid War in Eastern Ukraine", *PONARS Eurasia*, 30 September 2014. www.ponarseurasia .org/article/defense-conspirology-rejoinder-serhiy-kudelias-anti-political-analysis -hybrid-war-eastern; Sergiy Kudelia, "Reply to Andreas Umland: The Donbas Insurgency Began At Home", *PONARS Eurasia*, 8 October 2014. www.ponarseurasia .org/article/reply-andreas-umland-donbas-insurgency-began-home; Lawrence Freedman, "Ukraine and the Art of Limited War", *Survival* 56, no. 6 (2014-15): 7-38; Nikolai Mitrokhin, "Infiltration, Instruction, Invasion: Russia's War in the Donbass", *Journal of Soviet and Post-Soviet Politics and Society* 1, no. 1 (2015): 219-250; Oleksandr Zadorozhnii, "Hybrid War or Civil War? The Interplay of Some Methods of Russian Foreign Policy Propaganda with International Law", *Kyiv-Mohyla Law and Politics Journal*, no. 2 (2016): 117-128; Andrew Wilson, "The Donbas in 2014: Explaining Civil Conflict Perhaps, but not Civil War", *Europe-Asia Studies* 68, no. 4 (2016): 631-652; Ivan Katchanovski, "The Separatist War in Donbas: A Violent Break-up of Ukraine?", *European Politics and Society* 17, no. 4 (2016): 473-489; Serhiy Kudelia, "The Donbas Rift", *Russian Politics and Law* 54, no. 1 (2016): 5-27; Gwendolyn Sasse and Alice Lackner, "War and Identity: The Case of the Donbas in Ukraine", *Post-Soviet Affairs* 34, nos. 2-3 (2018): 139-157; Elise Giuliano, "Who Supported Separatism in Donbas? Ethnicity and Popular Opinion at the Start of the Ukraine Crisis", *Post-Soviet Affairs* 34, nos. 2-3 (2018): 158-178; Andreas Umland, "The Glazyev Tapes, Origins of the Donbas Conflict, and Minsk Agreements", *Foreign Policy Association*, 13 September 2018. foreignpolicyblogs.com/2018/09/13/the-glazyev-tapes-origins-of -the-donbas-conflict-and-minsk-agreements/.

24 Several years before the start of the war, a prescient warning against separatism and praise for decentralization was published in Ukrainian: Hennadiy Poberezhnyy, "Detsentralizatsiya yak zasib vid separatyzmu", *Krytyka*, no. 11 (2006): 3–7. http://krytyka.com/ua/articles/detsentralizatsiya-yak-zasib-vid-separatyzmu.

the targeting and planning of irredentist operations like those carried out in Simferopol, Donetsk and Luhansk in 2014. As regional capitals and governments gradually lose political relevance, it becomes more difficult for the Kremlin to clearly delineate territories where it may want to support a secession or/and prepare an annexation.

In a properly decentralized Ukraine, a successful coup in an eastern or southern Ukrainian *oblast* center by some Moscow-supported "people's governor" would be of limited use. A hypothetical Kremlin-installed warlord in this or that regional capital would have to persuade all of the region's municipal and communal legislative and executive bodies to join his (much less likely: her) cause. Russia could, in March 2014, install the present Prime Minister of Crimea, Sergei Aksenov in Simferopol, in spite of the fact that Aksenov's Russian Unity party received only 4 percent of the vote in the preceding local elections of 2010. Had strong local (rather than regional) self-government been in place by February 2014, Russia's takeover of the Crimean peninsula would arguably have been more difficult to plan, and more complicated to execute.

After the Russian Federation's open invasion of Ukraine and its temporary occupation of some territories, like the Kherson *oblast*, it discovered that it was not enough to appoint a "regional governor" to control the system of governance in the whole region. Due to Ukraine's decentralization reform, mayors and city councils are not fully and directly subordinate to regional governors. In part, Ukraine's subnational governance system continued to function even after the Kremlin attacked Ukraine on 24 February 2022, and Russia occupied Ukrainian territories:

> "[M]ayors and sub-state councils have been making decisions that undermine the enemy's attempts to stage 'referenda' on the occupied territories. In response to democratically elected councilors' fears about potential attempts by the Russian military to do so in occupied Kherson oblast, the regional council held a session on 12 March 2022 to address the president, parliament, government and people of Ukraine. It announced that it would not approve any attempts to hold a potential referendum proclaiming any kind

of 'people's republic' in the region. The Mykolaiv regional council made a similar decision on 26 April 2022".[25]

To the degree that local government reforms have helped to support Kyiv's independence and to stabilize the Ukrainian state, they have undermined the ideology and rhetoric of Russian revanchism, in general. The stronger Ukraine is, the less plausible does Moscow's neo-imperial project look, to say nothing of the Kremlin's pretense to hegemony in the former Tsarist or Soviet space. As Zbigniew Brzezinski quipped in 1997, "without Ukraine, Russia ceases to be a Eurasian empire".[26]

This geostrategic character of Ukraine's nation-building reforms, including decentralization, is for many Ukrainians a trivial fact, if not simply self-evident and hardly worth mentioning. They may find an outline, like the one above, of—for them—commonplaces and obvious truisms redundant. It is, however, an aspect sometimes overlooked by Western observers operating within the coordinates of generic prerogatives and traditional aims of decentralization reforms. As with other projects that help to strengthen the Ukrainian state, the significance of Ukraine's decentralization for the entire post-Soviet area can, given its anti-colonial repercussions, hardly be overstated.

Decentralization Supports Europeanization

A third geopolitical aspect of Ukraine's decentralization is that it supports Ukraine's ongoing integration into the EU's political and legal space. Initially, this was linked mainly to the Eastern Partnership program, which started in 2009, and to the Association Agreement signed by the EU and Ukraine in 2014, along with the establishment of the Deep and Comprehensive Free Trade Area. For instance, the EU-Ukraine Association Agreement encourages transborder regional cooperation (Chapter 27), which presupposes properly empowered local and regional authorities. More recently,

---

25 Romanova, "Ukraine's Resilience to Russia's Military Invasion in the Context of the Decentralisation Reform".
26 Zbigniew Brzezinski, *The Grand Chessboard: American Primacy and Its Geostrategic Imperatives* (New York: Basic Books, 1997), 46.

this aspect has been linked to Ukraine's EU candidacy, obtained on 23 June 2022, by the decision of the European Council. The start of EU accession has serious implications for EU-Ukraine bilaterial relations and Ukraine's domestic reform agenda. Decentralization is one of the reforms that will help prepare Kyiv for eventual full membership in the Union.

To a certain extent, Ukraine's decentralization is a more fundamental aspect of Ukraine's gradual Europeanization than other aspects of this process often heavily influenced from the outside. Much, if not most, of the past and current revision of the Ukrainian state's laws and institutions has been triggered, conditioned or/and modified by Western institutions. They include, for instance, such reform drivers as the EU's Visa Liberalization Action Plan, the IMF's stand-by agreements, and the Council of Europe's interventions through the opinions of the Venice Commission or of the European Court on Human Rights regarding Ukraine.

In contrast, the ongoing transformation of Ukraine's system of local self-governnment has, as already indicated, originated from within the country rather than from the outside. To be sure, a number of concepts in the new Ukrainian legislation were inspired by examples from abroad, above all by Poland's decentralization, which started as early as 1990. Moreover, various Western countries, like Switzerland, the UK, Sweden and Germany, had already provided funding for the preparation, discussion and formulation of reform plans, before their implementation began in April 2014.[27] Once the reform started, it quickly became a major focus of international developmental organizations like America's USAID, Germany's GIZ or Sweden's SIDA. The latter two have implemented an especially comprehensive and systematic support project called U-LEAD with Europe (U-LEAD = Ukraine Local Empowerment,

---

[27] See, for example, Oksana Myshlovska, "Democratising Ukraine by Promoting Decentralization? A Study of Swiss-Ukraine Cooperation", *International Development Policy Working Papers*, 4 May 2015. http://journals.openedition.org/poldev/2010; Duncan Leitch, "International assistance to democratic reform in Ukraine: An opportunity missed or an opportunity squandered?", *Democratization* 24, no. 6 (2017): 1142-58.

Accountability and Development Program), principally funded by the EU.

Nevertheless, the particular design and specific synthesis of templates in Ukraine's decentralization reform is largely a native product owing no specific debt to Warsaw, Brussels, Washington, Berlin or Stockholm. Ukrainian decentralization is thus, in a way, *not* part of Ukraine's "Europeanization", in the narrow and more technical sense of the word. It is *not* an aspect of the mechanical transposition of the EU's *acquis communautaire* into domestic law, within the ongoing implementation of the 2014 Association Agreement between Kyiv and Brussels. Yet, at the same time, Ukrainian decentralization– precisely because of its national rather than foreign impetus—can be seen as a particularly profound aspect of Ukraine's *deep* Europeanization, in the broader sense of the word, i.e., in terms of the country's gradual approximation to general EU governance norms and principles, as a result of the victory of the Revolution of Dignity in 2014.

As a Ukrainian project inspired by, but not modeled on, foreign examples, and thus a national undertaking that does not follow a pre-defined Western algorithm, decentralization is significant for two reasons. First, it is the visible manifestation of Ukraine's turning away from the centralist Tsarist and Soviet traditions of its past within the former Russian empire. Both the idea and the initiation of the Ukrainian decentralization reforms document the "European" character of Ukraine. It is practical proof of the civil, pluralist, and open character of Ukraine's political tradition and culture.

Second, the transition's accumulating results are making Ukraine more and more compatible with the EU, whose member countries are all more or less decentralized.[28] To one degree or

---

[28] Liesbet Hooghe, Gary Marks, Arjan H. Schakel, Sandra Chapman Osterkatz, Sara Niedzwiecki, and Sarah Shair-Rosenfield, *Measuring Regional Authority* (Oxford: Oxford University Press, 2016); Andreas Ladner, Nicolas Keuffer, Harald Baldersheim, Nikos Hlepas, Pawel Swianiewicz, Kristof Steyvers, and Carmen Navarro, "The Local Autonomy Index (LAI)", in: Andreas Ladner et al., eds., *Patterns of Local Autonomy in Europe: Governance and Public Management* (London: Palgrave Macmillan, 2019).

another, they continue to decentralize further as we write. They follow the well-known subsidiarity principle in their relations with Brussels and their own regions, as well as with their municipalities. Thus, the more deconcentrated and subsidiary power in Ukraine becomes, the more will it look like the polities of other European nations. And the better will it be prepared for full accession to the EU.

Beyond introducing the principle of subsidiarity, Ukraine has transformed its subregional units in a way that largely corresponds to the NUTS-3 level used in the EU. Notably, this was not a requirement imposed on Ukraine. As soon as the policy of local amalgamation was finalized in 2020, the government proceeded to further enhance the state's public administration capacity at the subnational level, in agreement with EU standards. For these purposes, in mid-2020, it merged 490 *rayons* into 136 novel subregional entities.

Another example of such Europeanization is Ukraine's attempt to foster regional development and reduce regional disparities in line with EU practices. In 2014, the parliament approved the so-called "State Strategy for Regional Development to 2020", and in 2020 the "State Strategy for Regional Development in 2021-2027". These were aimed at improving multi-level institutional coordination and applied planning and budgeting standards and methods consistent with those used in the EU.

Ukraine did again not blindly copy the way such institutions foster regional development in the EU. Ukraine's State Fund for Regional Development is, in contrast to similar organs in the EU, not a separate institution.[29] "In order to support medium-term regional development projects aligned with the [State Strategy for Regional Development], as well as to minimize cronyism and corruption in project selection, central government budgets have to commit at least 1 per cent of central revenues to the [State Fund for Regional Development] each year, with the fund co-financing projects on a

---

29 The State Fund for Regional Development was launched before the decentralization reform; however, the reform has modified it significantly.

competitive basis".[30] In practice, the amount of its annual funding often depends, however, on the interests of MPs, and especially of those MPs elected in majoritarian districts. There is thus still a lot of work to be done to advance Ukraine's multilevel governance and the framework of regional development so as to comply with EU rules and practices.

The national origins and Europeanizing effects of Ukraine's decentralization are important not only in terms of the spread of Western values and principles. They also have a larger geopolitical dimension. To the extent that Kyiv's local government reform expresses and advances the "European" character of Ukraine, it demonstrates that it belongs to the Western normative and cultural hemisphere. That, in turn, makes Ukraine's ambition to enter the EU and NATO more natural than it may otherwise have appeared.[31]

This dimension appears especially relevant when seen in the context of the various centralistic tendencies in Russia and other post-Soviet republics, for instance those in Central Asia, in the last two decades. After more or less serious democratization and decentralization attempts following the break-up of the USSR in the early 1990s, many post-Soviet republics have again regressed towards authoritarianism and centralism, albeit under new nationalist slogans. Against this background, Kyiv's claim to be different from the other more autocratic and even partly totalitarian successor states of the USSR sounds more plausible. While this has not been its primary aim, decentralization supports Ukraine's European integration and inclusion in the Atlantic community. Moreover, to the degree that Ukrainian local government reform furthers Kyiv's Western integration, it may also contribute to a general reshaping of the geopolitics of Eastern Europe.

---

30 Valentyna Romanova and Andreas Umland, *Ukraine's Decentralization Reforms since 2014: Initial Achievements and Future* Challenges (London: Chatham House, 2019). 15.
31 On 30 September 2022, Ukraine's president announced that Kyiv is officially applying for NATO membership.

Ukraine's Decentralization as a Model

This final — and still speculative — geopolitical aspect of the ongoing transformation of Ukrainian local self-government concerns its cross-national diffusion potential. Decentralization in Ukraine could, in the future, provide policy directions and institutional templates for use by other currently highly centralized post-Soviet states, as they undertake reform efforts. Above all, Russia itself may one day find it relevant to pursue decentralization along the Ukrainian localist, rather than the older Russian federalist, paradigm.

As time goes by, ever post-Soviet republic will be affected by gradual social modernization, cross-national norm dispersion, democratizing intra-elite divisions, as well as international economic integration. These processes will bring more and more changes to all the still politically underdeveloped and culturally regressive post-communist countries. When government crises, competitive disadvantages, and general backwardness create sufficient pressure for deep reform in Russia, Belarus, Armenia, Azerbaijan and/or Central Asia, their nations will look for ideas and experiences that could help them to reconstitute their immobile societies and remake their inefficient states.

In the case of such a turn of events, the Ukrainian post-Euromaidan experience will, to be sure, not be the only reference point for Minsk, Moscow, Yerevan, Baku or Astana. Yet, once a greater post-Soviet search for successful reform templates starts, Ukraine may — because of her size and history as a founding republic of the USSR — attract special attention from the Soviet Union's successor states.[32] Whatever sustainability, dynamism and progress this or that aspect of Ukraine's current transformation produces in the next years could, at some point, also become attractive to other reform-minded states — perhaps even to those outside the post-Soviet space.

---

32 Andreas Umland, "Für eine neue Osteuropa-Politik: Europas Weg nach Moskau führt über Kiew", *Internationale Politik* 66, no. 4 (2011): 86-92.

The possibility and even the intention of cross-border diffusion is explicitly entailed by many reform concepts and efforts around the world. The Ukrainian local government reform may, however, have even greater geopolitical salience because of its above-mentioned nation-building and anti-secessionist effects.[33] Ukrainian decentralization is not only an instrument for improving state-society relations; it can also function as a tool to stabilize regionally divided states threatened by separatist tendencies. In the same way that devolving power to municipal levels helps Ukraine to hold its territory together, an application of its decentralization model may one day also help other post-Soviet states remain unified. This is a concern not least for Russia, whose sheer size and multi-ethnic character make it especially vulnerable to autonomism and secessionism.

During the last 15 years, the formally federalist Russian state has become more and more centralized under President Vladimir Putin. Russia is today de facto once again a unitary state for which the label "Federation" looks like a misnomer. This authoritarian centralized state uses liberal-democratic language and manipulates elections to present itself as a supposedly federal multi-ethnic democracy. Yet, as history has shown, centralization is no guarantee against secessionism. The pseudo-federal and centralist constitution of the supposed Soviet federation did not prevent the USSR's

---

[33] Relevant analyses of generic aspects of this issue include, in chronological order: Ugo Panizza, "Decentralization as a Mechanism to Prevent Secession", *Economic Notes* 27, no. 2 (1998): 263-267; Bruno S. Frey and Simon Luechinger, "Decentralization as a Disincentive for Terror", *European Journal of Political Economy* 20, no. 2 (2004): 509-515; Dawn Brancanti, "Decentralization: Fueling the Fire or Dampening the Flames of Ethnic Conflict and Secessionism?" *International Organization* 60, no. 3 (2006): 651-685; Axel Dreher and Justina A. V. Fischer, "Government Decentralization as a Disincentive for Transnational Terror? An Empirical Analysis", *IZA Discussion Papers*, no. 4259 (2009); François Vaillancourt, Edison Roy-Cesar and Richard Miller Bird, "Is Decentralization 'Glue' or 'Solvent' for National Unity?" *Andrew Young School International Studies Program Working Paper*, no. 3 (2010); Jürgen Ehrke, *Zur Stabilisierung fragmentierter Staaten: Dezentralisierung, Entwicklungszusammenarbeit und das Gespenst des Separatismus* (Potsdam: Universitätsverlag Potsdam, 2011); Jörn Grävingholt and Christian von Haldenwang, "The Promotion of Decentralization and Local Governance in Fragile Contexts", *DIE Discussion Papers*, no. 20 (2016).

break-up. On the contrary, it helped to generate the centrifugal tendencies that eventually broke apart the "Union".

A similar prospect may be looming for the Russian so-called Federation. In times of crisis, not only the ethno-nationalized republics, but even certain self-sufficient Russian regions may start to entertain plans of weakening or even leaving the Russian pseudo-Federation to become partly or fully sovereign. A more or less successful departure of even one Russian official federal subject—such as those recently annexed and, according to international law, illegitimate as well as illegal, in any way—could trigger a domino effect among regions believing that they will better off as separate states.

Many in Ukraine today would not mind such a development—a standpoint understandable in view of Moscow's aggressive behavior vis-à-vis Kyiv since 2014 and especially since 2022. Yet, the assumption that a collapse of Russia would be unambiguously beneficial to Ukraine could be too optimistic. It is not clear that the new quasi-states separating from, or replacing, the current Russian Federation would be more friendly towards Kyiv and the West than Putin's regime is today.

Worse, one cannot be sure that all of Russia's WMDs would remain under the control of more or less sane political forces, if the huge country splits apart. In a chaotic situation on the territory of the current Russian Federation, a fanatically anti-Ukrainian and anti-Western warlord like could get control of, say, tactical nuclear weapons. Such a development could have disastrous consequences for other countries, Ukraine first of all.

Against this background, it may be worth considering a scenario in which the current Russian federal set-up, with its subnational authoritarian institutions, autonomistic undertones and unintended promotion of regional self-sufficiency, may one day be replaced by a governance mechanism modeled on Ukraine. This would mean a devolution of power to Russia's local rather than regional level. Such a deconcentration of political decision-making away not only from Moscow, but also from the republican and *oblast* to the urban and rural levels may be in everybody's interest.

A decentralized Russia with strong local self-governments — i.e., a Russian Federation where cities and territorial communities rather than Moscow, federal districts and *oblast* capitals control substantive prerogatives and finances — would probably be far less imperialistic and internationally ambitious than Putin's regime is today. When Russian municipal communities have the last word in much political decision-making, the appetite for great power grandeur and expansion may give place to more mundane concerns of socioeconomic advancement in the vast underdeveloped territory of Russia. Education, public health, road building, energy efficiency, investment, environmental protection etc. could become the new primary tasks of the day, rather than claims of continental hegemony, global power, or new territory.

A properly decentralized rather than regionalized state would also be a more stable entity than the current Russian Federation. The current macro-regional and regional administrative division of Russia may, in a crisis situation, facilitate secessionist moves. As the quoted former Ukrainian parliamentary speaker Parubiy put it, Kyiv's decentralization reforms has been "sewing the Ukrainian space".[34] In a similar way, a deep municipalization of its governance system could one day help Moscow to keep the Russian state together. In view of its considerable centrifugal potential, the Russia may, in fact, find it even more imperative to implement a Ukrainian-type decentralization reform than Ukraine does.

Decentralization as an Underestimated Reform Agenda

The above list does not mean to suggest that local government reform is a panacea for Ukraine and other post-Soviet states. Yet its Europeanizing, anti-separatist and diffusion potential makes it an especially salient, interesting, and consequential aspect of Ukraine's ongoing socio-political transformation. In the context of specifically post-Soviet political challenges, the empire-subverting, nation-building, and state-supporting dimension of decentrali-

---

34 "How European Ukraine is being sewn of amalgamated hromadas".

zation endow this particular reform in Ukraine with a greater meaning than other substantively similar processes of devolution have in other parts of the world. Neither the overcoming of the Tsarist-Communist empire nor the formation of democratic nation states is yet completed, in the post-Soviet area. Decentralization may do the trick—or, at least, be one of the principal instruments in achieving these daunting tasks.[35]

This illustrates that Ukraine's decentralization, despite its present limitations and unknown future prospects, has produced a model for center-periphery relations. When local communities—whether within an urban, rural or mixed context—take over major political tasks and public funds, both imperialism and separatism lose their allure. Decentralization can help to contain radical nationalism and facilitate European integration. Ukraine's local government reform thus deservers greater attention from national governments, the mass media, civil society, and academic researchers around the world. Deeper study of the concepts, elements and experiences of the current Ukrainian reset of local self-government may reveal useful ideas and lessons for administrative reform advocates in other post-Soviet countries and beyond.

---

35 We are aware, so far, of only one scholarly work that considers Ukraine's post-2014 decentralization reform as a potential model for reforming center-periphery relations (in the UK), based on its success in reducing fragmentation at the municipal level and providing stimuli for local development, namely: Breach and Bridgett, "Centralisation Nation".

The Contributors

Aadne Aasland, Ph. D., is a Research Professor at the Norwegian Institute for Urban and Regional Research (NIBR) at Oslo Metropolitan University.

Max Bader, Ph. D., is a University Lecturer at the Department of Russian and Eurasian Studies at Leiden University.

Oleksandra Deineko, Ph. D., is a Guest Researcher at the Norwegian Institute for Urban and Regional Research (NIBR) at Oslo Metropolitan University, and Associate Professor of Sociology at the V. N. Karazin National University of Kharkiv.

Igor Dunayev, Dr. Sc., is Director of the Research Center of Blockchain Solutions in Kyiv, and Professor of Economic Policy and Management at the V. N. Karazin National University of Kharkiv.

Melanie G. Mierzejewski-Voznyak, Ph. D., is a Visiting Research Fellow at the Aleksanteri Institute - Finnish Centre for Russian, Eurasian and Eastern European Studies at the University of Helsinki.

Yuriy Palekha, Dr. Sc., is Deputy Director for Research at the Ukrainian State Research Institute of Urban Design "DIPROMISTO", and Associate Professor of Urban Planning at the Kyiv National University of Construction and Architecture.

Maryna Rabinovych, Ph. D., is Assistant Professor of Public Administration and Governance at the Kyiv School of Economics, and Research Fellow in Political Science and Management at the University of Agder.

Valentyna Romanova, Ph. D., is a Research Fellow at the Institute of Developing Economies—Japan External Trade Organization (IDE-JETRO).

Oleksii Sydorchuk, Ph. D., is a Development and Research Manager at the International Foundation for Electoral Systems in Ukraine.

Andreas Umland, Ph. D., is an Analyst at the Stockholm Centre for Eastern European Studies at the Swedish Institute of International Affairs (UI), and Associate Professor of Political Science at the Kyiv-Mohyla Academy.

SOVIET AND POST-SOVIET POLITICS AND SOCIETY
Edited by Dr. Andreas Umland | ISSN 1614-3515

1   Андреас Умланд (ред.) | Воплощение Европейской конвенции по правам человека в России. Философские, юридические и эмпирические исследования | ISBN 3-89821-387-0

2   Christian Wipperfürth | Russland – ein vertrauenswürdiger Partner? Grundlagen, Hintergründe und Praxis gegenwärtiger russischer Außenpolitik | Mit einem Vorwort von Heinz Timmermann | ISBN 3-89821-401-X

3   Manja Hussner | Die Übernahme internationalen Rechts in die russische und deutsche Rechtsordnung. Eine vergleichende Analyse zur Völkerrechtsfreundlichkeit der Verfassungen der Russländischen Föderation und der Bundesrepublik Deutschland | Mit einem Vorwort von Rainer Arnold | ISBN 3-89821-438-9

4   Matthew Tejada | Bulgaria's Democratic Consolidation and the Kozloduy Nuclear Power Plant (KNPP). The Unattainability of Closure | With a foreword by Richard J. Crampton | ISBN 3-89821-439-7

5   Марк Григорьевич Меерович | Квадратные метры, определяющие сознание. Государственная жилищная политика в СССР. 1921 – 1941 гг | ISBN 3-89821-474-5

6   Andrei P. Tsygankov, Pavel A.Tsygankov (Eds.) | New Directions in Russian International Studies | ISBN 3-89821-422-2

7   Марк Григорьевич Меерович | Как власть народ к труду приучала. Жилище в СССР – средство управления людьми. 1917 – 1941 гг. | С предисловием Елены Осокиной | ISBN 3-89821-495-8

8   David J. Galbreath | Nation-Building and Minority Politics in Post-Socialist States. Interests, Influence and Identities in Estonia and Latvia | With a foreword by David J. Smith | ISBN 3-89821-467-2

9   Алексей Юрьевич Безугольный | Народы Кавказа в Вооруженных силах СССР в годы Великой Отечественной войны 1941-1945 гг. | С предисловием Николая Бугая | ISBN 3-89821-475-3

10 Вячеслав Лихачев и Владимир Прибыловский (ред.) | Русское Национальное Единство, 1990-2000. В 2-х томах | ISBN 3-89821-523-7

11 Николай Бугай (ред.) | Народы стран Балтии в условиях сталинизма (1940-е – 1950-е годы). Документированная история | ISBN 3-89821-525-3

12 Ingmar Bredies (Hrsg.) | Zur Anatomie der Orange Revolution in der Ukraine. Wechsel des Elitenregimes oder Triumph des Parlamentarismus? | ISBN 3-89821-524-5

13 Anastasia V. Mitrofanova | The Politicization of Russian Orthodoxy. Actors and Ideas | With a foreword by William C. Gay | ISBN 3-89821-481-8

14 Nathan D. Larson | Alexander Solzhenitsyn and the Russo-Jewish Question | ISBN 3-89821-483-4

15 Guido Houben | Kulturpolitik und Ethnizität. Staatliche Kunstförderung im Russland der neunziger Jahre | Mit einem Vorwort von Gert Weisskirchen | ISBN 3-89821-542-3

16 Leonid Luks | Der russische „Sonderweg"? Aufsätze zur neuesten Geschichte Russlands im europäischen Kontext | ISBN 3-89821-496-6

17 Евгений Мороз | История «Мёртвой воды» – от страшной сказки к большой политике. Политическое неоязычество в постсоветской России | ISBN 3-89821-551-2

18 Александр Верховский и Галина Кожевникова (ред.) | Этническая и религиозная интолерантность в российских СМИ. Результаты мониторинга 2001-2004 гг. | ISBN 3-89821-569-5

19 Christian Ganzer | Sowjetisches Erbe und ukrainische Nation. Das Museum der Geschichte des Zaporoger Kosakentums auf der Insel Chortycja | Mit einem Vorwort von Frank Golczewski | ISBN 3-89821-504-0

20 Эльза-Баир Гучинова | Помнить нельзя забыть. Антропология депортационной травмы калмыков | С предисловием Кэролайн Хамфри | ISBN 3-89821-506-7

21 Юлия Лидерман | Мотивы «проверки» и «испытания» в постсоветской культуре. Советское прошлое в российском кинематографе 1990-х годов | С предисловием Евгения Марголита | ISBN 3-89821-511-3

22 Tanya Lokshina, Ray Thomas, Mary Mayer (Eds.) | The Imposition of a Fake Political Settlement in the Northern Caucasus. The 2003 Chechen Presidential Election | ISBN 3-89821-436-2

23 Timothy McCajor Hall, Rosie Read (Eds.) | Changes in the Heart of Europe. Recent Ethnographies of Czechs, Slovaks, Roma, and Sorbs | With an afterword by Zdeněk Salzmann | ISBN 3-89821-606-3

24 *Christian Autengruber* | Die politischen Parteien in Bulgarien und Rumänien. Eine vergleichende Analyse seit Beginn der 90er Jahre | Mit einem Vorwort von Dorothée de Nève | ISBN 3-89821-476-1

25 *Annette Freyberg-Inan with Radu Cristescu* | The Ghosts in Our Classrooms, or: John Dewey Meets Ceauşescu. The Promise and the Failures of Civic Education in Romania | ISBN 3-89821-416-8

26 *John B. Dunlop* | The 2002 Dubrovka and 2004 Beslan Hostage Crises. A Critique of Russian Counter-Terrorism | With a foreword by Donald N. Jensen | ISBN 3-89821-608-X

27 *Peter Koller* | Das touristische Potenzial von Kam''janec'–Podil's'kyj. Eine fremdenverkehrsgeographische Untersuchung der Zukunftsperspektiven und Maßnahmenplanung zur Destinationsentwicklung des „ukrainischen Rothenburg" | Mit einem Vorwort von Kristiane Klemm | ISBN 3-89821-640-3

28 *Françoise Daucé, Elisabeth Sieca-Kozlowski (Eds.)* | Dedovshchina in the Post-Soviet Military. Hazing of Russian Army Conscripts in a Comparative Perspective | With a foreword by Dale Herspring | ISBN 3-89821-616-0

29 *Florian Strasser* | Zivilgesellschaftliche Einflüsse auf die Orange Revolution. Die gewaltlose Massenbewegung und die ukrainische Wahlkrise 2004 | Mit einem Vorwort von Egbert Jahn | ISBN 3-89821-648-9

30 *Rebecca S. Katz* | The Georgian Regime Crisis of 2003-2004. A Case Study in Post-Soviet Media Representation of Politics, Crime and Corruption | ISBN 3-89821-413-3

31 *Vladimir Kantor* | Willkür oder Freiheit. Beiträge zur russischen Geschichtsphilosophie | Ediert von Dagmar Herrmann sowie mit einem Vorwort versehen von Leonid Luks | ISBN 3-89821-589-X

32 *Laura A. Victoir* | The Russian Land Estate Today. A Case Study of Cultural Politics in Post-Soviet Russia | With a foreword by Priscilla Roosevelt | ISBN 3-89821-426-5

33 *Ivan Katchanovski* | Cleft Countries. Regional Political Divisions and Cultures in Post-Soviet Ukraine and Moldova | With a foreword by Francis Fukuyama | ISBN 3-89821-558-X

34 *Florian Mühlfried* | Postsowjetische Feiern. Das Georgische Bankett im Wandel | Mit einem Vorwort von Kevin Tuite | ISBN 3-89821-601-2

35 *Roger Griffin, Werner Loh, Andreas Umland (Eds.)* | Fascism Past and Present, West and East. An International Debate on Concepts and Cases in the Comparative Study of the Extreme Right | With an afterword by Walter Laqueur | ISBN 3-89821-674-8

36 *Sebastian Schlegel* | Der „Weiße Archipel". Sowjetische Atomstädte 1945-1991 | Mit einem Geleitwort von Thomas Bohn | ISBN 3-89821-679-9

37 *Vyacheslav Likhachev* | Political Anti-Semitism in Post-Soviet Russia. Actors and Ideas in 1991-2003 | Edited and translated from Russian by Eugene Veklerov | ISBN 3-89821-529-6

38 *Josette Baer (Ed.)* | Preparing Liberty in Central Europe. Political Texts from the Spring of Nations 1848 to the Spring of Prague 1968 | With a foreword by Zdeněk V. David | ISBN 3-89821-546-6

39 *Михаил Лукьянов* | Российский консерватизм и реформа, 1907-1914 | С предисловием Марка Д. Стейнберга | ISBN 3-89821-503-2

40 *Nicola Melloni* | Market Without Economy. The 1998 Russian Financial Crisis | With a foreword by Eiji Furukawa | ISBN 3-89821-407-9

41 *Dmitrij Chmelnizki* | Die Architektur Stalins | Bd. 1: Studien zu Ideologie und Stil | Bd. 2: Bilddokumentation | Mit einem Vorwort von Bruno Flierl | ISBN 3-89821-515-6

42 *Katja Yafimava* | Post-Soviet Russian-Belarussian Relationships. The Role of Gas Transit Pipelines | With a foreword by Jonathan P. Stern | ISBN 3-89821-655-1

43 *Boris Chavkin* | Verflechtungen der deutschen und russischen Zeitgeschichte. Aufsätze und Archivfunde zu den Beziehungen Deutschlands und der Sowjetunion von 1917 bis 1991 | Ediert von Markus Edlinger sowie mit einem Vorwort versehen von Leonid Luks | ISBN 3-89821-756-6

44 *Anastasija Grynenko in Zusammenarbeit mit Claudia Dathe* | Die Terminologie des Gerichtswesens der Ukraine und Deutschlands im Vergleich. Eine übersetzungswissenschaftliche Analyse juristischer Fachbegriffe im Deutschen, Ukrainischen und Russischen | Mit einem Vorwort von Ulrich Hartmann | ISBN 3-89821-691-8

45 *Anton Burkov* | The Impact of the European Convention on Human Rights on Russian Law. Legislation and Application in 1996-2006 | With a foreword by Françoise Hampson | ISBN 978-3-89821-639-5

46 *Stina Torjesen, Indra Overland (Eds.)* | International Election Observers in Post-Soviet Azerbaijan. Geopolitical Pawns or Agents of Change? | ISBN 978-3-89821-743-9

47 *Taras Kuzio* | Ukraine – Crimea – Russia. Triangle of Conflict | ISBN 978-3-89821-761-3

48 *Claudia Šabić* | „Ich erinnere mich nicht, aber L'viv!" Zur Funktion kultureller Faktoren für die Institutionalisierung und Entwicklung einer ukrainischen Region | Mit einem Vorwort von Melanie Tatur | ISBN 978-3-89821-752-1

49 Marlies Bilz | Tatarstan in der Transformation. Nationaler Diskurs und Politische Praxis 1988-1994 | Mit einem Vorwort von Frank Golczewski | ISBN 978-3-89821-722-4

50 Марлен Ларюэль (ред.) | Современные интерпретации русского национализма | ISBN 978-3-89821-795-8

51 Sonja Schüler | Die ethnische Dimension der Armut. Roma im postsozialistischen Rumänien | Mit einem Vorwort von Anton Sterbling | ISBN 978-3-89821-776-7

52 Галина Кожевникова | Радикальный национализм в России и противодействие ему. Сборник докладов Центра «Сова» за 2004-2007 гг. | С предисловием Александра Верховского | ISBN 978-3-89821-721-7

53 Галина Кожевникова и Владимир Прибыловский | Российская власть в биографиях I. Высшие должностные лица РФ в 2004 г. | ISBN 978-3-89821-796-5

54 Галина Кожевникова и Владимир Прибыловский | Российская власть в биографиях II. Члены Правительства РФ в 2004 г. | ISBN 978-3-89821-797-2

55 Галина Кожевникова и Владимир Прибыловский | Российская власть в биографиях III. Руководители федеральных служб и агентств РФ в 2004 г.| ISBN 978-3-89821-798-9

56 Ileana Petroniu | Privatisierung in Transformationsökonomien. Determinanten der Restrukturierungs-Bereitschaft am Beispiel Polens, Rumäniens und der Ukraine | Mit einem Vorwort von Rainer W. Schäfer | ISBN 978-3-89821-790-3

57 Christian Wipperfürth | Russland und seine GUS-Nachbarn. Hintergründe, aktuelle Entwicklungen und Konflikte in einer ressourcenreichen Region| ISBN 978-3-89821-801-6

58 Togzhan Kassenova | From Antagonism to Partnership. The Uneasy Path of the U.S.-Russian Cooperative Threat Reduction | With a foreword by Christoph Bluth | ISBN 978-3-89821-707-1

59 Alexander Höllwerth | Das sakrale eurasische Imperium des Aleksandr Dugin. Eine Diskursanalyse zum postsowjetischen russischen Rechtsextremismus | Mit einem Vorwort von Dirk Uffelmann | ISBN 978-3-89821-813-9

60 Олег Рябов | «Россия-Матушка». Национализм, гендер и война в России XX века | С предисловием Елены Гощило | ISBN 978-3-89821-487-2

61 Ivan Maistrenko | Borot'bism. A Chapter in the History of the Ukrainian Revolution | With a new Introduction by Chris Ford | Translated by George S. N. Luckyj with the assistance of Ivan L. Rudnytsky | Second, Revised and Expanded Edition ISBN 978-3-8382-1107-7

62 Maryna Romanets | Anamorphosic Texts and Reconfigured Visions. Improvised Traditions in Contemporary Ukrainian and Irish Literature | ISBN 978-3-89821-576-3

63 Paul D'Anieri and Taras Kuzio (Eds.) | Aspects of the Orange Revolution I. Democratization and Elections in Post-Communist Ukraine | ISBN 978-3-89821-698-2

64 Bohdan Harasymiw in collaboration with Oleh S. Ilnytzkyj (Eds.) | Aspects of the Orange Revolution II. Information and Manipulation Strategies in the 2004 Ukrainian Presidential Elections | ISBN 978-3-89821-699-9

65 Ingmar Bredies, Andreas Umland and Valentin Yakushik (Eds.) | Aspects of the Orange Revolution III. The Context and Dynamics of the 2004 Ukrainian Presidential Elections | ISBN 978-3-89821-803-0

66 Ingmar Bredies, Andreas Umland and Valentin Yakushik (Eds.) | Aspects of the Orange Revolution IV. Foreign Assistance and Civic Action in the 2004 Ukrainian Presidential Elections | ISBN 978-3-89821-808-5

67 Ingmar Bredies, Andreas Umland and Valentin Yakushik (Eds.) | Aspects of the Orange Revolution V. Institutional Observation Reports on the 2004 Ukrainian Presidential Elections | ISBN 978-3-89821-809-2

68 Taras Kuzio (Ed.) | Aspects of the Orange Revolution VI. Post-Communist Democratic Revolutions in Comparative Perspective | ISBN 978-3-89821-820-7

69 Tim Bohse | Autoritarismus statt Selbstverwaltung. Die Transformation der kommunalen Politik in der Stadt Kaliningrad 1990-2005 | Mit einem Geleitwort von Stefan Troebst | ISBN 978-3-89821-782-8

70 David Rupp | Die Rußländische Föderation und die russischsprachige Minderheit in Lettland. Eine Fallstudie zur Anwaltspolitik Moskaus gegenüber den russophonen Minderheiten im „Nahen Ausland" von 1991 bis 2002 | Mit einem Vorwort von Helmut Wagner | ISBN 978-3-89821-778-1

71 Taras Kuzio | Theoretical and Comparative Perspectives on Nationalism. New Directions in Cross-Cultural and Post-Communist Studies | With a foreword by Paul Robert Magocsi | ISBN 978-3-89821-815-3

72 Christine Teichmann | Die Hochschultransformation im heutigen Osteuropa. Kontinuität und Wandel bei der Entwicklung des postkommunistischen Universitätswesens | Mit einem Vorwort von Oskar Anweiler | ISBN 978-3-89821-842-9

73　*Julia Kusznir* | Der politische Einfluss von Wirtschaftseliten in russischen Regionen. Eine Analyse am Beispiel der Erdöl- und Erdgasindustrie, 1992-2005 | Mit einem Vorwort von Wolfgang Eichwede | ISBN 978-3-89821-821-4

74　*Alena Vysotskaya* | Russland, Belarus und die EU-Osterweiterung. Zur Minderheitenfrage und zum Problem der Freizügigkeit des Personenverkehrs | Mit einem Vorwort von Katlijn Malfliet | ISBN 978-3-89821-822-1

75　*Heiko Pleines (Hrsg.)* | Corporate Governance in post-sozialistischen Volkswirtschaften | ISBN 978-3-89821-766-8

76　*Stefan Ihrig* | Wer sind die Moldawier? Rumänismus versus Moldowanismus in Historiographie und Schulbüchern der Republik Moldova, 1991-2006 | Mit einem Vorwort von Holm Sundhaussen | ISBN 978-3-89821-466-7

77　*Galina Kozhevnikova in collaboration with Alexander Verkhovsky and Eugene Veklerov* | Ultra-Nationalism and Hate Crimes in Contemporary Russia. The 2004-2006 Annual Reports of Moscow's SOVA Center | With a foreword by Stephen D. Shenfield | ISBN 978-3-89821-868-9

78　*Florian Küchler* | The Role of the European Union in Moldova's Transnistria Conflict | With a foreword by Christopher Hill | ISBN 978-3-89821-850-4

79　*Bernd Rechel* | The Long Way Back to Europe. Minority Protection in Bulgaria | With a foreword by Richard Crampton | ISBN 978-3-89821-863-4

80　*Peter W. Rodgers* | Nation, Region and History in Post-Communist Transitions. Identity Politics in Ukraine, 1991-2006 | With a foreword by Vera Tolz | ISBN 978-3-89821-903-7

81　*Stephanie Solywoda* | The Life and Work of Semen L. Frank. A Study of Russian Religious Philosophy | With a foreword by Philip Walters | ISBN 978-3-89821-457-5

82　*Vera Sokolova* | Cultural Politics of Ethnicity. Discourses on Roma in Communist Czechoslovakia | ISBN 978-3-89821-864-1

83　*Natalya Shevchik Ketenci* | Kazakhstani Enterprises in Transition. The Role of Historical Regional Development in Kazakhstan's Post-Soviet Economic Transformation | ISBN 978-3-89821-831-3

84　*Martin Malek, Anna Schor-Tschudnowskaja (Hgg.)* | Europa im Tschetschenienkrieg. Zwischen politischer Ohnmacht und Gleichgültigkeit | Mit einem Vorwort von Lipchan Basajewa | ISBN 978-3-89821-676-0

85　*Stefan Meister* | Das postsowjetische Universitätswesen zwischen nationalem und internationalem Wandel. Die Entwicklung der regionalen Hochschule in Russland als Gradmesser der Systemtransformation | Mit einem Vorwort von Joan DeBardeleben | ISBN 978-3-89821-891-7

86　*Konstantin Sheiko in collaboration with Stephen Brown* | Nationalist Imaginings of the Russian Past. Anatolii Fomenko and the Rise of Alternative History in Post-Communist Russia | With a foreword by Donald Ostrowski | ISBN 978-3-89821-915-0

87　*Sabine Jenni* | Wie stark ist das „Einige Russland"? Zur Parteibindung der Eliten und zum Wahlerfolg der Machtpartei im Dezember 2007 | Mit einem Vorwort von Klaus Armingeon | ISBN 978-3-89821-961-7

88　*Thomas Borén* | Meeting-Places of Transformation. Urban Identity, Spatial Representations and Local Politics in Post-Soviet St Petersburg | ISBN 978-3-89821-739-2

89　*Aygul Ashirova* | Stalinismus und Stalin-Kult in Zentralasien. Turkmenistan 1924-1953 | Mit einem Vorwort von Leonid Luks | ISBN 978-3-89821-987-7

90　*Leonid Luks* | Freiheit oder imperiale Größe? Essays zu einem russischen Dilemma | ISBN 978-3-8382-0011-8

91　*Christopher Gilley* | The 'Change of Signposts' in the Ukrainian Emigration. A Contribution to the History of Sovietophilism in the 1920s | With a foreword by Frank Golczewski | ISBN 978-3-89821-965-5

92　*Philipp Casula, Jeronim Perovic (Eds.)* | Identities and Politics During the Putin Presidency. The Discursive Foundations of Russia's Stability | With a foreword by Heiko Haumann | ISBN 978-3-8382-0015-6

93　*Marcel Viëtor* | Europa und die Frage nach seinen Grenzen im Osten. Zur Konstruktion ‚europäischer Identität' in Geschichte und Gegenwart | Mit einem Vorwort von Albrecht Lehmann | ISBN 978-3-8382-0045-3

94　*Ben Hellman, Andrei Rogachevskii* | Filming the Unfilmable. Casper Wrede's 'One Day in the Life of Ivan Denisovich' | Second, Revised and Expanded Edition | ISBN 978-3-8382-0044-6

95　*Eva Fuchslocher* | Vaterland, Sprache, Glaube. Orthodoxie und Nationenbildung am Beispiel Georgiens | Mit einem Vorwort von Christina von Braun | ISBN 978-3-89821-884-9

96　*Vladimir Kantor* | Das Westlertum und der Weg Russlands. Zur Entwicklung der russischen Literatur und Philosophie | Ediert von Dagmar Herrmann | Mit einem Beitrag von Nikolaus Lobkowicz | ISBN 978-3-8382-0102-3

97　*Kamran Musayev* | Die postsowjetische Transformation im Baltikum und Südkaukasus. Eine vergleichende Untersuchung der politischen Entwicklung Lettlands und Aserbaidschans 1985-2009 | Mit einem Vorwort von Leonid Luks | Ediert von Sandro Henschel | ISBN 978-3-8382-0103-0

98 *Tatiana Zhurzhenko* | Borderlands into Bordered Lands. Geopolitics of Identity in Post-Soviet Ukraine | With a foreword by Dieter Segert | ISBN 978-3-8382-0042-2

99 *Кирилл Галушко, Лидия Смола (ред.)* | Пределы падения – варианты украинского будущего. Аналитико-прогностические исследования | ISBN 978-3-8382-0148-1

100 *Michael Minkenberg (Ed.)* | Historical Legacies and the Radical Right in Post-Cold War Central and Eastern Europe | With an afterword by Sabrina P. Ramet | ISBN 978-3-8382-0124-5

101 *David-Emil Wickström* | Rocking St. Petersburg. Transcultural Flows and Identity Politics in the St. Petersburg Popular Music Scene | With a foreword by Yngvar B. Steinholt | Second, Revised and Expanded Edition | ISBN 978-3-8382-0100-9

102 *Eva Zabka* | Eine neue „Zeit der Wirren"? Der spät- und postsowjetische Systemwandel 1985-2000 im Spiegel russischer gesellschaftspolitischer Diskurse | Mit einem Vorwort von Margareta Mommsen | ISBN 978-3-8382-0161-0

103 *Ulrike Ziemer* | Ethnic Belonging, Gender and Cultural Practices. Youth Identitites in Contemporary Russia | With a foreword by Anoop Nayak | ISBN 978-3-8382-0152-8

104 *Ksenia Chepikova* | ‚Einiges Russland' - eine zweite KPdSU? Aspekte der Identitätskonstruktion einer postsowjetischen „Partei der Macht" | Mit einem Vorwort von Torsten Oppelland | ISBN 978-3-8382-0311-9

105 *Леонид Люкс* | Западничество или евразийство? Демократия или идеократия? Сборник статей об исторических дилеммах России | С предисловием Владимира Кантора | ISBN 978-3-8382-0211-2

106 *Anna Dost* | Das russische Verfassungsrecht auf dem Weg zum Föderalismus und zurück. Zum Konflikt von Rechtsnormen und -wirklichkeit in der Russländischen Föderation von 1991 bis 2009 | Mit einem Vorwort von Alexander Blankenagel | ISBN 978-3-8382-0292-1

107 *Philipp Herzog* | Sozialistische Völkerfreundschaft, nationaler Widerstand oder harmloser Zeitvertreib? Zur politischen Funktion der Volkskunst im sowjetischen Estland | Mit einem Vorwort von Andreas Kappeler | ISBN 978-3-8382-0216-7

108 *Marlène Laruelle (Ed.)* | Russian Nationalism, Foreign Policy, and Identity Debates in Putin's Russia. New Ideological Patterns after the Orange Revolution | ISBN 978-3-8382-0325-6

109 *Michail Logvinov* | Russlands Kampf gegen den internationalen Terrorismus. Eine kritische Bestandsaufnahme des Bekämpfungsansatzes | Mit einem Geleitwort von Hans-Henning Schröder und einem Vorwort von Eckhard Jesse | ISBN 978-3-8382-0329-4

110 *John B. Dunlop* | The Moscow Bombings of September 1999. Examinations of Russian Terrorist Attacks at the Onset of Vladimir Putin's Rule | Second, Revised and Expanded Edition | ISBN 978-3-8382-0388-1

111 *Андрей А. Ковалёв* | Свидетельство из-за кулис российской политики I. Можно ли делать добро из зла? (Воспоминания и размышления о последних советских и первых послесоветских годах) | With a foreword by Peter Reddaway | ISBN 978-3-8382-0302-7

112 *Андрей А. Ковалёв* | Свидетельство из-за кулис российской политики II. Угроза для себя и окружающих (Наблюдения и предостережения относительно происходящего после 2000 г.) | ISBN 978-3-8382-0303-4

113 *Bernd Kappenberg* | Zeichen setzen für Europa. Der Gebrauch europäischer lateinischer Sonderzeichen in der deutschen Öffentlichkeit | Mit einem Vorwort von Peter Schlobinski | ISBN 978-3-89821-749-1

114 *Ivo Mijnssen* | The Quest for an Ideal Youth in Putin's Russia I. Back to Our Future! History, Modernity, and Patriotism according to Nashi, 2005-2013 | With a foreword by Jeronim Perović | Second, Revised and Expanded Edition | ISBN 978-3-8382-0368-3

115 *Jussi Lassila* | The Quest for an Ideal Youth in Putin's Russia II. The Search for Distinctive Conformism in the Political Communication of Nashi, 2005-2009 | With a foreword by Kirill Postoutenko | Second, Revised and Expanded Edition | ISBN 978-3-8382-0415-4

116 *Valerio Trabandt* | Neue Nachbarn, gute Nachbarschaft? Die EU als internationaler Akteur am Beispiel ihrer Demokratieförderung in Belarus und der Ukraine 2004-2009 | Mit einem Vorwort von Jutta Joachim | ISBN 978-3-8382-0437-6

117 *Fabian Pfeiffer* | Estlands Außen- und Sicherheitspolitik I. Der estnische Atlantizismus nach der wiedererlangten Unabhängigkeit 1991-2004 | Mit einem Vorwort von Helmut Hubel | ISBN 978-3-8382-0127-6

118 *Jana Podßuweit* | Estlands Außen- und Sicherheitspolitik II. Handlungsoptionen eines Kleinstaates im Rahmen seiner EU-Mitgliedschaft (2004-2008) | Mit einem Vorwort von Helmut Hubel | ISBN 978-3-8382-0440-6

119 *Karin Pointner* | Estlands Außen- und Sicherheitspolitik III. Eine gedächtnispolitische Analyse estnischer Entwicklungskooperation 2006-2010 | Mit einem Vorwort von Karin Liebhart | ISBN 978-3-8382-0435-2

120 *Ruslana Vovk* | Die Offenheit der ukrainischen Verfassung für das Völkerrecht und die europäische Integration | Mit einem Vorwort von Alexander Blankenagel | ISBN 978-3-8382-0481-9

121 *Mykhaylo Banakh* | Die Relevanz der Zivilgesellschaft bei den postkommunistischen Transformationsprozessen in mittel- und osteuropäischen Ländern. Das Beispiel der spät- und postsowjetischen Ukraine 1986-2009 | Mit einem Vorwort von Gerhard Simon | ISBN 978-3-8382-0499-4

122 *Michael Moser* | Language Policy and the Discourse on Languages in Ukraine under President Viktor Yanukovych (25 February 2010–28 October 2012) | ISBN 978-3-8382-0497-0 (Paperback edition) | ISBN 978-3-8382-0507-6 (Hardcover edition)

123 *Nicole Krome* | Russischer Netzwerkkapitalismus Restrukturierungsprozesse in der Russischen Föderation am Beispiel des Luftfahrtunternehmens „Aviastar" | Mit einem Vorwort von Petra Stykow | ISBN 978-3-8382-0534-2

124 *David R. Marples* | 'Our Glorious Past'. Lukashenka's Belarus and the Great Patriotic War | ISBN 978-3-8382-0574-8 (Paperback edition) | ISBN 978-3-8382-0675-2 (Hardcover edition)

125 *Ulf Walther* | Russlands „neuer Adel". Die Macht des Geheimdienstes von Gorbatschow bis Putin | Mit einem Vorwort von Hans-Georg Wieck | ISBN 978-3-8382-0584-7

126 *Simon Geissbühler (Hrsg.)* | Kiew – Revolution 3.0. Der Euromaidan 2013/14 und die Zukunftsperspektiven der Ukraine | ISBN 978-3-8382-0581-6 (Paperback edition) | ISBN 978-3-8382-0681-3 (Hardcover edition)

127 *Andrey Makarychev* | Russia and the EU in a Multipolar World. Discourses, Identities, Norms | With a foreword by Klaus Segbers | ISBN 978-3-8382-0629-5

128 *Roland Scharff* | Kasachstan als postsowjetischer Wohlfahrtsstaat. Die Transformation des sozialen Schutzsystems | Mit einem Vorwort von Joachim Ahrens | ISBN 978-3-8382-0622-6

129 *Katja Grupp* | Bild Lücke Deutschland. Kaliningrader Studierende sprechen über Deutschland | Mit einem Vorwort von Martin Schulz | ISBN 978-3-8382-0552-6

130 *Konstantin Sheiko, Stephen Brown* | History as Therapy. Alternative History and Nationalist Imaginings in Russia, 1991-2014 | ISBN 978-3-8382-0665-3

131 *Elisa Kriza* | Alexander Solzhenitsyn: Cold War Icon, Gulag Author, Russian Nationalist? A Study of the Western Reception of his Literary Writings, Historical Interpretations, and Political Ideas | With a foreword by Andrei Rogatchevski | ISBN 978-3-8382-0589-2 (Paperback edition) | ISBN 978-3-8382-0690-5 (Hardcover edition)

132 *Serghei Golunov* | The Elephant in the Room. Corruption and Cheating in Russian Universities | ISBN 978-3-8382-0570-0

133 *Manja Hussner, Rainer Arnold (Hgg.)* | Verfassungsgerichtsbarkeit in Zentralasien I. Sammlung von Verfassungstexten | ISBN 978-3-8382-0595-3

134 *Nikolay Mitrokhin* | Die „Russische Partei". Die Bewegung der russischen Nationalisten in der UdSSR 1953-1985 | Aus dem Russischen übertragen von einem Übersetzerteam unter der Leitung von Larisa Schippel | ISBN 978-3-8382-0024-8

135 *Manja Hussner, Rainer Arnold (Hgg.)* | Verfassungsgerichtsbarkeit in Zentralasien II. Sammlung von Verfassungstexten | ISBN 978-3-8382-0597-7

136 *Manfred Zeller* | Das sowjetische Fieber. Fußballfans im poststalinistischen Vielvölkerreich | Mit einem Vorwort von Nikolaus Katzer | ISBN 978-3-8382-0757-5

137 *Kristin Schreiter* | Stellung und Entwicklungspotential zivilgesellschaftlicher Gruppen in Russland. Menschenrechtsorganisationen im Vergleich | ISBN 978-3-8382-0673-8

138 *David R. Marples, Frederick V. Mills (Eds.)* | Ukraine's Euromaidan. Analyses of a Civil Revolution | ISBN 978-3-8382-0660-8

139 *Bernd Kappenberg* | Setting Signs for Europe. Why Diacritics Matter for European Integration | With a foreword by Peter Schlobinski | ISBN 978-3-8382-0663-9

140 *René Lenz* | Internationalisierung, Kooperation und Transfer. Externe bildungspolitische Akteure in der Russischen Föderation | Mit einem Vorwort von Frank Ettrich | ISBN 978-3-8382-0751-3

141 *Juri Plusnin, Yana Zausaeva, Natalia Zhidkevich, Artemy Pozanenko* | Wandering Workers. Mores, Behavior, Way of Life, and Political Status of Domestic Russian Labor Migrants | Translated by Julia Kazantseva | ISBN 978-3-8382-0653-0

142 *David J. Smith (Eds.)* | Latvia – A Work in Progress? 100 Years of State- and Nation-Building | ISBN 978-3-8382-0648-6

143 *Инна Чувычкина (ред.)* | Экспортные нефте- и газопроводы на постсоветском пространстве. Анализ трубопроводной политики в свете теории международных отношений | ISBN 978-3-8382-0822-0

144 *Johann Zajaczkowski* | Russland – eine pragmatische Großmacht? Eine rollentheoretische Untersuchung russischer Außenpolitik am Beispiel der Zusammenarbeit mit den USA nach 9/11 und des Georgienkrieges von 2008 | Mit einem Vorwort von Siegfried Schieder | ISBN 978-3-8382-0837-4

145 *Boris Popivanov* | Changing Images of the Left in Bulgaria. The Challenge of Post-Communism in the Early 21st Century | ISBN 978-3-8382-0667-7

146 *Lenka Krátká* | A History of the Czechoslovak Ocean Shipping Company 1948-1989. How a Small, Landlocked Country Ran Maritime Business During the Cold War | ISBN 978-3-8382-0666-0

147 *Alexander Sergunin* | Explaining Russian Foreign Policy Behavior. Theory and Practice | ISBN 978-3-8382-0752-0

148 *Darya Malyutina* | Migrant Friendships in a Super-Diverse City. Russian-Speakers and their Social Relationships in London in the 21st Century | With a foreword by Claire Dwyer | ISBN 978-3-8382-0652-3

149 *Alexander Sergunin, Valery Konyshev* | Russia in the Arctic. Hard or Soft Power? | ISBN 978-3-8382-0753-7

150 *John J. Maresca* | Helsinki Revisited. A Key U.S. Negotiator's Memoirs on the Development of the CSCE into the OSCE | With a foreword by Hafiz Pashayev | ISBN 978-3-8382-0852-7

151 *Jardar Østbø* | The New Third Rome. Readings of a Russian Nationalist Myth | With a foreword by Pål Kolstø | ISBN 978-3-8382-0870-1

152 *Simon Kordonsky* | Socio-Economic Foundations of the Russian Post-Soviet Regime. The Resource-Based Economy and Estate-Based Social Structure of Contemporary Russia | With a foreword by Svetlana Barsukova | ISBN 978-3-8382-0775-9

153 *Duncan Leitch* | Assisting Reform in Post-Communist Ukraine 2000–2012. The Illusions of Donors and the Disillusion of Beneficiaries | With a foreword by Kataryna Wolczuk | ISBN 978-3-8382-0844-2

154 *Abel Polese* | Limits of a Post-Soviet State. How Informality Replaces, Renegotiates, and Reshapes Governance in Contemporary Ukraine | With a foreword by Colin Williams | ISBN 978-3-8382-0845-9

155 *Mikhail Suslov (Ed.)* | Digital Orthodoxy in the Post-Soviet World. The Russian Orthodox Church and Web 2.0 | With a foreword by Father Cyril Hovorun | ISBN 978-3-8382-0871-8

156 *Leonid Luks* | Zwei „Sonderwege"? Russisch-deutsche Parallelen und Kontraste (1917-2014). Vergleichende Essays | ISBN 978-3-8382-0823-7

157 *Vladimir V. Karacharovskiy, Ovsey I. Shkaratan, Gordey A. Yastrebov* | Towards a New Russian Work Culture. Can Western Companies and Expatriates Change Russian Society? | With a foreword by Elena N. Danilova | Translated by Julia Kazantseva | ISBN 978-3-8382-0902-9

158 *Edmund Griffiths* | Aleksandr Prokhanov and Post-Soviet Esotericism | ISBN 978-3-8382-0963-0

159 *Timm Beichelt, Susann Worschech (Eds.)* | Transnational Ukraine? Networks and Ties that Influence(d) Contemporary Ukraine | ISBN 978-3-8382-0944-9

160 *Mieste Hotopp-Riecke* | Die Tataren der Krim zwischen Assimilation und Selbstbehauptung. Der Aufbau des krimtatarischen Bildungswesens nach Deportation und Heimkehr (1990-2005) | Mit einem Vorwort von Swetlana Czerwonnaja | ISBN 978-3-89821-940-2

161 *Olga Bertelsen (Ed.)* | Revolution and War in Contemporary Ukraine. The Challenge of Change | ISBN 978-3-8382-1016-2

162 *Natalya Ryabinska* | Ukraine's Post-Communist Mass Media. Between Capture and Commercialization | With a foreword by Marta Dyczok | ISBN 978-3-8382-1011-7

163 *Alexandra Cotofana, James M. Nyce (Eds.)* | Religion and Magic in Socialist and Post-Socialist Contexts. Historic and Ethnographic Case Studies of Orthodoxy, Heterodoxy, and Alternative Spirituality | With a foreword by Patrick L. Michelson | ISBN 978-3-8382-0989-0

164 *Nozima Akhrarkhodjaeva* | The Instrumentalisation of Mass Media in Electoral Authoritarian Regimes. Evidence from Russia's Presidential Election Campaigns of 2000 and 2008 | ISBN 978-3-8382-1013-1

165 *Yulia Krasheninnikova* | Informal Healthcare in Contemporary Russia. Sociographic Essays on the Post-Soviet Infrastructure for Alternative Healing Practices | ISBN 978-3-8382-0970-8

166 *Peter Kaiser* | Das Schachbrett der Macht. Die Handlungsspielräume eines sowjetischen Funktionärs unter Stalin am Beispiel des Generalsekretärs des Komsomol Aleksandr Kosarev (1929-1938) | Mit einem Vorwort von Dietmar Neutatz | ISBN 978-3-8382-1052-0

167 *Oksana Kim* | The Effects and Implications of Kazakhstan's Adoption of International Financial Reporting Standards. A Resource Dependence Perspective | With a foreword by Svetlana Vlady | ISBN 978-3-8382-0987-6

168 *Anna Sanina* | Patriotic Education in Contemporary Russia. Sociological Studies in the Making of the Post-Soviet Citizen | With a foreword by Anna Oldfield | ISBN 978-3-8382-0993-7

169 *Rudolf Wolters* | Spezialist in Sibirien Faksimile der 1933 erschienenen ersten Ausgabe | Mit einem Vorwort von Dmitrij Chmelnizki | ISBN 978-3-8382-0515-1

170 *Michal Vít, Magdalena M. Baran (Eds.)* | Transregional versus National Perspectives on Contemporary Central European History. Studies on the Building of Nation-States and Their Cooperation in the 20th and 21st Century | With a foreword by Petr Vágner | ISBN 978-3-8382-1015-5

171 *Philip Gamaghelyan* | Conflict Resolution Beyond the International Relations Paradigm. Evolving Designs as a Transformative Practice in Nagorno-Karabakh and Syria | With a foreword by Susan Allen | ISBN 978-3-8382-1057-5

172 *Maria Shagina* | Joining a Prestigious Club. Cooperation with Europarties and Its Impact on Party Development in Georgia, Moldova, and Ukraine 2004–2015 | With a foreword by Kataryna Wolczuk | ISBN 978-3-8382-1084-1

173 *Alexandra Cotofana, James M. Nyce (Eds.)* | Religion and Magic in Socialist and Post-Socialist Contexts II. Baltic, Eastern European, and Post-USSR Case Studies | With a foreword by Anita Stasulane | ISBN 978-3-8382-0990-6

174 *Barbara Kunz* | Kind Words, Cruise Missiles, and Everything in Between. The Use of Power Resources in U.S. Policies towards Poland, Ukraine, and Belarus 1989–2008 | With a foreword by William Hill | ISBN 978-3-8382-1065-0

175 *Eduard Klein* | Bildungskorruption in Russland und der Ukraine. Eine komparative Analyse der Performanz staatlicher Antikorruptionsmaßnahmen im Hochschulsektor am Beispiel universitärer Aufnahmeprüfungen | Mit einem Vorwort von Heiko Pleines | ISBN 978-3-8382-0995-1

176 *Markus Soldner* | Politischer Kapitalismus im postsowjetischen Russland. Die politische, wirtschaftliche und mediale Transformation in den 1990er Jahren | Mit einem Vorwort von Wolfgang Ismayr | ISBN 978-3-8382-1222-7

177 *Anton Oleinik* | Building Ukraine from Within. A Sociological, Institutional, and Economic Analysis of a Nation-State in the Making | ISBN 978-3-8382-1150-3

178 *Peter Rollberg, Marlene Laruelle (Eds.)* | Mass Media in the Post-Soviet World. Market Forces, State Actors, and Political Manipulation in the Informational Environment after Communism | ISBN 978-3-8382-1116-9

179 *Mikhail Minakov* | Development and Dystopia. Studies in Post-Soviet Ukraine and Eastern Europe | With a foreword by Alexander Etkind | ISBN 978-3-8382-1112-1

180 *Aijan Sharshenova* | The European Union's Democracy Promotion in Central Asia. A Study of Political Interests, Influence, and Development in Kazakhstan and Kyrgyzstan in 2007–2013 | With a foreword by Gordon Crawford | ISBN 978-3-8382-1151-0

181 *Andrey Makarychev, Alexandra Yatsyk (Eds.)* | Boris Nemtsov and Russian Politics. Power and Resistance | With a foreword by Zhanna Nemtsova | ISBN 978-3-8382-1122-0

182 *Sophie Falsini* | The Euromaidan's Effect on Civil Society. Why and How Ukrainian Social Capital Increased after the Revolution of Dignity | With a foreword by Susann Worschech | ISBN 978-3-8382-1131-2

183 *Valentyna Romanova, Andreas Umland (Eds.)* | Ukraine's Decentralization. Challenges and Implications of the Local Governance Reform after the Euromaidan Revolution | ISBN 978-3-8382-1162-6

184 *Leonid Luks* | A Fateful Triangle. Essays on Contemporary Russian, German and Polish History | ISBN 978-3-8382-1143-5

185 *John B. Dunlop* | The February 2015 Assassination of Boris Nemtsov and the Flawed Trial of his Alleged Killers. An Exploration of Russia's "Crime of the 21st Century" | ISBN 978-3-8382-1188-6

186 *Vasile Rotaru* | Russia, the EU, and the Eastern Partnership. Building Bridges or Digging Trenches? | ISBN 978-3-8382-1134-3

187 *Marina Lebedeva* | Russian Studies of International Relations. From the Soviet Past to the Post-Cold-War Present | With a foreword by Andrei P. Tsygankov | ISBN 978-3-8382-0851-0

188 *Tomasz Stępniewski, George Soroka (Eds.)* | Ukraine after Maidan. Revisiting Domestic and Regional Security | ISBN 978-3-8382-1075-9

189 *Petar Cholakov* | Ethnic Entrepreneurs Unmasked. Political Institutions and Ethnic Conflicts in Contemporary Bulgaria | ISBN 978-3-8382-1189-3

190 *A. Salem, G. Hazeldine, D. Morgan (Eds.)* | Higher Education in Post-Communist States. Comparative and Sociological Perspectives | ISBN 978-3-8382-1183-1

191 *Igor Torbakov* | After Empire. Nationalist Imagination and Symbolic Politics in Russia and Eurasia in the Twentieth and Twenty-First Century | With a foreword by Serhii Plokhy | ISBN 978-3-8382-1217-3

192 *Aleksandr Burakovskiy* | Jewish-Ukrainian Relations in Late and Post-Soviet Ukraine. Articles, Lectures and Essays from 1986 to 2016 | ISBN 978-3-8382-1210-4

193 *Natalia Shapovalova, Olga Burlyuk (Eds.)* | Civil Society in Post-Euromaidan Ukraine. From Revolution to Consolidation | With a foreword by Richard Youngs | ISBN 978-3-8382-1216-6

194 *Franz Preissler* | Positionsverteidigung, Imperialismus oder Irredentismus? Russland und die „Russischsprachigen", 1991–2015 | ISBN 978-3-8382-1262-3

195 *Marian Madeła* | Der Reformprozess in der Ukraine 2014-2017. Eine Fallstudie zur Reform der öffentlichen Verwaltung | Mit einem Vorwort von Martin Malek | ISBN 978-3-8382-1266-5

196 *Anke Giesen* | „Wie kann denn der Sieger ein Verbrecher sein?" Eine diskursanalytische Untersuchung der russlandweiten Debatte über Konzept und Verstaatlichungsprozess der Lagergedenkstätte „Perm'-36" im Ural | ISBN 978-3-8382-1284-5

197 *Victoria Leukavets* | The Integration Policies of Belarus and Ukraine vis-à-vis the EU and Russia. A Comparative Analysis Through the Prism of a Two-Level Game Approach | ISBN 978-3-8382-1247-0

198 *Oksana Kim* | The Development and Challenges of Russian Corporate Governance I. The Roles and Functions of Boards of Directors | With a foreword by Sheila M. Puffer | ISBN 978-3-8382-1287-6

199 *Thomas D. Grant* | International Law and the Post-Soviet Space I. Essays on Chechnya and the Baltic States | With a foreword by Stephen M. Schwebel | ISBN 978-3-8382-1279-1

200 *Thomas D. Grant* | International Law and the Post-Soviet Space II. Essays on Ukraine, Intervention, and Non-Proliferation | ISBN 978-3-8382-1280-7

201 *Slavomír Michálek, Michal Štefansky* | The Age of Fear. The Cold War and Its Influence on Czechoslovakia 1945–1968 | ISBN 978-3-8382-1285-2

202 *Iulia-Sabina Joja* | Romania's Strategic Culture 1990–2014. Continuity and Change in a Post-Communist Country's Evolution of National Interests and Security Policies | With a foreword by Heiko Biehl | ISBN 978-3-8382-1286-9

203 *Andrei Rogatchevski, Yngvar B. Steinholt, Arve Hansen, David-Emil Wickström* | War of Songs. Popular Music and Recent Russia-Ukraine Relations | With a foreword by Artemy Troitsky | ISBN 978-3-8382-1173-2

204 *Maria Lipman (Ed.)* | Russian Voices on Post-Crimea Russia. An Almanac of Counterpoint Essays from 2015–2018 | ISBN 978-3-8382-1251-7

205 *Ksenia Maksimovtsova* | Language Conflicts in Contemporary Estonia, Latvia, and Ukraine. A Comparative Exploration of Discourses in Post-Soviet Russian-Language Digital Media | With a foreword by Ammon Cheskin | ISBN 978-3-8382-1282-1

206 *Michal Vít* | The EU's Impact on Identity Formation in East-Central Europe between 2004 and 2013. Perceptions of the Nation and Europe in Political Parties of the Czech Republic, Poland, and Slovakia | With a foreword by Andrea Pető | ISBN 978-3-8382-1275-3

207 *Per A. Rudling* | Tarnished Heroes. The Organization of Ukrainian Nationalists in the Memory Politics of Post-Soviet Ukraine | ISBN 978-3-8382-0999-9

208 *Kaja Gadowska, Peter Solomon (Eds.)* | Legal Change in Post-Communist States. Progress, Reversions, Explanations | ISBN 978-3-8382-1312-5

209 *Pawel Kowal, Georges Mink, Iwona Reichardt (Eds.)* | Three Revolutions: Mobilization and Change in Contemporary Ukraine I. Theoretical Aspects and Analyses on Religion, Memory, and Identity | ISBN 978-3-8382-1321-7

210 *Pawel Kowal, Georges Mink, Adam Reichardt, Iwona Reichardt (Eds.)* | Three Revolutions: Mobilization and Change in Contemporary Ukraine II. An Oral History of the Revolution on Granite, Orange Revolution, and Revolution of Dignity | ISBN 978-3-8382-1323-1

211 *Li Bennich-Björkman, Sergiy Kurbatov (Eds.)* | When the Future Came. The Collapse of the USSR and the Emergence of National Memory in Post-Soviet History Textbooks | ISBN 978-3-8382-1335-4

212 *Olga R. Gulina* | Migration as a (Geo-)Political Challenge in the Post-Soviet Space. Border Regimes, Policy Choices, Visa Agendas | With a foreword by Nils Muižnieks | ISBN 978-3-8382-1338-5

213 *Sanna Turoma, Kaarina Aitamurto, Slobodanka Vladiv-Glover (Eds.)* | Religion, Expression, and Patriotism in Russia. Essays on Post-Soviet Society and the State. | ISBN 978-3-8382-1346-0

214 *Vasif Huseynov* | Geopolitical Rivalries in the "Common Neighborhood". Russia's Conflict with the West, Soft Power, and Neoclassical Realism | With a foreword by Nicholas Ross Smith | ISBN 978-3-8382-1277-7

215 *Mikhail Suslov* | Geopolitical Imagination. Ideology and Utopia in Post-Soviet Russia | With a foreword by Mark Bassin | ISBN 978-3-8382-1361-3

216 *Alexander Etkind, Mikhail Minakov (Eds.)* | Ideology after Union. Political Doctrines, Discourses, and Debates in Post-Soviet Societies | ISBN 978-3-8382-1388-0

217 *Jakob Mischke, Oleksandr Zabirko (Hgg.)* | Protestbewegungen im langen Schatten des Kreml. Aufbruch und Resignation in Russland und der Ukraine | ISBN 978-3-8382-0926-5

218 *Oksana Huss* | How Corruption and Anti-Corruption Policies Sustain Hybrid Regimes. Strategies of Political Domination under Ukraine's Presidents in 1994-2014 | With a foreword by Tobias Debiel and Andrea Gawrich | ISBN 978-3-8382-1430-6

219 *Dmitry Travin, Vladimir Gel'man, Otar Marganiya* | The Russian Path. Ideas, Interests, Institutions, Illusions | With a foreword by Vladimir Ryzhkov | ISBN 978-3-8382-1421-4

220 *Gergana Dimova* | Political Uncertainty. A Comparative Exploration | With a foreword by Todor Yalamov and Rumena Filipova | ISBN 978-3-8382-1385-9

221 *Torben Waschke* | Russland in Transition. Geopolitik zwischen Raum, Identität und Machtinteressen | Mit einem Vorwort von Andreas Dittmann | ISBN 978-3-8382-1480-1

222 *Steven Jobbitt, Zsolt Bottlik, Marton Berki (Eds.)* | Power and Identity in the Post-Soviet Realm. Geographies of Ethnicity and Nationality after 1991 | ISBN 978-3-8382-1399-6

223 *Daria Buteiko* | Erinnerungsort. Ort des Gedenkens, der Erholung oder der Einkehr? Kommunismus-Erinnerung am Beispiel der-Gedenkstätte Berliner Mauer sowie des Soloveckij-Klosters und -Museumsparks | ISBN 978-3-8382-1367-5

224 *Olga Bertelsen (Ed.)* | Russian Active Measures. Yesterday, Today, Tomorrow | With a foreword by Jan Goldman | ISBN 978-3-8382-1529-7

225 *David Mandel* | "Optimizing" Higher Education in Russia. University Teachers and their Union "Universitetskaya solidarnost'" | ISBN 978-3-8382-1519-8

226 *Mikhail Minakov, Gwendolyn Sasse, Daria Isachenko (Eds.)* | Post-Soviet Secessionism. Nation-Building and State-Failure after Communism | ISBN 978-3-8382-1538-9

227 *Jakob Hauter (Ed.)* | Civil War? Interstate War? Hybrid War? Dimensions and Interpretations of the Donbas Conflict in 2014–2020 | With a foreword by Andrew Wilson | ISBN 978-3-8382-1383-5

228 *Tima T. Moldogaziev, Gene A. Brewer, J. Edward Kellough (Eds.)* | Public Policy and Politics in Georgia. Lessons from Post-Soviet Transition | With a foreword by Dan Durning | ISBN 978-3-8382-1535-8

229 *Oxana Schmies (Ed.)* | NATO's Enlargement and Russia. A Strategic Challenge in the Past and Future | With a foreword by Vladimir Kara-Murza | ISBN 978-3-8382-1478-5

230 *Christopher Ford* | Ukapisme – Une Gauche perdue. Le marxisme anti-colonial dans la révolution ukrainienne 1917-1925 | Avec une préface de Vincent Présumey | ISBN 978-3-8382-0899-2

231 *Anna Kutkina* | Between Lenin and Bandera. Decommunization and Multivocality in Post-Euromaidan Ukraine | With a foreword by Juri Mykkänen | ISBN 978-3-8382-1506-8

232 *Lincoln E. Flake* | Defending the Faith. The Russian Orthodox Church and the Demise of Religious Pluralism | With a foreword by Peter Martland | ISBN 978-3-8382-1378-1

233 *Nikoloz Samkharadze* | Russia's Recognition of the Independence of Abkhazia and South Ossetia. Analysis of a Deviant Case in Moscow's Foreign Policy | With a foreword by Neil MacFarlane | ISBN 978-3-8382-1414-6

234 *Arve Hansen* | Urban Protest. A Spatial Perspective on Kyiv, Minsk, and Moscow | With a foreword by Julie Wilhelmsen | ISBN 978-3-8382-1495-5

235 *Eleonora Narvselius, Julie Fedor (Eds.)* | Diversity in the East-Central European Borderlands. Memories, Cityscapes, People | ISBN 978-3-8382-1523-5

236 *Regina Elsner* | The Russian Orthodox Church and Modernity. A Historical and Theological Investigation into Eastern Christianity between Unity and Plurality | With a foreword by Mikhail Suslov | ISBN 978-3-8382-1568-6

237 *Bo Petersson* | The Putin Predicament. Problems of Legitimacy and Succession in Russia | With a foreword by J. Paul Goode | ISBN 978-3-8382-1050-6

238 *Jonathan Otto Pohl* | The Years of Great Silence. The Deportation, Special Settlement, and Mobilization into the Labor Army of Ethnic Germans in the USSR, 1941–1955 | ISBN 978-3-8382-1630-0

239 *Mikhail Minakov (Ed.)* | Inventing Majorities. Ideological Creativity in Post-Soviet Societies | ISBN 978-3-8382-1641-6

240 *Robert M. Cutler* | Soviet and Post-Soviet Foreign Policies I. East-South Relations and the Political Economy of the Communist Bloc, 1971–1991 | With a foreword by Roger E. Kanet | ISBN 978-3-8382-1654-6

241 *Izabella Agardi* | On the Verge of History. Life Stories of Rural Women from Serbia, Romania, and Hungary, 1920–2020 | With a foreword by Andrea Pető | ISBN 978-3-8382-1602-7

242 *Sebastian Schäffer (Ed.)* | Ukraine in Central and Eastern Europe. Kyiv's Foreign Affairs and the International Relations of the Post-Communist Region | With a foreword by Pavlo Klimkin and Andreas Umland| ISBN 978-3-8382-1615-7

243 *Volodymyr Dubrovskyi, Kalman Mizsei, Mychailo Wynnyckyj (Eds.)* | Eight Years after the Revolution of Dignity. What Has Changed in Ukraine during 2013–2021? | With a foreword by Yaroslav Hrytsak | ISBN 978-3-8382-1560-0

244 *Rumena Filipova* | Constructing the Limits of Europe Identity and Foreign Policy in Poland, Bulgaria, and Russia since 1989 | With forewords by Harald Wydra and Gergana Yankova-Dimova | ISBN 978-3-8382-1649-2

245 *Oleksandra Keudel* | How Patronal Networks Shape Opportunities for Local Citizen Participation in a Hybrid Regime A Comparative Analysis of Five Cities in Ukraine | With a foreword by Sabine Kropp | ISBN 978-3-8382-1671-3

246 *Jan Claas Behrends, Thomas Lindenberger, Pavel Kolar (Eds.)* | Violence after Stalin Institutions, Practices, and Everyday Life in the Soviet Bloc 1953–1989 | ISBN 978-3-8382-1637-9

247 *Leonid Luks* | Macht und Ohnmacht der Utopien Essays zur Geschichte Russlands im 20. und 21. Jahrhundert | ISBN 978-3-8382-1677-5

248 *Iuliia Barshadska* | Brüssel zwischen Kyjiw und Moskau Das auswärtige Handeln der Europäischen Union im ukrainisch-russischen Konflikt 2014-2019 | Mit einem Vorwort von Olaf Leiße | ISBN 978-3-8382-1667-6

249 *Valentyna Romanova* | Decentralisation and Multilevel Elections in Ukraine Reform Dynamics and Party Politics in 2010–2021 | With a foreword by Kimitaka Matsuzato | ISBN 978-3-8382-1700-0

250 *Alexander Motyl* | National Questions. Theoretical Reflections on Nations and Nationalism in Eastern Europe | ISBN 978-3-8382-1675-1

251 *Marc Dietrich* | A Cosmopolitan Model for Peacebuilding. The Ukrainian Cases of Crimea and the Donbas | With a foreword by Rémi Baudouï | ISBN 978-3-8382-1687-4

252 *Eduard Baidaus* | An Unsettled Nation. Moldova in the Geopolitics of Russia, Romania, and Ukraine | With forewords by John-Paul Himka and David R. Marples | ISBN 978-3-8382-1582-2

253 *Igor Okunev, Petr Oskolkov (Eds.)* | Transforming the Administrative Matryoshka. The Reform of Autonomous Okrugs in the Russian Federation, 2003–2008 | With a foreword by Vladimir Zorin | ISBN 978-3-8382-1721-5

254 *Winfried Schneider-Deters* | Ukraine's Fateful Years 2013–2019. Vol. I: The Popular Uprising in Winter 2013/2014 | ISBN 978-3-8382-1725-3

255 *Winfried Schneider-Deters* | Ukraine's Fateful Years 2013–2019. Vol. II: The Annexation of Crimea and the War in Donbas | ISBN 978-3-8382-1726-0

256 *Robert M. Cutler* | Soviet and Post-Soviet Russian Foreign Policies II. East-West Relations in Europe and the Political Economy of the Communist Bloc, 1971–1991 | With a foreword by Roger E. Kanet | ISBN 978-3-8382-1727-7

257 *Robert M. Cutler* | Soviet and Post-Soviet Russian Foreign Policies III. East-West Relations in Europe and Eurasia in the Post-Cold War Transition, 1991–2001 | With a foreword by Roger E. Kanet | ISBN 978-3-8382-1728-4

258 *Paweł Kowal, Iwona Reichardt, Kateryna Pryshchepa (Eds.)* | Three Revolutions: Mobilization and Change in Contemporary Ukraine III. Archival Records and Historical Sources on the 1990 Revolution on Granite | ISBN 978-3-8382-1376-7

259 *Mikhail Minakov (Ed.)* | Philosophy Unchained. Developments in Post-Soviet Philosophical Thought. | With a foreword by Christopher Donohue | ISBN 978-3-8382-1768-0

260 *David Dalton* | The Ukrainian Oligarchy After the Euromaidan. How Ukraine's Political Economy Regime Survived the Crisis | With a foreword by Andrew Wilson | ISBN 978-3-8382-1740-6

261 *Andreas Heinemann-Grüder (Ed.)* | Who Are the Fighters? Irregular Armed Groups in the Russian-Ukrainian War in 2014–2015 | ISBN 978-3-8382-1777-2

262 *Taras Kuzio (Ed.)* | Russian Disinformation and Western Scholarship. Bias and Prejudice in Journalistic, Expert, and Academic Analyses of East European, Russian and Eurasian Affairs | ISBN 978-3-8382-1685-0

263 *Darius Furmonavicius* | Lithuania Transforms the West. Lithuania's Liberation from Soviet Occupation and the Enlargement of NATO (1988–2022) | With a foreword by Vytautas Landsbergis | ISBN 978-3-8382-1779-6

264 *Dirk Dalberg* | Politisches Denken im tschechoslowakischen Dissens. Egon Bondy, Miroslav Kusý, Milan Šimečka und Petr Uhl (1968-1989) | ISBN 978-3-8382-1318-0

265 *Леонид Люкс* | К столетию «философского парохода». Мыслители «первой» русской эмиграции о русской революции и о тоталитарных соблазнах XX века | ISBN 978-3-8382-1775-8

266 *Daviti Mtchedlishvili* | The EU and the South Caucasus. European Neighborhood Policies between Eclecticism and Pragmatism, 1991-2021 | With a foreword by Nicholas Ross Smith | ISBN 978-3-8382-1735-2

267 *Bohdan Harasymiw* | Post-Euromaidan Ukraine. Domestic Power Struggles and War of National Survival in 2014–2022 | ISBN 978-3-8382-1798-7

268 *Nadiia Koval, Denys Tereshchenko (Eds.)* | Russian Cultural Diplomacy under Putin. Rossotrudnichestvo, the "Russkiy Mir" Foundation, and the Gorchakov Fund in 2007–2022 | ISBN 978-3-8382-1801-4

269 *Izabela Kazejak* | Jews in Post-War Wrocław and L'viv. Official Policies and Local Responses in Comparative Perspective, 1945-1970s | ISBN 978-3-8382-1802-1

270 *Jakob Hauter* | Russia's Overlooked Invasion. The Causes of the 2014 Outbreak of War in Ukraine's Donbas | With a foreword by Hiroaki Kuromiya | ISBN 978-3-8382-1803-8

271 *Anton Shekhovtsov* | Russian Political Warfare. Essays on Kremlin Propaganda in Europe and the Neighbourhood, 2020-2023 | With a foreword by Nathalie Loiseau | ISBN 978-3-8382-1821-2

272 *Андреа Пето* | Насилие и Молчание. Красная армия в Венгрии во Второй Мировой войне | ISBN 978-3-8382-1636-2

273 *Winfried Schneider-Deters* | Russia's War in Ukraine. Debates on Peace, Fascism, and War Crimes, 2022–2023 | With a foreword by Klaus Gestwa | ISBN 978-3-8382-1876-5